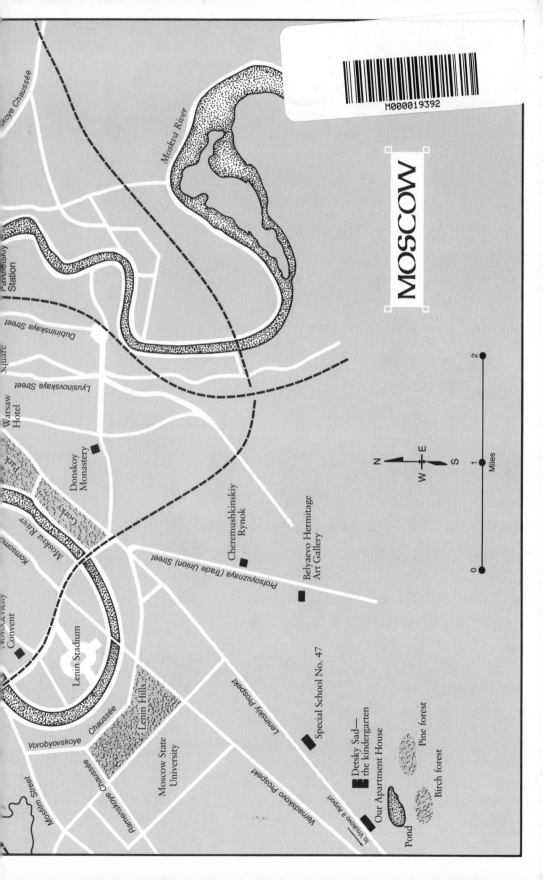

MOSCOW

Moskva River

Paveletsky Station

Dubininskaya Street

Lyusinovskaya Street

Square

Warsaw Hotel

Donskoy Monastery

Gorky Park

Cheremushkinskiy Rynok

Profsoyuznaya (Trade Union) Street

Belyaevo Hermitage Art Gallery

Komsomol

Moskva River

Novodevichiy Convent

Lenin Stadium

Special School No. 47

Vorobyovskoye Chaussée

Lenin Hills

Leninskiy Prospekt

Moscow State University

Ramenskoye Chaussée

Moslim Street

Detsky Sad—the kindergarten

Our Apartment House

Vernadskovo Prospekt

to Vnukovo II Airport

Pond

Pine forest

Birch forest

N
W — E
S

0   1   2
       Miles

89-547

947.085 Schecter, Jerrold
SCH   L.

Back in the USSR

89-547

947.085 Schecter, Jerrold
SCH   L.

Back in the USSR

$24.95

DATE	BORROWER'S NAME	
4 03 D	Hedgeo	
4 24	NUTILE JENNIFER M	
	92-146518	
NOV 21 '90		NUTLES

6

Other books by Jerrold Schecter

The Palace File (1986), co-authored with Nguyen Tien Hung

An American Family in Moscow (1975), co-authored with Leona, Evelind, Steven, Kate, Doveen, and Barnet Schecter

The New Face of Buddha (1967)

To Miriam Schecter, and the memory
of Edward Schecter, Belle and Barnet Protas

CONTENTS

CONTENTS

ACKNOWLEDGMENTS

Our thanks and appreciation go to our Russian friends who welcomed us back to Moscow as if time had stood still and we had left yesterday. Their lives and how they have changed are what this book is about. In seeing them again we better understood ourselves and why the Soviet Union and its future is a part of our lives. Despite *glasnost*, or openness, in describing our friends we felt it best to change some of their names and occupations. In every other way this is as it was for us in Moscow.

Our colleagues and friends in the press corps were stimulating and helpful; we want to thank Mark D'Anastasio, Peter Arnett, Felicity Barringer, Ann Blackman, Louise Branson, Stanley Cloud, Dusko Doder, Bill Eaton, Robert Evans, Jim Jackson, Bill Keller, Gary Lee, Mike Putzel, Paul Quinn-Judge, Walter Rodgers, Felix Rosenthal, Thomas Shanker, Edmund Stevens, Anastasia Stevens-Ferrari, Strobe Talbott, Phil Taubman, and Gerlind Younts. Ludmilla Alexeyeva, Valery Chalidze, Murray Feshbach, Grisha Friedin, Kirsten Goldberg, Paul Goldberg, Marc Leland, Sherrod McCall, and Richard Solomon made helpful suggestions and generously offered the benefit of their experience and scholarship. Ian McLeod of *The Sunday Times* graciously lent us their Moscow apartment. Alan Loflin and Pan American Airways cooperated in expediting our travel. David Fanning, executive producer of *Frontline*, had the vision and determination to sponsor our idea and see it through. Sherry Jones, Hans Roland, Nancy Sloss, Hugh Walsh, and Foster Wiley brought it to life on film with skill and sensitivity. Boris Semenov and Valentine Yegorov of *Gosteleradio* taught us the pleasures and pitfalls of making a documentary film in the U.S.S.R.

Our editor, Edward T. Chase, encouraged the initial idea with enthusiasm and made valuable editorial suggestions. He nourished us with positive responses to our ideas and helped to focus the book. Charles Flowers patiently and diligently kept the book on track. Ravin Korothy's attention to detail and style was helpful in the final editing.

Back
in the
U.S.S.R.

Going Back

By the summer of 1970, after I'd spent two years as *Time-Life* bureau chief, Moscow had become a dead end. We had come to try to understand the Soviet system and the wellsprings of Communist power. What we saw was the living past in a stagnant society that could not accommodate to change. "Looking at America from Moscow made us want to move on to where the action was, where the society, for all its faults, was changing, groping, experimenting; where historical prejudices against blacks, women, and other minorities were being budged. The real social revolutions, to which the Marxists lay claim, were occurring not in the Soviet Union but in America. We felt drawn home to take part in them," Leona wrote.

By the spring of 1987 it appeared as if Mikhail Gorbachev was breathing new life into the dying Russian revolution. We wanted to return and see if it was really happening.

Our five children, ages five to thirteen when we arrived in 1968, went to Soviet Special School 47. They learned to speak Russian and did not let the pejorative stereotype of "capitalist Americans" handicap their efforts to make friends with young Russians, who quickly learned to love chewing gum, Beatles' records, and the kids' Monopoly set. Despite periodic vigilance campaigns in the Soviet press against spies under cover as foreign journalists, Leona and I were accepted by Russians as *bogatye Mama i Papa*, "rich mother and father," because we had five children.

The intensity of a correspondent's life in Moscow drew us closer together as a family, and we formed deep personal friendships with Soviets. We skied, picnicked, hunted for mushrooms, and went to parties together. The family knew about the stories and the big project, Nikita Khrushchev's memoirs. I was instrumental in the acquisition of the Khrushchev memoirs and contributed to editing and annotating them when we returned to America. Our lives, for better or worse, were governed by border wars, expulsions, and deadlines. Tapped telephones, erasable plastic slates for messages between us to avoid bugging, and care not to expose Soviet friends and sources, even to American Embassy officials, were part of living in Moscow.

When we returned to the United States we settled in Washington, D.C., and I became *Time*'s White House correspondent. We spent hours discussing our experiences in the Soviet Union, and together we wrote *An American Family in Moscow*, which was published in 1975. Leona's work on the book led her to a career as a literary agent; her Washington-based network of authors soon included friends of friends from the Soviet Union. Evelind majored in economics and Russian studies at Yale. Steven studied advanced Russian and Soviet filmmakers at Harvard. Kate is working on a Ph.D. at the Averell Harriman Institute for Soviet Studies at Columbia University. She and Steve made a TV documentary of the Chautauqua Conference in Yurmala, Latvia, in September 1986. Doveen majored in English at Barnard and traveled the Trans-Siberian railroad from Beijing to Moscow in the summer of 1985, returning from a year when she worked with Cambodian refugees in Thailand. Barney, who is studying sculpture, immersed himself in the early Soviet painters and sculptors. Our sons-in-law, Michael Shafer and Ari Roth, and our daughter-in-law, Suprabha Schecter, had never been to the Soviet Union, but they had their own areas of interest—education, theater, and spiritual development—with which to explore *glasnost*. Ari is a playwright and songwriter, Michael is a professor of political science at Rutgers University, and Suprabha is a long-distance runner and disciple of the spiritual leader Sri Chinmoy.

As White House correspondent for *Time* I covered the détente years of Richard Nixon and Henry Kissinger, and returned to Moscow for the summit of 1972. As *Time*'s diplomatic editor (1972–76) the Soviet Union was a primary interest. When I moved to the Carter White House in 1977 as spokesman for the National Security Council and associate White House press secretary I carried my Soviet interests with me and handled press coverage for the Vienna summit in 1979. The pattern of Brezhnev's leadership was the same as I had seen it in Moscow: dogged, repressive, unpredictable, and lawless. When he died in November 1982 Brezhnev was succeeded by Yuri Andropov, and there was talk of reform; but Andropov suffered from a mortal kidney disease and he died in February 1984, too soon for his tree of changes to take root. The ailing Konstantin Chernenko's brief rule until his death in March 1985 was a gridlock before Gorbachev's succession.

We stayed in touch with friends in Moscow despite the freeze on relations after the Soviet invasion of Afghanistan in 1979. Every reporter who has served in Moscow returns critical of the Soviet system but attached to the country and its people; we all feel that we are a part of Moscow and that its story belongs to us. Viewing Gorbachev's audacious consolidation of power from a distance, we felt left out and wanted to take part in the biggest story of the decade. When Gorbachev personally called Andrei Sakharov on the telephone in December 1986 and invited him to return to Moscow after seven years of internal exile in Gorky it was apparent that a new-style Soviet leader was in charge. In Moscow we would hear Gorbachev compared to Peter the Great and Lenin.

In the spring of 1987 my family and I decided that we would try to return to the Soviet Union to do a book and television documentary on how life had changed since our days in Moscow. The focus would be on our friends and the children's school. Each of us would also look at that part of Soviet life which corresponded with our own interests. I would see how covering the Soviet Union had changed under Gorbachev's *glasnost* and what had happened to the Soviet press and the KGB, which plays so large a role in the lives of foreign correspondents. Leona would look at changes in publishing and how the lives of our writer and poet friends had changed. Evelind, who specializes in strategic planning and factory automation, would look at a Soviet factory and *perestroika*, restructuring, in action. Her husband, Michael Shafer, is working on a Vietnam War study program for high schools. Comparing Soviet and American education was his project. Steve would look at Soviet TV and movies, and compare his life to that of his old friends, especially his childhood mentor, Lyokha, who had initiated him into the Moscow street life. Kate, who has done research on Soviet medicine for her Master's degree and Ph.D., would talk to Soviet doctors. Her husband, Ari Roth, was anxious to see the new directions of Soviet theater. Doveen, who worked as an editor for First Boston Corp., would look at fashion and trends among young people in their mid-twenties. Barney took a semester off from finishing his Master of Fine Arts degree at Queens College to explore the Moscow and Leningrad art scene.

Steve and I had lunch with an old acquaintance at the Soviet Embassy in Washington, the deputy chief of mission, Oleg Sokolov. Oleg said, "So much is happening in Moscow I want to be back there now instead of in Washington." He was enthusiastic about our ideas and turned us over to Oleg Benyukh, the embassy's head of information, who edits their magazine, *Soviet Life*, and handles foreign media projects. "You'll need a detailed written proposal, copies of your book and the reviews, personal résumés for the whole family, and letters of support for the project," Benyukh explained. He sent off six copies of the proposal in the diplomatic pouch.

In April I traveled to the Soviet Union for ten days on a writing assignment and met with Novosti Press Agency officials to confirm their interest and cooperation in the project. Aleksei Pushkov, deputy chairman of Novosti, received me in his office. He listened politely and said he liked the idea for a television show. "But," he added, "our schedule is full for this year. We'd like to do it next year."

I was stunned. The embassy in Washington was enthusiastic and had supported the project. I had been led to understand that all I would have to do in Moscow was to make the final arrangements. Pushkov was friendly, but said, "Novosti is really not prepared to take part in that kind of television project. We are fully occupied with the picture book *A Day in the Life of the Soviet Union*, but let's think about your project for next year."

"But we are a family of seven people all of whom are working or in school. I can't organize them a year from now. The time for us to come is this summer, otherwise I'm afraid it will be impossible. Please discuss it again with your board," I pleaded.

I left Pushkov's office in despair. All the efforts to get the project launched were wasted. I returned to the *Time* magazine office on Kutuzovskiy Prospekt and talked to my old friends and colleagues there. "Forget about Novosti. Let's call Gosteleradio, the State Committee for Television and Radio. They'll be interested in this kind of project," suggested the wisest of the group. He called, and I went to see Boris Semenov, deputy head of the international relations department, that afternoon. "We have the contacts and promises of cooperation from our old friends," I assured him. I mentioned the poet Andrei Voznesensky, Steve's old school friend, and our family friends. We would come back and look them up, explain the project to them, and then give Gosteleradio a list of what we proposed to shoot.

Semenov listened carefully and said he could not find room in his schedule for us until August. "Everybody will be on vaction by then," I said.

"Don't worry. We'll be able to film then," replied Semenov.

Semenov works hard to create the appearance of a joking, easy-going, always amiable expediter. To our meeting he had invited Valentin Yegorov and Vitaly Syphan, who would be the coordinators working with us. Normally, Gosteleradio makes all the arrangements. Visiting Americans submit a request. Gosteleradio contacts the Soviet organization in charge. If the hospital, school, factory, or military unit responds with interest, Gosteleradio helps produce the program. We were hoping to work around the system by going back to see old friends and finding our own people to interview. Under the rules of the Soviet system, Gosteleradio would still have to obtain the formal permissions. Semenov told me he would try to get them in one month.

If he approved our revised proposal we would be able to film in August. When I again raised the problem of August as a vacation month, Semenov assured me that he would be able to handle us. "It's not vacation for us. We work all the time," he joked. He had CBS and ABC coming before us, and Billy Joel on tour of the Soviet Union.

At Novosti, Pushkov had said that our request to see leading members of the Politburo to discuss their roles in the reforms would not be possible because they were "too busy for the rest of the year." I explained to Semenov that we could do the project without the highest level Politburo interviews and that I would revise the proposal and get back to him.

We began the search for a TV outlet through our old friend Tom Ross, senior vice president at NBC News. The network was interested in the idea of an American family returning to Moscow, but after careful consideration turned us down. The reason: NBC had already approached the Soviets for an anchor and other interviews. They did not want us to compete with their stars. Then Bill Garrett, editor of *National Geographic*, put us in touch with his film people. We had long, inconclusive meetings until they said the film needed a six-year shelf life and they were busy filming circuses in the Soviet Union. "You really should go to David Fanning of 'Frontline' at WGBH in Boston. We'll call and introduce you," they suggested. We had watched "Frontline" shows on the Public Broadcasting Network and were impressed with them. Judy Woodruff, the host, is an old friend. I called Fanning, and he was immediately receptive to the idea. So were Henry Grunwald and Jason McManus at Time Inc.

In Washington we met with David Fanning and he was enthusiastic. His famous talent was quickly apparent as he visualized for us how we could work together to make a film that would probe beneath the surface of *glasnost* ("openness") and *perestroika* ("restructuring"). He explained that we would be the subjects of the film and that he would sponsor our trip to the Soviet Union. We could not be both subjects and producers. Steve, however, could make his own film and would be given partial support. We worked out a budget and a contract for a ten-week stay, seven weeks to prepare for three weeks of shooting. We would have no control over the content of the film or its editing, except for factual accuracy. The book would be an entirely separate project. Gosteleradio would have to approve the final list of subjects to be filmed. We would have three weeks after we arrived to see if our plan was realistic and to get Gosteleradio's approval.

If we could not come to terms with Gosteleradio on the shooting schedule, "Frontline" would not renew our support for the remaining seven weeks to make the film. It would be expensive to live in a hotel with ten people in Moscow. We would need to find an apartment. Fanning said the project hinged on his finding a producer who would be willing to work with us. Up to that point he had only met Steve and had no idea whether the rest of the "kids" were nagging brats or geniuses. Sherry Jones, the prize-winning producer, came to breakfast on the front porch to see if the chemistry was right and made plans to meet the rest of the family.

After a lunch in New York with Kate, Ari, Barney, and Doveen that went on for hours, Sherry and the kids became friends—and a working team. Sherry signed on for the project. After ten weeks in Moscow she knew them as well as if she were their aunt.

You cannot go to Moscow and move in with friends, nor can you just rent an apartment. You need government permission. You can't hire a real estate agent and go into the market. There is no market for foreigners because of the acute shortage of living space.

We told each other that we were going to have to land on our feet running. We would have to work hard in those first three weeks to visualize and organize the whole film. We had the background of having lived in Moscow before, but this time it would be different. The timid schoolchildren of the 1960s were now twenty-four to thirty-two years old, grown up and able to operate in their fields of interest and experience. They had become educated about the Soviet

Union far beyond that knowledge they had brought to it in 1968. We did not have the formal support system and backup of a major news organization, but we were still distant relatives of the Time Inc. family, and the Moscow bureau was a base for messages and mail. We didn't have a car and a driver and an expense account, but we lived in the center of the city and found a new freedom using the metro, trolley buses, and taxis. The five-kopeck fare for a ride to any part of the city was convenient, but like all Muscovites, when we really needed a cab in a hurry we put up two fingers, indicating we would pay double the fare on the meter.

The bureaucratic American Embassy press officer defined us as nonmembers of the press corps and said we could not use embassy facilities during our stay. Only grudgingly did he relent to have our mail forwarded when I told him I had already given the address to family and friends.

The politically alert members of the staff were willing to share experiences and trade stories. Discussing Moscow moves and the new rules with such experts as Shaun Burns, Anton Kasanof, Priscilla Clapp and Kathy Kavalec was a delight.

The morale of the embassy staff was low as a result of the U.S. Marine security scandal and the bugging of the new chancery by the Soviets. The new chancery stands deserted and unfinished in the middle of the new American compound. Daily business is still carried on in the old, overcrowded quarters on Tchaikovsky Street.

Leona had turned from "the perfect *Time* wife" into an independent literary agent with her own agency. In Moscow she had to be like Soviet women. She worked on her part of the book all day, then stood on line to shop for food and organize dinner.

We had first seen the Soviet Union during the Brezhnev era, a period of stagnation and corruption in Soviet life. From détente relations had passed through the confrontation and embargoes following the invasion of Afghanistan. By the summer of 1987 relations had improved. An arms-control agreement on intermediate-range nuclear weapons and a summit looked promising.

When Gorbachev came to power he said the country was "verging on crisis." He insisted he was going to change the system, though he is a product of it. The inertia of the Soviet system remains stronger than the individual, even the general secretary of the Communist party.

Now we would be comparing *glasnost* and *perestroika* to intellectual and economic standards in the West. Where was the Soviet Union heading, and could it really accomplish the economic and social changes Gorbachev advocated?

When we lived in Moscow the first time it was a period of great intensity in our lives, but the children felt they were missing out on the exciting pleasures of life as teenagers in America: rock music, the rebellion of the 1960s, high school dances, and sports were parts of the wonder of life they were being denied in the U.S.S.R. Even so, the return to America after ten years abroad was not as easy as they had anticipated. Nobody trusted kids. The frozen foods didn't taste as good as the ads promised, and the children had to make decisions for themselves. Friendship was different in America. People were more private and withheld their feelings. The kids looked back fondly on the friendships they had formed in Moscow. They felt they had left something of themselves back in the U.S.S.R. that they needed to find again.

Settling In

When I set off for Moscow in August 1987, after a gap of seventeen years, I feared that I would find a totally alien, incomprehensible environment. We had lived there from 1968 to 1970 with a measure of comfortableness about ourselves in that strange land. We learned to speak some Russian, we had some idea of how to dress so as not to stand out too much in a crowd. We formed close friendships that were a mixture of easygoing camaraderie and fear: we could never let down our guard in protecting our friends from their own countrymen, never involve them so much in our activities that they would be called in for questioning about why they were trucking with dangerous foreigners. There was a half-secret quality to our meetings, like children playing spies. We did not arrive places at the same time, did not speak to each other in their entrance hallways so their neighbors would not know they had foreign visitors; we invited them to our house when we knew the maid and the driver would not be present. However, the apparatus was always watching. To enter our building our friends had to pass a checkpoint where the militiaman on duty might or might not ask to see their internal passports. So with all our care they still arrived at our apartment each time with churning innards. We called only a few friends from our apartment telephone; for others we used pay phones chosen at random so as not to form a clear pattern. Every exotica has its own habitat, in which it is a familiar native—we took on the coloration and walking style of the locals and we got along.

In 1970 we came back to the United States and settled into a big house in Washington's upper northwest. Slowly our stories of two years in Moscow came together in print and thus became legends in our own minds. Moscow became a distant place alongside the images of childhood, to be cherished as a memory, but a place in time to which we could never return. Thus, when the idea took shape to revisit Moscow to see what had changed since Gorbachev took over, I was torn between wanting to go back—to recapture a couple of years that were of a younger me, to draw my children around me again as if they were still the ages they had been in 1968—and a fear that it is unholy, at least impossible, to refind an experience through which you have already lived.

Where would I find again the tools that had gotten me through the first time: patience, a self-forgiveness about speaking broken Russian, a willingness to live on their terms of secrecy and fear, an ability to make mistakes and not get rattled by them? I'm nearly twenty years older; can I still put up with inconvenience and making do? My locus in the world is different now; can I leave my office and literary clients for three months? I am free of childrearing but not of the responsibilities of my job. Can I handle the job I have agreed to do, to tell about literary Moscow? Can I make my tongue speak those sounds again and conjure up enough Russian words to communicate even a simple idea?

The first contingent of five—Steve, Kate and Ari, Jerry and I— arrived at Sheremetievo Airport on August 11, 1987, and gathered our luggage in preparation for going through Soviet customs. Missing were two red umbrellas that had stuck out of the nylon zipper case, which was too short for them. Jerry assumed they were gone forever, but an axiom learned long ago came back to me: Your umbrellas never get stolen in a totalitarian country. Ordinary thieves can't do much with them. The authorities don't steal your belongings, they only leave evidence that they have been there, as a warning to you that you are under surveillance. They might peruse your papers and scan the books in your luggage for hours, but they won't steal your umbrellas. Sure enough, they had been put aside so they wouldn't get broken by the baggage handlers. The customs official did spend twenty minutes leafing through Kate's books, asking her questions about the authors, asking if she carried anti-Soviet literature, but it is hard to know whether he just liked looking at her or whether he was trying her patience. If she became jumpy under the scrutiny of his questions, he would begin to look for illegal currency, rubles bought at their natural cheap rate outside the country, or something more serious than Western analyses of Soviet political history. She answered his queries with a tired but benign smile, and he let us all through without another look.

After customs our first stop was at the Intourist desk to collect the two cars (for which we had paid in advance) to take us to our hotel and bring us back to the airport when we left. This charge was added to our hotel bill, which we also paid in advance. The Soviets don't take a chance on bouncing checks or cancelled reservations. The dollars are too important. "You have so much baggage you will never get five people in two cars. We will have to hire a third car for you," the Intourist woman said as soon as she saw us.

"We'll do fine with two cars. I'll help you load them to make sure it all fits," Jerry said.

The two drivers, standing around waiting for us, were impatient to get going. Their faces registered sullen skepticism toward the Intourist agent. She made one more try. "Sign here for the third car," she said, and threw up her hands in annoyance when we refused to accept the third car. The drivers began pushing the dollies loaded with eighteen pieces of luggage that had been checked through and nine hand-carried bags. An often-mended duffel bag was stuffed with the protruding edges of a stew pot, a frying pan, a padded picnic ice chest, a thermos, and whatever sneakers didn't fit elsewhere. These in turn were filled with a supply of instant noodles, granola bars, and tissues.

The monster duffel bag slipped with ease into the huge Volga trunk and still left room for the biggest luggage. All of the small pieces went onto the front seat of the Intourist taxi, leaving Jerry and me a leisurely space, which could have held a third person, in the backseat. The drivers quickly loaded the second car, which had plenty of space for Steve, Kate, and Ari. Off we drove, the driver grumbling about the bureaucrats who have grown so fat working for Intourist that they never think about the poor drivers who want to get finished with their work and go home to their families. "Trying to suck some more money out of you so they can give themselves some more perks," he said.

"Will that change with *perestroika?*" Jerry lost no time getting started; the reporter's first story always comes from the taxi driver coming in from the airport. I have always been dubious about these representatives of the body politic, but as it turned out this one expressed views that we were to hear many times in the months that followed. "So far *perestroika* is a lot of talk, not much action. I'm not so sure we should change everything. Some things are better left alone."

The broad expanse of Leningradskoye Chaussée was clean and grimly gray in the summer twilight as we drove toward the center of the city. Then colorful red, yellow, and orange billboards came into view on the grassy islands between the driving lanes. "Quality Is the Goal of *Perestroika*," "The New Emphasis Is on Hard Work," and a quote from Lenin: "Film Is Our Most Important Educational Tool." These were a change from the clichés of the late 1960s that exhorted all workers of the world to unite under socialism, but their presence was the first familiar note and made me feel suddenly at home in the sense that this alien city had once been home.

In the last week before we left for Moscow, Intourist changed our rooms from the Belgrade Hotel to the Berlin Hotel. We weren't sure where we were going. Our first months in 1968 at the old-fashioned Ukraine Hotel were attached to happy sentiments; we hoped our new location would be equally convenient and the rooms would not be too coldly modern. The drivers took us through Red Square and then around the circle that encloses the lofty statue of Felix Dzerzhinsky, father of the KGB, past the rocky battlements of Lubyanka Prison, past Detsky Mir (Children's World) department store, facing the statue, and deposited us at the Berlin Hotel, only a half block off Dzerzhinsky Square. These were all landmarks we knew well. "Look, next door to Detsky Mir." "Right in front of KGB headquarters. They won't have any trouble keeping track of us." "We'll be able to hear the asses braying at night." This last comment was a reference to a Moscow joke of earlier years in which Dzerzhinsky's ghost is heard at midnight asking for a horse. The next night Kosygin brings Brezhnev to verify that the statue has spoken. In a hollow voice Dzerzhinsky says, "I asked for a horse and you brought me an ass." The familiar square oriented us immediately. We were plumb in the center of Moscow.

The lobby of the Berlin Hotel is barely big enough to hold the seven-foot stuffed bear that greets all guests as they emerge from the revolving door, two souvenir counters, a newsstand, and an un-adorned reception counter. The gentle ladies who manage the Berlin soon had us in our rooms: "For tonight you will be on two different floors but tomorrow we can move you to the same floor." The suites each contained a bedroom, a sitting room with a large dining table, a bathroom with an ample tub and tiled walls, and a small foyer with a luggage bench, a small refrigerator, and an old-fashioned wooden wall fixture with room to hang a number of coats. The furniture, all with carved hardwood frames copied from an indeterminate French period, was upholstered in blue-flocked velvet that matched the heavy bedspreads. A blue-flowered rug covered the sitting room floor. We would not appreciate until morning the rush of sunlight that flooded the sitting room from a wall of tall windows in the shape of an arch.

"I'm so tired. I'm getting hungry. We'd better eat dinner or we'll wake up starving in the middle of the night. Have you seen the dining room?" I asked.

The restaurant of the Berlin Hotel, most Muscovites agree, is the best in the city. Gold and pastel-colored vines and flowers in plaster relief wind their stately way up the walls and around the lintels of doors and windows. A fountain lit with underwater lights is famous for the live fish that have in the past been offered to the restaurant's clientele, fresh from swimming under the mirrored ceiling into the frying pans of the kitchen, but there were no fish in the indoor pond all the time we were in Moscow.

A five-piece band played ersatz swing music, and a singer in a body-hugging lamé dress chanted into the microphone. We tried a little of everything on the menu: caviar with dark bread and butter, smoked salmon, mild smoked sturgeon, small pots of mushrooms baked in a cheese sauce until the top was browned, tomatoes from Bulgaria, and spears of crisp cucumbers. The children ordered halves of small chickens, pounded flat and broiled, that were stringy and dry. "Road-runners," we laughed, and chewed the tough meat off the bones.

Just as we arrived back in our room after dinner I realized that I had left my jacket on the back of the dining room chair. Jerry set off to retrieve it for me, but he had gone only a few steps down the hall when he met the waiter who had served us dinner, returning my jacket.

We slept hard and woke before the sun was up. It was warm under the Russian comforters, which were blankets stuffed into heavily starched white linen covers through an oval opening on the top side so that the blanket pattern showed like an emblem in the center of the bed. "Are you awake?" we whispered to each other, and talked with the slow wonder of finding ourselves in an unfamiliar bed half a world from Washington. We watched the city come alive beneath our window and when it was late enough we called the desk to ask for breakfast in our room. From the first day we formed the habit of all eating together, because it would be our only way of keeping track of each other's activities.

The breakfast came on a rolling wagon: *syrniki*, pancakes made of dry pot cheese, eggs, and sugar, slightly browned on each side, with individual plastic containers of strawberry jam, white and dark bread, coffee, and tea. The coffee and tea were lukewarm by the time we gathered at the table. The next days' breakfasts were omelets with a few cubes of ham and fatback, fried eggs and ham, crepes with jam folded inside them, or pale pink hot dogs with green peas. Almost every day there was a large platter of sliced mild cheese or sausage dotted with white fat. "Can't face it. Let's put it away for lunch." "They don't seem to have heard of cholesterol." "Just pop out the fat with the tip of your knife." By the end of the week we had solved our minor complaint about breakfast by asking the waiter to fill our thermos bottles with boiling water (*kipyatok*) from the kitchen. We could add hot water to the coffee and tea to make them hotter or make our own tea and instant coffee. In the Women's Store, two blocks from the hotel, we purchased a one-burner hot plate for seven rubles with which we could reheat the eggs and get a little crisp on the hot dogs when we brought them out for lunch.

The next day we moved our clothes on their hangers and our suitcases downstairs to a room on the same floor as the room occupied by Steve and Kate and Ari—the couple in the bedroom, Steve in the sitting room. I had a quick look at their suite, and they showed off the polished bronze statue of a nymph and a ring of porcelain ladies with parasols and long skirts dancing around the base of their bedroom lamp. They had a small balcony with a good view of the street, onto which thousands of workers streamed from the two nearby metro stations on their way to offices in the central district.

When we entered our new room I was silent for a while, not sure what to do about the narrow, irregular shape of the room and the dull view into the hotel courtyard filled with air ducts and large gray garbage bins, on the opposite side of the building from the morning sun. There was the smell of stale cooking oil rising from the restaurant kitchen below. An old reserve, an avoidance of making a fuss, a passivity that subtly weighed what I want against what is good for Jerry and the children, momentarily overtook me. I had to break through it, remind myself that I had discarded that kind of acceptance years ago. "Jerry," I said quietly, "I'm not going to be happy in this room. Can't we have the room back that we had upstairs?" There it was, out in the open. Jerry immediately picked up the phone and conveyed my request to the front desk. Meanwhile, his eyes took in what I had seen and felt, and they relayed a silent thanks for getting us out of there. "Yes, of course you can have the other room. We were only trying to give you rooms together." The bellhop and the maids were surprised by the sudden reversal of the rooms, but they put the suitcases, duffel bag, and clutch of clothes on hangers back on the dolly, back into the elevator and up to the fourth floor, back into the sunny suite that would be our home for the next ten weeks.

At breakfast I was amazed to see that Kate, Ari, and Steve each had long lists of Moscow telephone numbers they had gathered from friends in New York, Boston, and Washington. Kate had readied herself with contacts through the Russian Research Center at Harvard, from which she received her master's degree, and the political science department at Columbia University, where she is a candidate for a doctorate. Ari, a playwright, had introductions to theater people, and together they had numbers for Jewish refuseniks, would-be emigrants to the United States who had been waiting eight and ten years for exit visas. Their friends had also given them names and numbers for artists and filmmakers, "for your brothers and sisters to meet." An émigré friend in the States had given me the names of the most interesting writers, and Jerry had his own list of current foreign journalists and the new faces in the foreign ministry. Steve's first call was to his childhood friend Lyokha, whom he had managed to find on a filming trip the year before. Jerry had been in Moscow for three days in April, so our old friends Yuri and Nadya, Pyotr and Natasha, Dmitri, Ed Stevens, and Andrei Voznesensky and his wife, Zoya Boguslavskaya, were expecting us.

I called Larisa Bogoraz, whom I had never met during our first stay in Moscow, but who was well known for her daring dissident activities. A close friend of hers, an émigré friend of mine in Washington, had written ahead to introduce me. It was less than a year since her husband, Anatoly Marchenko, had perished in a labor camp.

We had names of relatives of friends in the United States, and gifts from Americans who had served in Moscow and who wanted us to take these tokens to Russian staff members with whom they still exchanged greetings.

It became evident at once that we were the beneficiaries of a network that formed between the United States and the Soviet Union, a result of the wave of emigration that began in the early 1970s and continues to this day. A large group of Jews fled the upsurge of anti-Semitism that we witnessed as we were leaving in the summer of 1970. Nixon's and Kissinger's quiet diplomacy, coupled with the threat of the Jackson-Vanik amendment, had pushed the Brezhnev regime to allow 35,000 Jews to leave for Israel and the United States in 1973. (The amendment, attached to a trade bill, denied most-favored-nation trade status to countries restricting emigration. Once it passed in 1974 emigration dropped sharply.) Most of the dissidents we knew in the late 1960s, who had been forced to leave as an alternative to labor camps, were now living comfortably in the United States and England. Even as late as 1985, after Gorbachev's rise to power, critics of the Brezhnev regime were forced to leave the country as a condition of their release from the camps or Siberian exile.

Among the talents lost to the Soviet Union by forced emigration are such names as Josef Brodsky, the Nobel Prize–winning poet; Yuri Orlov, physicist and human rights leader; Anatoly (Natan) Shcharansky, Jewish activist; Pavel Litvinov, physicist grandson of the Soviet Union's first foreign minister; and Valery Chalidze, physicist and publisher of the *Chronicle of Current Events*, a collection of *samizdat* or self-published articles and essays on human rights in the Soviet Union. A substantial group of mathematicians, medical researchers, and computer experts, both Jewish and members of other minorities, have left in these fifteen years. During this long migration thousands of people who could have contributed to the restructuring of the Soviet economy sadly turned their backs and left in frustration. Gorbachev has called the migration "a brain drain," but in fact these people were either forced to leave or were not allowed to work in their professions in the Soviet Union.

The United States is now blessed with their abilities from coast to coast, teaching, doing research, publishing, creating computer software. It hasn't taken them long to become Americans, but like all immigrants, they have within them a yearning to visit their birthplace. With the speed of transatlantic telephones and Pan American flights into Moscow there is a stream of conversation and visitation in both directions. Only shortly before we arrived in Moscow there occurred the first visits by emigrants with American passports who came back to visit family and friends.

We witnessed the scrutiny with which Soviet customs officials greet former Soviet citizens at Sheremetievo Airport. No scrap of clothing, no pocket was left unexamined. A Georgian woman with four suitcases filled with still tagged clothing and shoes, which she said were gifts for her large family, argued, wept, and shouted at the inspector who insisted that she pay duty on all of it. Her relatives came to calm her, and the inspector brought in his superior to support him. The drama, in full view of a line of travelers waiting behind her, continued from 5:30 P.M. to 9:30 P.M. We waited for Evelind, who was stuck in the line.

Émigrés who return to see relatives must come as tourists and pay in advance for hotel rooms booked through Intourist, the government travel agency, even if they stay with their relatives. A Russian friend described the painful departures of their exiled friends in the 1970s and their surprising return to Gorbachev's Moscow: "My very close friends in the human rights movement were forced to leave in 1978 and 1979. When they walked behind the customs curtain to leave for the plane I was sure we would never see each other again. Now, ten years later, they come back and they cannot believe their eyes. They look at the same Moscow that they left, but they cannot believe that they were once part of it. They have become totally American and cannot remember that they once lived under KGB restrictions and food shortages."

When my father emigrated from Byelorussia in 1906 it took weeks of dangerous travel across closed borders and heaving seas to reach New York. Few if any Russians went back for a visit. Russians now emigrating have some of the same fears, which might best be illustrated by describing a dream my father had over and over again after he came to America. In the dream a bridge appeared across the Atlantic, all the way to his native village near Pinsk. He walked all the way there and had a joyous reunion with his parents and childhood playmates. However, when he bade them farewell and started back to New York, the bridge had disappeared. The returnees wonder how long the visas to visit Moscow will be forthcoming. The Muscovites we know are watching and waiting to make sure there are no repercussions against the first travelers who try the new rules.

There is another possibility and potentiality to the inadvertent network that has formed between the two countries. The Soviets who have become Americans but still have ties in Russia can help us understand their countrymen. Will this network create an exchange of ideas? Will it help keep peace between the superpowers? Will these Russian-Americans form a new political constituency in the United States that will work to protect the community they left behind? Until now we have received mostly warnings from the ex-Soviets not to be naive about Soviet intentions, but Gorbachev's image has softened their bitterness and many are speaking out to support him.

I soon learned to wear comfortable shoes and carry a *sumka*, or carryall bag, with me whenever I went out. Down the street I could see two lines of Soviet shoppers, mostly women with a few men, waiting to buy tomatoes at one table and bell peppers at another, from vendors who had set up impromptu stands on the sidewalk. Wooden crates, stacked one upon another, all filled with Bulgarian tomatoes, surrounded a young woman clerk. Her head was wrapped in a towel-like scarf to keep her hair from falling onto the produce, and she wore a tattered grocery smock over her clothes. She filled a plastic tub over and over again, weighing out tomatoes on a scruffy balance scale with iron kilogram weights to offset the filled bucket. The price was low—fifty, sixty, or seventy kopecks a kilo (2.2 pounds), with a kopeck equalling about 1.6 cents—set by the state ministry in charge of fruits and vegetables. I walked up close to the weighing operation to have a look at the quality of the tomatoes. The seller was conscientious about removing the worst of them and tossing them into a crate at her feet. Roughly one third of them had to be thrown away. The rest were not beautiful, but they looked edible, so I got in line. The women in front of me were buying four and five kilos each, which required the seller to refill the bucket two or three times. One couple bought ten kilos. There was a rustling of discontent on the line, an impatience at how long it took to measure out their big purchase, but there was no limit to how many tomatoes one person could buy. Behind me, a young woman of about twenty was bored and vexed that her mother had enlisted her in their shopping; her mother stood in the bell pepper line nearby. I wanted to converse with the young girl, but I wasn't yet sure enough of my Russian. "How do I say it?" I whispered to her. "*Dve* kilos or *dva* kilos?" (Meaning was the word for kilos masculine or feminine?) "*Dva kilogramma,*" she answered haughtily, slightly amused but still impatient.

Then a man of about forty joined the line, and he had a strategy to get the best tomatoes and save time doing it. "*Devushka* ("young lady")," he said, smiling, "all those crates are too heavy for you. Let me help you carry them closer." The clerk was familiar with the tactic and at first resisted him, but when he made a move to carry the crates, and there was no real opposition among the other shoppers, she let him have his way. He lifted one crate after another off the piles and stacked them close to her weighing table. When he came to a box that had particularly good tomatoes, he placed it aside for himself. The faces of the women in line showed clearly that they saw him put his favorite box out of reach, but they shrugged and accepted it because they hoped his help to the clerk would get them their tomatoes faster.

"I've become a real Muscovite," I joked with my friend Yadviga a few days later, "I always carry a *sumka*."

"No, not yet," she said. "To be really Russian you have to carry two, one for each arm."

Everything about Moscow was familiar. Even the inconveniences fit like an old shoe. This time I knew the way. It seemed perfectly natural to stand on line to buy some treasured fruit or vegetable in short supply, to cook meals in one pot on the one-burner stove in the hotel room, to make good use of the *kipyatok* (boiled water) stored in the thermos. Russians have a fondness for *kipyatok* because when you are cold and hungry even boiled water tastes good. They tell the story of the worker who saves his money and goes on vacation. In the train station he shows off by asking, "Comrade, where is the restaurant?" drawling out the word *restaurant*. At the end of his vacation, his money spent, the worker returns to the train station and asks in a meek voice, "Say, comrade, please tell me, where is the *kipyatok*?"

We returned to habits from our first months in Moscow in 1968, again washing dishes in the bathroom sink and stacking them in the bathtub to dry. The second time around I was a little better at it. After I found the way to the Beriozka food store, where you pay in dollars with good American plastic credit cards, I figured out how to make potted duck with apple-and-plum gravy in the single stew pot, how to add the doggy bags from restaurant meals to a pot of rice to make a tasty pilaf that would satisfy starch-hungry family members thirty years old and under. Even in the Beriozka there was not much variety and no consistency to the supply. For two weeks there was good German breakfast cereal, then it never appeared again. They had bananas twice while we were there, and I bought as many as I could carry because our Russian friends were as hungry for them as we were. There was usually good smoked salmon and sturgeon, but smoked eel, my favorite, appeared only once, and the lampreys that I remembered with pleasure weren't very good this time. The water from boiling a tongue could be left in the pot and used for pea soup the next day. A lot of pork loin fit into the covered frying pan, and it tasted fine cooked with onions and garlic.

We saved the large restaurant platters that held cheese at breakfast to lay out the food for dinner in an attractive way. There was no lettuce, but sliced cabbage with apples made a good salad, and everyone liked the olives stuffed with hazelnuts, an outlandish luxury I probably wouldn't buy at home. In Moscow we bought what we could get and barely looked at the price.

The hard-currency food Beriozka that we shopped in when we lived in Moscow was no longer open to us. That one was now only for diplomats. Journalists who wanted to buy food for hard currency could only use this new warehouse on the riverfront. Every other place I wanted to get to in Moscow was near a metro stop or on a tram line that passed a metro station, but there was no public transportation to the food Beriozka. I had to either order an Intourist car well in advance or find a taxi driver who was willing to wait for me in return for American cigarettes. Every trip there was difficult; one time I forgot that their lunch hour is from two to three, and I had to wait forty-five minutes to get in.

The Beriozka shops sell food, imported luxury consumer goods, and top-of-the-line Soviet products that are unavailable in ordinary stores: American and British cigarettes, vodka, scotch, French wine, Japanese TV sets and cassette recorders, cosmetics, and perfumes. The Beriozkas are closed to Soviet citizens except for a small, privileged elite who earn hard currency abroad. The system of having luxury goods available for dollars amid chronic shortages has bred resentment and discontent. In the Soviet Union that is followed by humor. A Soviet worker visits the United States and returns to tell his friends, "Everything is the same as in Moscow. All the good things have to be paid for in dollars." Twenty years ago our maid Lyuba found it hard to believe that there was only one kind of store in America—where anybody could enter and buy what they wanted.

Not much had changed in the years we were away from Moscow, but even in the first week it became clear that the food supply was less than in the 1960s. It had become more difficult to put together a meal. It was August, the middle of the summer fruit-and-vegetable season, yet there were only a few things to buy either in the Beriozka or on the street. There were heads of cauliflower one day, but the next week they disappeared; one day I walked into a regular, ruble food market where a line had formed to buy the few crates of cauliflower they had received, and an argument was raging between the women in line and a man who had tried to push his way in.

The Soviet women we met who worked at jobs all day refused to wait in lines two hours each day to shop. "If I see a stall without a line I always have a *sumka* with me, but if there is a long wait I skip it. We just do without fresh vegetables," said a schoolteacher friend. My professional women friends told me they could buy fresh meat, milk, and some canned goods at a special counter for women at their office cafeteria. Other friends described prepackaged market baskets they could order through their place of work before holidays. For twenty-five rubles ($40) they could choose from an A or B list of hard-to-obtain canned fish, vegetables, pickles, and fruit. The problem was that in order to get the package with a small can of red caviar one had to also take ten rubles ($16) worth of a dry salted fish that was hard to give away.

Because getting ourselves out of Washington had been such a frantic effort, we promised ourselves a few days of rest when we arrived in Moscow, but it was not to be. Every lunch and dinner became a meeting with old friends we were eager and curious to see after so many years. The first night we had dinner with Yuri at an Uzbek restaurant where we ate lamb shashlik and spicy noodle soup under the din of the orchestra playing central Asian folk songs and Jewish dance music. The dance floor was lively with circles of dark-haired men and women bending, swirling, and kicking in traditional patterns. Then the music stopped and there was shouting and a rush of bodies as the crowd struggled to pull apart two hot-tempered men who were jabbing and snarling at each other. The one who was considered the troublemaker was still shouting epithets as his friends pulled him off the dance floor and pushed him out the door into the street. The other diners smiled, as if they considered the fight social life as usual, but the angry men didn't see the humor in it.

The next day Jerry's old friend Dmitri had us all to lunch at the Foreign Ministry Press Center, a newly built, modern cement-block building only four metro stops from the hotel. In the dining room we were served a lavish meal by an English-speaking waiter whose skills at presenting the meal were impressive. The red caviar and veal shashlik were delicious, but we grew restive listening to a party line so optimistic it would be hard to discover a country to which it would apply in any reality. "There are less than one thousand refuseniks now, either Jewish or other. Under Gorbachev they have all changed their minds and want to stay. Even a few who got as far as Vienna realized they didn't really want to leave, and turned back. . . . In the old days we did not allow young people to have summer jobs that pay real money. That of course was wrong because they didn't learn the value of money. Now they earn good salaries at construction jobs. They've become independent and say whatever they please. You can't tell them how to dress."

In Dmitri's view the Soviet Union under Gorbachev was fast becoming the best of all possible worlds.

That same night Phil Taubman, Moscow bureau chief of *The New York Times*, and his wife, Felicity Barringer, also a correspondent in the bureau, who are our longtime friends from the years they lived in Washington, managed to add all five of us to a dinner party they were giving in their apartment. The other guests were newspaper correspondents from the United States and Europe, and diplomats from Western countries. I asked about recent reports that the Soviets had gotten ahead of the United States in space development. "It's all 1950s technology, just a lot of it. They're not ahead in quality, just in quantity. And it doesn't do anyone on the ground much good because it's so secret and compartmentalized that there are no civilian spin-offs from which the population can benefit. The one exception is beautifully built baby prams made by an airplane factory," said a British diplomat.

We were already thinking ahead about our own needs, one of which was to find a factory undergoing the rigors of *perestroika*, because Evelind wanted to show the process by interviewing a manager on camera. At the party, a correspondent from a business magazine told us the difficulties of getting into a factory. Unless the factory made products it hoped to export to the United States it had nothing to gain by letting us in to film its travails during a difficult transition. We might see how primitive it really was in manufacturing. The business correspondent also told us that the only way he got in was to arrive on the factory's doorstep; if management didn't let him in he came back until they did.

"How about *glasnost*?" we asked. It was obvious to all of us who read the daily papers that the press was filled with thoughtful stories that could never have been printed under Brezhnev. "But no one has tested the limits yet. It's all pretty tame by our standards," our dinner companions all agreed.

Pyotr met us outside the Pushkinskaya metro station and hugged us each separately. We stared into his face, looking for the changes of seventeen years. His full, neatly rounded brown beard was mixed with gray, and his eyes were calmer; perhaps he looked the same to us because we had undergone a similar transformation. He walked us across Gorky Street and through back streets and a building site to reach his apartment on Alexsei Tolstoy Street. He proudly pointed to historical buildings and told us how happy he and Natasha were to have gotten this apartment in the center of the city. When we left them in 1970 they had just gotten married and were living on the edge of the city in an old *izba* (a log cabin) that had been condemned to make way for a major highway expansion. He was working as a part-time translator of English into Russian. Natasha was attending music school. They had a roof over their heads on borrowed time and their income was just as unreliable. "But we were young then, what did it matter?" Pyotr said in his first toast welcoming us back as if we were family returning from an extended journey.

At his apartment to greet us were Yuri and Nadya, she in the kitchen working side by side with Natasha on dinner, just as we remembered them when they were two young couples who often came to our apartment in Yugo Zapad together. Now Pyotr and Natasha had a seven-year-old son, Anton, whom they had recently adopted and who had brought more than a quiet joy to their life. Yuri and Nadya have a thirteen-year-old daughter, Anya, who did not join us that first evening. "And we have a dog," Yuri said. "Timofey is home with Anya." Yuri had not changed except for the gray in his beard. He was still tall and vigorous, filled with ideas and enthusiasm. Nadya was more beautiful than we remembered, her long fine blond hair framing delicate, reposed features and extraordinary fine skin. She had grown serene, more devoted than ever to her activities in the Russian Orthodox Church. Her occasional smiles flashed like brightly colored flowers in a pastel field.

Pyotr and Natasha had given up their bedroom to Anton, and it now looked like a boy's room, with shelves for model airplanes and cars. There was a schedule board on the wall that laid out his daily activities (beginning with "breakfast and five minutes of conversation with parents" before setting off for school). They slept in the living room, a standard practice in Moscow, where a one-bedroom apartment is divided among parents and children and often a grandparent.

We sat around a large table in the middle of their living room, which was lined with bookshelves and an old upright piano with a swinging candlestick to light the score. The four sat on one side of the table, pulled up to a sleeping sofa. There was room for eight more chairs. They laughed about what we had written about them in the first book and they understood without our having to explain that we had come to do a sequel. We hesitated to talk about the television documentary. We wanted to give them more time before we asked them if they wanted to be on camera.

Seventeen years before neither they nor we would have considered putting them in such a vulnerable position, where even their most patriotic statements could have been twisted against them during a period of reaction. Now Pyotr and Natasha, Yuri and Nadya wanted to speak out to convince us that Gorbachev's hopes for the Soviet Union were their hopes. Now both the leader and his supporters could speak openly of errors and shortcomings in their common attempt to bring about reform. However, there is opposition, and no one knows how long Gorbachev's thaw will last. Could they take the chance of putting their support for Gorbachev onto film?

We did not want to press them just then, and left the question open for the many more nights we would sit around this table.

Jerry called a couple we were not sure would welcome us because they had always kept their foreign contacts at a minimum and kept their distance from the dissident movement. We knew them only because they were friends of friends, who now told us that Elena and Slava would be more open to receiving us. Elena warmly invited us to come the next evening.

We arrived with a gift of instant coffee, which is like a Russian bringing caviar to a friend in the United States, and we brought regards from their friends who had long since emigrated to America. We took off our coats and hung them on the hooks that are at the entryway to every Moscow apartment, then went straight to the kitchen. We crowded around the small table, my back against a large hardwood breakfront. Above my head, carved lions upheld a cabinet with leaded glass doors in which the family dishes were stored. Elena and Slava are both athletically trim, both good-looking, with the quiet manner of their profession—both are scientists who have always wanted to keep out of politics and do their research. It was therefore all the more surprising when the doorbell rang and another couple arrived. The husband was a well-known dissident, Sergei Kovalev, who had only recently been released from a labor camp.

Elena kept a kettle boiling on the stove and repeatedly refilled the teapot from which we all kept replenishing our cups. The Russians at the table enjoyed the granola bars we had brought. We shamelessly ate every crumb of the slices of bread Elena took out of the oven with cheese melted over them, a can of salmon, and sweetened pot cheese with raisins in it, which Katie called a "Proust cookie" because we had forgotten how much the children loved that cheese when we lived in Moscow. It was a good thing that Elena fed Katie well, for in the next hour she worked hard translating back and forth views and arguments that were at the core of the Soviet Union's attempt to pull itself out of its long years of lethargy under Brezhnev. We were all awake and at attention because Kovalev, who we would meet again during our stay, presented the issues with a clarity and openness we had never heard in Moscow before.

All the Russians at the table supported Gorbachev's efforts for nuclear disarmament, but Kovalev warned that neither the United States nor the Soviet Union should destroy all of their bombs. "If a war starts they will build their nuclear rockets again. It is better that both sides stay armed and afraid of each other. That will keep the peace, the way it has until now." He admonished us as Americans for not fighting harder and longer in Vietnam. "You were not the aggressors," he said, somewhat to our surprise.

Kovalev said we all, Americans and Soviets alike, must help Gorbachev because he offers a glimmer of hope for change. "The Soviet system cannot sustain itself without constant aggression." Then he explained that the Soviet Union feels insecure because of food shortages, which makes it want to hold on to the food-growing countries it dominates and seek to control others. "Russia's food problem is a problem for the whole world," he said.

We asked what the average Soviet citizen thinks about disarmament. They all laughed. "There is no body of public opinion here. All we know is what our leaders think and what our own personal friends think. We don't know anything about Afghanistan and we hear very little about it. It only becomes a conscious problem if you have a son or a relative who is sent there."

We remarked how much they, and all Russians, smoke cigarettes. "Don't you worry about lung cancer? Don't you have a lot of deaths from lung cancer the way we do in the United States?"

"We don't have public opinion and we don't have statistics. It makes life much easier," Slava said, and they all laughed in agreement.

Ed Stevens and his daugher Anastasia invited us for lunch on Saturday. The big house and garden in the middle of Moscow, where everyone else we know lives in a high-rise apartment, still stands in rambling luxury, as it did when we last visited it seventeen years ago.

Plums were nearly ripe on a tree next to beds of lettuce and cucumbers. A rectangular gazebo large enough to seat a banquet, which was not yet built when I was last there in the sixties, sits on a knoll overlooking the shrubbery. Ed's wife, Nina, had just left on a trip to the States, so we all pitched in to cook the lunch of pasta, fresh mushrooms, and a whole beef filet. It was the same cut of beef and the same kind of champignons that we had lived on in the sixties. The steaks we cut from the filet were luxuries, but it was the only beef we could buy. Ed laughed, saying, "I got them at the Beriozka. That hasn't changed." Ed is a distinguished American journalist who has lived in Moscow since the 1930s, when he met and married Nina, a Siberian beauty who worked in the same publishing house where Ed got his first job. Ed and Nina left during World War II, but then returned in 1946 when Ed became bureau chief for the *Christian Science Monitor*. He won a Pulitzer Prize in 1950 for his articles "Russia Uncensored." He also worked with *Look* magazine and *Time*, *Newsday*, the *Sunday Times* (London), and the *Boston Globe*, to which he contributes while he is writing his memoirs.

First there was the necessary conversation concerning the whereabouts of mutual friends, then we got to the same question that was on the minds of everyone. "*Glasnost* is real. All you have to do is look at the newspapers and magazines. Gorbachev is sincere. Reagan and Gorbachev should get together and solve the problems of the Persian Gulf," Ed said. Stasia retorted, "Bah, it's a joke. A lot of hot air in the newspapers, but there is no real change. Look at the lines at the stores." Again we heard families disagreeing about the burning issue of their time.

That night we hired a car and drove to Peredelkino to visit the poet Andrei Voznesensky and his wife, Zoya, friends from our first time in Moscow. Andrei comes to Washington from time to time, so it had not been long since we last saw each other. However, Andrei's life had changed markedly in recent months, for reasons directly related to *glasnost*. "We dreamed of freedom for so many years. I could never imagine what problems would come with it."

With *glasnost* free speech applied to everyone. Old worms long hidden in the woodwork had come out to see the light of day, with the same right to speak up and express their anti-Semitic views as their countrymen with democratic views. *Pamyat* ("Memory") began as an organization to promote preservation of historic buildings and recognition of traditional Russian culture. Praiseworthy enough, but with its laudable aims came one of the vicious aspects of traditional

Russia: anti-Semitism. A small group of fanatics took over the leadership of *Pamyat* and they had latched on to Andrei as a target; articles against him appeared in the provincial press and he received threatening telephone calls.

Real or not, *glasnost* was everywhere. The newspapers, magazines, literary journals, and television broadcasts were filled every day with discussions of subjects that had not been discussed publicly in twenty years. "You could skip reading the press for days and not miss anything before, but now so much is printed every day that is truly interesting that we can't keep up with it," a young lawyer told me.

The first step each of the five of us had to make was to divide our lists of phone numbers into those we believed it was safe to call from the phone in our hotel room, which we assumed was tapped, and those we thought we had to protect from the tappers by calling them from outside pay phones. We wondered whether or not the KGB monitored all the pay phones near the hotels, so that even if we chose one at random it would be within the range of their tape recorders. We played the TV loud when we discussed friends, assuming that the wires around the ceiling, which might be a fire alarm system, were really listening devices. "Can they really be listening to us all the time?" we asked each other. No, they can't, but they can sample the tape, and thereby keep you in a state of apprehension. The KGB has always kept the population in line by creating an atmosphere of danger in which Russians restrain themselves from contacts with foreigners out of fear of the consequences.

The clearest change is the freedom with which our friends now speak their minds. After a week of making calls to refuseniks and former dissidents from pay phones outside the hotel, our old and new friends all scoffed at our caution and told us to call them from our hotel room. They assured us that anyone who might be listening already knew that they had frequent contact with foreign visitors. Even friends with whom we had been excruciatingly careful in the old days now were willing to drop by for drinks or dinner in our hotel room.

The KGB Today

It was past midnight when Leona, Steve, and I walked out of the metro station onto Dzerzhinsky Square. After a long, intense evening with friends searching for Gorbachev's motivations, we were sleepy and eager to walk the one block to the Berlin Hotel and warm beds. But there before our eyes was an eerie sight that forced us to wake up and take notice. High above us, in a circle of light, Felix Edmundovich Dzerzhinsky, the first chairman of the KGB, was getting his face washed. A bright blue crane stood at attention parallel to the pedestal of the seventy-foot-high statue, and workmen labored on a platform suspended from the tip of the crane. With heavy bristle brushes they scrubbed the residue of exhaust fumes, bird droppings, and grime from the bronze likeness of Dzerzhinsky, the benefactor of orphans. A fire truck stood by, pumping water to wash down the night's work and leave the forefather's face gleaming for the forthcoming anniversary of his birth and the morning traffic that jams the square. The brilliant blue of the crane, with the stark circle of its spotlights, and the dark, looming figure in the night were a surreal painting come alive. We on the ground were part of it. Steve wanted to rush back and get his camera to record the moment, but I urged him not to since he would also be photographing the KGB headquarters. The aide assigned to us from Gosteleradio warned repeatedly against taking video film of the headquarters. The heavy symbolism of trying to clean up the KGB's image could not be avoided, and we laughed out loud, noting that it was being done in the dark after midnight and not in the broad daylight of *glasnost.*

Behind Dzerzhinsky's back, like a frame, stands the central headquarters of the KGB, the Lubyanka, named after the prison in its basement. The main entrance, which I never saw anybody use to enter or exit, faces onto the square. People do not walk on the street in front of the headquarters. The building is seven stories high and has a yellow-and-pink stone front. Built in prerevolutionary days as the headquarters for the Rossia insurance company, it was noted for the fine architecture of its public rooms and the opulence of its furnishings. There is always a light on in the second-floor office on the right side of the building facing the square. On the left wall at street level is a memorial plaque commemorating that Yuri Andropov "worked in this building from 1967 to 1982" when he was head of the KGB. We often saw a bouquet of carnations left on the ledge over the plaque. When Steve mentioned to a friend that this seemed to be evidence of the people's affection for Andropov, his friend laughed and said, "Are you kidding? Only the Chekists would dare to put flowers there." *Cheka* is the abbreviation for *Chrezvychaynaya Komissiva po Borbe s Kontrarevolutsivei i sabotazhem* ("Extraordinary Commission to Combat Counterrevolution and Sabotage"), founded by Lenin on December 20, 1917. The Cheka is the forerunner of the KGB (*Komitet Gosudarstvennov Bezopasnosti*), Committee for State Security.

The KGB has expanded on both sides of the square with a set of low, heavy, black marble boxy buildings on the left and a pink-and-yellow stone annex on the right. (The First Chief Directorate, responsible for foreign intelligence and espionage operations, has a facility fifteen miles south of Moscow off the ring road, not unlike the CIA facility at Langley, Virginia.) In the back of the main building is a parking lot for official black cars, the initials MOC on their license plates. The tall wooden doors of the back entryways swing open as dark-suited men and uniformed border guards, part of the 250,000-man KGB army, enter and leave. The offices of the Organs, as the KGB's directorates are known, are busier than ever with the influx of foreign visitors coming to observe the new openness. The KGB has an estimated 90,000 staff officers supported by 150,000 technical and clerical workers. Its annual budget is estimated at more than $10 billion dollars.[1]

The KGB is the enforcer of ideology and the guardian of the Party's interpretation of truth. In the 1960s it listened to telephone conversations, harassed individuals who made contacts with foreign correspondents, and invaded our lives so that we felt watched even if

---

1. *U.S. News & World Report*, June 18, 1986, p. 31.

we were not watched. We used the plastic bubble in the embassy to talk about dissidents and we scratched out conversations on a child's Magic Slate so our thoughts could be erased by lifting the plastic film from its backing. That left no written record and nothing to be plucked from the telephone wires. We played Beatles' records loudly so our conversations could not be overheard. Even though we were doing nothing illegal the idea of being subjected to surveillance was an indignity, and we sought to thwart our tormentors.

There are many levels of trying to understand *glasnost*, and its limits. The KGB still permeates Soviet society and maintains control, but its profile is less apparent. Our most vivid initial impression was that our friends no longer feared the KGB the way they had during our first tour in Moscow. The biggest difference is that under Gorbachev people are no longer being arrested and imprisoned for carrying *samizdat*, materials that were judged to be anti-Soviet propaganda. (*Samizdat*, or self-publishing, is the arduous process of typing an essay or article with carbon paper on onionskin to make half a dozen copies at a time for distribution. Forbidden books and ideas were circulated in *samizdat*.) People can express themselves without fear of arrest, internal exile, and imprisonment in insane asylums. In 1987 there were no arrests in Moscow or Leningrad for violations of Article 70, "anti-Soviet propaganda," and Article 190-1, slandering the Soviet state. That, our dissident friends said, is a major accomplishment under Gorbachev.

Today the KGB is under orders to appear more benign in daily life. "The party wants the Organs to be less visible internally, but to do what needs to be done internationally. People should not be conscious of the KGB listening to them," explained a knowledgeable old contact, who was reputed to be a KGB major himself. The limits of dissent have been extended, but at the same time they are not clearly defined. The militia breaks up protest demonstrations by cutting the cords on the TV network's cameras, or it will detain protesters and foreign correspondents as a warning. The heavy hand of KGB harassment has lightened in the daily lives of many of our friends. Phones are still tapped and foreigners watched, but the number of visitors has increased to more than one million a year, including more than 100,000 Americans, so the KGB must resort to selective sampling of key individuals on its watch lists and careful telephone monitoring with computerized responses to specific key words and phrases, such as *Gorbachev, Afghanistan, human rights,* and *strategic arms.*

*　　　　*　　　　*

We had been in Moscow about ten days when an unexpected morning visitor walked into our room while the maid was cleaning and had the door open. He clutched in his hand a slip of paper with our name written on it in Russian, so there was no mistaking that we were his destination. He wore a tattered and dirty brown nylon parka with a hole in the sleeve. His fingernails were broken and lined with black grease, but his most telling features were his clouded over and rheumy eyes that spoke of illness and pain. He smoked a heavy-tobacco Russian cigarette with a strong smell, and his lower lip hung open revealing stained teeth and a difficulty in keeping his saliva under control.

"Are you sure you are looking for us?" I asked as he pushed his way into the room, highly agitated.

"You are an American journalist. I got your name from the In-tourist driver. I want you to write my story."

He began to describe his problem: He had contracted syphilis during a vacation at a Volga River resort. He had passed it on to his family of sixteen people, including nine children. He said he was given some medication but no continuing treatment. Now he was refused even medication. He said he felt he needed three or four months of hospital treatment to cure the disease. His family also needed hospital treatment or they would die.

We could not seem to get futher details from him, so Leona picked up the phone and asked Steve to come up to our room immediately, to interpret for us. The man pleaded with Steve to help him. He said he had been to the Ministry of Health, the Central Committee, and his local hospital: "They all took me for a fool." Only by revealing his story in the Western press, he thought, would he get any response to his needs.

We explained to him that his problem was an internal Soviet matter and we could not help him. Steve told him to go to *Izvestia* or *Pravda*, both of which have departments to deal with citizens' complaints. He did not believe that he would get any help there and made no move to leave. There was an immediate unspoken understanding among Steve, Leona, and me that this was not a case in which our compassion could have any effect and that the reverse might well be true, that this was a provocation designed to lure us into taking up this man's case as a human rights issue, thereby trivializing the head-line cases of refuseniks, divided families, and prisoners of conscience still in labor camps. It is always a touch-and-go question when a Western journalist receives a human appeal in the Soviet Union.

Can I help this man, or can he hurt me by getting me off on a tangent that is irrelevant to the main agenda of human rights? Does this man have a case or is he simply a misfit in the Soviet system for whom I can do nothing to help? I had no way of knowing if he was really ill with syphilis. Clearly he was disturbed and agitated. Our collective instinct told us there was nothing we could do to help him and that we should ask him to leave. Steven repeated firmly that the Western press would not write about his story and he should instead go to the Soviet press, which could help him and put pressure on the necessary authorities. Reluctantly, in frustration, he left.

We complained to the hotel administration for giving this man a pass to come up to our room without calling us first. Nina at the desk apologized profusely and explained that since he had our name she thought we knew him. It would not happen again. The effect, however, was that from that day onward everyone, including our friends, had to give his or her name at the desk before entering the elevator to visit us. This put a cooling effect on Soviet friends who did not want to be identified visiting foreigners. It took some work on our part to reassure them that they would not have to run the gauntlet if we accompanied them into the hotel. From then on our friends always called us from outside the hotel and we went down to greet them so they would not be stopped and checked by the hotel administration.

The incident made us aware that we and our visitors were watched. We could never decide whether or not the syphilitic man was a trap and a warning to us. We learned that his story was most unlikely because Soviet health authorities are very alert to syphilis cases and will go to extreme effort to learn an individual's contacts. They will follow up any known case and treat it aggressively to wipe out the spread of venereal disease. In the Soviet Union, even under *glasnost,* one never knows for sure whether there is any connection between an illogical visit and the logic of KGB control by instilling fear and uncertainty.

In April 1987 *Moscow News* carried a story quoting an East German scientist's report that the AIDS virus had been produced for the first time in the U.S. Army's biological warfare laboratories at Fort Dettrick, Maryland. This was the KGB's disinformation arm at work against the United States. Reports of the story had been carried in

Izvestia and the Associated Press filed a report from Moscow that was used on the CBS Evening News. The State Department protested to the Ministry of Foreign Affairs. When the Soviets suggested a joint Soviet-American research effort against AIDS later in the year, American ambassador Jack Matlock told them no cooperation would be possible until they stopped spreading the lie that the AIDS virus had been produced in America.

When I visited the *Moscow News* on September 15, I made a note to ask Deputy Editor Yuri Bandoura why they had published the AIDS story, which was a blatant example of disinformation to discredit the United States. *Moscow News*, under the leadership of editor-in-chief Yegor Yakovlev, is the point newspaper for *glasnost*, drawing fire from conservative critics for its articles on previously blank pages of history. The AIDS story was either an aberration or a command performance for the KGB. Deputy Editor Bandoura, fifty-three, is a former foreign correspondent based in Japan, where I also served and about which we compared experiences. He was friendly and open as he offered tea, cookies, and chocolates in his modest office, furnished with simple, old, wooden furniture, overlooking Pushkin Square. He spoke with passion on the need for *glasnost* to "move in all directions or not move at all to bridge the gap between generations." When I asked about the AIDS story he was evasive. "It doesn't mean our publishing house has the same point of view. We have not received anything contrary even from the Americans. We are ready to publish a story about the origin of AIDS from an American scientist," Bandoura said. Later I discussed his offer with Ambassador Matlock.

I also discussed the AIDS story with a high-ranking Soviet journalist who thought that making up such an egregious charge was "stupid and would only hurt the Soviet Union in its attempt to present itself as a willing partner in reducing the tensions between the U.S. and the U.S.S.R." In the past my Soviet colleagues would not challenge disinformation stories planted in foreign publications to discredit the United States and then reprinted in the Soviet press. With *glasnost* there was an opportunity for open criticism of such shabby tactics. "We had a big argument over how to handle the AIDS story," the journalist explained. "I warned them that it would undercut what we are trying to achieve with the U.S. When I told a colleague to tone down an article that inflated the story, he got excited and said, 'We have to keep up the pressure,' making an obscene gesture with his forearm. 'Don't forget, we are fighting a class war.'"

Secretary of State George Shultz raised the AIDS issue with Mikhail Gorbachev in their meeting on October 23, 1987, and told him bluntly that the Soviets had been peddling "bum dope" on the subject. A week later *Izvestia* carried an article quoting two leading Soviet scientists who protested the appearance of Soviet articles alleging that Americans had artificially cultured the AIDS virus.[2] I never saw a retraction or correction in *Moscow News*.

Disinformation originates in Department D of the First Chief Directorate of the KGB. Disinformation programs blossomed during Yuri Andropov's years as head of the KGB (1967 to 1982). Under Andropov's leadership the KGB cracked down hard on dissidents and the human rights movement. Those who openly advocated ideas not in conformity with the Communist party line set by the Central Committee were declared insane and sent to mental hospitals, where they were heavily drugged and "treated" for schizophrenia, dementia, and other conjured-up psychiatric ailments. While such tactics had been used before, the systematic perversion of psychiatry to deal with political dissent was perfected under Andropov's leadership—his contribution to the KGB's history. He also moved the KGB into the world of modern communications and computers.

Andropov's chosen successor as the head of the KGB is Viktor Mikhaylovich Chebrikov, a sixty-four-year-old full general with a marshal's star, the badge of distinction for army generals. He commands the KGB's border guards, in effect his own army, and is a member of the National Defense Council. As head of the KGB, Chebrikov directs the Soviet Union's worldwide espionage programs. Chebrikov was named KGB chief in December 1982 by Yuri Andropov and was approved by the Politburo.

He has had powerful patrons, first Leonid Brezhnev and then Andropov. Chebrikov came to Brezhnev's attention as first secretary of the Dnepropetrovsk party organization in the Ukraine. Brezhnev, who had also been the party's first secretary, maintained his power base in Dnepropetrovsk.

In 1967, as a trusted Brezhnev protégé, he was called to Moscow to become chief, Administration of Cadres in the KGB, the top administrative position inside the security apparatus, and the Communist party's watchdog. Chebrikov proved himself a skillful operator, balancing between Brezhnev and Andropov and then shifting to Andropov as Brezhnev's health failed.

---

2. *The New York Times*, November 5, 1987, p. A31.

Chebrikov and Andropov first met in the 1950s, when they served together for two weeks on a promotion board. Although ten years older, Andropov took a liking to Chebrikov, and when Andropov became ambassador to Hungary in 1954 he requested that Chebrikov be assigned as his deputy.[3] When Andropov was named general secretary of the Communist party he appointed Chebrikov the head of the KGB. Chebrikov has maintained a low public profile and, unlike Andropov, he has not been known to privately meet with poets, writers, or intellectuals.

When I suggested to a high-ranking Central Committee member that *glasnost* would be taken more seriously in the West if Chebrikov granted me an interview, he laughed. We were meeting in his austere office on the third floor of Central Committee headquarters on Staraya Ploshchad (Old Square) to discuss my proposal for a TV documentary. I explained that the director of the American CIA gave interviews and that I would ask Chebrikov about the problems of modern Soviet youth and the morality of the younger generation. "He is not in a position to give advice about morality," said the official, no longer smiling, his discreet expression a symbol of an attitude of distaste toward the KGB and its dirty tricks. When I discussed the possibility of meeting Chebrikov with Aleksei Pushkov, a deputy chairman of the Novosti Press Agency, he squirmed and slid away from the subject, saying only, "They have their place now." It was as if I had said something forbidden or dirty when I mentioned the KGB, a subject not to be mentioned in public.

I got the same uncomfortable reaction at all levels of society. When my taxi stopped for the light on Dzerzhinsky Square I looked at the KGB building and nodded to the driver. "*Strashno* [scary]," said the driver. "FBI, CIA," he said, equating them.

The idea that the Committee for State Security is the home of the indomitable Chekists, the knights of duty "who are in service at the front line of struggle against the class enemy," was never expressed to us by friends or Soviet officials.

The power of the KGB is undiminished, but the weight of its hand on foreigners seems lighter under Gorbachev and it is less openly oppressive for our Soviet friends. The long arm of the KGB still reaches into their mail, telephone calls, and visits to the American Embassy to watch American movies. Those known to be in contact with foreigners

3. See William R. Corson and Robert T. Crowly, *The New KGB* (New York: William Morrow and Co., Inc., 1985), p. 382.

are called in, interrogated, and urged to compromise their contacts. The class war has not diminished inside the KGB. Chebrikov and his men still are the guardians of ideology, and they have not weakened their will to defend the omnipotence of the party. Gorbachev may say that survival in the modern world transcends class interests, but that is not the line followed by Chebrikov and his subordinates.

On September 11, 1987, the 110th anniversary of the birth of Felix Dzerzhinsky, Chebrikov celebrated the occasion with a speech. While praising Dzerzhinsky's efforts to build the Soviet economy as chairman of the U.S.S.R. Supreme Council of the National Economy in 1924, Chebrikov failed to mention that Dzerzhinsky opposed Stalin's mass collectivization and favored a more gradual approach to developing the Soviet Union as an industrial power. Stalin's model, with forced collectivization of agriculture and the end of individual private farms, has crippled the Soviet Union to this day. Dzerzhinsky, who favored an expansion of cooperatives, is seen by Western scholars as a backer of Nikolai Bukharin, who was executed by Stalin in 1938 after a "show" trial featuring Bukharin's confession of guilt. Bukharin was finally rehabilitated in February 1988 by a state commission set up by Gorbachev. In Arthur Koestler's classic novel, *Darkness at Noon*, based on Bukharin's case, the hero, Rubashov, signs his confession and is told by the state prosecutor: "The Party promises only one thing: after the victory, one day when it can do no more harm, the material of the secret archives will be published. Then the world will learn what was in the background of this Punch and Judy show—as you called it. . . . And then you, and some of your friends of the older generation, will be given the sympathy and pity which are denied to you today."[4]

When he collapsed in the middle of a speech and died in 1926, Dzerzhinsky was leading the New Economic Policy, or NEP, which made concessions to private enterprise in agriculture, trade, and industry in an effort to restore the economy. It was successful, and by 1927 the production level of 1913 had been regained. In 1929 Stalin introduced collectivization of agriculture and ended the NEP. As one Soviet expert on Stalin said: "If Dzerzhinsky had lived he most likely would have suffered the same fate as the others," referring to Stalin's purges in the 1930s.

In his speech Chebrikov praised Dzerzhinsky for opposing red tape and urging high labor productivity, but he never referred to his role

---

4. New York: Macmillan, 1941, pp. 238–39.

in the NEP and the crucial issue of how to develop the Soviet economy.

Although Chebrikov praised Gorbachev and paid lip service to *glasnost*, he warned:

> A clear awareness is needed that *perestroika* is taking place in our state and society under the leadership of the Communist party, within the framework of socialism and in the interests of socialism. This revolutionary process will be reliably protected against any subversive intriguers.

Chebrikov then argued that human rights activists are being subverted by "Western Special Services" and that "there are many who have thrown off the mask of 'fighters' for human rights, have exposed themselves fully as implacable enemies of socialism and Communist ideology."

He blamed the riots in Alma Ata at the end of 1986, demonstrations by the Crimean Tartars in the summer of 1987, and "the recent provocative sorties by nationalists in the capitals of the Baltic republics" on "imperialist reaction," which "channels considerable efforts into undermining the international unity and fraternal friendship of our country's peoples."

Chebrikov warned of "extremist elements penetrating the leadership of certain independent associations." He added:

> All strata of our country's population are the targets of the imperialist special services. The Soviet creative intelligentsia is no exception. The works of writers, movie makers, artists, musicians, theater figures—in a word all creative workers—have a tremendous power of emotional influence on people. Realizing this, our opponents are trying to push individual representatives of the artistic intelligentsia into positions of carping, demagogy, nihilism, the blackening of certain stages of our society's historical development and the abandonment of the main purpose of socialist culture—the spiritual elevation of the working person.

Gorbachev relies on Chebrikov to maintain order during the difficult period of restructuring. What the Soviet leadership fears most is *besporyadok*, disorder, the loss of control. In unguarded moments friends and high-ranking officials warned that Gorbachev's most difficult task is to prevent discontent from spilling over into the streets and ending his rule. Right now Gorbachev has the intellectuals, most of the press, and the propaganda arms of the party supporting him. The hard decisions on changing the price structure, laying off inefficient workers, and rewarding initiative are still ahead. Gorbachev has moved to subordinate the military to the civilian leadership. In the process he has weakened the role of the military and is said to have alienated its top generals. He has not criticized the KGB or shifted personnel there. When it comes time to end demonstrations or detain the editors of *Glasnost*, a new dissident magazine, the KGB is on the job.

Chebrikov is the first head of the KGB since Beria to hold the title of Marshal of the Soviet Union. He is a powerful force behind Gorbachev and is a voice for orthodoxy within the framework of *glasnost*. Chebrikov's speech on Dzerzhinsky had the ring of the old-line dogmatist.

"Now we know who the real enemy of *glasnost* and *perestroika* is," said a dissident after reading Chebrikov's speech in *Pravda*.

In an earlier article, in *Molodoy Kommunist* (April 1981), Chebrikov warned of the threat of Western ideas to Soviet young men and women. These included "bourgeois nationalism"; religion, which was being used to confuse young people and "cut them off from active social life"; consumerism, including the fad of sexual freedom; and provocation, which he said came from agents in the service of foreign powers. Chebrikov suggested that counterpropaganda be strengthened, because "ideological sabotage by imperialism succeeds only where the propagation of the hostile ideology does not meet with the rebuff it deserves, where young people are not provided with clear and exact answers to the questions that trouble them."[5]

Chebrikov's first deputy, Filipp Denisovitch Bobkov, wrote a detailed article titled "Political Vigilance—A Requirement of the Times."[6] In the midst of *glasnost* in 1986 Bobkov stressed the importance of the Leninist party and "THE NEED FOR REVOLUTIONARY VIGILANCE . . . UNDER THE CONDITIONS OF . . . THE VERY ACUTE CONFRONTATION BETWEEN TWO SOCIOPOLITICAL SYSTEMS—SOCIALISM AND CAPITALISM." Bobkov also charged that "THE MOST FANATICAL CIRCLE OF IMPERIALISM, PRIMARILY THE UNITED STATES, USES THE MOST VAR-

5. Martin Ebon, *The Andropov File* (New York: McGraw-Hill, 1983), pp. 84–85.

6. In *Politicheskoye Samoobrazovaniye*, no. 6, June 1986, pp. 25–33.

IED FORMS OF PRESSURE ON THE SOVIET UNION AND OTHER SOCIALIST COMMUNITY COUNTRIES ON A GLOBAL SCALE AND IN ALL AREAS—MILITARY, IDEOLOGICAL AND ECONOMIC [capital letters in the original]."

Bobkov warned his readers that "Western special services are seeking to infiltrate the system of the Soviet Union's foreign economic relations and use them not only for intelligence purposes, but also to undermine the Soviet economy and to create an obstacle for its successful development."

He cited (again in capital letters) "THE PROVOCATIVE ANTI-SOVIET CAMPAIGN THAT IS SUPPOSEDLY BEING CONDUCTED IN DEFENSE OF HUMAN RIGHTS IN THE USSR IS AN EXAMPLE OF THIS DEMAGOGUERY."

Bobkov charged that religious and philosophical groups are the focus of "the intensification of subversive acts" and warned of efforts to weaken unity and "instigate national dissension and separatist dispositions . . . The carriers of these phenomena, as a rule, turn into moneygrubbers, accumulators and carefree consumers trying to take more from the state than they deserve."

The Central Committee Propaganda Department is in charge of foreign correspondents. Under Gorbachev propaganda and disinformation have come under tighter party control from the Central Committee, specifically from the Propaganda Department shop headed by Politburo member Alexander Yakovlev. In the 1970s and early 1980s, until Gorbachev took over in 1985, foreign correspondents were under the jurisdiction of the Ministry of Foreign Affairs Press Department, the Central Committee Propaganda Department, and the KGB Second Chief Directorate, which deals with foreigners inside the Soviet Union. The KGB, which was the lead organization in charge of control and harassment of foreign correspondents, watched them carefully and let them know they were being watched. Now the tapping of phones continues but there are fewer instances of harassment. Yet there is always the possibility of a surprise move to use a journalist as a trading pawn for the exchange of a spy.

The arrest of *U.S. News & World Report* Moscow correspondent Nicholas Daniloff in August 1986 by the KGB is a case in point. Daniloff was arrested on phony charges and held in prison for thirteen days. He was released in exchange for the freeing of Soviet spy Gennady Zakharov, but both sides denied there was a trade. Soviet officials suggested to me privately that the Daniloff case had not been handled well. By holding him in prison they generated waves of sympathy for Daniloff and created an international celebrity who was offered an advance of more than $600,000 for his book when he returned to the United States. For correspondents in Moscow, however, Daniloff is more a reminder of their occupation's hazards than its rewards.

Foreign correspondents receive their housing, drivers, and office employees from UPDK. The initials stand for *Upravlenie po obslu-zhivaniyu diplomaticheskogo korpusa*, or Diplomatic Corps Service Bureau. It is pronounced "oou-pe-de-ka," after the sounds of its initials in the Russian alphabet. UPDK comes under the jurisdiction of the KGB, and its employees are required to report on the activities of their employers. When it is determined by the Organs, UPDK is used to pressure diplomats or journalists.

In the summer of 1987 the Soviets and Japanese were feuding over the expulsion from Tokyo of two Soviet attachés for spying. In retaliation the Soviet employees of the Japanese Embassy in Moscow, all supplied by UPDK, resigned en masse, ostensibly of their own volition. When Japanese reporters spoke to the employees they admitted they had been ordered to leave their jobs.

Having employees with divided loyalties creates paranoia for some and difficulties for others. For years the American Embassy hired Soviet employees through UPDK to serve as cooks, drivers, and secretaries in the embassy. In Washington and other overseas posts Soviet embassies use only Soviet nationals; embassy wives must serve dinner and perform menial tasks. In 1987 the State Department cut down the number of Soviets who could serve in the Washington and New York embassies to make the number reciprocal with the number of Americans who serve in Moscow and Leningrad. In retaliation the Soviets withdrew their employees in the American Embassy in Moscow. Now private contractors hired by the State Department send Americans to Moscow to work in the embassy and do the jobs the Russians did. Following the scandal involving a Marine guard with a Russian KGB girl friend, security has improved, but life in the embassy remains under the cloud of a fortress mentality.

Soviet militiamen stationed in front of the chancery stop all visitors and demand to see their identification before allowing them to enter. There are eight militia guard posts spaced at intervals around the new American Embassy compound, and Ambassador Jack Matlock has protested the number as excessive to maintain security.

One day when I rang our room at the Berlin Hotel more than ten times from a pay phone a voice answered and said, "There is no one there now." In the old days one never used the office phone to make appointments with friends. They would be followed, and if they were delivering *samizdat* materials such as the *Chronicle of Current Events*, could be arrested for possessing anti-Soviet propaganda. Under Article 70 of the criminal code they would be subject to imprisonment for up to seven years and/or exile for from two to five years. Now, most of our friends were not concerned if we called them from our hotel phone. However, if we spoke certain key words—such as *Afghanistan*, *Gorbachev*, or *human rights*—the phone line began to buzz or was disconnected. This is a standard practice, according to foreign correspondents. Mostly there is an annoying buzzing on the line. Gerlind Younts, of Cable News Network, returned from a Foreign Ministry–sponsored trip to Afghanistan in the summer of 1987 and tried to call in her story. Twice she was interrupted by buzzing on the line when she mentioned Afghanistan. The third time she shouted into the phone: "I have just returned from a trip to Afghanistan with the Foreign Ministry and I'm trying to file my story." The buzzing stopped.

When television correspondents send their news scripts on the telex, sensitive copy—on Gorbachev or Afghanistan—is monitored. "You can feel it happening. Somebody pulls the switch and the telex stops while they call a supervisor and ask, 'What do you think of this?' After it has been read the machine goes back on and you can refile and the copy goes through," explained Peter Arnett of Cable News Network. For most correspondents it is just another of the idiosyncrasies of doing business in Moscow, which, while they do not halt operations, interfere with them, slow them down, and make work more difficult.

Leona and I went to a dinner party at which all the guests were American journalists. "This is like stepping back into a time capsule," Leona told our host, Peter Arnett. "The only difference in the conversation is the word *computer*. You are all still talking about tapes in a secret attic room of the apartment house where the KGB listens to us exchange recipes over the telephone. You are still talking about the ambulance that comes every week to change the tapes. You are still wondering if the maids are reporting family arguments at the compulsory debriefing they must attend."

Individual correspondents are still singled out to be followed and photographed, but such instances, correspondents told me, are the exception—not the rule, as in previous years. "They appear more of the nature of a reminder rather than a systematic campaign," said Mark D'Anastasio of *The Wall Street Journal*. "In the late 1970s and early 1980s correspondents were watched and the KGB had devious ways of letting people know of their presence. There would be phone calls in the middle of the night from irate citizens complaining about a story. Before Gorbachev took power, Press Department officials would not-too-subtly let correspondents know they were familiar with the content of their conversations."

There are still dirty tricks campaigns to indicate displeasure or intimidate correspondents. Tom Shanker, of the *Chicago Tribune*, who has written consistently about the plight of Jewish refuseniks, returned home one evening to find the water turned on and running full force in all the faucets in his apartment. Another American correspondent found all the books in his office rifled and replaced in a different order than he had left them. Correspondents have returned home to find all their electric lights turned on or their best china and glassware placed on the edges of shelves so they could easily fall. Address books disappeared.

Some harassments have abated. *New York Times* and CBS correspondents are no longer regularly followed in two brown Moskvich station wagons stationed outside their Sadovaya Samotechnaya (which the Americans nicknamed "Sad Sam") apartments. The Novosti Press Agency effort to coopt reporters by providing them with *mamkas* (slang for "little mothers," or baby-sitters) has ended. No longer does Novosti try to influence a correspondent's files by providing him with these KGB officials in the roles of Soviet newsmen. This practice has been abandoned in favor of the briefings twice a week by the Press Department of the Ministry of Foreign Affairs. The *Christian Science Monitor* correspondent, Paul Quinn-Judge, said he had inherited a *mamka* who worked for Gosteleradio; but he found the man badly informed and nothing more than a propaganda conduit, so he stopped seeing him. In the days when there was no access to Soviet sources, an official *mamka* could be used to obtain details that were unavailable otherwise. A good *mamka* would provide the tips for checking out a good story. The challenge of seeing who could use whom more was part of the territory for a Moscow correspondent.

Another big change is in the role of the dissidents, who were a major source of news in the 1970s; today they are overshadowed by the informal organizations that have grown up as part of *glasnost*. By the early 1980s most of the dissidents were either in labor camps or in exile abroad. Their relationship to the KGB has also changed under Gorbachev. In place of trials and labor camps they are harassed on a lesser scale by brief arrests and warnings; their goal is to enter into a dialogue with the government.

We spent an afternoon discussing the changes with Sanya Daniel, the son of Larisa Bogoraz and Yuli Daniel, at his mother's apartment. Yuli Daniel and Andrei Sinyavsky were charged in 1965 with anti-Soviet propaganda for publishing in the West under the pseudonyms Abram Tertz and Nikolai Arzhak. Their trial marked the end of the Khrushchev thaw. When I arrived in Moscow in August 1968, Larisa Daniel and Pavel Litvinov were arrested for protesting in Red Square against the Soviet invasion of Czechoslovakia. Their trial rallied the dissident community, but they were sentenced to internal exile for five years. Larisa Bogoraz and Daniel were divorced, and Larisa married Anatoly Marchenko, author of *My Testimony*, a book about his life in the post-Stalin labor camps, which received worldwide acclaim. I met Marchenko briefly in 1969, when he was released from jail and was in Moscow. A worker from a small village, he had a direct manner of speaking with no masks or pretense. I liked him immediately for his openness and still have the picture he gave me. Marchenko was in and out of prison and internal exile for twenty years of his life. He had lived with Larisa in the same apartment, where we were now meeting Sanya Daniel, before his last arrest. Marchenko died in prison in 1986 after undergoing a long hunger strike and beatings by camp guards.

Also present at the afternoon meeting were Sergei Kovalev, who spent seven years in a labor camp and three in internal exile for delivering the *Chronicle of Current Events*. (The *Chronicle* was first issued in *samizdat* in April 1968, and reported human rights violations of individuals and national groups and prisoner mistreatment in labor camps. Possession of the *Chronicle* was grounds for arrest, and it was the backbone of the dissident and human rights movements. The KGB's goal was to prevent the *Chronicle* from appearing and circulating.)

Kovalev was joined by Arseny Roginsky, a Leningrad historian, and Katya Velikanova, the sister of the mathematician Tatyana Velikanova, who is still in exile for working with Kovalev to publish the *Chronicle of Current Events* in 1974.

We squeezed around the table into the small kitchen. Kovalev, whose face has weathered and whose hair has thinned from his ordeal in the camps, said, "Our work and the human rights movement is changing under Gorbachev. Previously it was simpler because it was clear that any interaction with the authorities was impossible. Before no matter what we might have thought ourselves it was impossible for us to have a political position. We could not deal with the government. It was a case of moral incompatibility. We knew that if we said what we thought we would go to jail. It was a very simple approach. We would try to make our views known to the West. No intelligent person could expect practical results, except going to jail, but we also knew that the long-term result would be to let the truth be known. The West called us Don Quixotes on Russian soil. That was a true image.

"It is harder now because we have a special responsibility. Before it was enough just to say 'This is what I believe,' and not be concerned with the results. Now that is not possible. Now there is the hope for a constructive and fruitful dialogue. Every one of us must feel responsibility for what is said. One cannot just be occupied with exposing things, even though, as in the past, there is still a lot to be exposed. Now you have to contribute something positive as well."

Leona asked what alternatives are being offered by the former dissidents. Kovalev was quick to reply: "The intention of the authories to change the lawmaking process has been made public. This intention should be welcomed, but it also means one has to take action so these changes take place in the necessary way. This is very important. We have become accustomed in our history that very little is determined by the law. But if we are to become a cultured and truthful nation then it is important that the laws be changed . . . if we are to have a civilized, modern country we must have the rule of law.

"We can also try to publish our point of view in the newspapers. Not long ago a group of Muscovites spoke out in support of a Soviet proposal for a government-level conference, within the framework of the Helsinki Accords, in Moscow, on humanitarian questions. They also proposed to have an international meeting of nongovernmental human rights groups before the government meeting. They call it an international public seminar on humanitarian questions. As far as we know this proposal is being supported by the Helsinki Commission, the Helsinki group, the International Helsinki Association . . . About fifty independent international organizations have supported this initiative. In the Soviet Union we hope some of the new informal organizations will support the initiative. I am not a member of any of these organizations, but I have some friends who are and I was recently asked to speak at a group called Press Club

Glasnost about lawmaking and some other issues as well. There is no membership there. It is just a place where anyone who thinks he has something to say can say what he wants. It is very recent. It just began this summer."

Leona asked if the discussion groups are an important political force. Can they be compared to the single-interest groups that have an influence on legislation in the United States? Is this possible in the Soviet Union, where there is only one political party?

"The formation of *neformalnyye obyedineniya* (informal organizations) is very important," said Arseny Roginsky, as he drank tea. "It may be the most important and most interesting development in this country in recent years. Young people began to unite by themselves, many of them, and many of those groups emerged. Nobody knows how many of them exist. Maybe there are a few hundred, maybe there are a few thousand. A group may have five or ten members, but at their meetings there are many more. One group in Leningrad had a thousand people at its gathering. . . . We can definitely say there are thousands of groups at this time. They can be divided into three categories. The first is ecology oriented. The second is interested in what is now called the ecology of culture—the preservation of monuments, and defense of the old, and even some new, architecture. The third type of group has political directions, and there are less of them. But even the first two types of group have an enormous political potential, and those groups exhibit a tendency toward self-politicization. Let's say a group is organized to defend a church or defend some house where a famous person lived. Soon that group comes into conflict with the authorities. Then the group begins to exhibit an entirely new tendency. Professionally I have been interested in gauging their direction. Here is their idea: We have been fortunate to have a new leader who wants to change the face of the nation. He is being opposed by the bureaucrats' various machines: the state, the economy, all of them, and the leader has no support. They think they, the informal groups, must form the social base to support Gorbachev. They have a right wing, they have a left wing, but their common ground is their belief that they form the support base for Gorbachev."[7]

---

7. *Pravda*, December 27, 1987, in an editorial titled "Democracy and Initiative," said there are 30,000 *neformalnyye obyedineniya* (informal groups). According to a study by Ludmilla Alexeyeva, an expert on Soviet internal affairs, 70 percent of the 67.5 million Soviet youths ages fifteen to thirty belong to informal groups and spend their free time together in more than 3 million informal groups of ten to

Kovalev chimed in: "These groups are forming a social base for the changes that Gorbachev wants to make. They are not a party or a government apparatus. This is important because they are politicizing themselves."

Sanya explained to us that in the 1970s "dissidents were people who openly expressed the opinions that were held privately by the majority of the intelligentsia. That movement has consistently attempted to talk to the authorities in a specific language: the language of law.

"It was like a chess match, where one of the players, recognizing that he is losing, throws one of the opponent's figures off the board. In the final analysis, how many figures can you throw off the board? The movement was very ruthlessly destroyed in the early 1980s and in the years before Gorbachev. Well, now what? The problems dissidents talked about have remained. That means something must be done about these problems. Forcing dissidents into emigration, putting them into camps and exile, is not a complicated task for this state. Something must be done about the problems, because the problems are real, they aren't made up. Naturally, when the government had to face the question of what was to be done, this Gorbachev fellow emerged. He apparently put to his own use the twenty-year experience of criticism from the outside. So you could say the human rights movement, the dissident movement, the intelligentsia, has won a victory.

"Now, here is another interesting question: What's left for those people who over all these years have been in opposition to the authorities, essentially demanding what is now taking place? The people who were in that movement are now facing a serious psychological problem, to find a place for themselves in the new situation. For some people I know that place remains the same: the opposition. It is understandable psychologically. It's simply that people who have for so long been part of a specific group cannot change their reflexes. For so many years the situation was expressed as 'us' and 'them' and it is indeed difficult to get out of that framework.

"One way out of this situation is the constructive dialogue, which now appears possible. This dialogue could wipe out the division between 'us' and 'them,' and a new relationship could emerge. It does not mean that there would be unity or that there would be total

---

fifteen members. Those associating with public and political aims are estimated at 300,000, ten times the official *Pravda* estimate.

agreement, but just that the dialogue, apparently, has become possible. They remain the opposition. Now it is not only a task for the dissidents, but for all people."

"Is it only Gorbachev? Does he have enough people around him to continue this process?" I asked.

Sergei Kovalev replied: "Gorbachev has his team around him. The place of the Russian intelligentsia is in the opposition. It has always been so. It will always be so. But that does not preclude a dialogue, provided there is respect between partners. Traditionally the intelligentsia fought for change, and they will continue to lead. The dialogue between the dissidents and the government does not exist yet. Basically there is not that kind of respect on the part of the government. At this point all that the intelligentsia can do is urge a dialogue."

"Does the fact that Gorbachev is a lawyer give you more hope for respect for the law?" Leona asked.

Kovalev smiled. "There are so many lawyers," he said. Laughter.

"For the past two years under Gorbachev nobody has been tried and sentenced under Article 70, which provides for penalties of labor camp and exile for distributing anti-Soviet propaganda. What does that mean?" I asked.

"That's the most important development. You have to agree, my friends, that is a colossal development. It's more important than the publication of books by Rybakov and Pristavkin; it's more important than publication of twenty books," said Arseny Roginsky.

"How has that changed things?" I asked.

Arseny said, "There are still people in prison, and as long as they are in prison there cannot be a dialogue. It is a prologue to the prologue. Some were given the opportunity to confess the guilt of their crimes. There are estimates of four hundred to four thousand political prisoners. We think there are about twenty in psychiatric prisons. But we don't know. One political prisoner is too many."

"Why are they still holding them?" we asked.

"People are in prison because they have refused to sign a document admitting their wrongdoing and asking to be released. Velikanova refused to sign," said her sister, Katya.

Katya said Tatyana Velikanova, who represented the Initiative Group for Human Rights, was arrested in November 1979. She was sentenced to four years in a strict-regimen labor camp and five years of internal exile.

"While these people are there, how can we talk about *perestroika*? That's why we call it the prologue to the prologue," said Roginsky.

"If the West agrees to participate in a human rights conference in Moscow, they will have to let these people free," said Kovalev. "But that's a guess. An educated guess, but still a guess."

We drank more tea, ate *pirozhki* (fried dough filled with chopped cabbage), and listened carefully to their warnings that a human rights conference should not be held in Moscow unless a series of conditions are met. These include the need to allow nongovernmental groups to be represented and for there to be a preconference meeting to discuss the agenda, with nonofficial groups included. In the past, human rights activists had been spirited out of town or kept under house arrest when foreign delegations interested in human rights issues were in Moscow. "The challenge of *glasnost* is for Gorbachev to take action, not only to express his good intentions," they argued.

Sanya Daniel, in carefully measured phrases, said, "We have a moral obligation to those still in prison. I should remind you that we are meeting in the apartment of a man [Anatoly Marchenko] who died in prison one year ago after a hunger strike, fighting for the freedom of all political prisoners."

Thus far, the government has not invited any of the dissidents to take part in preparations for a human rights conference. Sergei Kovalev wanted to tell us his views: "I'm afraid to be prematurely optimistic, but the fact that there have not been any arrests for anti-Soviet activities and people are being freed are definite signs. The things our leader is saying now are things we have not heard in the seventy years of Soviet power. Gorbachev has said that there is something higher than class interest, namely survival in the modern world. We never heard that before. If you said these things very loudly five years ago you would be put in jail, but so far nobody has put Gorbachev in jail." We all laughed.

"Of course, they can backtrack, but it would be difficult for them to turn back. It is not that simple."

"Yes," I agreed. "If you look at the history of the past seventy years there are periods of reform and then periods of repression. Things open and close."

"It seems to me," said Sergei, "that what is happening now is a unique period in history. Nothing like it has happened before. Gorbachev will never say this, but I don't think Gorbachev is really interested in communism.

"If you compare what is happening now to the 1920s, there was a period where we went from openness to being closed and repression, but I don't think you can really make a comparison between then and now. The comparison with the Khrushchev era seems more formidable, but the problem is that I think Khrushchev believed, quite naively, that as soon as the cult of personality was out of the way everything would be in order. Everything would be fine in the country. Its political theory is the most progressive in the world. Its economy is the most progressive, as is its science and its art. Everything is beautiful. Only Stalin lies in the way. Throw him the hell out and that's it. In 1980 we'll live under communism. Personally, I believed then [in 1960] that in twenty years communism would come."

Katya interjected to say, "Well, maybe we *are* living under communism." Laughter.

Kovalev said, "The thing is that Gorbachev understands that we don't live under communism. He has understood that communism isn't here. That's how it is."

I said I had heard a story that when Gorbachev was on a trip to Riga he was asked, "When will we have communism?" He replied: "Comrades, we have had communism. Now we have to work."

They all laughed.

Sanya said, "Sometimes I get the impression from reading the press that Gorbachev, or perhaps his group upstairs, is not too certain about socialism, either. They ask if what we have built is really socialism.

"Gorbachev has told us that what is happening is a revolution, not just cosmetic changes. What that means is the replacement of old institutions with new institutions, and there is a dialectic in a revolution. So far this has been a bloodless revolution from above."

Katie, who had been busy translating, ate a *pirozhok* and asked, "Have you tried one of these?" It was time to wind up our meeting.

I was fascinated with how Khrushchev's image had changed from that of disgraced buffoon in 1970, when I left Moscow to work on editing his memoirs with Strobe Talbott, to that of a brave reformer who had denounced Stalin's crimes and his cult of personality. Khrushchev was slowly being rehabilitated, and there were rumors that his body might be moved from its resting place in Novodevichiy Convent to a deserved place of honor in the Kremlin wall. But the most significant development was the growing role of the *neformalnyye obyedineniya*, the informal organizations, and their impact.

Kovalev told us that on Constitution Day a club called Democracy and Humanism demonstrated on Kropotkinskaya Square with slogans that read: "The Constitution Is for the People Not the Party," "Down with Partocracy," and "Down with the Power of the Party."

The day before, *Vechernaya Moskva* published a notice saying that the demonstration would not be permitted. Those who showed up were arrested and held for four hours.

Kovalev, who had served nine years for distributing the *Chronicle of Current Events*, smiled bitterly and asked, "Can you imagine what would have happened to them a few years ago?"

Russia Asleep

At the end of a searching discussion of Gorbachev's aims and his chances for success we were still probing for historical answers, but we were also ready for a bit of Russian humor. "You want to know why Khrushchev was overthrown? It's very simple," Arseny Roginsky said, keeping a straight face with difficulty. "Those under him were all very tired. They wanted to be able to sleep at night." Then he explained the Sleep Theory of Soviet History.

"Stalin worked all night, and his aides had to stay awake with him. When Stalin was on vacation they still couldn't sleep because eventually he began to think they were plotting against him. One by one they were shot. At night they would listen for footsteps on the stairs and hope the KGB were coming for their neighbors, not them. Then Khrushchev took over and the *apparatchiki* were very relieved, but they soon found that even though it was better they still could not sleep at night. Khrushchev was always reforming. So a member of the *nomenklatura* could be the head of a ministry at night and in the morning find out he was chairman of a collective farm.[1] Khrushchev was always moving things around. He was always restless. The *apparat* wanted to sleep. They wanted nothing so much as a little peace.

"Brezhnev came in and gave them what they wanted. Everyone loved him. One never went down, only up. Once they had a position they stayed there, went up, or died there. Nothing changed, year after

---

1. *Nomenklatura* positions are designated by the Communist party and are under party control. There are an estimated three million *nomenklatura* positions in the Soviet Union, and those on the list are given special party privileges and constitute a ruling class in a classless society.

year. Not only could you feel confident about your own job but you could depend on your friend still being the chief of the Ministry of Health five years in the future when your son had to get into medical school. It was like a sleeping kingdom. Brezhnev gave himself medals and then personally pinned them on his friends. He was the kind poppa on the top. He had one call: 'Fight for peace.'

"Then came Andropov and he never smiled. He told them everything is bad because everyone is stealing and we have no discipline. His idea was simple: get rid of the thieves. He cleaned up the *apparat* and got rid of the most guilty ones. People loved Andropov. Most important to them, he was the strict father who told them what they had to do to make the country right again. They were confident in him, as you would be in your own father. So we were willing to make the sacrifices that we all knew were necessary. The Soviet people cried real tears when Andropov died.

"Then came Chernenko. He was old and senile, a jester to Brezhnev. He had no time to figure out who he was before he died.

"When I was in the camps a frightening thing happened to me. There was a special room for political information. One of the posters that hung in the room was a moral code for the building of communism. The day that Gorbachev came to power I was sick and was in the barracks. The drunken political officer came in with the head of the camp police. I was lying in bed. 'Come here and help me take down the moral code,' he ordered.

" 'Citizen director, why?' I asked.

" 'Everything has gotten old now,' he replied, and pulled down the code, tucked it under his arm and walked off. I knew that a new revolution had come and the *apparat* would not sleep again.

"Gorbachev must now create a restructuring of the economy without moving people around too much. We don't want to see him test his strength too much because we are not sure he is strong enough to do what is necessary. He knows that he must not make the *nomenklatura* feel insecure. It's a paradox for him." We all laughed and told Arseny he should write a fairy tale called "The Sleeping Kingdom of Socialism."

When we lived in the Soviet Union in the late 1960s we had a picture of Khrushchev that was very different from the way Russians see him now. Five years after his demotion from general secretary of the Communist party to pensioner even the maid spat on his memory. Khrushchev was known as a buffoon, a wild experimenter whose virgin lands agricultural policy collapsed in disarray. He was given little credit for de-Stalinization or for increasing the size of private plots or liberalization in the arts. He was identified with the Cuban missile crisis and building the Berlin Wall, two reckless adventures that nearly led to world war. Khrushchev's efforts to decentralize the economy, the forerunner of Gorbachev's reforms, were mocked as "harebrained schemes."

Arseny's description of Andropov as a stern, beloved father, for whom the whole nation wept when he died in February 1984, was also a revelation to us. Watching Andropov from the West we could not imagine such a benign image.

The next morning was a beautiful Indian summer day. From our hotel room the sky was clear and blue with bright sunshine. Andropov was still on my mind when Dmitri called to say that he had gotten a tennis court for us at Sokolniki Park at noon. It was too late to order the sauna there, but we would have a bite to eat afterward. Soon after he and Irina picked us up it became clear that the car was not going to make it all the way to the park. "Damn it," he said, "I just had the car fixed. Now I'll have to take the car back. I can't even get mad at the mechanic because I don't want to lose him. This happens every time I take the car in for service, but what can I do? There are no good garages. Now I'll have to invite him again for dinner and an American western on videotape."

He drove the sputtering Lada until he could find a wide avenue where parking was allowed. "We're not going to let the car waste *babye leto* ["Grandmother's summer," the Russian expression for Indian summer]." He hailed a taxi, transferred the bags of tennis gear and cold beer, and we rode to Sokolniki Park without further mishap. On the way we gossiped about Gorbachev's speech in Murmansk foreshadowing an increase in food prices.

"I heard that *Pravda* and the other newspapers were four hours late the next morning," Jerry said.

"That's not unusual," Dmitri said, laughing. "It often happens with a major speech because Gorbachev departs from the prepared text. *Pravda* has to print the full text and it has to be checked against what he says. By the time it is transcribed, edited, and approved, the deadline is past."

At first Jerry and Dmitri played singles while Irina and I warmed up on another hard clay court. My fears of her being a better player than I was were soon dispelled when she and I hit and missed about an equal number of shots. Then we played doubles. It was a close and tense game, and they did not like losing. For a fleeting moment the game became a symbol of national pride, but we were soon over that—laughing, opening Danish beers that we had wrapped in layers of *Pravda* to keep cold, and looking forward to lunch. We passed the central building of the sports complex and laughed heartily at a woman on a scaffold who was shouting choice curses at her male partner, who had gone off to a long lunch, leaving her to wash the plate glass windows of the gymnasium with no way to get down.

We returned to Dmitri and Irina's apartment, where the meal she had prepared was waiting. Irina had made my favorite dish, whole sweet peppers filled with a mixture of egg and *tvorog* (a dry pot cheese) and cooked in a frying pan until the peppers are soft and the cheese has formed a firm cake. Dmitri poured their home-flavored lemon vodka and offered us an array of homemade pickles, cabbage, tomatoes, and garlic cloves. "It's after two o'clock, so we can drink vodka," Dmitri said, smiling, referring to the new law against drinking vodka in restaurants before 2 P.M.

The phone rang. It was Dmitri's son, a journalist, who said he was on his way to join us for lunch. "It's wonderful to be a young man today. All the major newspapers and journals—*Pravda*, *Izvestia*, and *Ogonyok*—are competing for the reporters who have spent time abroad. What a time to be a journalist! You can say so much more than you could three years ago. But now you really have to report and say something. The old boys don't know how to tell a story. All they ever did was sit around and think up variations on how to praise Brezhnev. It was like a jazz session but there were no new ideas or criticism."

Jerry and I had the afternoon off from filming because Sherry and the crew were shooting a scene with the children and a group of avant-garde artists. Dmitri was curious about what we had been shooting, and we were hesitant to say that we had filmed a session with dissidents the day before. But Arseny's image of Andropov popped back into my mind, and I wanted to test it on Dmitri. "We filmed a discussion yesterday in which Andropov was portrayed as a beloved father," I said with a question mark in my voice.

"Of course. Andropov was wonderful. Everyone, including the critics and the dissidents, the whole country, loved him. He was a very special leader. He had imagination and a fierce strength. We were ready to follow him into the fire. He was both kind and strict. We were willing to do whatever he said needed to be done to reform the country because we knew that it was good for us. There never would have been all this hesitation and questioning if Andropov had lived to accomplish *perestroika*."

Dmitri's face grew solemn as he spoke slowly and with emotion to emphasize his sincerity. Only to such a close friend as Dmitri could I speak the truth as I saw it. "That's not the Andropov we know in the West. We hold two things against him." Dmitri's eyes widened as he sat back to listen. He could hardly believe that we did not love Andropov the way he did. "For us Andropov is the butcher of the 1956 Hungarian revolution who lured his victims with food, drink, and smiles. He made promises to the Hungarian leaders, then arrested and executed them."

"But he was young then and he was only an ambassador who took orders from the Center."

"He did his job awfully well," Jerry said sardonically.

"And what is the second thing?" Dmitri asked.

"He will go down in history for saying that dissidents were crazy and forcing them into insane asylums to crush their ideas. He used drugs to turn people into vegetables and systematically crushed dissent this way," said Jerry.

"He did not start it," said Dmitri.

"No, but he institutionalized it."

Dmitri shook his head wonderingly. "Such a great man. I can't imagine that you would pick out these two small things to characterize him. He was much bigger than that."

Andrei Sakharov: The Collective Conscience

Before I called Andrei Dmitrievich Sakharov I asked a friend who knew him well to pave the way. Although I had written about him often I had only met him once because when I was a correspondent in Moscow Sakharov did not meet with the press. Now I was anxious to obtain his views on Gorbachev and *perestroika*. "Only call between eleven A.M. and four P.M. or from six-thirty P.M. to eight-thirty P.M.," Bill Eaton of the *Los Angeles Times* advised. "His wife is trying to give him some time to himself."

Sakharov answered the phone, and he was friendly and polite. He sounded as if he remembered my name, but he complained how busy he was. "Call back in two weeks," he said.

Sakharov, sixty-seven, has been a major part of the story since I began covering Moscow on August 21, 1968, the day after the Soviet Union invaded Czechoslovakia. Shortly after I arrived, I learned that Sakharov was under heavy fire at the Academy of Sciences. In the spring and summer of 1968 his essay titled "Progress, Coexistence and Intellectual Freedom" was circulated in Moscow among intellectuals. In July it was published in *The New York Times* and created a sensation. Sakharov had two major themes: "civilization is threatened by a universal thermonuclear war" and "intellectual freedom is essential to human society—freedom to obtain and distribute information, freedom for open-minded and unfearing debate and freedom from pressure by officialdom and prejudices." Andrei Sakharov was making the first plea for *glasnost* or openness. By publicly raising the need for freedom of information, he set the stage for Mikhail Gorbachev's campaign for *glasnost* seventeen years later.

In the Brezhnev era of strict conformity to Communist party intellectual control, Sakharov's views were heresy. Reports quickly spread that the then-forty-seven-year-old physicist, known as the father of the Soviet hydrogen bomb, had been denied his security clearances and his laboratory for experiments. Sakharov was dropped from his government positions and isolated by his colleagues. A year later, in the summer of 1969, Sakharov was given a job as a senior scientist at the Physics Institute of the Academy of Sciences, where he had done his graduate work. It was the lowest possible rank for an academy member and a punishing comedown for the man who, at age thirty-two, had been named a Doctor of Science and the youngest full member in the academy. The drop in prestige was accompanied by a loss of pay and perquisites. The head of the Academy of Sciences, meeting with Time Inc. editors Hedley Donovan and Henry Grunwald in October 1969, called Sakharov "naive," but he assured his visitors that Sakharov was still a member of the academy.

Sakharov did not meet with foreigners or Western correspondents in those days because of the secrecy restrictions placed on his scientific work. His punishments and abasement by the authorities were not revealed until later, but his ideas were made available in writing through *samizdat*, or self-publishing. It was an arcane process. In those days, Sakharov did not want to be in the position of directly providing his essays to Western correspondents. If they were circulating in Moscow and the correspondents obtained copies of them then Sakharov could not be charged with disseminating anti-Soviet propaganda.

On one occasion Dusko Doder, then with United Press International, and I were given a *samizdat* document attributed to Sakharov. We read it carefully and considered filing a story on it. "How do we know Sakharov wrote this?" I asked Dusko.

"We don't. It was left at the office," he replied.

"Can't we call him and check or get a friend to get through to him?" I asked.

"We can try, but it will take a day or so."

"I think we had better do that. I just don't like the sound of the language. It may not be Sakharov and it is very critical of official Soviet policy."

Fortunately, we waited. Two days later word came back from a friend of a friend who had checked with Sakharov. He had not written the protest and it was clearly a provocation, the first of many. Had we filed stories and had our editors published them Sakharov could have been accused of anti-Soviet propaganda activities. The purity of his position would have been muddied with a trumped-up story. *Time* and UPI would have been accused of printing any anti-Soviet material they could lay their hands on.

Sakharov continued to speak out, and in November 1970, with physicists Valery Chalidze and Andrei Tverdokhlebov, he founded the Moscow Human Rights Committee. Sakharov became a public activist. He dictated appeals to foreign correspondents on behalf of dissidents who were on trial for anti-Soviet behavior. He personally went to the courts to attend the trials or stood outside in silent protest when the authorities refused him permission to enter.

He was still a member of the academy, but he was shunned by his establishment colleagues. He found a new world of human rights advocates, and his committee became the focal point for protest. In 1973 Sakharov was attacked publicly in the Soviet press for his actions.

I first met Andrei Sakharov in 1974, during Henry Kissinger's visit to Moscow for a meeting with Leonid Brezhnev. It was the first time I had been back since the fall of 1970. We were there for only a few days in March, a quick in-and-out visit during which Kissinger would present Brezhnev with a proposal for strategic arms reductions. The press accompanying Kissinger was invited to the Kremlin for a photo opportunity at the beginning of their meeting. This would give us a chance to observe Brezhnev up close and provide a layman's opinion of his health, which was rumored to be deteriorating. Brezhnev had put on weight and his voice was raspy, but he gave an impromptu performance of good cheer and strength. He even had a prop, his wooden cigarette box with the built-in timer that opened a lock on the box every two hours, so he would not chain smoke through the day. Brezhnev confessed that he was smoking too much despite the box. We stood around the green-felt-covered table laden with mineral water, crisp white notepads, and freshly sharpened pencils. Kissinger and Helmut Sonnenfeldt, his expert on the Soviet Union, joked with Brezhnev. It seemed a world of reason and possible agreement on SALT II. Kissinger was concentrating on strategic arms reductions and was careful not to link them to human rights. In his grand design, human rights were to be dealt with in "quiet diplomacy" and prevented from becoming a public issue.

Six weeks earlier, on February 14, Alexander Solzhenitsyn had been forcibly deported from the Soviet Union to West Germany and deprived of his citizenship. Kissinger showed little interest in Solzhenitsyn's plight and said, "The necessity for détente does not reflect approbation of the Soviet domestic structure. The necessity of détente is produced by the inadmissibility of general nuclear war under present conditions. Our human, moral, and critical concern for Mr. Solzhenitsyn and people of similar convictions should not affect the day-to-day conduct of our foreign policy."[1]

The scene in the Kremlin was carefully structured to create the atmosphere of cooperation, reasonableness, and the possibility of mutual agreement. Human rights, trade, and Soviet support for the war in Vietnam would not be openly linked to strategic arms control.

That same evening I was invited by Russian friends to go to a farewell party for Solzhenitsyn's wife, Natalia Svetlova, who was leaving with her mother and children to join her husband in Switzerland. She had gathered his writings and arranged for them to be smuggled to the West. Then she packed what would pass the customs and made the final arrangements to leave. The party in her apartment on Kozitskiy Pereulok, off Gorky Street in downtown Moscow, was a wake. Many of the leading Soviet dissidents were there, including Lev Kopolev, Yuli Daniel, and Alexander Ginzburg, along with Svetlova's first husband, Andrei Tiurin. (Sakharov does not like the term *dissidents*. He prefers the old Russian word, *volnomyslyashchiye*, "freethinkers.")

The rooms were poorly lit and the air was heavy with cigarette smoke. There was little to eat or drink, but the combination of emotional songs and deep unity of purpose was intoxicating. The songs were traditional Russian dirges, slow and rolling with sorrow. The atmosphere was one of mourning. Although Natalia Svetlova was joining her husband with her children, they were being forced to leave the motherland they loved. "It is painful to part from Russia, painful that our children are condemned to a life without a homeland, painful and difficult to leave friends who are not protected," said Svetlova.

During the evening I was introduced to Sakharov. He was tall and

---

1. *The Washington Post* and *Baltimore Sun*, February 15, 1974.

thin with stooped shoulders. He seemed particularly sad and tense as he sang with the group. Yet, there was an energy and resonance about him that distinguished him from others in the room. I had read that in December 1973 Sakharov and Yelena Bonner had entered a Moscow hospital. He was suffering from high blood pressure and a heart condition. She had a thyroid problem. They were released from the hospital in January 1974. We talked briefly of his health and he said he was feeling better. I told him I felt I had known him through his statements and explained what it was like making sure we had the real documents before he had started to meet with the press. He smiled and thanked me and the other correspondents for the careful handling of his statements. He was friendly but cautious. With Solzhenitsyn gone, Sakharov now spoke for the collective conscience of the Soviet Union. I could see that he preferred to make statements in writing.

In the summer of 1974 *Sakharov Speaks*, a collection of his statements and interviews, was published in the United States. In his introduction Sakharov reiterated the importance of his 1968 book, *Progress, Coexistence and Intellectual Freedom*. He noted that "the general tenor of the book was affected by the time of its writing—the height of the 'Prague Spring.'" He called the work "eclectic, and imperfect ['raw'] in terms of form. Nonetheless its basic ideas are dear to me. In it I clearly formulated the thesis (which strikes me as very important) that the rapprochement of the socialist and capitalist systems, accompanied by democratization, demilitarization, and social and technological progress, is the only alternative to the ruin of mankind."

In 1975 Sakharov was awarded the Nobel Peace Prize but was forbidden to travel to Stockholm to accept it. When Jimmy Carter was elected president of the United States Sakharov sent him a telegram of congratulation. In January 1977, after the inauguration, Sakharov wrote to Carter congratulating him on his commitment to human rights and pointing to the human rights problems in the Soviet Union. I was the spokesman for the National Security Council at the time and discussed the president's response with National Security Advisor Zbigniew Brzezinski. "Sakharov is a Nobel prize winner and the president would do no less with a letter from a Nobel Laureate from any country," Brzezinski said. A bad precedent had been set by President Ford, who refused to meet with Alexander Solzhenitsyn when he came to Washington after forced deportation from the Soviet Union. Carter's reply was polite and pointed to his universal concern for human rights. Sakharov received Carter's letter at the American Embassy in Moscow. The day that the president's letter was released in Moscow, the Soviet ambassador to Washington, Anatoly Dobrynin, called at the State Department to protest. In a personal letter to Carter on February 25, 1977, Brezhnev described the letter as "correspondence with a renegade who proclaimed himself an enemy of the Soviet state."[2] In a speech on March 22, 1977, Leonid Brezhnev denounced "outright attempts by official American agencies to interfere in the internal affairs of the Soviet Union."

In 1980 Sakharov protested the Soviet invasion of Afghanistan and he was stripped of his Soviet medals and awards (the Order of Lenin, three times Hero of Socialist Labor, the Lenin Prize, and the State Prize) and banished to Gorky. He languished there, going on hunger strikes to protest his circumstances and that of his family, until called on the telephone by Mikhail Gorbachev in December of 1986. Gorbachev asked Sakharov to return to Moscow "to continue his patriotic activity."

In February of 1987 Sakharov, back from internal exile in Gorky, appeared at the govenment-sponsored international Forum for a Nuclear-Free World and the Survival of Mankind in Moscow. He gave three speeches on human rights, the nuclear arms race, and U.S.–Soviet relations. In March Sakharov edited the speeches and published them in *Time* magazine because the main points of his remarks were not published in the Soviet press and "Western radio stations reported my views imprecisely and incompletely." He summed up the progress of *glasnost* and *perestroika* with his usual candor:

> Despite the continuing process of democratization and the increasing openness in the country, the situation remains contradictory and unsettled, and in some areas instances of backward movement can be observed (for example, the new decree on emigration). Without a resolution of political and humanitarian problems progress in disarmament and international security will be extremely difficult, if not impossible.
>
> Conversely, democratization and liberalization in the U.S.S.R.—and the economic and social progress closely associated with them—will be impeded unless the arms race slows down. Gorbachev and his supporters, who are waging a difficult struggle against ossified, dogmatic and self-seeking

2. Zbigniew Brzezinski, *Power and Principle* (New York: Farrar, Straus and Giroux, 1983), p. 155.

forces, have an interest in disarmament, in making sure that huge material and intellectual resources are not diverted to producing new and more sophisticated weapons.[3]

Sakharov also established his own position on Ronald Reagan's Strategic Defense Initiative (SDI). He voiced deep skepticism that SDI would ever be workable. Yet he does not favor the Soviet negotiating position that links a strategic arms agreement to what amounts to abandonment of SDI. Sakharov persists in his call for freedom of information. "We need," he said, "the unconditional and complete release of prisoners of conscience; the freedom to travel, to choose one's country and place of residence; effective control by the people over the formulation of domestic and foreign policy."

When I got back to Sakharov on the phone Steve spoke with him, and they chatted in Russian about how I had covered him in Moscow and then dealt with the press in the Carter White House when his letter was received and answered by the president. He was still on a tight schedule, he said. "Come this evening at nine P.M."

The Sakharovs' seventh-floor apartment at 48B Chkalova Street is modest by American standards, spacious by Moscow standards, where ten square meters is the official norm per person. There was a large hall, a bedroom, a living room, the kitchen, and another room. Yelena Bonner, Sakharov's wife, invited Leona, Steve, and me into the kitchen, where she prepared tea. She was wearing a black sweatshirt emblazoned with "I read *Harper's Bazaar*" on the front. It was a souvenir collected during her recovery from a heart bypass operation in 1986 in the States.

The kitchen is the meeting room for Russians, informal and cozy. Sitting around the kitchen table with tea and cakes and bread and sausage is more conducive to good honest talk than being in a formal living room setting. In practice, most apartments are so small that the living room serves as a bedroom and the kitchen is for meeting friends. For Russians, talk goes with tea and whatever food is available and in season. Russians are proud of their homemade jams from black currants, raspberries, apricots, or gooseberries. A heaping spoon of jam is stirred into the tea instead of sugar.

Sakharov's first wife died in 1968. He met Yelena Bonner at a protest vigil and they were married a year later. She is half Armenian

---

3. *Time*, March 16, 1987, p. 41.

and half Jewish, with a forceful personality. I asked if Sakharov had seen the television movie about his life starring Jason Robards and Glenda Jackson. He said he had not. Yelena Bonner said she had seen it while in the United States. "Don't see it," she cautioned Sakharov. "You'll fall in love with Glenda Jackson and leave me, she's so beautiful."

"Don't worry," he said. He laughed and embraced her.

Sakharov is a tall man. He was wearing a cotton plaid shirt with a pullover sweater. His eyes looked tired, and although he was friendly there was a quietness within him that was hard to reach. He had spent much of the week meeting with foreign visitors: New York governor Mario Cuomo, members of a visiting French delegation. He had told them all that Gorbachev is the last hope.

Like the writers who have flourished under Gorbachev's *glasnost*, Sakharov now leads a relatively normal life. Although still ostracized by members of the Academy of Sciences, his international stature and support for Gorbachev have made him a key figure in the reform. "Gorbachev," explained Sakharov, "is trying to accomplish reforms before there is a conservative reaction. He is making changes step by step so that the reactionary forces cannot rally to stop him. He is not announcing the whole program so that his plans will be revealed and an opposition can form against them."

Yelena Bonner served tea from a chinaware pot, pouring the strong essence into the cups, then adding boiling hot water from a metal kettle she took from the stove. There were biscuits and a large jar of her own apricot jam on the table. Sakharov stirred jam into his tea, then poured it into the saucer to cool and sipped it. We talked of his grandson living in America and attending Andover, where he had to take swimming lessons. The grandchildren had been allowed to return to Moscow for the summer, and when they arrived it was apparent that they had started to lose their Russian, he said. By the end of the summer they had gotten it back.

We discussed Gorbachev's plans and the political climate. While we talked, Yelena Bonner took several phone calls from friends and people who were having problems with their visas to the West. The Sakharovs' apartment had become a center for the human rights movement in the Soviet Union before he was exiled to Gorky. When I ventured that he was "the conscience of the Soviet Union," Sakharov replied with discomfort, "It is too big a burden for one man."

Although he is a strong supporter of Gorbachev, he continues to press for human rights. "The first priority is the release of prisoners of conscience and political prisoners in psychiatric hospitals. The second priority is the end of the war in Afghanistan, and the third is to allow people to live in whatever country they want to or whatever place they want to live," he said.

Sakharov believes "Gorbachev shares these priorities, but he cannot move faster than the people who work with him. If he gets out ahead of them he will lose their support." We talked about Afghanistan, and Sakharov said he believes there are pressures on Gorbachev from the military. "There is a fear that if they end the war in Afghanistan there will be a bloodbath between those who fought against them and those who cooperated with the Russians. I think it is necessary to take that chance because it [the war] is having a terrible effect on the morale of our country, especially the young," he said.

What struck us most about Sakharov was that, despite his intellectual edge and his willingness to speak out when asked, he has become a supporter of Gorbachev. No longer is Sakharov a total outsider. He has been allotted a special category. He can speak from within the Soviet Union, but he cannot travel abroad. In 1975, while negotiating for permission for his wife to visit the United States for her heart operation, he signed a statement acknowledging the right of the state to decide when he can go abroad. His right to travel abroad has become a litmus test for the issue of whether scientists who possess classified information can leave the Soviet Union. Is there enough *glasnost* to permit the collective conscience of the U.S.S.R. to travel to the West?

Sakharov has been on the ramparts for twenty years and he is weary of battle. Intellectually he remains a catalyst, determined to persevere, but he appears to have lost his taste for combat. He will not compromise, but no longer does he lead the charge. There is a new strategy: to build a base of support for Gorbachev, who has coopted the mantle for change from the dissidents. Still, Sakharov speaks out, even when his remarks are likely to incur official ire. But he is working within the system; no longer is he outside.

In analyzing the difficulties facing *perestroika*, we discussed the underlying fear of change in the Soviet Union. Unlike America, where change is seen as offering new opportunities for development and growth, in the Soviet Union change has brought hardship and dislocation. Sakharov mused over the psychological motivation for change. "People are not motivated because the current arrangement is convenient. They do not have to work hard. They will have to work harder. They live by comparing themselves to their neighbors. As long as their standard of living is not lower than their neighbors' they are satisfied. They particularly like the idea that they can never lose their job. There is a Russian saying: 'You pretend you are paying me and I'll pretend I'm working.' That is what exists today."

There is still no realistic system to reward high-quality workers; the newly established State Quality Control Commissions reject shoddy goods but do not issue rewards for higher-quality output. Gorbachev is undertaking to change the nature of the psychology of socialism, which has deteriorated to satisfaction with the lowest common denominator. For Sakharov this is unspeakable, and a perversion of his vision of socialism. In *My Country and the World* (1975) Sakharov quoted the late Soviet literary critic Arkady Belinkov, who wrote: "Socialism is the kind of thing it's easy to sample but hard to spit out." Sakharov agrees: "And indeed, by virtue of its inherent qualities of imminent stability and the inertia of fear and passivity, totalitarian socialism (which may be called 'pseudosocialism') is a kind of historical dead end from which it is troublesome to escape." But Sakharov does not believe that is the future socialism. He explained that:

> Heretofore socialism has always meant a one-party system, power in the hands of a grasping and incompetent bureaucracy, the expropriation of all private property, terrorism on the part of the Cheka or its counterparts, the destruction of productive forces, with their subsequent restoration and expansion at the cost of countless sacrifices by the people, and violence done to free consciences and convictions.[4]

Sakharov does not believe this is inevitable. "I believe that in principle 'socialism with a human face' is possible, and represents a high form of social organization. But it is possible only as a result of extraordinary collective efforts plus wisdom and selflessness exercised by a great part of the people. . . . The total nationalization of all means of production, the one-party system, and the repression of honest convictions—all must be avoided or totalitarianism will prevail."

His direct struggle is to fill the blank pages of the past and to press for human rights. He is concerned that the human rights movement

---

4. Andrei D. Sakharov, *My Country and the World* (New York: Alfred A. Knopf, 1975), p. 91.

does not become divided and conquered. "You Americans are willing to trade Jewish flesh for trucks," he said angrily, indicating that all human rights cases must be given equal priority, not only Jewish emigration. Sakharov has warned against making deals for lifting trade restrictions in the United States in exchange for increased Jewish emigration.

He has urged Western leaders not to cooperate with the Soviet proposal for an international human rights conference in Moscow until the Soviet Union frees all political prisoners and restores their good names, changes the legal code to prevent persecution of dissenters, opens its borders, and removes its troops from Afghanistan.

While we were eating a sweet yellow melon served by Yelena Bonner, the phone rang. She answered and told Sakharov a friend was calling about a visa problem. He said, "Call the Jews to find out." She laughed and told the friend they would call back.

Sakharov has cut back on direct involvement in individual cases, but he remains committed to the freeing of two hundred prisoners of conscience still in prisons. In January of 1988 Sakharov had his first face-to-face meeting with Gorbachev at the Kremlin and appealed for their release. Sakharov handed Gorbachev a list of names of those in prison camps, psychiatric hospitals, and exile. He met Gorbachev as a member of the board of the International Fund for the Survival of Humanity, a private research group. At a press conference after the meeting Sakharov also called for the withdrawal of Soviet troops from Afghanistan "without any conditions whatsoever." These are the two main issues for which he continues to use his influence.

He remains close to his old friends who have struggled for human rights and are still carrying the torch in the Soviet Union. At a dinner in January 1988 for human rights activists in Moscow, Sakharov summed up his views: "Up until now the situation was very difficult, but it was a clear one. It was clear that there were problems with human rights, and it was clear there were problems with peace. . . . Now I would say that the situation has become more complex. It has become complex because it has become better."[5]

---

5. Gary Lee, "Sakharov Quietly Stays the Course," *Washington Post*, February 8, 1988, p. A-24.

A Second Party

Democracy in the Soviet Union is based on Lenin's "inalienable principle" of Communist party dictatorship over the political life of the nation. The party, through "democratic centralism," is the source of all knowledge and power. At lunch in the Berlin Hotel with an old friend we talked about the source of political power in the Soviet Union. My friend, a senior official, reminded me that the writer Fyodor Dostoyevsky defined political power as mystery, authority, and secrecy.

During the celebration of the seventieth anniversary of the October Revolution, in November 1987, top party officials held an unprecedented series of press conferences. At one, Alexander Yakovlev, the Politburo member who is chief of the Central Committee Propaganda Department, was asked why there was no coverage of Communist party deliberations in the Central Committee on the case of Boris Yeltsin, the Moscow party chief who had to resign because he protested the slow pace of change. Yakovlev told correspondents the Yeltsin affair was an internal matter and did not belong in the public domain. "If all internal party matters are discussed by one and all, then there will be no sense in having a party," Yakovlev said. "This I think is understood." At that point the Soviet press had barely covered the story, which had been leaked to Western correspondents. Yakovlev was asked if there were two kinds of *glasnost*: one for the Western press and another for the Soviet media. He rebuked the American journalist who asked the question. That evening on the television news Yakovlev's comments on Yeltsin were excluded from accounts of his press conference. The next day Tass put out an abbreviated version of his remarks on Yeltsin.

Earlier, on Saturday, October 31, following heated debate in the Central Committee, Tass filed an account of Yeltsin's offer to resign. It was followed nineteen minutes later by a notice to editors warning: "It is categorically recommended not to publish" the report. Western journalists got the story from their Soviet sources, but Soviet citizens got the news only over the Voice of America, BBC, or Radio Free Europe. The internal workings of the Communist party remain sacrosanct and not subject to *glasnost*.

In Stalin's time, talk of a second political party in the Soviet Union to challenge the paramount authority of the Communist party would be grounds for deportation to a labor camp or for execution. Even in the reform period of Nikita Khrushchev's rule there was no questioning of the dominant role of the party. When Khrushchev tried to weaken party control by giving more autonomy to factory managers and local officials he created a strong opposition within the party that was capable of removing him from office. Andrei Sakharov suggested party reforms to Leonid Brezhnev in 1971, but his letter went unanswered for a year before Sakharov allowed it to be published in the West.

Today Gorbachev walks a tightrope to maintain the support necessary to sustain the momentum for his reforms. Does he want his reforms to weaken party control, or are the reforms a subterfuge to strengthen party rule? For former dissidents and intellectuals, such as Andrei Sakharov, Gorbachev represents an opportunity that must not be missed. He is the last chance for reform, they say. The lines of the struggle are drawn, and the central issue is control by the Communist party, which deliberates in secret and maintains its authority with police and military force.

Talk of a second political party is not part of the public discussion of *glasnost* and *perestroika*, but such heresy is regularly raised among the intelligentsia. They see a second party as a logical next step emerging from the growth of public discussion groups, the so-called informal organizations that have developed as part of *glasnost*. Thousands of such groups have sprung up across the Soviet Union, largely in major population centers such as Moscow, Leningrad, and Kiev. The groups advocate action on environmental, social, and political issues. They are an outgrowth of *glasnost* manifested in letters-to-the-editor columns in the press and in the enlarged boundaries of discussion for the intelligentsia. They are the results of *glasnost* at the grass roots level.

In the summer of 1987, for the first time, there was a meeting of these independent groups to discuss their causes and ideas. An environmental group in Leningrad is trying to prevent the construction of a flood-control dam, which the members believe will ruin the city's water flow and create a swamp in the canals that have made Leningrad "the Venice of the North." Another group is advocating building a war memorial to honor the victims of Stalin's terror. In Moscow the human rights activist Lev Timofeyev organized Press Club *Glasnost*, an unofficial human rights advocacy group. Former political prisoner Sergei Grigoryants, a leading voice of dissent, started an unofficial *samizdat* magazine called *Glasnost*. Several Moscow groups organized a letter-writing campaign in support of Boris Yeltsin.

The presence of conservative groups urging traditional Slavophile ideas has also emerged with *glasnost*. There are unconfirmed reports that the conservative group *Pamyat* ("Memory") is infiltrated and supported by the KGB. There is still lingering suspicion at how real the openness really is and whether it represents a fundamental change in the Soviet Union or a deliberate deception, where new ideas and dissent are encouraged to bloom only to be cut down when they emerge into the open.

Intellectuals recall that the first legal trade union in Russia was founded in 1901 by Sergei Vasilyevich Zubatov, the head of the Moscow branch of the Okhranka, the Czar's secret police. With the help of former Social Democrats and Moscow University professors, Zubatov organized the Society of Mutual Help of Workers in Mechanical Production. Known as police socialism, Zubatov's scheme attempted to prevent workers from being influenced by revolutionary socialism through the establishment of a legal workers' movement largely controlled by police agents. Zubatov was able to control the movement in Moscow, but elsewhere it got out of hand and was used by Social Democrats for revolutionary purposes. Zubatov was forced to resign in 1903.[1]

The KGB's role in infiltrating, sponsoring, or controlling the informal groups has still to be defined. Ostensibly they are unaffiliated and meet only informally with each other. They represent a new wave of intellectual thought and are not linked to any Western organizations. Unlike dissident groups in the 1960s and 1970s and

---

1. S. V. Utechin, *Everyman's Concise Encyclopedia of Russia* (London: J. M. Dent & Sons Ltd., 1961), pp. 425, 622.

1980s, they prefer to stay away from foreign correspondents and work within the Soviet system. They are a new phenomenon in the Soviet Union, roughly akin to single-interest groups in America.

In the 1960s and 1970s dissidents relied on the publicity of the foreign press and radio to get their ideas back into the Soviet Union. Under Gorbachev ideas can be discussed openly, although not without official harassment of such publications as Grigoryants's *Glasnost*.

In Moscow in the summer of 1987 the groups met under the auspices of the newspaper *Komsomolskaya Pravda* and discussed the question of a national organization. The new phenomenon has brought a response from the Komsomol, the youth organization of the Communist party. The Komsomol is concerned that it will lose control over youth and their ideas. In a secret draft proposal the Komsomol argued that "the creative quest of young people should be secured above all within the framework of existing Komsomol organizations and committees. There is no need for the creation of alternative organizations."

In an ideal world such alternative organizations could form the basis for new political parties in the Soviet Union, but such a transformation is hard to imagine. A senior journalist at *Pravda* told me, "We need a new political culture," but the shape of that culture remains unclear. Another political party would deny the infallibility of the Communist party and raise major philosophical and psychological doubts of its historical omnipotence. It would undermine the edifice of Marxism-Leninism and change the nature of communism.

In the ABC-sponsored television debate on human rights between the United States and the Soviet Union that aired simultaneously in both countries in October of 1987, Senator Daniel Patrick Moynihan (D.–N.Y.) criticized the Soviet Union as a one-party state, a "dictatorship of the proletariat, which means the intellectuals. How the word *proletariat* turned out to be intellectual, I don't know, but you guys did it." Moynihan's comment enraged his debating partner, Vadim Zagladin, first deputy of the International Department of the Central Committee, who asked Moynihan: "Don't you think this is a call to overturn the government in the Soviet Union? If you don't think so, then tell us. But it looks like a call to overturn the government."

Senator Moynihan replied: "No sir, it is not, and if you ever start thinking like that I think we're all going to have great problems. We don't want to interfere in your system, and we don't want you interfering in ours or others. And Mr. Gorbachev has made the point. But in your own interest, don't you see that you can't have a free economy if you don't have free government? At least have free churches. Next year [1988] is the jubilee, the millennia of Christianity in Russia, in the Ukraine. Can't you let your churches open? Can't you let people have Sunday schools where they can teach their children the Bible? Can't you let the Baptists have a seminary? You'd feel better. You'll be stronger."

Zagladin defended the dictatorship of the proletariat and told Moynihan: "Mr. Senator, there are countries in which there are twenty-five parties. We can't say that just because you have two in America and they have twenty-five that they have twelve and a half times greater democracy there. That's not serious. And it's not the number of parties, but the policies which they have. Our policies have led to the fact that in only seventy years a country which was backwards, which was agrarian, turned into a modern state. Our people who did not have any rights—80 percent were illiterate, did not know what a doctor was in many corners of the country—turned into people whose very culture was protected in all areas in society. This is the result of the work of our party and our un-free government, as you call us. And our people value this appropriately. It doesn't mean we are happy with everything. We're far from being happy with everything."

For Soviet citizens to listen to such a discussion on national television was astounding. Our friends called and asked what we thought of the program.

For the first time the question of Jewish immigration was discussed openly: numbers and specific cases were addressed by high-ranking government officials. With Zagladin was Ivan Laptev, editor-in-chief of *Izvestia*. "The program means that the issue of Jewish immigration is no longer taboo and can be discussed," explained a Soviet journalist. "Yes," I agreed, "the genie is out of the bottle and it cannot be put back in."

The idea of a second political party, or a group of parties, is an idea whose time has not yet come in the Soviet Union. A second party would be an invigorating and democratizing move, but for orthodox Communists it would destroy the intent of the Revolution to create a dictatorship of the proletariat and instead create the pluralism that Soviet leaders have traditionally characterized as weakness in Western democracies. The Communist system and its infallibility are at stake in Gorbachev's reforms. Gorbachev has preempted Sakharov's banned 1968 calls for *glasnost*, but he has still to accept the conclusion to Sakharov's essay, *My Country and the World*: the proposal of a multiparty system in the Soviet Union.[2]

When we talked with Sakharov a second party was less of an immediate priority than was the withdrawal of Soviet troops from Afghanistan. We were anxious to hear about the war straight from the mouths of the young veterans.

2. Andrei D. Sakharov, *My Country and the World* (New York: Alfred A. Knopf, 1975), p. 102.

J E R R Y

Afghanistan: International Duty

Artyom Borovik, the twenty-eight-year-old foreign editor of *Ogonyok*, the Soviet equivalent of *Life* magazine, became a celebrity after the publication of his three articles on Afghanistan in 1987. For the first time since the Soviet Union invaded Afghanistan in December 1979 a Soviet journalist was permitted to publish a personal, on-the-scene account of the wartime life and death of Soviet troops.

The war in Afghanistan was a defeat for the Soviet Union, marked by the withdrawal of Soviet troops that began in May 1988. The cost of the war is still being tallied but its impact on the Soviet psyche continues to mount, much as the aftermath of the Vietnam war did in America.

There were 115,000 to 120,000 Soviet troops in Afghanistan, and Soviet casualties since 1979 totaled 49,098, of which 13,310 were killed in action, 35,478 wounded, and 310 missing. These official Soviet numbers come close to the Western estimates of 12,000 to 15,000 killed and upward of 30,000 wounded.[1] Borovik spent a month with the Soviet blue berets, the *Spetsnaz*, or special forces, an elite, all-volunteer group that is the pride of the Red Army. I heard Borovik describe his experiences in Afghanistan on September 30, 1987, at a forum sponsored by *Ogonyok* in October Hall on Kalinina Prospekt. It was billed as an evening for the readers of the magazine to meet its editors and contributors. Everybody understood it was

---

1. See *Strategic Survey 1986–1987* (London: International Institute for Strategic Studies), p. 134. *Washington Post*, May 26, 1988, p. 1.

an evening for the audience to ask the editors tough questions and to diagnose from their answers the health of *glasnost*. Written questions were carried to the platform from the audience. Borovik was on the stage with *Ogonyok*'s high-spirited editor-in-chief, Vitaly Korotich, and poets Andrei Voznesensky and Robert Rozhdestvensky.

Under Korotich's leadership, *Ogonyok* has become a leading practitioner of *glasnost*, and its weekly issues often set the standard for the new openness. *Ogonyok* tries to fill the blank pages in Soviet history. The magazine published a letter to Mikhail Gorbachev from the widow of Nikolai Bukharin, the Bolshevik leader executed by Stalin in 1938. In the letter, Anna Larina appealed for her husband's political rehabilitation. For the past fifty years Bukharin has been portrayed as a traitor and enemy of the people. Now he has been redeemed.

Afghanistan has been a blank spot in Soviet press coverage. Borovik's articles, which would be considered good reporting from the field in an American magazine, were a sensation in the Soviet Union. The war had been going on since 1979, but nothing like them had been written before. Borovik lived for a month with the *Spetsnaz* troops. He went on operations with them and described the Afghanistan war with sharp detail. His diary told of listening to rock music and fearing death. It was a human story that glorified Soviet soldiers, but it also conveyed the frustration of combat in a guerrilla war. ("Even if they built ten ski lifts up there, they couldn't get me to set foot back in this place," says one young soldier, gazing at the snowy peaks of the Hindu Kush. Another Soviet soldier looks at the corpse of a guerrilla and says, "Allah didn't help you.")[2] The articles also disclosed that the Afghans were selling Soviet arms on the black market and that it is possible to buy your way through a checkpoint. Borovik now follows the line that if Soviet troops leave before the "rebel bands decide what they want" there will be a holy war and a bloodbath.

On stage, Borovik told the audience, which included military men in uniform, of his fear of ambushes while climbing 8,000-meter-high mountains in the Afghan heat. He made the war real, and he was applauded loudly when he told of the hardships and dangers faced by the Soviet troops in the field. His description of a war without front lines and an enemy without uniforms, who attacked and re-

---

2. *Ogonyok*, no. 30, p. 19.

treated at will, sounded very much like *Life* magazine's coverage of Vietnam in the 1960s. It repeated the elements of international duty: "It's a tough, dirty job, but somebody's got to do it" and "Our boys are doing well under difficult circumstances." The overall theme is still upbeat.

We met backstage, and I told Artyom I had covered the Vietnam war in the early 1960s. We talked briefly, comparing notes, and I suggested we meet. He agreed to dinner at the Berlin Hotel.

Artyom has a fresh-faced, intelligent look that is searching and eager. His manner is open and friendly and he lacks the jaded air of most Soviet journalists who have traveled abroad and seen it all. The war in Afghanistan had become an obsession for him, and he was commissioned to write a play describing the life of Soviet troops in Afghanistan. Borovik speaks English well because he was educated in New York City. His father, Genrikh Borovik, the political observer, served there as a correspondent for Novosti, the Soviet press agency. "After two years in the Soviet UN mission school in New York I was permitted to attend an American private school, the Dalton School, and that helped my English," explained Artyom. "I wanted to be a journalist like my father, but he urged me to become a diplomat and have what he said was a 'real career.' I studied at the Moscow Institute of International Relations and joined the Ministry of Foreign Affairs. I was posted to South America as a consular officer but I couldn't stand the work. It was too boring. When I returned to Moscow I decided to go into journalism." He joined Korotich at *Ogonyok* in January 1987.

For our dinner at the hotel, Leona laid out an assortment of cold tongue, fresh sauerkraut, sliced tomatoes, cheese, radishes, butter, and white and dark bread. We drank cold vodka with Danish Carlsberg beer for chasers. Artyom was fascinated with the Vietnam war. He questioned us about the American role there and how the Americans lived and fought. He had read Michael Herr's *Dispatches* (New York: Alfred A. Knopf, 1977) and found many parallels between the United States war in Vietnam and the Soviet war in Afghanistan. His writing style shows Herr's influence. Herr describes an old map of French Indochina on the wall of his Saigon apartment; Borovik has a map of Afghanistan in the 1950s, a gift from a veteran British correspondent. On his first trip to a combat zone, Herr is fitted out with a dead paratrooper's helmet; Borovik received a dead captain's jacket. American soldiers in Herr's book listen to Jimi Hendrix while under fire in a rice paddy; Borovik's *Spetsnaz* troops played Rod Stewart tapes before going out on an ambush.[3]

Of course, Artyom never acknowledged that the Soviet Union had invaded Afghanistan; but neither did he use the usual clichés about American aggression in Vietnam. Instead, we talked about the common nature of both wars. How both the United States and the Soviet Union were fighting a war outside their own borders against an elusive enemy. These were wars with constantly shifting front lines and hostile populations. In Vietnam the Americans found civilians who might be friends today but became enemies tomorrow. The same was true in Afghanistan. It was often impossible to tell who was a guerrilla and who a civilian.

At home the war was unpopular, but the Soviet public knew less about the Afghanistan war than the American public knew about Vietnam. There was more to read about AIDS in the Soviet press than about Afghanistan. Still, with returning veterans, alienation was beginning to spill over publicly. There were letters to *Pravda* from parents who had lost their only sons, complaining that the newspapers would not print their obituaries or indicate they had died in Afghanistan. Other letters exposed poor treatment of returning Afghan veterans by local officials and even ordinary citizens. I told Artyom how we had all gone to the movie *Is It Easy to Be Young?* by the Latvian director Juris Podnieks, and were surprised by the frankness and disillusionment of the Afghan veterans who were interviewed on camera. This documentary, about troubled Soviet youth who are without a sense of purpose, has shocked audiences and stirred angry debate. It was shown at the American Film Institute in Washington, D.C., in early 1988.

While watching the film I saw distinct parallels between Vietnam and Afghan war veterans. The experiences and reactions of the Soviet soldiers echoed those of their American counterparts. The first Afghan veteran talked about deceitful press coverage of the war. "Only the victories are publicized, with barely a few lines about the losses and the hardships of the soldiers. There was nothing said about my friend who has been given all possible medical care but will never really be able to walk properly again. I drank a lot," the veteran said, "but that didn't help because the tension remains in your subconscious." Then he found a job as a fireman, which he likes. "It is

---

3. See Aaron Trehub, "Popular Discontent with the War in Afghanistan," Radio Liberty Research, November 30, 1987.

similar to war in that you are confronting the unknown, the dangerous. Coming back you feel that the time in Afghanistan is when you lived, and now you are just waiting out the rest of your life. You come back and you are just a second-year student at normal life."

Another Afghan veteran in the film talked about how the privation of war creates a common purpose and lifelong bond among the soldiers. They shared small crusts of bread equally among six or seven men. "The Soviet people today have everything compared to this and so they are not conscious of and do not value everyday things. The experience there cannot be communicated in words. Seeing your comrades shed their blood hardens something inside you."

A third veteran said, "I feel like I was associated with something dirty and foul." He has a medal for valor but doesn't wear it. He doesn't think he was heroic. "I just did what was necessary at the time. People won't understand the medal. Maybe someday I'll wear it."

The first veteran summed up: "It's hard to carry the complexity of the experience around inside, but people don't want to hear about it. They don't want to see you lost and confused. They want to see you healthy and strong. 'Do some work and put some fat on you. War matures a young man,' they say. This is false. It makes you old. But they treat us like children and don't let us take responsibility. This is infuriating."

Artyom said these veterans were not typical. The ones he knew were doing well and had adjusted.

"I'd like to meet some Afghanistan veterans," I suggested.

"I'll talk to my friends and see if I can set it up at my office," Artyom replied. The next morning he had it all arranged. He would tape the discussion and then edit it for an article in *Ogonyok*. I told him I would bring Evelind and her husband, Michael.

The editorial offices of *Ogonyok* are in the *Pravda* Publishing House, a six-story building that is the headquarters for several magazines, at 14 Bumazhnyy Proyezd ("Paper Street"). Michael was eager to join me because he teaches a course at Rutgers University called "The Vietnam War in the American Imagination" and is currently heading an investigation of the war's political, social, and cultural legacy. He has interviewed and worked with Vietnam vets, and knows their moods and feelings, especially their differing political views. Some support the war; others believe it was a mistake. There is no common position, which the Russians were to find surprising.

In the *Ogonyok* conference room, Artyom introduced us to three vital, handsome young men, all highly decorated for valor. The two younger men, in blue blazers, were Dmitri and Alexander, who had served as volunteers with the *Spetsnaz*. They had each spent a two-year tour in Afghanistan, twice as long as the American tour in Vietnam, and Alexander had been wounded. Alexander, Artyom told us, had wanted to have a military career from the time he was a schoolboy. He had volunteered for parachute training in the summer paramilitary program for Soviet youth, and when the time came for his compulsory service he joined the blue berets. Dmitri was brought up in Siberia, where as a boy he hunted with his father. Like Alexander he was in excellent physical condition and handled himself well in the outdoors. He was a prime candidate for the blue berets when he volunteered at age eighteen. The third veteran, Sergei, age twenty-six, wore the khaki-and-blue uniform of a Soviet air force captain. His insignia indicated he had been seriously wounded and had won the Order of the Red Star for valor. Sergei's jet had been shot down on a bombing mission against the Afghan rebels, explained Artyom. Although badly wounded, Sergei managed to parachute to the ground. There he was surrounded by thirty Afghan guerrillas. When he saw the situation Sergei hid a hand grenade underneath his body. If the Afghans turned him over the grenade would explode, killing them all. Soviet rescue helicopters picked up his beeper signals and found him. They were also under attack from the guerrillas, but drove the Afghans off with heavy fire. When the rescue team saw him bleeding and badly wounded, Sergei did not have the strength to tell them he had placed a grenade, ready to explode, underneath himself. However, when he was moved one of the rescuers spotted the grenade and threw it out of range before it exploded. Sergei had been in the hospital for a year for reconstructive work on his leg.

After friendly introductions Dmitri and Alexander lit cigarettes. We drank tea and ate soft pretzels with poppy seeds. Then we turned the tape recorders on and the Russians delivered a well-prepared criticism of the Vietnam war. Alexander, blond and handsome, had seen a picture of the Vietnam War Memorial and said, "From above it looks like there is a crack in the rock of America. A crack means a mistake. I've heard it interpreted as a symbol of America's mistakes, a symbol of America's defeat."

Michael countered: "Our understanding is that the feeling in the Soviet Union toward Afghanistan is the same as our attitude toward Vietnam. We have read letters in *Pravda* from men who had come back from Afghanistan and found that nobody was interested in the war they had fought. For ten years after defeat in Vietnam the American people did not want to think about the war. They did not want to hear about the war. There is a connection here between our Vietnam war and your war in Afghanistan."

Dmitri interpreted Michael's remarks narrowly and avoided a direct answer. He denied that the men who fought in Afghanistan "were thinking about what they would get when they returned. In Afghanistan, I never met anyone who was forced to serve there. And when they come home, they don't think about honors. When they return, they return as people who had fulfilled their duty."

"Then what are they thinking about?" I asked.

"Military service in the army is considered to be an honorable thing," said Alexander.

"So is it in the United States," I replied.

"When you are in Afghanistan you are absolutely sure what you are doing is necessary," said Alexander.

"How do you know?" I asked. "What makes you sure?"

"I was brought up in this country with its propaganda. From childhood I knew that black is black and white is white. But if life experience says black is not black or white is not white, then it would be up to me to correct these mistakes. As for Afghanistan, while I was there I never doubted what I was doing," said Alexander.

"That sounds like many American veterans," said Michael. "But later it was difficult to explain what they had been doing in Vietnam and why."

Michael pointed out that "one of the common experiences of American Vietnam vets was to be criticized by World War II vets who would say, 'We entered the war in December of 1941 and by June 1945 the war was over and we won over a much tougher enemy. For years you have been fighting these peasants with small weapons.' "

"You know, we too hear the same thing from our veterans of the Great Patriotic War," said Alexander. "The older men shake my hand and say, 'You are a good lad.' They bowed their gray heads before me and said, 'I did my job and you are doing your job, but you are doing it worse than we did it.' It is hard to explain, but many of the people have a feeling of vanity. They think this war cannot be compared with that war."

Then Dmitri tried to explain how hard it was to tell people about the war in Afghanistan. "While I was still in Afghanistan, a journalist asked me what I was thinking about, what I was dreaming about Afghanistan," said Dmitri. "I told him my only dream was to have enough time to sleep, enough good things to eat, and to be able to stand upright knowing that I would not be shot."

Dmitri, now twenty-one, studies law at the Moscow Institute for International Relations.

We talked about the differences between World War II as a total war, with the whole nation being mobilized, and Vietnam and Afghanistan as limited wars, with only a very small number of men between eighteen and twenty-one called to serve. "In America it was a question of equality—who goes, how do you choose?" said Michael.

"The state chooses," replied Dmitri.

"But how?" I asked.

"This question of why somebody went and somebody didn't arises only after he has passed his service in Afghanistan," said Alexander.

Michael agreed. "That is one of the primary complaints Vietnam vets have as well. While they were serving in Vietnam their peers were finishing college, getting jobs, and getting married, going ahead with their lives. They had been left behind and all the anger from what they had seen was inside them, building up. It was the feeling of living in the dirt for a year and not being able to stand up, the way you described you felt in Afghanistan. Vietnam was similar to Afghanistan; there were no safe grounds and no front."

Dmitri: "Morally I do not think I have lost something. My peers went on but I'm not late."

Alexander: "The state tries to take into account our experience and integrate us into life. I do not feel excluded from life."

Michael said he had read a letter in *Pravda* from a father whose son was killed in Afghanistan, but his gravestone did not say where he died.

Dmitri explained: "On the graves it is written, 'This person lost his life in fulfillment of his international duty.' "

Alexander quickly added, "In Kabul a memorial is being built to Soviet soldiers who died in Afghanistan. Members of the Orenburg Komsomol will build a memorial in the Soviet Union to the Soviet Internationalists who gave their lives in Afghanistan." They also said a fund for Afghan veterans was being started and a museum is being organized by Komsomol members in the town of Lyubertsy, on the outskirts of Moscow, dedicated to those who died while "fulfilling their international duty" in Afghanistan. *Lyubari* is also a new word for the young punks who come from Lyubertsy to pick fights with and beat up hippies and Jews in Moscow. They belong to body-building clubs and roam in gangs that operate as Soviet-style neo-Nazis.

'Don't you want a memorial in the Soviet Union and the place named where your son died on his grave?" I asked.

Dmitri said, "Three years ago the press did not write openly about Afghanistan. People had very little information and did not know our soldiers were fighting there. People here never understood what we passed through. We lived one life and they another. Now thanks to *perestroika* and openness people are getting to know more and more what is happening. People did not know we were participating in a war there. Now the press is writing about real combat actions. The attitude of the people here is developing thanks to the press coverage."

Dmitri asked, "Did American veterans feel better or worse personally as a result of their Vietnam experience?"

Michael: "They became better people. There are a wide variety of opinions on whether the war was politically correct. They cover the political spectrum, but when veterans get together there is a tremendously strong sense of brotherhood. They survived. They stood together."

Dmitri listened carefully, then he stopped challenging us and asked sincerely, "If we didn't send our troops to Afghanistan would there be Americans there?"

"No," I replied, "that, frankly, is propaganda. That is the argument Brezhnev used, that the CIA was stirring up trouble on the Afghanistan border, but there is no supporting evidence."

Michael said, "We all remember the date of the Soviet invasion of Afghanistan. It came on the night of December 27, 1979, the wedding night of Evelind's brother Steve to Suprabha. Dr. Brzezinski attended the wedding reception and had to leave to return to the White House."

Alexander, reflecting what he had been told, said, "If America stops helping the rebels, they cannot continue. If the financial support is stopped the problem will be stopped immediately."

"That sounds good," I said, "but in practice it does not work that way. The Afghan tribal rivalries are such that they never tolerated rule by any foreign power. They drove the British out and fought the Russian Czars for their freedom. Today there are real parallels to Vietnam. The war is continuing and neither side is victorious. The answer is not a military victory, but a political compromise."

Michael added: "The war goes deeper than the provision of equipment to the participants. Their equipment is primitive and simple, certainly by comparison to the military might of the Soviet Union. The key to the Afghans' success, like the key to the success of the North Vietnamese against the United States, has to do with the deep belief on the part of the guerrillas. They will fight with almost nothing, walking, not taking helicopters, eating very little and doing without medical assistance, giving their lives when there is nothing else to give against a country that is larger and stronger. The Afghans don't know anything about America. They are not fighting for us. They are fighting for a belief, just as the Vietnamese fought against us. You have to be able to enter into the mind of your enemy and realize that belief is a very powerful weapon."

Sergei, the jet pilot, smiled bitterly and said, "Yes, I know their minds. If they captured me they would cut my head off and the man who brought it back would be paid a prize of one million Afghani ($20,000). None of our pilots are returned alive, but American pilots returned from Vietnam."

We discussed the way American pilots were treated in Vietnam: those captured near Hanoi were usually jailed there, but pilots captured in the South were often killed because the Viet Cong did not take care of prisoners in the jungle.

"In Afghanistan it doesn't make any difference if you are shot down near Kabul or not; the end is the same," said Sergei.

Michael: "American soldiers went into the jungle in Vietnam and found their comrades nailed to trees."

"The M-16 and the Stinger are not primitive weapons. The ammunition has recently been stamped U.S. Army, and there is a year marked on them. I've seen M-22 hand grenades, and there are Italian mines," said Dmitri.

"But they have no air force, no helicopters or armored cars," said Michael. "We are still talking about a fundamental difference. The Soviet military is one of the great military forces in the world."

"Yes, but the ways of fighting in the mountains make the sides equal. The rebels are accustomed to traveling fifty miles at a crack in the mountains. Soviet jets and helicopters do not bomb *kishlaks* (villages), only the rebels in the field," said Alexander. He insisted that he saw American military advisors with a transmitter in the field in Afghanistan.

"What would happen in the Soviet Union if the war was on television every night on your prime time evening news program?" I asked. "How would people react? What would they think of the war?"

The question stunned them. They admitted that the interest of the Soviet people in the events in Afghanistan is high, but said, "Our cameramen are forbidden to be in combat there. Everybody is afraid if a cameraman or journalist is killed the officer who commanded the unit he was with would immediately lose the stars off his shoulders."

Sergei said, "Press coverage would be okay. It would not be like the Vietnam war because in Afghanistan there is not combat and fighting every day."

Michael pointed out that was true in Vietnam too and compared it with periods of waiting for the North Vietnamese to attack. Sergei said the longest period of waiting he had experienced was three weeks.

What did they do while they were waiting or off duty? Alexander said he had read in Michael Herr's *Dispatches* that American soldiers drank whiskey, had women, and went freely through the streets of the city. At the same time they lived with a fear of reprisal. "Comparing this with our soldiers the difference is like earth and sky. We heard on the Voice of America that all Soviet officers were alcoholics and drug users—that's not true. We had a pool we could bathe in or go to the river, but usually we were in contact with battalions of rebels fighting us. In the evening we read books or went to a movie or a concert with artists from Moscow."

"Were drugs a problem?"

"The rebels grow poppies in the fields and they sell them. Sometimes it happens among the service personnel. There is a real difference between the airborne troops and the service troops. They stay in the battalion headquarters and don't go anywhere. It is pretty hard to imagine the men who go into the mountains using drugs. You have to have a bear's health. I even quit smoking because it is hard to breathe climbing those hills. You can't drink vodka or whiskey. I had to carry seventy kilograms in the mountains; it is impossible to use anything."

Sergei shifted the talk away from drugs and asked, "Can you imagine American pilots building houses or kindergartens for the Vietnamese the way we did in Afghanistan? When we were building various structures around the airstrip, I was thinking that when these problems are over and the Soviet troops are pulled out, the new buildings will be used as *sanatoriy* [rest homes]."

"The American special forces did that. They had a civic action program. Americans spent their spare time building schools and medical aid centers for the Vietnamese," I explained.

Dmitri said, "We never used chemical weapons in Afghanistan the way you did in Vietnam."

"The record shows that chemical weapons were used in the early days of the war in Afghanistan. The evidence of yellow rain was not bee pollen, but a poison gas that burned the skin. Once this was pointed out and evidence was made public it appears that the use of these weapons was stopped. I was in the government at the time and saw the intelligence reports," I said.[4]

Again, they listened carefully. Alexander shifted the argument: "Chemical grenades were used against us by the rebels and we were given special masks to protect ourselves."

Michael said he was surprised that nothing had appeared in the press, because "the Soviet government, which is quick to note the use of chemical weapons, has not made any public outcry." Michael argued that it was important to distinguish between the use of chemical defoliants aimed at destroying crops and ground cover and the use of chemical warfare against individuals. The defoliants poisoned American soldiers and Vietnamese people, but they were not intended to do so. That is an issue that is important in the United States today.

"We should not try to take the positions of our governments in this discussion," I said. "Let's talk about our human feelings and what we can learn from this kind of experience. To many Americans, the United States made the mistake in Vietnam that the French made in Algeria and that you are now making in Afghanistan. Of course there are some differences, but the basic similarity is that people's beliefs motivate them and that is what drives them to fight. That is what we have to understand as the political reality in the twentieth century."

"We are just soldiers. Why should we make a political comment?" said Alexander.

"That comment could have come from any Vietnam veteran," said Michael. " 'I didn't start this war. I'm not responsible for American foreign policy. Nobody is going to ask me if this is right or wrong.

---

4. Sterling Seagrave, *Yellow Rain: A Journey Through the Terror of Chemical Warfare* (New York: M. Evans and Company, Inc., 1981), p. 141. Details Soviet use of chemicals in Afghanistan in January 1980, which caused vomiting, constriction of the chest, blindness, paralysis, and quick death.

I'm here because I am a soldier for my country. If they tell me to walk or carry heavy weapons I will do it. I will walk fifty miles.' I have heard over and over again from American vets what you just said: 'I am not responsible for this war. I am just a soldier.'

"I am looking for the human connection. My friend was nineteen when he went to Vietnam from our town of Enfield, New Hampshire, where we have two hundred and fifty people and a thousand cows. One day he was put on an airplane and flown for eighteen hours to Cam Ranh Bay. The next week he was killed in battle."

Alexander and Dmitri avoided talking about battle losses. Instead they asked us how veterans are treated in America, and Michael explained the G.I. Bill of Rights, which provided college educations for veterans.

"Our veterans get more privileges than those who served in the Patriotic War. They get more rights. They are first on the list for apartments, for travel, theater tickets, sanatoriums, and rest homes," said Alexander. He took out a card from his wallet to show us that he was a veteran who was entitled to these privileges.

Are there unemployed Vietnam veterans in America? they asked. "Yes," answered Michael. "The veterans' organizations are particularly annoyed by the image created by Hollywood of veterans as violent and as drug addicts. If you look at the statistics you find that Vietnam vets are not more likely than an average person to be violent or to be drug addicts. The problem is that it makes a very exciting Hollywood movie to show a drug-crazed Vietnam vet. In fact, the average Vietnam veteran today is a forty-one or forty-two-year-old man with two or three children, a wife, and a dog, just like everybody else."

We had relaxed now and the questions came freely. Curiosity overcame posturing. They asked professional questions and wanted to know about the attitude of American soldiers toward North Vietnamese troops.

Michael said the Americans had a tremendous amount of respect for both the North Vietnamese and the guerrillas in the South. "American G.I.s called him Mr. Charlie, out of respect, meaning that he was an extraordinarily good soldier. As Dmitri said about the Afghanis, they could walk all night and fight all day, they were tough."

Dmitri said, "The rebels are really good. First of all the rebels, like the North Vietnamese patriots, are fighting on their own territory. They know the terrain well and are accustomed to it."

Dmitri is from Siberia and likes a cold climate. In Afghanistan it is hot, plus 40 or 50 degrees Celsius (104 to 122 degrees Fahrenheit). The rebels use stimulants to help them in the mountains.

Michael asked, "Wasn't the constant patrolling frustrating? Never holding a place, only fighting and moving on, losing friends? American soldiers expressed constant frustration at having to walk through an area and then return to it, walk through and leave it."

"Of course, sometimes you don't want to go into the mountains," said Alexander, "but orders are orders, there's no discussing them. But as far as shooting . . . you want to know if one feels fear, right? The sense of fear is something you regain later, after the battle is over. When I capture weapons, it's a delight as far as I am concerned. Or you take a prisoner. Then there is the simple physical satisfaction. You look at a mountain and its top is in the clouds. You feel that you have climbed down from atop that mountain. It is a pleasure to reaffirm your confidence in your physical powers.

"The most pleasant thing is to hear a rebel radio transmission which is contacting the leaders sitting in Pakistan that they are without supplies, without men. They can no longer continue military actions. And they are radioing, 'Help us. Help us. We have no weapons. The paratroopers came and took everything. We have suffered losses . . .' It's a pleasure to hear it. You feel some results, that they won't shoot at you as much."

Artyom contrasted the air war to the ground war. He had climbed the mountains with the blue berets and flown with the Soviet Air Force on a bombing mission. "Flying in a jet is like sitting on a sofa. When you fly at seven thousand meters you don't feel insecure, but when you dive to one thousand meters you feel strange when the pilot says, 'On this mountain one of our pilots was killed last week.' "

It was late and we had to break. I had found the veterans predictable, but also forthcoming in a human way. I was particularly curious as to why Alexander, who told us he had dreamed of a military career, had left the blue berets. All he would answer was, "It is hard to explain."

Borovik: "Why?"

Alexander sighed.

Borovik: "Still, try."

Alexander: "It's hard to say. I wanted to stay in the army. But I was wounded. Now I would have returned."

Although well briefed, they conveyed a realistic sense of the war. They are aware that the United States is supporting the Afghans. Yet there was no animosity. Rather, there was fascination. "We know very little about you really. This was very valuable because we have a stereotype about you, just as you have of us," said Alexander. "You know, you are the first Americans we have ever met."

Artyom took down details about my background and Michael's, and we discussed the ground rules for printing the exchange in *Ogonyok*. I said I would like to see the text in Russian. If one side raised a point on such controversial issues as chemical warfare, veterans' rights, and drugs, the other side's answer had to be included. Artyom agreed. I wondered how they would handle the controversial material on the yellow rain poison gas and our view that the Afghans were fighting for their freedom.

A few days later I met a senior editor of *Ogonyok* at a dinner party and asked him how the piece was coming along. "Oh," he said, "we are not going to run it. There is nothing new in it. We will just run our own interview with the veterans." Clearly we had been found wanting in our knowledge of the accepted truths of the war against Afghanistan. We had also tested the limits of *glasnost* and found it wanting.

Dmitri

Dmitri had changed since I last saw him when he had traveled to Washington as part of an official journalists' delegation in the 1970s. He had fallen on bad days toward the end of the Brezhnev era for criticizing an official with connections near the top. His contact with foreigners had been limited and he was banished to a desk job at a government publishing house. With *glasnost* and the need for skilled professionals in the press he has been rehabilitated and moved ahead.

Dmitri still believes in socialism, but he has grown older and, at age fifty-five, his dreams are smaller, more realistic. He wants to be able to travel to his *dacha* along the Iskra River on weekends and out of the country in the summertime. His children are grown, and he remarried after his first wife died of cancer. The wife who died was a Communist party member, an intellectual goddess, blond and full-bodied, but moody, politically ambitious, and demanding. Dmitri suffered trying to live up to her expectations and his own, but he told me the pain was sweet and he was fascinated by the heights and depths to which she could drive him. He totally collapsed when she died. Then he met Irina at the wake. She consoled him and they began living together. She swims and jogs and has fine skin, so she looks at least ten years younger than her age. She does not make demands on him and has her own friends; she is outside the power curve of party competition and promotion. Their life is less complicated.

Physically Dmitri has not changed except that his hair is thinner. If anything his energy and zest for life have increased, but the pace is less frantic than I remember. He jogs or plays tennis to maintain a stocky, powerful build that has not gone to fat. When he can get away he skis. He does not smoke and he has cut back on his drinking.

Most of his mentors have moved on or out of positions of power, but he is valued for his professional experience and his charm.

Flexibility and the ability to quickly adjust to change has enabled him to survive. He never openly expressed his reservations about *glasnost* or *perestroika*. That is not his style. Rather, over a long lunch, he explained how "in the old days you could get things done. All you had to do was say, 'Do it,' and it was done. Nowadays there is criticism and arguing about how to deal with a problem. Everybody gets a chance to offer an opinion and it goes back and forth. There is too much autonomy. Everybody has his own area of responsibility, and coordination is difficult. In theory the idea of individual initiative is excellent, but in practice how do you make it work unless somebody is in charge?"

Gorbachev's rise to power had come quickly, too quickly, according to Dmitri, who was an Andropov man. Andropov understood the people's need and respect for a "strict father" as their leader. To Dmitri, the reform had come from Andropov. It was Andropov who had moved to renovate the economy, improve quality, and cut back on alcoholism. Dmitri had been part of Andropov's team, and if Andropov had lived Dmitri would have been marked for promotion. With Gorbachev, the old team in Moscow was out and the new boys from Stavropol and Krasnodar were in. Along with their slogans of openness, restructuring, and new thinking had come a massive administrative purge.

We were having a late lunch together in the restaurant of the Foreign Press Center of the Ministry of Foreign Affairs on Zubovsky Boulevard. The restaurant opens at 2:00 P.M., and it was just like old times except that there was no 300-gram flask of vodka on the table, no wine, and there would be no cognac with our coffee. We each had a bottle of watery Moscow beer to go with the *zakuski*, hors d'oeuvres of smoked sturgeon, fresh tomatoes, and heavy black bread with butter. Dmitri raised his glass and wryly toasted our not-too-blatant violation of the rules against daytime drinking. Then he told me the story about how Brezhnev returned to Moscow from heaven and was given a guided tour by Gorbachev, who showed him the new construction and refurbishing of old landmarks. Brezhnev was impressed by it all, except that wherever he went he saw long lines for vodka. "You know, Mikhail Sergeyevich," Brezhnev said, "in my time we did not drink so much."

Periodically, Dmitri is excited by *glasnost* and the opportunities it has provided him to build a new career before retirement at age sixty-

five. Gorbachev and his new leadership "feel a tremendous excitement that possibly we have come to the end of a period of long hostility. They personally are having a hand in a great stroke for peace." Dmitri wants to be a part of this, but he has a long memory. His father was a victim of the Stalin purges, and he vows, "That is something I will never forget." Are Gorbachev and his team really changing the system, or are his reforms another campaign to seize control in a time of desperation after the stagnation of Brezhnev and Chernenko? Is he really carrying on a program of reform started by Andropov or are his people taking over where the old guard ended and substituting new slogans for old?

Gorbachev's strength remains an enigma to Dmitri and others of his generation. Gorbachev does not get on well with the military, and the base of his power remains unclear. His real organizational strength comes from the party and the backing of the KGB, yet there remains a strong conservative opposition. Intellectual support comes from the press and the arts, but playwrights, journalists, novelists, and artists are limited by conservatives in the Politburo who have created an atmosphere of ambiguity.

The momentum of Gorbachev's reforms carry him forward, then the conservative opposition stalls them. Ironically, it is this old mentality of going along with the leadership out of fear, ingrained from Stalin's day, that has made the reforms possible. Gorbachev is the general secretary; he has the power, and the conservatives must go along while fighting their rear guard action. The younger generation of careerists follows because to get ahead one must go along. There is still no real general belief in the reforms. They are the new general line to be followed and tested with skepticism.

Dmitri told me of a classic form of rebellion: making an obscene gesture in front of a high official with your fist deep inside your pocket—what the Russians call "a fuck-you gesture in your pocket," in Russian, *figa v karmane*. "This is an important part of people's character. How do you change people who have been brought up to be passive, raised not to question or debate, who rebel with their hands in their pockets?" he asked. "People do not challenge or fight back."

Gorbachev speaks of the need for people to accept responsibility and act on their own to speak up, make mistakes, and move ahead. In practice, everyone works for the state, and the party bureaucracy fights to maintain its perquisites, not diminish or share them. In Dmitri and others of his generation there was less resilience and willingness to do battle; more concern with their apartments, *dachas*, and the quality of their lives. They have been waiting for socialism and communism all their lives, and now they realize they had better do what they can to take advantage of whatever is available. They are tired and bored with shoddy television sets whose picture tubes explode, jars of fruit with tops that have to be pried off and cannot be screwed back on, and tough hunks of beef butchered with an ax. They want cold beer, sweatsuits, and quality tennis rackets. They want the system to work, but it is getting late.

Dmitri says he is optimistic for his children. They are doing well and know how to move ahead in the system. He sees small signs of change. His wife's friend is starting a restaurant under the new law permitting cooperatives. "She is an ordinary, not very successful person, but she is trying to start a vegetarian restaurant where they will serve cabbage that does not give you heartburn and an ulcer the next day. She is learning to drive a truck, and whether she is successful or not really does not matter. What is important is that she has been motivated to try to do something and change her life."

We talked shop and mentioned that dealing with the foreign press has changed. Press briefings by the Central Committee staff for key Soviet journalists have been discontinued. "We used to be given reports from ambassadors to read. Now the general line is put out in the press briefings twice a week and the political observers write what they think will fly. They face the music the next day after it appears in print," Dmitri said.

We agreed that there is no debate in foreign policy. There was no discussion in the press about possible political alternatives in Afghanistan or whether the Soviet Union should support an embargo on arms sales to Iran. Foreign policy is made by the Politburo and there are no checks and balances. Everybody is too busy trying to get the economy moving to engage in the luxury of a foreign policy debate. Dmitri follows the party line, and if he has reservations in private he is careful not to reveal them in public. He is sometimes sent by the news agency to lecture on current events outside Moscow. Often, he said, he is asked by audiences why Gorbachev does not go for an agreement with President Reagan and eliminate all nuclear weapons in spite of Star Wars. The elimination of nuclear weapons is Gorbachev's goal and is appealing to most Russians. "I warn them of the dangers of platforms in the sky and what will fall down on them," said Dmitri, smiling as our waiter brought heavy cast-iron skewers with crisp lamb *shashlik*.

"These days it is primarily the former dissidents who urge the United States to maintain a strong nuclear force in order to match Soviet power and negotiate effectively," I told Dmitri. "They are the biggest supporters of President Reagan."

"Yes, the dissidents have always been perverse," said Dmitri. "But don't you think backing Reagan is going too far?"

Dmitri writes well, and he is working on a novel about the future that he believes will be appealing to Russians. The plot centers around the building of space stations by the United States and the U.S.S.R. The countries end up cooperating in space instead of using it for war.

Dmitri's wife, Irina, is a free-lance children's book illustrator. Together they earn about 900 rubles a month (or $1,440). They have a one-bedroom apartment with a rent of 37 rubles ($59) a month, and a four-wheel-drive Lada recreation vehicle that is a cross between a Jeep and a Land Rover. He spends nearly 100 rubles ($160) a month on gas and upkeep for the car, but it is the lifeline to his *dacha*, to which he and Irina and their friends can escape from Moscow in two and a half hours.

Dmitri said we must arrange a visit to the *dacha* for a weekend. This time, unlike in the past, I sensed the invitation might be real. He said the presence of foreigners in his village might be possible under the new conditions; he lives in an area that is not closed to foreigners for military security.

True to his word, Dmitri called and invited us to Sunday lunch at his *dacha*. We drove from Moscow past the new satellite cities that are replacing woods and fields. Soon we were driving through small villages, the road lined on both sides with traditional wooden peasant homes with carved wood fronts and white curtains in the windows. There are hand pumps outside the houses that do not have running water. Old women had set up stands with buckets of newly harvested potatoes and bottles filled with gladiolus and fresh dill for sale. Cars pulled over to load up. Potatoes had been in short supply all year and these were the first of the new crop.

Dmitri's traditional wooden log cabin, or *izba*, is on the edge of a small village that grows potatoes. He and Irina get on well with the villagers, bringing them food and medicine from Moscow. The day we arrived the potato harvest was at its peak, and Dmitri pitched in to haul the sacks home for his neighbor, an old lady who could not carry them herself. The sky had cleared to a light blue and what had been rain and haze turned into a ripe autumn day with warm sunshine. The villagers seemed to brighten as Dmitri waved to them in front of their houses along the narrow dirt road that passes for the main street. From the front their *dacha* looks like the other ten houses in the village. There is a high wooden gate hiding the grounds from view. Inside is a private retreat with a garden of roses, wild-flowers, and fruit trees. Irina has a rock garden with ferns that she calls her Japanese garden.

Dmitri's pride is the sauna attached to the garage. There he exorcises worldly cares and body poisons with dry heat from the wood-fired stove and by beating his body with bunches of birch branches that leave his skin red and tingling. The smell of the woods is in the air here, and jumping from the dry heat of the sauna to an icy shower restores the circulation and clears the arteries.

Dmitri and I decided to avail ourselves of the sauna's relaxation. We performed a ritual of heating and cooling, then rested, swaddled in towels and robes, in an anteroom where there was tea and cold beer accompanied by *vobla*—dried, salted freshwater perch—to restore our body salts.

We took a walk before lunch along the path paralleling the shore of the nearby river. In the middle of the path and along its sides there were white domes growing from sandy soil. Dmitri identified them as puffballs, pure white mushrooms that are good to eat. We picked them carefully so as not to damage them, selecting only those that had no blemishes or splotches of green on them. Any color but white means the mushrooms have grown old and begun to spoil, explained Dmitri. With a week of rain behind us, there was a full crop to be harvested and we soon had enough for a feast. Irina fried them in butter, mixing them with orange-hued wild morels she had found in the woods.

We had a late lunch outdoors in the garden. The table was filled with an assortment of homemade pickled cucumbers, peppers, and squash. They all had an especially crisp and fresh flavor, which Dmitri said came from adding oak and cherry leaves to the pickling brine. There were mounds of bread and salads of fresh tomatoes and chopped dill, potatoes with vegetables, and pickled garlic bulbs and stems (the green stems are vinegary and chewy, with less of a kick than the actual garlic bulbs). Irina served borscht with heavy sour cream. Her niece, who had come for the weekend, said, "The borscht is *klass*." That was a term we were to hear often. The girls trying on a fur hat were *klass*, so was a new sweatsuit. We laughed because *klass* in the classless society was now used to describe the elegant or out of the ordinary. *Glasnost* has sprouted its own jargon.

For the main course Dmitri offered his smoked sausages. They were ordinary hot dogs marinated in sunflower oil with chopped coriander and a red pepper paste that gave them a rich, spicy flavor. He used a homemade smoker with wood chips heated over an open fire of logs. There was vodka flavored with a rare grass from the Caucasus Mountains. Dmitri had persuaded an old woman to give him some plants on one of his trips there, and had successfully transplanted the pungent greens to his own garden. The pale green vodka had an herbal scent and a smooth taste.

We joked about being able to finally see his *dacha* and enjoy life outside of Moscow. Dmitri and I talked about our careers and how we would like them to continue. I told him I wanted to continue writing books, but would consider returning to the government. "One must plan the last ten years of your career not to get swallowed up in the administrative machinery," he said.

Dmitri's niece and Barney, Doveen, Steve, and Suprabha were listening to the latest English and American rock on a boom box, Steve Winwood's "Back in the High Life." The kids had their language and we had ours.

Making a Movie

After we had been in Moscow for ten days, Evelind and Michael arrived with Sherry Jones, the producer of the film that "Frontline" would soon make of our return to the Soviet Union. They were due on Friday night, but in fact did not arrive until Saturday because of the fog around Moscow, which forced their Pan American plane from Frankfurt to detour overnight in Leningrad. Intourist had no rooms at the Berlin Hotel, so they were booked into the Belgrade Hotel, and when we went there to meet them we knew how lucky we were to be in the Berlin. The Belgrade is a gray stone-and-cement modern high rise with cramped, coldly modern rooms and dark hallways with low ceilings. A place to sleep, but not my taste.

We soon agreed that the three of them would come to our room in the Berlin for meals so we could plan our joint activities. Evelind and Michael went off on their own during the day, following up their lists of educators and business people.

With Sherry we plunged into the process of making a film in the Soviet Union, a new adventure for all of us. Steve had known Sherry for years in Washington, and he is a filmmaker himself, but we all faced a unique condition making a documentary under the watchful eyes of the State Committee for Television and Radio Broadcasting, Gosteleradio. We were technically their guests. The host-guest symbiosis has its own special qualities when the function of the host is to keep the guest's plate full at the same time that he watches to make sure the guest doesn't misbehave. Sherry, Jerry, and Steve made the trek to Ostankino on the north end of the city, where they met with Valentin Yegorov and his boss, Boris Semenov, to negotiate the dos and don'ts of their mutual contract.

The first step was for Sherry to provide Gosteleradio with a list of the locales and people we wanted to see; they would contact each subject and get permission for the camera crew to film. We agreed that we would contact our friends and sources and provide their names and places of work. Normally television documentaries are wholly organized by Gosteleradio, which provides the sites to be photographed and the subjects to be interviewed. Initial contact is not from the correspondent or the outside producer; all is arranged in advance by Gosteleradio. They were surprised that we thought we could line up an hour-long documentary without them providing the subjects, but they told us to go ahead and try. We would give them a list and they would obtain the official permissions. For example, Boris Semenov explained, "If you want to shoot on the metro or in Red Square you need permission from the city government and the metro authority. We have to write a letter for everything and go through all the appropriate ministries."

"What about friends?" Jerry asked.

"You can go anyplace as long as you are invited. The more friends who are willing to be on camera, the less we need to help you. You should keep in mind the Russian proverb 'If you have a hundred friends you don't need money.' "

We soon realized that getting permission to film worked both ways: until our friends, or a doctor in a polyclinic, or a factory manager, heard from Gosteleradio, they were taking a dangerous chance speaking to us. Gosteleradio's request gave them the protection they needed to appear on film, but they still had to watch what they said because there would be an irrefutable record that could be turned against them later.

Over breakfast around our dining table at the hotel, the seven of us by then in Moscow and Sherry drew up lists of possible segments she would shoot when the crew arrived at the end of September. During the day, Sherry stayed close to Steve or Katie as they moved around the city seeing art shows, visiting the school they attended when we lived in Moscow, or checking out the old neighborhood. On Sunday all of us followed Lyokha back to the open-air pet market where we had bought two rabbits years ago, and from there we all went for a walk through the Andronikov monastery, now a museum for Andrei Rublyov's icons. Next we went to the Moscow River for a scenic boat ride. Lyokha got us to the head of the boat line by introducing us as "an important American delegation." We got off at the last stop, Gorky Park. The park was alive with families throwing bread to ducks in the pond, lined up for ice cream, riding the ferris wheel, or gathered around their picnic baskets. Little girls with huge ribbons in their hair had their pictures taken with a Mickey Mouse look-alike, or with their heads peering out of the mouth of a cardboard dinosaur.

We watched the amazing feats of skateboarders racing through a slalom course in the late August warmth, and regretted that they were not likely to be out again in October when we would be filming.

In the evenings Sherry joined us for dinner with Pyotr and Natasha, where we also found Yuri and Nadya, the two couples still friends as they had been when we knew them at the end of the 1960s.

Sherry was terrified of taking the metro without one of us at her side, but she did manage to come back from a foray with Steve, Ari, and Katie to meet us at Ed Stevens's for dinner in the garden gazebo.

For two weeks Sherry moved around Moscow with us as part of the family. She became friends with our friends and visited the sites from which she would choose locales for her film. With Steve's and Katie's help she was preproducing her show: meeting the subjects of our interviews, visiting *Izvestia* and the art shows, seeing plays and films, scanning the subways and stores for the most representative visual ideas of this very foreign city.

It was not a leisurely tourist romp around the city, but rather an intense search for the right images to convey the real life of Moscow. Each member of the family would contribute two or three suggestions for segments that would be natural, uncontrived, but original and thought provoking. In the course of those weeks Steve and Katie were overworked and pressured to the limits of their patience. Inevitably, there were moments when they resented Sherry's demands. Doveen, too, was irked that Sherry wanted her to look up old school friends and teachers by telephone but not actually meet them until Sherry could record the emotional reunions on camera. Sherry upset Katie by asking her to lengthen her translations of conversations; since the English was shorter than the Russian, Sherry was sure that Katie was leaving out "the poetry." It took the reassurance of our friend Yuri to convince Sherry that Katie was giving her the full resonance of the Russian conversations. There were no public blowups. In the privacy of Jerry's and my suite at the Berlin, everyone vented their hurt feelings—you cannot make a movie without them. All I could do was massage their shoulders and promise that they would feel better after a night's sleep.

"I've never felt so at home on a foreign assignment before," Sherry said. "You've given me a rich list to choose from. You don't have to worry about making the choices—that's my job. But you have to pin all these people down and make sure they are going to be in the film. I have to go back to Washington, but I'll send you a shooting schedule. You'll have to firm up the dates because we won't have any time to lose once we start shooting." Every day at breakfast she handed each person handwritten lists on small sheets of lined paper torn from a miniature spiral notebook. The lists were reminders of the segments for which each person had offered to be responsible, with an admonition to find out whether or not the subject was willing to be on camera. She often signed these with a smile cartoon.

Her mood became more apprehensive, however, when David Fanning, the executive producer of "Frontline," arrived in Moscow to sign the final contract with Gosteleradio. Making a film on the U.S.S.R. had been Fanning's goal for years. He had put on "Frontline" shows about the Soviet Union that he had licensed from other producers, but this was "Frontline's" first show of its own on the U.S.S.R. For Fanning, the project he had assigned to Sherry was a long-awaited opportunity and a dangerous pit into which his funding and reputation could suffer with an inconclusive, mediocre film. He was the producer, but he wasn't on location with us; he was the boss, but he wasn't in control.

"I've really gone out on a limb for you guys," he said repeatedly. "No one else on my board wanted to do this film. I've staked a lot on you. I really want you to get inside."

Wasn't he as pleased with what we had accomplished in three weeks as Sherry seemed to be? We had gone beyond our promise of being the subjects of his film and were preproducing every scene so that the camera crew could get started as soon as they arrived at the end of September.

Fanning said he felt swamped by our numbers. Rather than looking on each member of the family as a contributor, he feared the total number as an amalgam of prima donnas who wanted to be seen on camera.

Doveen, Barney, and Suprabha arrived on September 1, just as Evelind and Michael left. Fanning was facing eight of us in our hotel room when he warned the troupe that he couldn't guarantee that everyone would appear in the final cut. We assured him that we understood that we had no control over the cutting, but we did want to know what this film was about. Did he have a point of view about the Soviet Union that he was trying to illustrate, or was this a film about an American family that had lived in the Soviet Union and was returning to look at *glasnost* and *perestroika*? The question went unanswered, but he repeated that he wanted "to get inside." Jerry assured him that through our friends old and new, and as a result of our expertise in special areas, he was getting as plugged-in a view as was possible through American eyes. I knew that Jerry was not exaggerating, because a longtime Soviet expert at the American Embassy had told me the day before, "It was a pleasure to meet with your husband. It's nice to discuss the issues with someone who has been around them for a long time, who knows what questions to ask." Fanning had not been privy to that conversation.

"What I am trying to tell you," he expostulated, "is that you have to go even further. After you have asked all the questions, you have to push yourself to dig even deeper." I could feel the edginess in the group, but they held their collective temper.

"Well, what is it that you imagine this film to be?" I asked him.

"I hope that through you we can get inside Soviet life. I wouldn't mind seeing the whole film take place in a series of Moscow living rooms," he answered.

"You mean around Moscow kitchen tables," I answered. "You'll get that and a lot more." I tried to reassure him.

Fanning and Sherry left the next day, leaving behind them an uncertainty that had not surfaced before his arrival. "What was that all about? Who did he think he was talking to?" Katie asked.

"Don't worry, it's a set speech he gives to all his producers and their subjects. He makes no distinction whether you are in kindergarten or graduate school. It's not based on anything we've done or will do, just a standard rah-rah he gives everybody. He sees it as a necessary but difficult part of his job," I told Katie.

The other difficult part of his job was approving budgets. He assured us before we left the States that he would not "leave us high and dry" if we could not find an apartment. The cost of keeping ten of us in a hotel for the whole stay pushed the budget $20,000 beyond what we had agreed upon. Fanning and I added up the number of days and the cost per day of keeping one of us in Moscow; the numbers were indeed startling.

By this time the question of commissioning the second part of the contract, which meant going ahead with preparations to make the film, was moot. We were already a week into it; he and Sherry had finished their bargaining with Gosteleradio. The shape of the film was visible in that all the contacts had been made. It was only a matter of cost overrun, which we all knew might happen before we signed the contract. Fanning was able to come up with half of it. We took the risk for the other half, with the hope that we would still find an apartment.

We also discussed with Fanning the possibility that our request for an interview with General Secretary Gorbachev, his family and ours in an informal setting, would be granted. We had applied in writing and received a visit from Vitaly Cherkin, an aide from the Propaganda Department of the Central Committee. Friends in the Foreign Ministry advised us to apply for the interview because, they said, "Gorbachev makes the choice himself, and the idea of meeting an American family may appeal to him." He had met with a group of American teachers of Russian and journalists from Indonesia, why not the Schecter family? Fanning encouraged us warmly and promised to cooperate fully to get the interview on film and distributed worldwide.

We did not get up at five to see Katie and Ari off on September 7, the day they left Moscow so that Katie could register and begin the term at Columbia. They would be back in three weeks for the shooting. When we awoke we found a pile of lists, imitating Sherry's style, set neatly beside our telephone by Ari and Katie. "For Barney: Cram eighty artists into a phone booth and interview them each intimately. Memorize the Moscow subway system. Ride it nonstop for six days to see if we want to film it. Make six busts of Lenin for possible reproduction in the United States. For Leona: How many authors can you cram into a telephone booth and interview intimately? Go shopping for two thousand people. Cook a gourmet meal for all of them on your hot plate and then we'll discuss possibilities for filming. Walk to every shop in Moscow that sells coats to check prices. For Doveen: Find two hundred fashion designers by Tuesday. Without going within a 200-mile radius of the school, find your old classmate Lena and tell her you want an intimate reunion with a lot of natural emotions."

We all had a good laugh and went back to getting ready for filming.

The Reality of Glasnost

There was a line of seventeen people waiting in the cold outside the high, double front doors of the Berlin Hotel on Zhdanov Street. From inside the hotel entrance I could see them standing silent and patient on their first line of the day. I checked the time on the clock across the street. It was ten minutes to eight. The sleepy doorman unlocked the doors for me to begin a jog to the Moscow River and around the Kremlin. The line was unusual, and before stepping outside I glanced back into the lobby and saw that the newsstand was empty. Since there were no newspapers yet the small lobby was being kept empty for hotel guests. Soviet citizens are not welcome in Intourist hotels for foreigners, and the doormen serve as bouncers.

When the papers are on time, people are admitted by the doorman and pass through the rickety revolving doors to line up for their morning black-ink fix of *Pravda, Komsomolskaya Pravda, Krasnaya Zvezda,* and *Sovietskaya Russiya.* On Wednesday mornings the line is always longer. The weekly editions of *Literaturnaya Gazeta* and *Moscow News* go on sale then. The people are waiting to find their past revealed in the light of *glasnost.* A blank page of history is filled in or a personality is returned from oblivion in articles that extend and test the limits of public debate and criticism.

In front of the newsstand is a huge stuffed black bear rearing on its hind legs, the symbol of the city of Berlin, after which the hotel was renamed in the 1960s. It was called the Savoy when it was built in the 1900s, with ninety rooms and an elegant restaurant with a mirrored dance floor and a pond in the middle from which guests selected live carp and perch for their meals. So old it is about to be restored, the hotel has a devoted staff and a long waiting list for its best rooms. The dining room is still a special high-priced treat. The Berlin Hotel is a Moscow institution, a quiet corner of conviviality with a lurid past. It is said that in Stalin's day the second-floor rooms were occupied by members of the Comintern, the Communist International that directed Communist parties around the world from Moscow. On Stalin's orders in the Great Purge of 1937 the Comintern members resident in Moscow were arrested and executed. Their rooms in the Savoy were sealed for months.

When I finished running forty minutes later the line outside was longer and not moving. In a flash I realized they were waiting to read the speech Gorbachev had given in Murmansk the previous evening. He had departed from his prepared text to discuss the need to raise prices for government-subsidized meat, milk, and bread. Gorbachev's remarks had to be transcribed and edited. Some of what he said was not printed. As is frequently the case, his informal, off-the-cuff remarks might be considered subversive.

Raising consumer prices is a critical part of the Gorbachev program of *perestroika*. As the program takes shape the accompanying shock waves are palpable. Price increases are at the heart of his reform program, yet they could be the catalyst for open political discontent. Rents for state apartments have not changed since 1928. Prices for bread, sugar, meat, milk, and eggs have been the same since 1954. In the past twenty-five years the cost of state subsidies to maintain these low prices has increased twenty times and now amounts to seventy-three billion rubles a year or almost seventeen percent of the total budget of the Soviet Union. In *Pravda* the people waiting on line would read where Gorbachev and the country were headed. The papers were four hours late.

Pravda ("Truth"), the newspaper of the Communist party of the Soviet Union, is the final word on official policy. It prints what the general secretary says and interprets what he means. What appears in *Pravda* is the Communist party line and is meant to be followed by the sixteen million party members who read the ten million copies of the newspaper published daily across the Soviet Union. *Pravda* prints the full text of every speech by a member of the Politburo, a custom that has not changed. "Too often the paper reads like your *Congressional Record*," complained a senior *Pravda* editor who worked in Washington.

Still there is always something new to read in the Soviet press—too much, my friends complained. The bland, boring diet of party communiqués has been supplemented with exposés of corruption in high places, calls for changes in the legal system and education, and the first glimmerings of pollution in the Soviet environment. No longer do all the newspapers read alike, filled with the same official communiqués and speeches. In the past even interpretations were cut from the same mold. While this holds true today on foreign policy matters, domestic issues are open for free discussion—up to a point. "When I was here there was little new to be found in the press. Now it's hard to keep up with the revelations and new ideas," said Dusko Doder, *The Washington Post*'s Moscow correspondent from 1981 to 1985, who was back for a brief visit. I had the same response, finding that there was a blizzard of material, much of it new and revealing.

The "blank pages of history," Stalin's policies toward Hitler and Stalin's purges, are being mentioned in print for the first time. The collective re-creation of history that started with the Bolsheviks' Great October Revolution is slowly starting to be chipped away. Reputations are being reestablished, and the great ideological battles that Stalin settled with show trials, labor camps, and purges are re-emerging in muted form. Gorbachev has cloaked his policies in the holy shroud of Lenin and takes him as the prophet to be followed. Still not out in the open are the questions of just how much *glasnost* is to be permitted and how far the ruling Communist party will go in relinquishing its own powers in the effort to foster individual initiative and expression.

The most lively and controversial newspaper is the weekly *Moscow News*, which has raised the curtain on the crimes of Stalin, ran reports of strikes in a bus factory, and published an obituary on the émigré writer Viktor Nekrasov that infuriated Kremlin conservatives. "We are the kamikaze pilots of *glasnost*," a top editor of the paper told a friend, comparing his staff to the Japanese suicide pilots of World War II.

Ogonyok, edited by Vitaly Korotich, is the most imaginative and probing weekly news magazine in the Soviet Union. Under Korotich, *Ogonyok* covered the war in Afghanistan with a personal approach that revealed for the first time some of the nature of the struggle. *Ogonyok*'s interviews and essays on the economy have been hard-hitting to the point of embarrassment. Its efforts to reveal the truth about the past stimulated official criticism from Yegor Ligachev, the second-ranking member of the Politburo.

The biggest change in the press I saw was the beginning of real debate over history. The editors of the leading Moscow newspapers and magazines were called together for a meeting by Ligachev in the fall of 1987 and urged to write "something positive because the seventieth anniversary is coming." The conference for leading editors and propagandists was held in the Central Committee headquarters on Staraya Ploshchad, overlooking the Moscow River. According to a participant in the meeting, Ligachev was soft-spoken, but rigid in his conservative interpretation of *glasnost*, supporting it only to the extent of preventing attempts "to hush up business like criticism." Ligachev said that the growing public interest in the press and television were "revolutionary transformations" that demonstrated the advantages of socialism over capitalism. He warned, however, that "certain publications, as is noted by the public, have not been able to orient themselves correctly organically to unite truthful coverage of our history with the resolving of presentday problems of restructuring. Moreover, individual periods of history are at times covered one-sidedly" (Tass, September 16, 1987).

Ligachev reiterated the point that "one could not permit a disrespectful attitude to our people, to those generations which built socialism." The message was clear. Stalin's crimes should be balanced against his economic achievements and there should be no further efforts to discredit Stalin. Ligachev called the meeting while General Secretary Gorbachev was on vacation; it was clear that Ligachev was trying to set limits on history and its interpretation. His speech was the raw material for those who argue that *glasnost* is nothing more than a sophisticated "Hundred Flowers" period, comparable to Chairman Mao's efforts to rejuvenate the Chinese Communist Revolution by eliciting opposition thoughts and then cutting them down.

Word of the meeting quickly leaked out, and Phil Taubman of *The New York Times* wrote a story. Tass carried quotes on its English-language wire, but nothing appeared in the Soviet press. In his column the following week, Yegor Yakovlev, editor of the *Moscow News*, wrote of the "braking mechanism" being placed on *glasnost*:

> To clear away the braking mechanism is a painful and complex operation . . . like a malignant tumor, this braking mechanism exists inside each one of us. It manifests itself in

our common bad habits, very often in the lack of courage to act according to our own conscience and convictions.[1]

Change is in the air. There are the usual exhortations in the press to work harder, combined with appeals to speak openly and honestly and warnings that those who do not work well will be out of jobs. Yet the old guard is still in place at *Pravda*. Of all the major papers, *Pravda* has undergone the fewest changes under *glasnost*. The noticeable exception is that its letters from readers appear to be honest reactions to the reforms to a degree unimagined in earlier days. Yet old friends at *Pravda* confide that they are not ready to lead. "There is no way to enforce *glasnost*," is the way one editor put it. "How can words make policy changes? There is no responsibility."

At *Pravda*, where Nikolai Bukharin was editor from December 1917 until February 1918, and again for ten years from July 1918 to 1928, Bukharin's name is still anathema. He was a victim of Stalin's 1937 show trial and he was executed in 1938. Bukharin remained a nonperson. The *Pravda* historical library did not include his portrait among the paper's editors. Nor is his position as editor mentioned in Soviet reference books.[2]

Among the major issues on which Bukharin split with Stalin was the New Economic Policy (NEP) of the 1920s, developed by Lenin. Under the NEP the Soviet Union returned to a modified form of capitalism in an effort to restore agricultural and industrial production, which had dropped to dangerous levels. Bukharin favored the development of cooperatives and a gradual approach to industrialization. He opposed Stalin on the collectivization of agriculture and the forced march to heavy industry. For Gorbachev to build a theoretical basis of support for his reforms it is necessary to move away from the Stalinist model of economic development.

Gorbachev opened the way to Bukharin's rehabilitation in his seventieth-anniversary speech, when he declared that "an important part in defeating Trotskyism ideologically was played by Nikolai Bukharin." A special commission of the Central Committee was established to prepare a new history of the Communist party. By mentioning Bukharin favorably, Gorbachev gave the go-ahead for his name and ideas to be mentioned publicly in plays, articles, and histories. Bu-

---

1. *Moscow News*, no. 29, September 27, 1987.
2. Angus Roxburgh, *Pravda* (New York: George Braziller, 1987), p. 28.

kharin was the Communist party's leading theorist until he was deposed by Stalin on phony charges and forced to confess before he was executed. Gorbachev's tepid, halfhearted rehabilitation of Bukharin left the way open for a full rehabilitation later. Vitaly Korotich, editor of *Ogonyok*, said that Gorbachev's speech opened little ground that Soviet editors were not already exploring; but he added with relief, "It did not close any either."[3] *Ogonyok* was then able to run a letter from Bukharin's widow urging his rehabilitation.

Rehabilitations continue. In June 1988, the Soviet Supreme Court annulled the sentences of Lev B. Kamenev and Grigory Y. Zinoviev, who were executed on charges of treasonous activities after the first of Stalin's show trials in 1936. Kamenev and Zinoviev were shot in August 1936. They were close collaborators of Lenin and members of the first Politburo after the revolution. The court also annulled the sentences of Yuri L. Pyatkov and Karl B. Radek, who were tried for treasonous activities in the January 1937 show trial. Pyatkov, who headed the State Bank and held other financial posts, was executed, while Radek, an early leader of *The Communist International*, was sentenced to ten years in a labor camp where he was believed to have died in 1939.

Izvestia, the official organ of the Presidium of the U.S.S.R. Supreme Soviet, has become the most interesting establishment newspaper under the leadership of Ivan Dimitrievich Laptev, who has a dynamic, bright personality similar to Gorbachev's. Laptev even resembles Gorbachev physically, except he has a full head of wavy, gray hair. *Izvestia* prints the Soviet equivalent of investigative reporting on everything from corruption in the armed forces to abuses in the legal system.

There is a sharp contrast between *Pravda* and *Izvestia* these days, and the joke that was popular when I was a correspondent—*Pravda ne izvestia i izvestia ne pravda* ("Truth isn't news and news isn't true")—is no longer heard. *Pravda* is still the standard-bearer of the Communist party and the last bastion of orthodoxy; but *Izvestia* has slipped the traces of total conformity and broken new ground in its columns.

Neither paper has open, noisy city rooms the way American newspapers do—instead, reporters and writers have their own offices and there are conference rooms for editorial meetings. The corridors of

3. *The New York Times*, November 3, 1987, p. A10.

power are silent. The give and take at *Izvestia* is at the morning conference, where the editors meet to discuss the paper's layout and the substance of stories.

At the morning meeting at *Izvestia* I attended with Steve and Evelind, we heard a round of criticism and discussion of forthcoming articles. Laptev, in gray suit, white shirt, and red-and-blue silk tie, ran the meeting from the head of the table around which were seated the major editors, some twenty in all. (Deputies and senior writers and political observers sit in rows of seats behind the editors.)

When we walked into the room Laptev introduced us as "American colleagues who will be with us for the day." One of the editors sarcastically asked, "Are they *blatniye zhurnalisty?*" not realizing we could understand what he said. It was unusual for Americans to sit in on the morning meeting, and the editor wanted to know if we had been allowed to attend because we had *blat* (influence). Everyone laughed. Laptev seemed shocked for a second, but then he laughed and said, "No, they are like us." (We had been given this rare opportunity to sit in on *Izvestia*'s editorial decision-making process thanks to my old contacts with political commentator Melor Sturua—whose first name comes from the first letters of Marx, Engels, Lenin, and October Revolution—and Laptev's willingness to extend *glasnost* to us.)

The editor for the day presented the pages and the stories planned for them. There was a discussion on whether to run an article on the use of nitrites and nitrates in meat and sausages and on what levels are unsafe for human consumption. "It's like Chernobyl," said one of the editors, urging that the story be run. "We have to tell people what's happening." It was decided that the story could wait until they had more detailed information comparing levels of chemicals present and could compare standards in the United States with the Soviet Union.

Under Laptev *Izvestia* has flourished. Circulation has jumped from 4.6 million before Laptev took over to more than 10 million daily. In 1986 the paper had a 1-million-copy increase in circulation and then added 2 million in 1987. In 1986 it turned a profit of 110 million rubles ($176 million). Laptev is presiding over the installation of a new printing plant, which will cost 40 million rubles ($64 million). (Within the monopoly state publishing system there is competition for subscriptions, and readers can exercise a choice when they sign up or cancel; but nobody starts their own publications except on a typewriter with carbon paper.)

Laptev is a prototype of the new generation of leadership. At age fifty-three he is vigorous, ambitious, and skilled in rising through the party bureaucracy. He began his career in Omsk as a dockworker, then graduated from an Auto Car Institute. After he won the bicycling championship of the Soviet Union, at age twenty-six, he came to Moscow and took evening courses at Moscow University. Laptev went to work as a journalist until he was marked for advancement and sent to the Central Committee's Academy of Social Sciences for advanced training. He wrote his thesis on the political and social problems of ecology, noting presciently in 1972 that environmental issues might form the basis for the building of political parties. (Some of the most powerful new informal groups formed under *perestroika* are concerned with environmental issues.) His thesis advisor questioned whether he wanted to make such an unorthodox claim and urged him to delete this part of his conclusion, but he persisted.

From 1972 to 1978 Laptev worked in the CPSU Central Committee apparatus, including a stint in the Propaganda Department. He returned to journalism in 1978, when he was named chief editor of the Propaganda of Marxist-Leninist Theory Department of *Pravda* and a member of the editorial board. He was named a deputy editor of *Pravda* in 1982, and held that post until being selected editor-in-chief of *Izvestia* in 1984, when Konstantin Chernenko was general secretary of the party. Journalists familiar with the selection process explained that Laptev was chosen by the Central Committee from a group of three candidates. Moving a *Pravda* man to *Izvestia* is much like taking the head of the FBI and making him director of the CIA. The two papers are strong rivals, but because of its party status *Pravda* remains paramount and could only be rivaled in power if there were more than one political party in the Soviet Union.

At *Izvestia* Laptev has the job of keeping the editorial line on the cutting edge of *glasnost* and *perestroika* while not digging his blade too deeply into the still-taboo issues of Stalinism, the role of the KGB, and human rights. Laptev has the style of a senior executive in an American corporation. He is smooth, reasoning, and not inclined to any display of emotion in print or in person. He gets on well with General Secretary Gorbachev, and often is called by him.

Laptev, instead of worrying about the bottom line of the paper's balance sheet, concerns himself with the ideological bottom line and how to remain lively and readable while pleasing the board of directors in the Central Committee.

Differences among editors of magazines and newspapers should best be resolved in private discussion, not in print, where they take on the quality of dirty linen being aired in public, he explained, as we sat in his office after the morning editorial meeting. As Steve and Evelind translated, I asked Laptev why Soviet leaders were still so furtive about their personal lives. Why, for example, was it not announced when and where General Secretary Gorbachev went on vacation? The rumors surrounding Gorbachev's health that grew out of the curtain of secrecy around him were an insight into how the system has not changed. Laptev said frankly, "Our image of the leader depends on the stereotypes hardened in our minds. If we readers know all the personal details of a leader's life not everybody is happy. We are not used to that. Not everybody wants his leader to be exposed. We try to become open step by step."

None of the Soviet papers printed that Gorbachev was vacationing at the former Imperial palaces in Livadia two and a half miles southwest of Yalta on the Black Sea. For fifty-two days, from August 7 to September 29, 1987, the general secretary was not seen in public, although statements were issued in his name. The diplomatic corps was told that the general secretary was on vacation, but there were no details of where he went and how long he would be gone. Then, on September 21, the West German newspaper *Bild Zeitung* published a story asserting that Gorbachev had suffered from food poisoning while vacationing in the Crimea and was temporarily hospitalized. The report, which cited no sources, said the general secretary had been seen being taken from a train and placed in an ambulance. *Bild* also said Soviet authorities were investigating whether the food poisoning might have been an attempt to assassinate Gorbachev.

Nothing was printed in the Soviet press, but Gary Lee, the *Washington Post* Moscow bureau chief, was asked to check out the *Bild* report. He filed a story saying the report could not be confirmed and officials "dismissed it as rumor." His story ran on page 15 under the headline RUMORS SAY GORBACHEV, LONG ABSENT, MAY BE ILL.

At the Foreign Ministry press briefing, Deputy Spokesman Boris Pyadyushev was asked to comment on Gorbachev's health. Reading from a prepared text, he said, "The general secretary is still on vacation." When pressed by foreign correspondents, Pyadyushev insisted that "the general secretary is in very good health."

Despite the official denials, rumors crackled like a firestorm. One account had his wife, Raisa, suffering from complications resulting from an emergency appendectomy. In Yalta, we were told by friends, people took to the streets. Men were upset and women were crying, afraid that Gorbachev was ill and dying. There was no way to check. The personal life of a Soviet leader is private and *glasnost* does not extend to a discussion of the leader's, or his wife's, health. Among our Soviet friends there was deep concern about Gorbachev's health. Without him they believe openness will end and conventional orthodoxy will return. He is seen as the last chance for the Soviet Union to turn away from the repressive social policies and economic stagnation of the post-Stalin era.

During his vacation Gorbachev spent his days preparing his speech for the seventieth anniversary of the Bolshevik Revolution and writing his book, *Perestroika* (New York: Harper & Row, 1987). His staff, which would have preferred to swim or walk in the elegant gardens of the Czars, was kept busy with a constant stream of work, according to Laptev. From Yalta, Gorbachev sent a greeting to the United Nations General Assembly that was published in full in *Pravda* and attracted attention because it predicted the possibility of agreement on limiting strategic nuclear weapons.

While Gorbachev was away the pace of reform slowed. There was quiet in the city and the newspapers relaxed from revelations and exhortations. There were no television pictures of the general secretary visiting a factory to urge quality control or discussing an "interconnected world" with American teachers. The Soviet leadership still has not learned how to portray a leader on vacation. Unlike the American president, the general secretary does not have a press secretary who gives daily briefings on his activities. Vacations are sacrosanct; yet a simple announcement that Gorbachev was going on a month's vacation would have limited speculation that he was under fire from his rivals in the Politburo.

With Gorbachev out of town it also seemed as if *glasnost* was on vacation. Yegor Ligachev, the second in command, gave a speech carefully pointing out that under Stalin the Soviet Union had become industrialized. It was a careful, firm effort to praise Stalin's economic policies. "In the 1930s, this country moved to second place in the world in terms of industrial output, collectivized agriculture, and attained unprecedented heights in developing culture, education, literature, and the arts," said Ligachev. He was signaling approval of Stalin's economic policies, including the brutal collectivization of agriculture. The limits of debate on Stalin were laid down. Stalin's economic policies were not to be attacked, even though his crimes against individuals and wartime record could be questioned.

The differences between Gorbachev and Ligachev have fueled speculation that they are rivals and that Ligachev's conservatism would make him an acceptable successor if Gorbachev's reforms fail. Gorbachev's skill as a politician has enabled him to sense when he has moved too quickly, and he has consolidated his power position by slowing the pace of reform. Gorbachev, however, has done nothing to weaken Communist party or Central Committee power. He has brought his supporters to power and moved out the old guard, but he is not changing the structure of control.

During our visit to *Izvestia* I was curious to see how the new openness was being reflected in editorial policy. If control remained at the top how did a newspaper reflect criticism and discontent? Who defined the limits? In our conversation Laptev made it clear that he had the confidence of those above him in the Central Committee and the Politburo. In part it is a question of style—no open bickering and recrimination among major newspapers and magazines. Disputes should be settled privately, not in print, Laptev explained. The best reflection of *glasnost* is through the letters department.

Since Gorbachev's *glasnost* began in 1985 *Izvestia* has received more than 500,000 letters a year from its readers. Letters to the editor are a unique institution in the Soviet Union because by law they are required to be acted upon. Each letter is registered with a number on a file card when it arrives in the eighth-floor offices of the Letters Department. The department is not computerized and all the work is done by hand. If a letter requires action from a ministry or government bureau a copy is sent by *Izvestia* and, by law, an answer is required within one month.

Vladimir Nadelin, editor of the Letters Department, is handsome and intense. He has seventy-five people in the department, of whom twenty are technical workers who open and register letters. There is a five-person "literary group" that, Nadelin said, "edits letters by shortening them but retaining their content and their way of thinking." Twenty-five people forward letters to local government and party officials for responses. Each week *Izvestia* prints a page 1 column of letters from readers, and Nadelin writes a weekly column discussing the mail he has received. He had just written a column summarizing the reactions to the four-year labor camp sentence for Mathias Rust, the West German youth who had landed a Piper Cub aircraft in Red Square. The readers' reactions ranged from calls for a tougher sentence to leniency. Some readers argued that "the military leaders who let him land are guilty." There was no consensus except that the incident was a major embarrassment to the Soviet Union. Gorbachev used the incident to fire Defense Minister Sergei Sokolov and replace him with Dimitri Yazov.

Nadelin told me that mail was increasing to up to ten thousand letters a week. Roughly 10 percent of the mail complains about abuses of power by militia, party, and government officials. *Perestroika* and its problems are a major subject of concern, as is the lack of apartments and the long waiting time to receive them. Medical care and school problems are also high on the list of subjects covered. Individuals can also raise cases of wrongdoing in the hope of having them investigated. Nadelin noted that readers "are more cautious in writing about local conditions than when referring to General Secretary Gorbachev." What emerges from the letters, he explained, is a pattern that shows local leaders are not changing to meet the demands of *perestroika*. "National leaders say local leaders must act; but many of these local officials are products of the Brezhnev times, when their job was not to complain and keep everybody quiet. If you complained you were a bad leader. Now local leaders cannot behave as they did five years ago, but the circumstances in which they work are the same as five years ago. The changes in spiritual and ideological life have not been matched quickly enough by changes in economic life."

The range of letters also includes comments on novels, songs, popular performers, television programs, and the war in Afghanistan. Veterans of the war complain of their treatment and mothers demand an immediate Soviet withdrawal. The letters serve as a pressure valve, a public opinion sampling service, and a court of last resort for citizens who believe they have been wronged by authorities.

I was curious if the editors at *Izvestia* believed there was a change in their coverage of the United States as a result of *glasnost*. "It would be an exaggeration to say our vision of the United States has been completely changed by *glasnost*, but there has been a breakdown in the image of the United States as the enemy. In the same way you have an image of us, we have an image of you. Now we are getting more social and economic information about the United States and a more objective picture of the internal political process in the United States. Fifty to sixty percent of our foreign coverage is devoted to the United States," Nadelin said.

The *Izvestia* staff gathers informally in the cafeteria on the second floor after the paper rolls off the presses, usually around 4:00 P.M. Along with a review of the new issue there is brainstorming for new

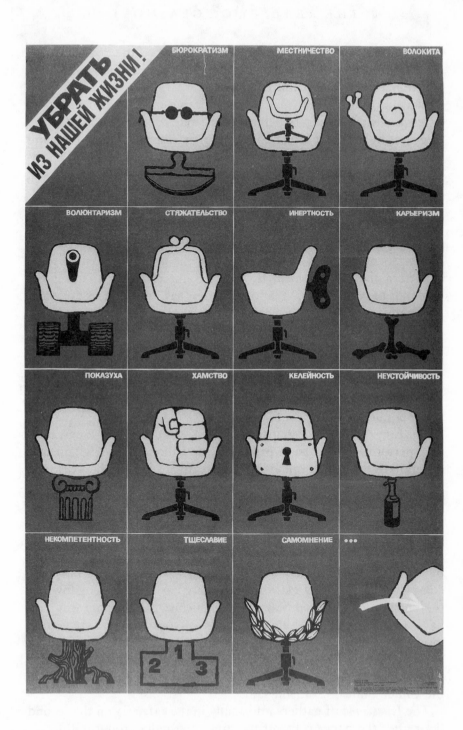

articles and features. A giant, four-foot-high electric samovar provides an endless supply of hot water for tea. The staff congregates according to its political preferences—conservatives, middle-of-the-roaders, and innovators. "The only time one changes his place is to sit beside an attractive woman," explained Melor Sturua, *Izvestia*'s senior political observer, a former Washington correspondent who has become rich and famous on his books critical of America. Sturua has capitalized on the Soviet fascination with American life, describing it in detail but with a heavy ideological spin.

It had been an exciting day and we had broken through the initial reserve of the editors. Now, over tea and sweet cakes, we talked about the pleasures of journalism and newspaper lore. Sturua asked me how I had started. I worked as a copyboy at the now defunct *New York Herald Tribune* in the summers of 1949 and 1950, and I regaled them with tales of bringing late-breaking copy to the great editors drinking beer in Bleeck's, the hallowed bar next to the paper's loading dock on 40th Street in Manhattan. Sturua said he started as a correspondent during the Stalin years. "In those days there was a beer bar on Gorky Street, across the street, where the reporters would go for drinks. If he received a byline for his article, the writer had to buy a round of drinks for his friends. Young reporters would be asked if they had any money to lend the older hands. They knew that the rubles would never be returned, but they anted up in order to be invited to the bar by their seniors. Drinking was part of the job in those days," he recalled.

"Given Stalin's late-night working habits, the paper would often come out at three A.M. One night the editor came looking for his staff only to find they were all at the bar drinking. However, the paper came out without mistakes and nothing was said. In those days you could get as drunk as you wanted to, but you could not make mistakes. Today mistakes are tolerated, but we cannot get drunk," said Sturua with a smile. The beer bar across the street is long since gone, and only coffee and tea are served in the cafeteria.

I asked Sturua and his colleagues their views on the debate over the record of crimes left by Stalin. "The supporters of the so-called cult of personality say it doesn't matter what Stalin did. In one hundred years he will be justified because it was necessary to apply surgery to our society. Otherwise it would be hopeless to build socialism in Russia." Then Sturua cited the examples of Ivan the Terrible and Peter the Great as nation builders.

"It is very dangerous to play such games with historic parallels that justify every massacre," warned a colleague.

I tried to bring us back to Gorbachev and all the questions that had been raised during his vacation.

"When he rests the whole country rests and *perestroika* stops," I suggested provocatively.

"I think you are right when you say that as a personality he creates a great momentum, but to say that when he is resting the whole country is resting is wrong."

"But doesn't it frighten you that so much depends on one man?"

"You see, we are again going back to our history. We put too much trust into a person and think that one person can find a solution to every question. Sometimes we forget that leaders are fine but the whole society must support them. The whole society must also move toward his progressive ideas, otherwise he will be isolated and in the end defeated. That happened with Khrushchev, for example," Sturua said.

"There is a fear of change here. Historically change has disrupted people's lives and not brought opportunity as it has in America. Isn't that a restraint?" I asked.

"Perhaps, but at the same time it is difficult to find words to describe how people desire change and how they cannot live without change," answered the letters editor, Vladimir Nadelin.

"You Americans prefer a leader who 'is one of us,' yet you are afraid of a genius, an Einstein, in the White House. I think you have a justification for this. For us if he is a leader he must be an outstanding personality. He must deliver. Marx and Lenin and Engels were great thinkers and leaders. Then came other leaders cut out of ordinary wood. Why not a genius? Why not know everything? This happened with Khrushchev and other leaders. Brezhnev was a stupid, lazy, power-lusting personality. That is what really disturbed people. We had another kind of leader like Stalin who misused our longing for a strong personality."

"It is very difficult to think that there is no universal leader in our time. It is very difficult," mused another editor, lighting a Marlboro cigarette.

"We need an honest, competent ruler, as does every nation. We need a built-in mechanism for change. Not the same as in your country, but built-in," suggested Nadelin.

"You need four years to change a leader. We need just one hour sometimes," added Sturua. "You talk about Americans being used to change. Our people have less material goods than yours do, but we have a lot of guarantees, such as the right to work, the right to have a place to live. This is what we are accustomed to. Now there is a proposal to change prices. Everybody worries what will happen to us if the prices of bread and milk are raised. That is why we are a bit hesitant about these changes. We have to endure it. There is no other way."

Sturua and his colleagues got into a heavy argument as he tried to explain the differences between change in the United States and the U.S.S.R.: "You Americans travel a lot. You are not hesitant to change a career or to change a profession. We are a more settled people. We don't like to move. If you live in one town you like to end your career in that town without going to other places. You are opportunists. You look for a place where you can realize your potentials better and live better. That is why you gamble. We don't gamble."

"I disagree," said Nadelin firmly. "We have restrictions on where you can live. You need a *propiska* [a pass] saying you can live in a city. It is against our constitution. We must get rid of this *propiska* system. It prevents us from going from one city to another, from one region to another. We can change places and jobs, but the *propiska* is a manifestation of our economic shortcomings. It is a manifestation of the way we distribute all we have.

"The way apartments are distributed is wrong, basically wrong, although we allow very poor people to receive as good apartments as rich people. You can't have anything without losing something. Apartments are one problem of *propiska*. There is another problem. People who live in Moscow enjoy a better life than people who live in small regional towns. If the *propiska* system is abolished Moscow becomes an overcrowded city. Everybody will try to come and live in Moscow. If you live in New York and move to Cincinnati you can have the same goods as when you lived in New York. Or you can order by mail. If you are used to Bloomingdale's and there is no Bloomingdale's in Cincinnati you can write and they will send something. Or you can take a Sears catalog and order by mail. In our country, because of our economic shortcomings, Moscow is better supplied than small towns. So are cities like Kiev, Tbilisi, and Leningrad. That is why when you go to live in a small town your standard of living drops drastically. That is why people try to come to Moscow. If you make it, you make it in Moscow. As Liza Minnelli sings, if you make it, you make it in New York.

"Now everything is free. Apartments are practically free. Health care is free. This has its positive and negative sides. It makes you a little bit passive, socially passive. You are too dependent on the state. That is why initiative does not develop. *Perestroika* takes into account this danger. *Perestroika* tries to introduce the old socialist slogan: If you work better you are paid better. This situation we have now, we call *voronolovka* [literally, a "loafer trap"]. You work poorly and I work well and we each receive the same salary. Where is my incentive? We each have a two-bedroom apartment, but your contribution to the newspaper and mine are not the same."

"What happens to the people who work poorly under the new conditions of *perestroika?*" asked Steve.

"Nobody will take away their apartments, but we want to develop another approach toward housing. Everybody must pay for it. To pay for it you must work better; an apartment is not a free lunch. Now rent is very low. I have a big apartment now. I had a smaller apartment in Washington and I paid almost one thousand dollars a month for it. For my apartment in Moscow, which is bigger and better, I pay only twenty-four rubles, about forty dollars. Why? Because the government supports me financially through this low rent. That is why we need a *propiska* system, otherwise everything will go upside down. It's a new paradox," explained Sturua.

I had seen this argument developing in other conversations we had. At stake is the nature of socialism and how the individual is treated in the Soviet state. If there is a return to a market economy for housing, then how will the state provide housing for all people? Yet, as the journalists pointed out, the housing system has developed its own inequalities.

The same argument applied in other areas, such as health care.

"In our health-care system some people are prepared to pay in order to receive better care. I am prepared to pay for my health care. Others say, 'We are a socialist country—invest more money in health care and provide better free care.' These two viewpoints are reconcilable," insisted Sturua.

Another paradox of restructuring is that the old psychology still dominates people's thinking and responses. "People are not used to the idea of individual initiative," said letters editor Nadelin. "There were more than one hundred letters on the new cooperative restaurant, Number Thirty-six Kropotkinskaya Cafe, and only one of them was favorable. The rest opposed the café. The café buys meat and vegetables in the market. People complain that it is driving up prices by taking the best products off the market. We are defending the restaurant and argue that if there are more cooperatives then there will be competition and prices will be lowered. If there are a thousand or two thousand cafés then competition will increase and prices will be lowered.

"Basically, those who opposed the café are jealous of what the owners are doing. They have an ingrained psychological and ideological barrier against a private enterprise. They write that 'those private operators are making double what we are. That is what we fought to get rid of.' If we are not well off and others around us are not well off, that is fine, but if somebody around us is doing better than we are, we are jealous," said Nadelin, explaining a problem of *perestroika* we were to hear repeated over and over.

It had been a remarkable day for me, beginning with the morning *planyorka* (planning meeting), and ending with a bull session in the cafeteria after the paper had been put to bed. I had always known Soviet journalists to speak their minds in private, usually when they were out of Moscow, but I had never before visited *Izvestia* and been able to discuss more than the current party line. The relaxing effect of *glasnost* changed the atmosphere and the content of our talks. It was like being at a newspaper.

In the 1950s there was censorship of all copy sent from Moscow. In the 1960s correspondents were required to make two copies of their stories to be transmitted by telegraph from the Central Post Office. Today computer tapes are sent through open phone lines that are centrally monitored. The only limit is the speed at which tapes can be sent, because the Soviet equipment cannot monitor at very high speeds. In my day we complained about not having enough briefings. Now correspondents only half-jokingly mutter, "There are so many briefings I can't get my work done."

The biggest change in the life of foreign correspondents covering Moscow is the twice-weekly press briefings given by Gennadiy Ivanovich Gerasimov, chief of the Press Department of the Ministry of Foreign Affairs. The briefings are held in the Foreign Ministry's Press Center on Zubovsky Boulevard, built for the 1980 Moscow Olympics. On days when there is breaking news as many as 200 of the 320 accredited foreign journalists will appear in the briefing theater with red sandstone walls. The seats are equipped with earpieces for simultaneous translation into English, French, Spanish, and Arabic.

Gerasimov's acerbic wit and strong adversarial thrust often transform dull propaganda into high theater. A briefing can become a happening. The mixture of Arabic, Chinese, Latin, American, English, Japanese, French, German, and Soviet correspondents is volatile. Their probing mixture of sarcasm, humor, and occasional rage can boil over into confrontation.

The format is for a Foreign Ministry spokesman, usually Gerasimov, to comment on topics of the day and then open the floor for questions in Russian or English. These questions range from the parochial ("Why were Soviet employees of the Japanese Embassy forced to resign?") to the cosmic ("What is the Soviet Union's latest position on the Strategic Defense Initiative?"). Any question can be asked, and there is usually a carefully prepared written answer to be read or a Gerasimov free-form reply.

Sample questions: "What is the Soviet position on the border hostilities between Peru and Ecuador?" "Why has the Oriental Institute of the Academy of Sciences invited a well-known Zionist to lecture there?"

Answers: "The Soviet Union favors peaceful settlement of disputes." "The institute invited a recognized scholar, Rabbi Arthur Hertzberg, Professor of Religion at Dartmouth College, to lecture."

As have his counterparts at White House or State Department daily briefings, Gerasimov has established a characteristic style: relentless, but brightened on occasion by humor and self-mockery. He insists that he will not be anonymous: "I speak on the condition that I am identified." There is no background or off the record at one of his briefings. Gerasimov or his deputies want to be quoted around the world and put out the Soviet position. Instead of relying on Tass, *Pravda*, or *Izvestia*, correspondents now are offered a direct official foreign policy line.

On one occasion during the briefing I attended he referred to an article by a correspondent for the Italian newspaper *Corriere Della Sera*, suggesting that the Foreign Ministry was being recaptured by the relatives of Czarist diplomats. Under the headline ARISTOCRATS COME BACK TO THE KREMLIN, it was noted that Deputy Foreign Minister Vladimir Petrovsky had a relative who was foreign minister under the Czars. Deputy Foreign Minister Yuli Vorontsov had a relative who was a Czarist diplomat. Ambassador to the United States Yuli Dubinin came from the family of Count Witte, who was minister of finance (1892–1903) and later prime minister (1903–1906). Nothing was said about Gerasimov and his Greek roots. "Maybe I came from Macedonia and have different roots," smiled Gerasimov. "Let me assure you that in trying to solve the problem of nepotism our diplomats have no relations with any dukes or nobility. Their roots go deep into hardworking families. Only kings and queens grant titles and financial privileges." We all laughed. He had not really denied the story, but he had disposed of it cleverly.

For the first time anyone could remember, the press was told yes when a correspondent asked if Foreign Minister Eduard Shevardnadze would be traveling to South America after the United Nations meeting in New York in the fall of 1987. In the past, travel plans for such events were considered state secrets. Now there is a growing realization that the traditional practices of not answering correspondents' queries is counterproductive and leads to negative speculation.

Gerasimov has a smooth, sophisticated appearance, with what Asians praise as a high, intelligent forehead, and sharp features that give his face an expression of suppressed intensity, not unlike a cobra waiting to strike. He dresses well and conservatively, usually gray or blue smooth-finish worsted suits with white shirts and imported silk ties. His years in New York (1972 to 1978) as a Novosti Press Agency correspondent helped develop a brittle, ironic style, a sophisticated understanding of the American press and the power of network television. He is best known to American audiences through his television appearances on ABC's "Nightline" and the CBS News show on the Soviet Union, "Seven Days in May." Gerasimov tangled with correspondent Ed Bradley and won the verbal battle on points.

During the December 1987 summit in Washington, Gerasimov smoothly handled the joint spokesman role with White House Press Secretary Marlin Fitzwater. After the first meeting of Reagan and Gorbachev he was asked how the chemistry was between the two leaders. Gerasimov replied, "It is too early for chemical analysis." At another briefing, when pressed on Soviet restrictions on Jewish emigration, Gerasimov said most of the Soviet Jews who wanted to leave did so in the 1970s.

When told of Gerasimov's remarks, Anatoly (Natan) Shcharansky, who spent nine years in Soviet prison before he was freed in 1986, recalled a story about Gerasimov. In the early 1970s, Shcharansky said, his parents attended a dinner party in Moscow at which Gerasimov and his wife were present. Gerasimov had been working in New York, and Shcharansky quoted him as saying at dinner how wonderful and what a great country the United States is and how unhappy he was to come back to Moscow. At the same time, the articles by Mr. Gerasimov were about how awful life in America was. Shcharansky added that Gerasimov is willing "to say all kinds of ridiculous things in his official capacity."

Gerasimov denied the story and said he did not know Shcharansky's parents. "I never dined with them, and I never said the things which he said I said," insisted Gerasimov.[4]

In person Gerasimov is careful, wary but interested. The look from behind his eyes is hard, cutting, and intelligent despite the smile. He is the new Soviet man: worldly, self-assured, and usually skillful in conveying an image of reasonableness and good intent. However, the substance of his remarks shows little flexibility except on command. His surface amiability masks an ideological toughness and combativeness. He has raised the image of the Foreign Ministry and shown himself to be a skilled and steely advocate of the Soviet line.

Gerasimov's veneer cracked only once, American correspondents told me, when he sought to portray *U.S. News & World Report* correspondent Nicholas Daniloff as a spy in the fall of 1986. Alexander Goldfarb, the son of scientist David Goldfarb, had emigrated to America and told of a KGB attempt to set up Daniloff through his father in 1984. The elder Goldfarb, a friend of Daniloff, refused and was denied permission to emigrate. When his son's account was published Gerasimov told a press briefing that Tass had interviewed David Goldfarb in the hospital in Moscow and that he had denied his son's account of the incident. In a letter to the *Washington Post* Alex Goldfarb wrote: "Mr. Gerasimov is lying. My father was indeed interviewed at his hospital bed by Tass and Novosti correspondents and confirmed the story of the unsuccessful attempt to frame Nick. My father also said that Nick is his good friend and he did not believe the spying charges against him."[5] As support for Daniloff mounted Gerasimov turned nasty, insisting repeatedly that Daniloff was a spy. Correspondents realized that they too could be set up by the KGB to become currency for the release of a Soviet spy.

Usually Gerasimov is smiling, calculating, and intense, exhibiting the tension of a man who does not suffer fools. Self-confident, he enjoys his work and often lingers at the podium after his briefing. Correspondents can question him about their individual requests for Foreign Ministry cooperation on projects or feel him out informally

4. *The New York Times*, "A Russian Says No, He Wasn't the Man Who Came to Dinner," December 22, 1987, p. A14.
5. *Washington Post*, Letter to the Editor, September 16, 1986.

on the issues. During these informal sessions Gerasimov is often inclined to be at ease and depart from the formal foreign policy line. One afternoon after his 3:00 P.M. briefing he was asked the difference between *glasnost* and the Czech spring of 1968, which led to the Soviet invasion in August of that year. Without hesitation Gerasimov replied, "Nineteen years." This was hardly the answer he would have given during a briefing, when he would dispense a line of argument that blames the United States for the world's troubles and praises the Soviet Union for its contributions to world peace.

Shortly after I arrived in Moscow I met with Gerasimov in a reception room behind the auditorium after one of his briefings. Steve and Katie joined me as we explained our project over tea, cookies, and chocolate candies. He was friendly and asked Katie to tell him in Russian what she is studying at Columbia University. In our small talk, I told Gerasimov that as a former White House spokesman on foreign policy I was sympathetic to the obscure question he received on the border tension between Peru and Ecuador. Didn't he have a briefing book with prepared answers? I asked. He smiled. "I was supposed to be briefed, but they missed that one." He had given a general answer and promised a more specific reply.

Gerasimov has written prepared guidance, which he reads in response to questions on critical issues such as arms control negotiations or the conflict in the Persian Gulf. Once a correspondent read off his questions, and Gerasimov replied, "Since you have read your question I will read my answer." Often Gerasimov offers a reply based on general notes, so that it appears he is not reading a prepared statement; but on any major issue he has a carefully prepared text.

This is a far cry from press conferences during my days in Moscow, when the elaborately staged conferences were like holidays: few and far between. There was little give and take aside from heavy doses of propaganda. Nowadays the briefing menu is varied, with press conferences on nuclear fusion, chemical warfare, and even an invitation to witness the burning of drugs seized by customs agents. There is a continuing effort to present the Soviet positions at the United Nations, the latest developments in Soviet-Chinese relations, and Soviet views on the Middle East and the Persian Gulf.

Gerasimov's operation is part of a general upgrading of the Foreign Ministry since the departure of Andrei Gromyko in July of 1985 after twenty-eight years as minister. Under Eduard Shevardnadze, a former KGB head in the Georgian Republic and close colleague of Gorbachev, the ministry has turned to a new team. The Communist party coordination of foreign policy is controlled by the former ambassador to Washington, Anatoly Dobrynin, who runs his shop at the Central Committee much as the National Security Council is run from the White House.

Dobrynin, who was ambassador to the United States for twenty-five years (1961 to 1986), learned much from Henry Kissinger and Zbigniew Brzezinski on how to manage and control issues. He is Gorbachev's closest foreign policy advisor when it comes to dealing with the United States. It was on Dobrynin's initiative that Gorbachev sought to gain concessions on the Strategic Defense Initiative before agreeing to a summit meeting in Washington with President Reagan. Those who attended the meeting between Secretary of State George Shultz and Gorbachev in the Kremlin reported a look of surprise and chagrin on the faces of Foreign Minister Shevardnadze and his deputy, Alexander Bessmertnykh, when Gorbachev told Shultz that he would not set a date for the summit because of a lack of movement on the problem of space-based weapons systems.

"I felt that Shevardnadze was definitely surprised and disappointed," said a senior American official who watched his reaction. In the old days there was never a hint through a smile, eye contact, or a loose word that there was a difference within the Soviet delegation. This time it was different, and most of the Americans were convinced Gorbachev had acted without telling his foreign minister.

Dobrynin's former deputies in Washington are in key roles at the Foreign Ministry. On American affairs he normally relies on Alexander Bessmertnykh, deputy foreign minister with responsibility for the United States and Canada. Yuli Vorontsov is the Kremlin's top negotiator. Key experts include Boris Petrov on European affairs, Igor Rogachev on China, and Viktor Karpov for strategic arms. Gerasimov can and does call on all of them, plus Yevgeny Velikov, vice president of the Academy of Sciences, to brief at press conferences.

Dobrynin has clearly established his seniority and dominance over Georgi Arbatov, head of the United States of America and Canada Institute. The USA Institute, as it is known, is the Soviet equivalent of an American research think tank except that its staff includes personnel with Soviet intelligence affiliation. Arbatov's institute serves as a choke point for invitations to the Soviet Union for American political leaders and intellectuals. In the 1970s, when Dobrynin was ambassador to Washington, Arbatov tried to set up his own back channel to the White House, sidestepping Dobrynin. Arbatov was quickly slapped down by Dobrynin, but he remains an ambitious secondary player. In his memoirs Henry Kissinger describes Arbatov as "especially subtle in playing to the inexhaustible masochism of American intellectuals who took it as an article of faith that every difficulty in U.S.–Soviet relations had to be caused by American stupidity and intransigence."[6]

The heavy volume of press conferences, however, does not lead to internal debate on foreign policy issues in the Soviet press. Most of it is for foreign consumption. *Glasnost* in foreign affairs, thus far, consists of running a statement by an American official on a key arms control issue, and a Soviet rebuttal in an adjacent column of *Pravda* or *Izvestia*. Soviet journalists do not argue among themselves in print on the pros and cons of the Strategic Defense Initiative or human rights. The political observers in *Pravda* and *Izvestia* have been telling people what to think since Stalin's time, and they are not about to change.

When I covered Moscow, ranking Soviet journalists were briefed at least twice a month at the Foreign Ministry on new developments. I remember calling the Press Department to ask for clarification on the Soviet position on China and being told: "Read *Pravda* or *Izvestia*. They carry the official position." Nowadays they still reflect the government line, but my Soviet correspondent friends insist that they are being told to make their own interpretations first. At *Pravda*, political observer Vselevod Ovchinikov recalled that when the Chinese prime minister was visiting Yugoslavia recently Ovchinikov called a high-ranking source at the Ministry of Foreign Affairs for guidance and was told: "You decide what you think and write it. Then we'll discuss it." At *Moscow News*, deputy editor-in-chief Yuri Bandoura said his natural instinct was to call a friend at the Central Committee for guidance on controversial issues. "Write what you think you should," he was told. "If we have any criticism we'll let you know."

Old behavior patterns do not change easily. The senior commentator Valentin Zorin, who is sometimes called the Walter Cronkite of Soviet television, has had trouble adjusting to *glasnost*. As we sat in his office Zorin explained: "Most important in *perestroika* is what is happening within us." Zorin told about a trip he took to England, where he was asked who specifically is opposing *perestroika*. "I told my English journalist friends, 'I am the opposition.' I am an ardent supporter of Gorbachev, but when I take up my pen I am burdened

---

6. Henry Kissinger, *White House Years* (Boston: Little, Brown and Company, 1979), p. 112.

by the weight of thirty years of hardened attitudes. It is terribly difficult. One has to give up old customs developed over several decades." *Pravda* editor Viktor Afanasyev is of the same generation as Zorin. He wrote: "Whether we like it or not, the weight of the past still hangs on our leg and we to one degree or another are responsible for the process of stagnation."

Caution on foreign policy issues remains the command for internal discussion; but some writers are beginning to speak out. Alexander Keikov, a reporter for *Literaturnaya Gazeta*, complained that information from the Foreign Ministry briefings is used "only on occasion and with caution" in the Soviet press. "Apparently, we continue to think that, in fact, the answers are intended for foreigners, and not necessarily to open the eyes of our countrymen."[7]

The enemies of *glasnost* have also become skilled in resisting freedom of information despite Gorbachev's injunction that it is a cornerstone of his reforms. Without open debate, Gorbachev has warned, managers will become isolated and corrupt, workers will lose interest, and the stagnation that has crippled Soviet industry will continue.

The Soviet media is Gorbachev's primary weapon to make his program work, and the central press is under continued pressure to maintain momentum. Gorbachev is the composer and Alexander Yakovlev, the Politburo propaganda chief, is the conductor. At a year-end meeting in 1987 Yakovlev warned journalists against abusing their frontline position with "carelessness and slipshod preparation of material."

One of our friends told us that his colleague, an editor, had written a story that said people had not made up their minds about the value of *perestroika*. (The editor quoted the results of a research poll he learned about, which showed 30 percent of those interviewed were in favor of *perestroika*, 20 percent were against it, and 50 percent were undecided. There is no systematic public opinion polling in the Soviet Union, and the major newspapers rely on their letters to editors to sample the public's views. Polling is in its early stages in the Soviet Union and is conducted by academic organizations. Stalin's legacy still looms large, and people are reluctant to state their views in public.) The editor who disclosed the poll results was told he had exercised poor judgment and was demoted. "In Stalin's time he would have been sent to a labor camp. Under Brezhnev, he would have been

---

7. *The Washington Post*, December 22, 1987, pp. A-1 and A-34.

fired; now he has lost his power for 'bad judgment,' " explained the friend.

The limits of *glasnost* thus far have been flexible and open to constantly changing definition. *Glasnost* is a tool for the conservatives as well as the reformers. The upholders of the status quo and its privileges have learned how to protect themselves by paying lip service to reform. As Yakovlev explained: "A kind of natural selection has taken place; the suppressors of criticism have become more clever and more stable and dodgy. If need be they themselves support criticism, but this does not change the essence of the matter—suppression means suppression."

Yet Yakovlev is himself a suppressor because he sets the limits to the debate. *Glasnost* is a tool of the party to achieve reforms, the New Revolution of Mikhail Gorbachev; but it is limited by the need to maintain party control. *Pravda* sets the party line and the more daring press tests its limits. The breadth of *glasnost* lengthens and shortens depending on the strength of the opposition. *Glasnost* could disappear. The ultimate arbiter of press freedom in the Soviet Union is not the law, the Soviet constitution, or the courts; it is one man, Mikhail Gorbachev, and the Central Committee of the Communist party. So far Gorbachev has not insisted on defining *glasnost* from the top down; he has told the press to create its own limits, a kind of self-censorship that is guided from the inner councils of the Central Committee. *Glasnost* is not freedom of the press as Americans know it, but it is a major change for the Soviet Union and the most visible of Gorbachev's reforms.

The Yeltsin Affair

On our second day in Moscow I was standing on the platform of the metro at Pushkinskaya Station reading heroic lines from Pushkin's poems, engraved in bronze to look like pages in a book. You can read his poetry on the station walls until the arriving train cuts off the page from view. Out of the corner of my eye I spotted a militiaman a few yards away stop a man to ask for his identification papers. The other metro riders on the platform glanced furtively at the encounter and quickly turned away.

Everybody carries a *propiska*, a residence permit, which shows their legal address. You cannot live in Moscow without a *propiska*, and they are given only if you have a job and a place to live, or find a mate with an apartment. You cannot legally move to the city and look for work. That is the way the population of Moscow is limited. That is why there are no homeless people in Moscow. Young workers who come to the city to find work must live in dormitories on the city limits for three years before they are hired permanently and given resident status. They are called *limitchiki* because they are over the limit set for the factory and must wait for permanent employment. The militiaman did not like what he saw in the *propiska* of the man on the metro platform, and took him away for questioning as our train arrived.

We were surprised by the incident, a jarring reminder of the limits on life in Moscow. In the summer of 1987 the city was changing. I could not help but compare it to 1968, when I first saw Moscow and was surprised at how run-down and drab it was. The streets were clean and washed every evening, but the buildings were crum-

128

bling. Even the prefabricated new apartment houses looked old before they were finished because the quality of construction work was so poor. The plate glass in the storefronts of our new apartment house was broken when we moved in and it stayed that way for two years. New construction seemed to take forever. They were still working on a Moscow circus building after more than two years of delays. The magic mile on Kalinina Prospekt, with its heroic size, glass-fronted stores, and restaurants, built as a showpiece by Nikita Khrushchev, was the only sign of prosperity. Under Brezhnev, Moscow reflected its leader: grand ideas moldering from neglect and corruption.

Now, wherever I looked there was scaffolding for repairs and painting. The old Metropole Hotel, a landmark meeting place for friends, spies, and KGB prostitutes, was closed for *remont* by a Finnish contractor who was carefully preserving the art deco plaster cherubs and flowers on the outer walls and building a glass atrium on the top floor.

Our hotel was located on Zhdanov Street. Although it is named after the Leningrad party boss, Andrei Zhdanov, one of Stalin's notorious cronies, the street offers a panorama of charm and history. I enjoyed walking along Zhdanov Street from where it begins on Marksa Prospekt. Across the street from the Berlin Hotel is the Sardine, a stand-up restaurant that serves *pelmeni* (chopped-meat-stuffed ravioli) in a watery soup with bread and coffee for forty-eight kopecks (seventy-seven cents). I never saw the doors open without a line standing outside. It began at 8:00 A.M. and ended at 8:00 P.M. Barney would check the size of the line from our hotel room window and dash down for a snack, slurping his bowl of *pelmeni* with army officers and clerks at the chest-high stands where the food was eaten.

Farther down the block was our local bakery. When we returned home on the metro at about midnight and passed the entrance there was a warming perfume of fresh-baked bread on the cold street as the truck driver unloaded wooden trays of black, white, and rye bread on open racks for sale the next morning. Inside the shop there was a long fork at the bottom of each rack to test the freshness of the loaves. Touching or squeezing the bread is considered *nekulturno* (uncultured or rude), like wearing or carrying a coat into a restaurant, but not a roll or slice of bread was wrapped. I quickly learned to bring a plastic bag for my purchases, like the other customers. The attractive blond cashier was so busy she was hard to flirt with, but occasionally, when my plastic bag was overloaded and I had to juggle a handful of rolls and a loaf of black bread, she would lift her curls from the cash register and smile.

Across the street is the Kuznetskiy Most metro station, lined with vendors on both sides of the entrance. The old women carry their vegetable business in suitcases or shopping bags and peddle fresh flowers, dill, parsley, radishes, carrots, lettuce, and pickles. "Taste my pickles, young man," said one smiling old lady as she thrust a sample in front of me on the end of a knife. The leathery-skinned woman selling parsnips told Katie that Peter the Great introduced parsnips and potatoes to Russia. Before Gorbachev such street sales were illegal, and the women would be harassed by the militia. They kept their vegetables in bags or suitcases that could be easily closed, and still do, for a quick getaway down the metro escalator.

Inside the archway leading to the metro there were stalls with books and calendars for sale. I always joined the crowd to see what new novelty was quenching the parched consumer spirit of Muscovites. One day I noticed a particularly large crowd around a table. For one ruble vendors were selling a map of all the major stores in Moscow, a favorite with out-of-town peasants and workers in search of food and clothing. Individually owned photocopying machines are not permitted for Soviet citizens, so all copies sold on the street are made on expensive photography paper. The only places in which photocopying machines are available to individuals are at a few libraries and notaries' offices. Every morning a line forms outside the Lenin Library to obtain tokens for the photocopying machine. After half an hour the line disappears because all the tokens have been given out.

Major scientific organizations have complained about the inability to make photocopies and how this hinders their work. Soviet officials have long feared that photocopying machines would be used to circulate Western publications and forbidden Soviet authors. The Soviet Union produces only about one thousand office copying machines a year—supplemented by several hundred machines from abroad. Production of copying equipment is limited almost exclusively to one factory. In contrast, Japan produces two million photocopying machines annually.[1]

On Zhdanov Street calendars with black-and-white pictures of rock stars sell for a ruble. On good days you can buy the Soviet

1. NTR (*Nauchno-technicheskaya Revolutsia*), no. 15.

equivalent of a hamburger from a street vendor, or a package of stew meat wrapped in plastic, or a chunk of smoked sturgeon. The same item is rarely there twice in a row, and shopping is a game of chance.

Farther up the street on the corner of Kuznetsky Most is an outdoor book market. People gather on the sidewalk and spill over into the street with books or small suitcases under their arms. They carry lists of books they have for sale. The crowd of buyers and sellers is suspicious and there is silence as people move quietly from one vendor to the next, looking at lists or asking to see a volume for sale. The books range from popular novels to scientific tomes, art books, and out-of-print histories. The scene is kinetic as buyers and sellers push against each other searching for bargains and rare finds. I couldn't find anything I wanted to buy as I scanned the lists and peeked into suitcases.

On the opposite corner was a store selling aerosol cans of household items—bug sprays and deodorants. Steve heard that in the remote provinces people were using bug spray for a high because vodka was so difficult to buy. Bug spray is applied on the back of the neck or on a shaven spot on the skull as an alcohol substitute. He told us the joke going the rounds: A man who was waiting to buy bug spray finally got to the head of the line and asked for a whole case. The others in line shouted at him, "Speculator, speculator." An old man standing behind the buyer raised his hand, quieted the crowd, and asked for forbearance: "Maybe he has a wedding," said the old man.

Steve also heard that in the north after-shave lotion is filtered through a slice of black bread to separate the perfume from the alcohol. The bread is then squeezed out and eaten; the squeezings are used as perfume. There were many jokes about the lack of alcohol. There were no liquor lines on Zhdanov Street, but any line would spur the latest vodka joke. My friends would ask: "Have you heard the one about the two men standing on line for vodka? After an hour one man said he was fed up and was going to the Kremlin to complain to Gorbachev. 'Good luck,' said his friend. Two hours later the man came back dejected. 'The line there is even longer,' he said."

On the next block, past the elegant State Bank (a private bank in Czarist days), the walls of the Architecture Institute were being restored. Aquamarine and salmon-pink paints were being applied to the walls of a nearby Asian research institute. Off the sidewalk plane trees rose from the courtyards of former townhouses. The dome of a Russian Orthodox church was being rebuilt. Down a cobblestone by-street the Sandunovskiye Bani, the famous old bathhouse, was being renovated. Three blocks from the center of Moscow we walked into the ambience of the nineteenth century.

Wherever I walked there were signs of the last-ditch effort to preserve some of the city's landmark buildings. On Gorky Street an attempt was under way to refurbish the prerevolutionary storefronts and window frames of Czarist-era buildings. Scaffolding adorned the Bolshoi Theater and GOSPLAN, the State Planning Committee Building. The struggle between decay and restoration, the conflict between those who favor the reform attempts of Mikhail Gorbachev and those who oppose them, was everywhere. As I walked through side streets with nineteenth-century townhouses and mansions it was hard to see who was winning the battle; the need for restoration work was far greater than the pace of restructuring.

The city seemed friendlier than I remembered it. Every café had outdoor tables and a stand that offered coffee, tea, soft drinks, cake, and sandwiches. Supplies permitting, outdoor markets with decorated wooden kiosks offered fresh fruits and vegetables and handicrafts from outlying republics. They are a far cry from outdoor cafés or gourmet food shops in Western Europe, but this modest start was appreciated by Moscow citizens.

Since shopping for food was a game of chance I always checked the lines to see what was being offered. After a briefing at the Ministry of Foreign Affairs Press Center I saw a short line for golden melons from Kazakhstan outside the Park Kultury metro station. It was a warm, early autumn afternoon, and the people appeared relaxed in the soft sun. There were workers in greasy coveralls, a smartly dressed woman in an English tweed skirt, and young mothers with children in carriages. The price of fifty kopecks (eighty cents) a kilo (2.2 pounds) was considered cheap for ripe melons of good quality. The truck driver was friendly and met the customers' demands for big or small melons with a smile, tapping the melons to assure the women the fruits were ready to eat. The attractive women who smiled with their eyes and the ripe fruit for sale made it the best line I found in Moscow.

Old ways are hard to change. I saw kitchen workers and clerks hand food to their friends through the service entrances of restaurants and food stores. A friend told us that she quit her job as the janitor at an academic institute just before it was going to move to new quarters. "I knew that supplies and equipment would be missing during the move. Since I was the one responsible, I would have to pay. The staff, all high-minded academics, steal the supplies for their *dachas*. They think it belongs to them."

Socialism as it is practiced in the Soviet Union today means sharing at the lowest common denominator. As long as one's neighbors live modestly on the same scale there is no discontent, but woe to those who try to get ahead by buying or selling on the side. That is speculation, prohibited by law.

When people buy or sell to earn extra money, the cry of "Speculation" fills the air. The role of the middleman and the salesman is shunned in Soviet society, yet the economic reforms underscore the need for individual enterprises to accept responsibility for their profits and losses. The concept of profit has been associated with capitalist exploitation of workers, and selling for gain is seen as immoral or criminal unless you sell something you grew, raised, or created.

When we went to the Central Market to take pictures of the meat counter, the heavyset women selling beef for eight rubles ($12.80) a kilo told us: "We are not speculators. We raised these cows ourselves." They were collective farmers who had used their private plots to raise cows. Once a year they brought the animals to Moscow for sale in the Central Market. Making money has a different value in the Soviet Union than in the United States. There are few consumer goods to buy and such big-ticket items as housing, health care, child care, education, and vacations are all paid for or subsidized by the state.

However, under Gorbachev's economic reforms the state encourages new independent cooperatives to provide consumer services. They are a throwback to the New Economic Policy of Lenin, which from 1921 to 1929 tried to stimulate individual enterprises and services after the economy stagnated under total state control. A group of individuals can start a cooperative business, some with government loans, to provide such services as cafés, restaurants, taxis, barbershops, beauty shops, or fast foods.

When the new law went into effect in the summer of 1987 there were 1,500 applications for cooperative enterprises. Of these, 440 were approved, including 118 restaurants and cafés. The number is disappointing compared to the 5,000 cafés and restaurants that flourished in Moscow during the heady days of the NEP in the 1920s, said Abel Aganbegyan, Gorbachev's leading economist.

Cooperatives are as close to free enterprise as the Soviet Union gets. To start a café you have to obtain a license and a government loan if you need capital. You cannot stay out of your regular job for more than four months while you start a business. Cooperatives must pay a tax of 35 percent on profits. Profits are shared among those who run the co-op. Despite difficulties the cooperative restaurants we visited required reservations and were usually full. Prices were high, five to thirty rubles ($48) per person for a meal without wine or beer (you can bring your own). The food was of good quality and it was usually well served.

One of Doveen's college student friends said she would not eat in a new cooperative restaurant because "the prices are so high only speculators and criminals can afford to eat there." She argued that "ordinary people do not earn enough money to eat in such places."

One of the new restaurants is a joint venture between Indian restaurant owners and a state organization. There are two sections to the restaurant, one where payment is accepted in hard currency, the other accepts payment in rubles. The hard-currency profits can be taken out of the Soviet Union, while the ruble income is used to pay the help and buy supplies inside the Soviet Union. Pepsico made a similar deal in Moscow in October 1987, when it agreed to a joint venture to build two Pizza Hut restaurants. One will sell pizzas for rubles, the other for hard currency.

McDonald's has been negotiating for years with the government to develop reliable sources of beef, potatoes, and chicken so McDonald's can open a fast-food operation in the Soviet Union; the first of twenty McDonald's in Moscow is scheduled to open in 1989. Hamburgers now are sold on the street by vendors from state restaurants. They bring out wooden cases filled with burgers in heavy buns, set them up on a stand, add a squirt of tomato sauce, and charge ninety kopecks ($1.45). When the supply is sold out there are no more until the following day.

While we were there, Moscow celebrated the 840th anniversary of its founding. I was struck by the oddity of the number 840 as a commemoration date and wondered why it had been chosen. Our friends laughed, and asked, "Doesn't everybody celebrate their 840th birthday?" It soon became apparent that the celebration was the creation of Boris Yeltsin, Communist party boss of Moscow and the man responsible for running the city of nine million people. The burly, fifty-six-year-old Yeltsin had decided on the holiday.

He had begun his career as a construction engineer in Siberia and had been brought to Moscow in 1985 by Gorbachev. Yeltsin's assignment was to cleanse the corrupt and feudal party structure that had grown encrusted in the Brezhnev years under Viktor Grishin, secretary of the Moscow City Party Committee since 1967. Grishin, a hard-line conservative, had been Gorbachev's rival for the top power position of general secretary of the Communist party. According to an unconfirmed account, Grishin's name was withdrawn from nomination when KBG chief Viktor Chebrikov indicated to the Politburo that he had evidence of corruption by Grishin.

The Moscow City Communist party membership, 1.2 million, is the largest and most powerful in the country. Most of its members work in government or party organizations. They are a key part of the 18 million bureaucrats in the Soviet Union who send down orders to only 500,000 plant and factory managers at some 250,000 enterprises across the country. The Moscow party organization protects its interests and those of the 18 million bureaucrats who fight to retain control from the center over the management of the Soviet economy. Gorbachev's reforms are aimed at the center.

To make an outsider from Siberia with a construction background the head of the most sophisticated and privileged party organization in the Soviet Union was a daring and, in hindsight, a foolhardy venture. As an outsider Yeltsin was a natural enemy to the entrenched *apparatchiki* in the center. The odds are high against a non-Muscovite, without a power base in the city, surviving in that job.

Yeltsin seemed to be doing well. We saw him often on the evening news, moving around the city visiting food stores, new housing projects, and factories. He was tall, beefy, and aggressive, making decisions on the spot. The anniversary celebration was his effort to show the city and its population that life could be better under *perestroika*.

To us the newly created holiday seemed like a circus without much bread. The center of the city was closed to traffic and snack stalls lined Marksa Prospekt. For the holidays there were increased food supplies. Yeltsin had made sure there was pressed black caviar for open sandwiches, and an abundance of sausages and soft drinks. There were speeches and acrobatic dancing in the Manezh Square next to the Kremlin. Yeltsin's team organized folk dancing, concerts, and fireworks. Muscovites told us that their skepticism about the holiday turned to approval.

Despite Yeltsin's efforts, Moscow is at the center of a classless society with too many privileged people. Shortly after he took office in December 1985 Yeltsin instituted a personnel reshuffle. At the Twenty-seventh Party Congress in 1986 he gave an impassioned speech citing the "urgent need for changes in the structure of the party apparatus as a whole" and the end of all forms of "special benefits" for party officials. Yeltsin was referring to the special stores for party officials, where they received food, clothing, and consumer goods that were not sold to ordinary workers.

He was made an alternate member of the Politburo at the Twenty-seventh Party Congress and became known as the most outspoken proponent of Gorbachev's reforms. But his burst of reform quickly burned out. He fired personnel who had friends in high places. He demanded results quickly. The bureaucracy retreated into its shell and held fast. At the same time Yeltsin practiced *glasnost* by allowing open street meetings and demonstrations. Permits were granted to commemorate the anniversary of Babi Yar, and *Pamyat* ("Memory"), the reactionary anti-Semitic group that has also flourished under *glasnost*, met with Moscow City Party officials. Yeltsin's open style and his tolerance of open meetings came into conflict with the strict constructionist views of *glasnost* insisted upon by KGB head Chebrikov. Then Yeltsin began a second-round personnel reshuffle despite a warning not to proceed.

His brash manner and ideological flexibility irritated Yegor Ligachev, the number-two man in the Politburo, who defended the privileges of party members. Ligachev wants reform to take place only gradually, under full party discipline and control. While Gorbachev was on vacation it was apparent that Ligachev was trying to moderate the pace of *glasnost*. KGB head Chebrikov also laid down a hard line on culture in his speech commemorating the 110th anniversary of the birth of Felix Dzerzhinsky in September. Yeltsin was caught in the middle. At the end of the summer Yeltsin told Gorbachev he wanted to resign. Gorbachev asked him to wait until after the 70th anniversary celebrations in November.

In October, at the Central Committee meeting of the Communist party that preceded the 70th anniversary, Yeltsin insisted on raising the problems of Moscow. Again he gave an impassioned speech highly critical of the pace of reform. He attacked the conservatives in the Politburo who prevented him from carrying out the programs needed to make the city work. Yeltsin's criticism, inside the Central Committee, with its 312 full members present, was a bombshell. He had to be answered, and he was put down. There were complaints about the quality of food and services in Moscow, all reflecting poorly on Yeltsin. Instead of taking the criticism and promising to do better, Yeltsin spoke out against the opposition that was preventing reforms. He wanted to move faster and he wanted to make changes.

Yeltsin quickly found himself the target of attack from Ligachev and Chebrikov. Yeltsin's undoing was his personal style, as well as his failure to build a base of support inside the Moscow party organization. With no defenders, he was forced to resign on October 21, 1987, citing lack of support from the Central Committee Secretariat. Western correspondents were given varying versions of what happened in the Politburo. Some reports even said that the strong-willed Raisa Gorbachev clashed with Yeltsin's wife. Others say Yeltsin attacked Gorbachev for developing a cult of personality around himself. The single consistent element is that Yeltsin and Ligachev clashed. Later, Politburo member Alexander Yakovlev gave a rare press conference to support the Central Committee censure of Yeltsin.

The Yeltsin experiments were over. As an outsider, Yeltsin was a threat to the entrenched hierarchy in the powerful Moscow City Party organization and they blocked him at every turn. Yeltsin's efforts to uproot corruption and privilege came too close to the top, and his emotional, open style pushed him beyond the bounds of Communist party discipline. His loss is a severe blow for Gorbachev because it represents a slowing of the pace of restucturing in Moscow, the model for the rest of the Soviet Union.

The ouster of Yeltsin and his recantation at a meeting of the Moscow Communist party organization that was attended by Gorbachev were reminiscent of the show trials of the 1930s, except that Yeltsin was not executed physically. Gorbachev described Yeltsin's alleged lack of support from the Central Committee Secretariat as "totally absurd and contradicting the reality." Yeltsin's removal from office and demotion to deputy minister of construction marked a personal disgrace, but even more important, it raised a caution signal for *glasnost* and warned that those who stand out in support of change may find themselves victims if power shifts.

Yeltsin was a Gorbachev choice, and his forced resignation undercut Gorbachev's ability to speed the pace of his reforms. Even more crippling was the message that innovation and openness have their limits, to be defined by the most conservative elements of the party. Yeltsin's example is bound to have a chilling effect on other would-be reformers testing the limits of *glasnost, perestroika,* and new thinking.

In newspapers, on posters, and on television, Gorbachev exhorts Soviet citizens to enter a period of new thinking, to reconstruct themselves in order to reconstruct the country. Citizens are constantly told that they must restructure themselves from within. They must create a new soul that is hardworking, innovative, and brave enough to think and speak out. Yet all this revolutionary thinking and acting is in direct contradiction to the rule of the Communist party. Even now the way to get ahead is to grasp the party line and run with it. For the individual who is a cog in a government machine, who must never offend those above him, and who must be careful to keep in their place those below him, it is difficult to embrace new thinking. When one is crowded into a role and has learned from childhood not to stand out but to conform, to be a good member of the collective, where does one start? If you are a particle in a smooth sheet of glass, to think in a new way is to shatter the pane. How does a factory or office worker respond to restructuring? All of life's training is directed to learning by rote and following party commands. The truth is revealed by the party. Now people are being asked to think for themselves and speak out. The contradictions are staggering and irreconcilable.

During the Gorbachev summit in Washington in December 1987, a Soviet journalist came by for dinner and we talked about the Yeltsin Affair. "Don't pity Yeltsin. He was power hungry," the journalist said. I repeated what I had learned about Yeltsin's ouster and reminded him how Yeltsin had tried to improve life in Moscow. I recalled the permission for street demonstrations and an open Arbat, the romanticized old quarter of Moscow. "What about the outdoor cafés he started?" I added.

"Yeltsin isn't responsible for the good things in Moscow. Outdoor cafés are wrong for Moscow. The weather is too cold. Let me tell you about him. Did you know that he forced two people to commit suicide?" Then he told us about the Moscow party official who was warned by Yeltsin to increase the food supplies in his section of the city within twenty-four hours or lose his job. The man shot himself, said the journalist. In another alleged case, Yeltsin told a party official who, following orders, had pulled strings for high officials' children to enter Moscow University and prestigious institutes of higher education, that he would be fired and disgraced. The man jumped from a window to his death.

"Yeltsin was moving too fast for his own good and for the good of Moscow," said my old friend, who had survived the purges of Stalin. Already Yeltsin had become a nonperson, and history was being rewritten as it happened.

The Yeltsin Affair, however, had not ended. Ligachev pressed his attack against Gorbachev in public in March 1988. While Gorbachev was in Yugoslavia and his key propaganda boss Alexander Yakovlev was in Mongolia, Ligachev organized and endorsed the publication in the newspaper *Sovyetskaya Russiya* of a pro-Stalin letter from a teacher in Leningrad. The letter called Gorbachev's reforms an ideological "mishmash" and took issue with the criticism of Stalin. Gorbachev was reported to be furious and ordered Yakovlev to draft a reply, a long pro-*perestroika* editorial printed in *Pravda* on April 5. Then Gorbachev went out of his way to appear publicly with Ligachev and avoid signs of a split.

In April 1988 Yeltsin suddenly came to public life again in an interview in the German-language edition of *Moscow News*. The nonperson was reincarnated unrepentant. Yeltsin urged greater democratization and continuation of the struggle. "I belong to those who are ready to tough it out and not to be afraid to take risks," Yeltsin said. The article was seen as a partial rehabilitation of Yeltsin, who refused to discuss the contents of his speech to the Politburo that got him fired.

In May, in the middle of the Moscow summit, Yeltsin gave two extraordinary interviews to the BBC and CBS in which he urged the removal of Ligachev from the Politburo. The idea of public criticism of Politburo members is still not accepted in the Soviet Union. Questions from Western correspondents on rifts in the leadership have been eliminated from transcripts of interviews with Gorbachev when they are used for internal publication or television broadcast. Yet there was Yeltsin, on camera, telling Dan Rather that Ligachev was an obstacle to Gorbachev's reforms. "In his words and speeches you can't find any opposition [to Gorbachev] but we all know [Ligachev's] style of work—not to work actively for reform. His style is the Stalinist command economy. Without Ligachev there would have been more progress on economic reforms and we would have had more democratization," Yeltsin said. Pressed by the BBC on whether Ligachev should be removed, Yeltsin replied: "Yes." The next day, May 31, 1988, Yeltsin told ABC correspondent Walter Rodgers that he had been misquoted and his words were being used out of context, but the record was clear. For Yeltsin to call for the dismissal of the second ranking member of the Politburo on American television was unprecedented. On June 1, Yeltsin again was interviewed by Rather on camera. This time Yeltsin said his remarks on Ligachev had been "misunderstood" and "exaggerated." Yeltsin said: "There are aspects of his [Ligachev's] work with which I disagree. I did not focus on his departure."

In his June 1 news conference at the end of the summit Gorbachev was asked to comment on Yeltsin's call for Ligachev's resignation. Gorbachev was stunned and angry, but he was on live television. There could be no editing or elimination of the answer this time. Gorbachev said he had not seen Yeltsin's interview and asked for the full, unedited texts from the correspondents who conducted the interviews. Then he said: "Comrade Yeltsin seems to be in disagreement with the decision taken by the Central Committee of the party. Well then, if that is so, we must ask him in the Central Committee, and we shall demand that he explain his position and what he's out for. It means that his opinion is at variance with the opinion of the Central Committee of the party.

"As for Comrade Ligachev and his retirement, that problem is simply nonexistent and that's all. That's what you should proceed from and that's the way it will be."

The public discussion of Politburo disagreements on television is unprecedented and marks a giant step toward a new political culture in the Soviet Union. As long as he survives, Yeltsin is a lightning rod for Gorbachev against the conservative opposition in the Politburo led by Ligachev; but Yeltsin is a high-risk player and he could be consumed in the struggle. The Yeltsin Affair is not over.

Supply and Demand

When Vitaly and Elena picked us up at noon on Constitution Day for a ride in the country, the Soviet problem of supply and demand was already on my mind. Only a few minutes before they arrived, while I stood on the corner outside the Berlin Hotel waiting and watching for their car, an older couple, perhaps in their early sixties, walked by me at a leisurely holiday pace. The woman pointed out to her husband that a box of Autumn Waltz chocolates was protruding from the *sumka* that hung from my fingers. After a few words to each other they circled back and asked me where I had bought the chocolates. "In the Beriozka," I replied. The husband, a short, squarely built man with graying hair and a smartly clipped mustache, tilted his head in an expression of disappointment. Of course, his expression said, where else would you find such a rare treat?

"We can't buy there. You must have dollars," he said. I nodded in agreement.

"Will you sell it to us?"

"No," I replied, "that's impossible." They were skeptical. "It's strictly forbidden, impossible," I said adamantly.

"It's not impossible," the man argued in subdued tones. "Quietly, quietly," he said between his teeth to enunciate emphatically. "No one will know. We're from Tbilisi, no one will know."

"I'm sorry. I can't do it. I'm on my way to my friends' and this is a gift for them." The reputation of the Tbilisi Georgians for deal making outside the system has another facet—respect for the host-guest relationship. A gift is a gift. For a fleeting moment I thought about giving them the box of candy, but then my host would not receive it, and he might be just as anxious to have it.

"Forgive us for asking," he said, lowering his eyes.

"And forgive me," I answered.

Just then the car pulled up with Elena and Vitaly. Jerry had gone back to the hotel room to get me a jacket and to make a phone call. I was laughing as I told them the story of the candy, but they didn't find any humor in it. Jerry's arrival changed the subject and ended the embarrassment on both sides, mine for telling a story that I realized as I told it was sad, not funny, theirs for one more instance of the absurdity of an economy in which citizens can't buy the best goods in their own country.

A half hour later the ridiculous struck us again. Vitaly stopped for gas at a roadside station, rare in itself, that had a sign announcing that they had gas to sell. However, Vitaly could not fill up his car because this gas was only for official government cars. "Then why did you put up a sign that you have gas?" he asked angrily.

The manager pointed to a delivery truck that was in the process of filling his storage tanks. "I have plenty of gas, but you don't have the coupons you need to buy it. Tough luck."

Vitaly mumbled that he should have taken some coupons from the office, but that didn't solve the immediate problem. Then he walked over to the delivery truck and spoke a few words to the driver. Vitaly got back into the car and drove it onto a weedy path behind the garage. He took out a large funnel from the boot and waited patiently, no longer anxious. He was, however, embarrassed for us. In a few minutes the truck driver arrived with a banged-up five-gallon tin full of gas, which he carelessly sloshed into the funnel stuck into the side of Vitaly's car. The driver never missed a beat of laughing and telling good-natured stories while he emptied the can and filled his pocket with the fistful of rubles Vitaly handed him. He wished us all happiness as he walked back to his truck with no indication that he had to hide the transaction from the eyes of the gas station manager. His actions fit Moscow's most common slang word—*normalno* (verbally equivalent in spirit to the American "no problem").

The rest of the way to the *dacha* we gossiped about the second marriages of mutual friends and commented frequently on the golden aura of the perfect fall day we had received as a gift from the Soviet state for our excursion. Hail to national holidays, yours and ours, especially if it doesn't rain.

The outside of the *dacha* had lintels carved fancifully under steep eaves lifted from the illustration for a fairy tale. The house and garden were bathed in gold and orange leaves that sprang like cushions underfoot. Elena proudly showed me the kitchen that contained an old enamel gas stove and a sink, but there was no running water. She helped her mother carry buckets of water from an outside well. On a wooden worktable Elena's mother was rolling out a yeast dough to be filled with chopped cabbage and hard-boiled egg, ready in a bowl next to the pastry board. In what seemed like no time at all she had the *pirozhki* cut, filled, their sides pinched together, onto a pan, and into the hot oven. Elena had brought a large cauliflower in a reed basket that now sat on the floor next to a *sumka* with more cabbage, pumpkin squash, and tomatoes. She knew that even in the country her mother would have a hard time finding fresh vegetables. Most produce went to Moscow; a farmer with a private plot might have something to sell, but it was chancy and expensive to rely on that.

Elena gave me a tour of the airy upstairs bedrooms under the sharply graded roof. There were still posters and sneakers left behind by her son, who was now in the army. "I didn't grow up in this house. My parents bought it when I was already grown, but my children spent all their summers here." She said it with love for the old house and an ambivalent longing that mothers often feel for a simpler past when children still lived at home. Then we went into a large living room with an oilcloth-covered table in the center. Her father sat at the table talking to Vitaly and Jerry, who were lounging on a soft couch against the wall.

The old pensioner, who had served in World War II and been a party official and an engineer, questioned Jerry in careful detail about his work, his range of travel, and the extent of his education. He spoke only Russian. I joined them and had to answer some of the same questions. Then he knew what to talk about and the conversation proceeded at ease. He was curious about our social security system, how we pay for health care, and why we have homeless people living on our streets. I explained that we pay some money out of earnings for our pensions and health insurance. It was harder to explain homelessness in America, and I tried to suggest some of the complicated crosscurrents that keep the problem from being solved. "We have ideological hang-ups, just as you do, that keep us from simply providing a roof over these people's heads." I said that I had read recently a front-page story in *The New York Times* that described how the New York Housing Authority would soon use land taxes on luxury property to guarantee loans for rehabilitating empty buildings in the Bronx. "That's capitalism: banks, loans, and bonds. The city couldn't just fix the buildings directly," I said with amusement.

Vitaly chuckled. "We don't even have the concept of loans here," he said. "We had to pay all cash for this *dacha*, and you must pay all cash for a car. It takes a long time to amass ten thousand rubles (sixteen thousand dollars) unless you're making illegal profits."

"What are illegal profits?" I asked, a teasing undertone to the question.

"Any profit is illegal. We are repelled by anyone making profit from the sale of goods he or she did not labor to make or grow personally," Vitaly answered, realizing as he said it that we had come to the core of the difference between our two ways of thinking.

"You put no value on the labor of selling." My statement was also a question.

"That's right. We think it is immoral to be a merchant," he answered, neither offensively nor defensively.

"That's why nothing gets to market," I said wryly. Just before coming to Moscow an historian in Washington pointed out to me that the reason the Chinese Communists have been able to embrace free market mechanisms is that before the Communist Revolution they had a long tradition of a merchant class. The Russian Revolution occurred before their merchant class could establish itself.

We had begun to speak English as we dug deeper into our differences. I posed a long question in English to Vitaly, which made the old man complain and demand that we return to Russian. Vitaly translated as we went along, which made the conversation slower but gave each of us time to think about what we deeply believed.

"In my country," I began, "the economy is a self-generating engine; it keeps going by itself. As soon as goods are sold, the seller asks for more and the supplier rushes in to fill the space with more goods. You can go to the grocery store or department store month after month and find a reliable supply of approximately the same goods for sale. The supplier can sell a good product indefinitely as long as he can sustain the supply. In Moscow you can't depend on anything appearing in the same place twice. The god of supply is whimsical —it decides where to send what little goods are available, and you have to guess where they are."

"We have no gods, only central planners," Vitaly interjected, bemused.

"In *Moscow News* I read an analysis of Soviet economic problems in which the writer referred to the wild runaway engine of capitalism. He didn't sound as if he favored it," I said, again starting to ask a question. "To us it would seem that you, too, would want to achieve this perpetual-motion machine of supply and demand, but this economist wrote what a frightening uncontrollable robot it is, the Soviet Union would not want to let it into the country."

Vitaly nodded and smiled as I posed this paradox. "Yes, that is how we feel. In such a system some people will fill their pockets and be able to buy more than others. We don't care how little we have so long as our neighbors don't have more than we do. If we had an uncontrolled market economy there would be more goods and everything would get sold. We are hungry for things to buy, but there would be more illegal millionaires and workers wouldn't be able to buy as much as people with higher salaries. Yes, we would like to find good food whenever we go to the store and be able to buy better clothing; we all want bigger apartments. But we don't want to copy you and become capitalists. If we have a market economy, and increase the differences between rich and poor, who will we be? If we are no longer socialists, who are we? What was the revolution all about if not to give equality to all workers?" he asked with thoughtful sincerity. Then his voice lightened. "We could get stores full of beautiful things, but what will happen to our socialism, our beloved Communist goals that have brought us to a standstill?"

Echoes of this conversation with Vitaly were repeated with other introspective friends in the weeks that followed. "In these seventy years since the revolution," Yuri said over dinner, "we have tried a wide range of social experiments to make life better for the average man and woman. They have all come to a dead end. How do we turn them backward so we can start over again?" A young Soviet journalist asserted emphatically, "We don't want to become clones of you. We are socialists, that is our self-identity. That doesn't mean we have to keep what we have now. There are other kinds of socialism. We should look at the social democracies of Europe. Perhaps we could adopt the Swedish form of socialism." Perhaps they could, but first the Soviet Union would have to accept a multiparty system. As long as the Communist party controls all levers of power, today's *glasnost* can disappear in the time it takes for the Politburo to give new orders clamping down on freedom of discussion.

We listened sympathetically to these expressions that demonstrated a crisis of socialist identity, and then I posed to these same friends

ПУСТЬ НАД ЗЕМЛЕЮ
СИЯЕТ ВСЕГДА
СИМВОЛ ВЕЛИКОГО
БРАТСТВА ТРУДА!

—Vitaly, the young journalist, and a researcher from the Academy of Sciences—what seemed to me was the core difference between our two ways of thinking. "We in the United States have geared our efforts to the creation of new goods and services. We compete with each other to originate something new all the time. That way we constantly create new wealth. That is the direction in which we place our energies. That's the thrust of capitalism. We are also concerned with the poor; we have had massive efforts to fight poverty, but we end up with the same percentage of poor people. We also try to achieve a minimum standard of living for everyone, but we hope that by creating new wealth we can benefit everyone. It seems to me that you are preoccupied with preventing poverty; as a result everyone is poor by comparison with living standards in the rest of the industrialized world."

In each case our friends nodded in agreement. "But you have all the chips on your side of the table," Vitaly protested. "We are a poor country; you are a rich country."

"Come on now, Vitaly. You have the same resources we have. Whatever advantage we have is wealth we have created," I said. Capitalism demands that its citizens create and produce, which is hard on the nervous system; socialism, Soviet style, demands sharing and conformity, which is hard on the economic system.

One of the jokes we heard in Moscow satirizes their lack of concern for productivity: One worker digs a hole and another fills it. They walk thirty feet and repeat the action, all the way down the side of the highway. A curious bystander asks what they are doing. "The guy who puts a tree in the hole is out drunk today, but that's no reason we should lose a day's work," explain the workers.

When we interviewed the economist Abel Aganbegyan, we asked if the paternalistic guarantees that the system gives to all workers had brought down their economy. "No," he answered, sitting up taller in his seat, as if I had ruffled his composure, "in the 1950s and early 1960s we had very satisfactory growth rates with the same guarantees. It was bad political decisions that brought the economy to a halt." When I repeated Aganbegyan's answer to Vitaly, he laughed heartily. "He knows very well the system doesn't work, but he's got to be careful what he says. He has to keep his good standing with the old guard and not embarrass Gorbachev by saying what he knows is true, that until we diminish central planning and let our factories compete with each other, nothing will change. We are torn between wanting a market economy and wanting to keep all our comfortable subsidies.

"We had lines to buy food when you lived here before, but the lines you see in the street now are different. These are supposed to be an improvement. Now the collective farms are allowed to drive a truckful of melons, grapes, apples, peppers, cauliflowers, cabbages, or pears up from the Ukraine or the Caucasus and sell their produce on the street. Before the new system they had to deliver the fruits and vegetables to production bases around the city to be distributed from there to the government shops. Most of it rotted before it ever got out of the bases. Even the collective farm trucks lose thirty percent to spoilage, but it gets to the consumer faster now. The people of Moscow are glad to see the trucks, but the government is still uneasy. They are sure that the truck drivers are making a profit the planners can't control.

"Yeltsin has made life in Moscow more humane. We like seeing the old ladies outside the metro stations selling their bunches of fresh dill, radishes, and yellow turnips. I like to buy a handful of fresh parsley on my way home. Before Yeltsin the militia used to run after the old *babushkas* and shut them down. The women kept their goods in open shopping bags that they could snap closed when they saw the militia coming. They would run into a doorway and pretend they hadn't been peddling. Yeltsin put a stop to the crackdowns. Now they are allowed to sell their private garden products. He argued that they are not speculators because they grew the dill and the radishes themselves. Since they had put their own labor into it they should not be illegal. If they bought and sold produce grown by others they would be profiteers."

In a conversation with a mutual friend of Vitaly's and ours the friend repeated Vitaly's warning that there is a paradox between profit and state subsidies. "How can you justify an individual becoming a millionaire when he sells goods made with wheat flour for which he pays a ridiculously low state-controlled subsidized price? Let me give you an example. A man and his wife sell their homemade jelly-filled doughnuts at a street stand for twenty-five kopecks (forty cents) each. The nearby state stand sells similar doughnuts for fifteen kopecks (twenty-four cents) each, but the line is longer for the better tasting, privately made pastries. With only their labor, the man and his wife clear a profit of three thousand rubles (four thousand eight hundred dollars) a month. This compares to a normal salary of four hundred rubles a month (six hundred forty dollars) for two workers

The Schecter family in the living room of the Berlin Hotel. Left to right, back row: Barney and Doveen.
Second row, left to right: Michael Shafer, Ari Roth, Kate Schecter, Sudakkha Steve Schecter, Suprabha Schecter, and Evelind Schecter. Front row, seated: Leona and Jerry Schecter. *(Didier Olivré)*

View from the Berlin Hotel looking down on a line of people waiting to buy *pelmeni* at the Sardine Café, corner of Pushechnaya and Zhdanova streets. *(Didier Olivré)*

Reading the latest edition of *Moscow News* on a billboard in front of its offices off Pushkin Square. *(Didier Olivré)*

A line presses forward to enter Moscow TSUM, Tsentralny Universalny Magazin, Central Department Store. *(Didier Olivré)*

Producer Sherry Jones and Ari Roth on the Moscow River. The apartment house on the right is an example of Stalinist architecture. *(Jerrold Schecter)*

Leona and Jerry discuss *perestroika* on the Moscow metro. *(Didier Olivré)*

Doveen and an elderly lady wait for the metro at Kiev Station. *(Didier Olivré)*

Leona buying vegetables in the Central Market. *(Sudakkha Steve Schecter)*

Suprabha purchases honey in the Central Market. *(Sudakkha Steve Schecter)*

Leona, Suprabha, and Jerry consider buying a pigeon at the outdoor Bird and Pet Market. *(Sudakkha Steve Schecter)*

Poet Andrei Voznesensky and Doveen outside his home in Peredelkino. *(Jerrold Schecter)*

Poet Andrei Voznesensky. *(Didier Olivré)*

Kate, Evelind, Suprabha, and Doveen in front of Boris Pasternak's Peredelkino home, which is to become a museum. *(Jerrold Schecter)*

Jerry, *Izvestia* editor Ivan D. Laptev, and Evelind in his office. *(Sudakkha Steve Schecter)*

Izvestia letters editor Vladimir Nadelin. *(Sudakkha Steve Schecter)*

Kate, Leona, and Anatoli Pristavkin with his wife, Marina. *(Jerrold Schecter)*

Kate and historian Arseny Roginsky. *(Jerrold Schecter)*

Michael (right) interviews Afghanistan Veterans at *Ogonyok* magazine. *(Jerrold Schecter)*

Vitaly Korotich, editor of *Ogonyok* magazine. *(Sudakkha Steve Schecter)*

Artyom Borovik, foreign editor of *Ogonyok* magazine. *(Jerrold Schecter)*

in a family. How much should the doughnut makers pay the government for the real cost of the flour they are using? Private enterprise skews the system." On more than one occasion Soviet friends contradicted themselves by praising incentives but at the same time cursing the new millionaires benefiting from the reforms. They cannot get used to the idea, as *Pravda* explained, that under the new system some people make "significant sums that did not correspond to their expended labor." Profit flies in the face of seventy years of ideals of the Soviet workers' state. This contradiction is a problem for Gorbachev. Tatyana Zaslavskaya, the Soviet Union's leading sociologist, who has spearheaded the economic reforms, warns: "Our fear that someone will earn too much can become a truly restraining factor."[1] However, when a question was put to her during a visit to the United States in 1987, the highest salary she could imagine was "let's say twelve hundred rubles a month" for someone who had formerly earned six hundred rubles a month, three times the average. She could not envisage a multiple of five or six times a worker's present income as an incentive to change into an entrepreneur who would put up with the difficulties he or she would encounter—licenses, bureaucratic payoffs, and unlimited hours.

The fear of profit is not the only restraining factor. Factories and enterprises are organized along such hierarchical lines that little innovation is possible. The press and intellectuals repeatedly appealed to Soviet men and women to dig deep inside their souls to find the strength to face change. In fact, it is very difficult for individuals to respond. Where does the individual begin *perestroika*? Everyone is afraid of making changes because even if the boss above likes the idea, it may be rejected further up the line and there will be a penalty for suggesting innovation. The measure of a new idea is how suitable it is ideologically rather than its promise for rational change and improvement. Bureaucratic self-protection and *perestroika* are mutually contradictory.

After standing in one line for tomatoes on Kuznetskiy Most, two blocks from our hotel, I quickly got into another line where Georgians were selling still-warm flat breads filled with melted cheese for one and a half rubles ($2.40). I couldn't see at first what was being sold, and it seemed that the price was high, so I checked with the woman standing next to me to affirm that it was Georgian bread and she

---

1. *The Washington Post*, February 4, 1988, p. A-29.

just shrugged her shoulders when I commented on the high price. Jerry and I were going out to dinner that night and I was pleased to leave such a good supper behind for whoever wandered back to the hotel room for dinner. Everyone in the line must have had a similar reason. When I moved forward to get mine I could see that the woman wrapping each bread in stiff paper and collecting the money was exhausted from the busy run on her stand. A large man stood by her, smiling with a hint of excitement at the large profits they were taking in. I looked again on other days but never found the Georgians and their delicious cheese-filled bread again.

On the other side of Dzerzhinsky Square, on 25 October Street, which led directly to Red Square, I joined another line one day where for ninety kopecks ($1.44) I bought a whole bread with its center filled with baked ground beef. The bread was greasy, so I had to hold it carefully until I got it home, where we reheated it in the frying pan on our single-burner electric hot plate. This was a government stand and we were able to buy the same bread again another day. I never saw these tasty filled breads in the regular state bakeries. These were small efforts to make life easier for the harassed Moscow homemaker who faced the daily challenge of standing on multiple lines to put a meal on the table for dinner. It was a long way from the infinite variety and ingenuity of convenience foods in the West.

Our Russian friends were defensive about the food shortages. One official told me that the reason there were shortages in shops outside Moscow was that the local managers saved the incoming supply of meat for themselves and their friends. He had no idea that outside the Soviet Union there would be enough for his friends and the rest of the townspeople too. Others were impatient with the out-of-town shoppers who flocked into Moscow in late summer to stock up on dry foods, canned goods, and children's clothing for the winter. "They are the reason there is nothing to buy in Moscow," explained one of Steve's friends when I complained that I could not find rice or macaroni in the state food stores within five blocks of the hotel. Every morning, seven days a week, we watched a line two blocks long form around the side of Detsky Mir, waiting for the doors to open at 9:00 A.M. The center of Moscow is attacked each day by shoppers from the countryside who descend like locusts and strip the stores of goods. It is no wonder when you hear stories of travelers who visited cities in the south that had not had any meat for five weeks or that in the month of May 1987 only Communist party members could buy potatoes.

Another friend took a train ride through the wheat-growing plains around Krasnodar and saw wheat left behind in the fields to rot because the farmers had already fulfilled their norms and the price the government pays over the norm was not great enough to serve as an incentive for them to work the extra hours required to bring in the full crop. If they harvested more wheat then the next year the norm for production would be raised; better to let it lay in the field.

One day I took a trolley bus farther than my destination and had to get out and walk back. Looking for the right street I was amazed to see a street sign spelling out the Russianized version of a Western name: Richard Sorge. There facing me was a life-size bronze statue of the German journalist and master Soviet spy in a trench coat, emerging from a sinister-looking doorway also in bronze. Sorge, under the cover of a German journalist in Tokyo, supplied the Russians with information from September 1933 to October 1941, when he was captured and hanged. Sorge's greatest coup was to advise Stalin of the day the Germans would attack the Soviet Union in June of 1941. Stalin ignored the warning.

When I lived in Tokyo I read the story of Sorge's life, and one scene remained fixed in my memory. It depicted Sorge taking a German friend on a tour of the Japanese farm country in the late 1930s. Sorge explained to his colleague why he was a Communist. He showed his friend the decay of the countryside, in which most of the food was lost on its way to market because of the lackadaisical and primitive distribution system. Sorge believed that Japan's aggressive thrust into the mainland of Asia was motivated by the need for a better food supply. Looking at Sorge and the Soviet Union today it was a chilling thought.

Gorbachev and his supporters are convinced that rebuilding the economy is the only way the Soviet Union can survive as a major world power. Their fears are that if they cannot move fast enough technological advances in the world will leave them further behind. We found that the majority of Soviet citizens were terrified of the changes that will come with *perestroika*. There is a sad joke that "after *perestroika* comes *perestrelka* ('a shootout')." When one of our Russian-speaking American friends was recently hospitalized in Moscow with a mild heart attack, he found that everyone in the cardiac ward feared the impact of economic reforms on his own position.

Optimistic Soviets are asking for two to three years before we judge if *perestroika* has had any success. They hope that the reforms of January 1988, in which factories were given more discretion in buying supplies and selling their products, will create enough competition to give them the semblance of a market economy. They call it making socialism work. The system is so topheavy, however, that change will be difficult. According to official Soviet estimates there are eighteen million bureaucrats in government and party positions that control the economy by giving orders to only half a million factory and enterprise managers. That means thirty-six central planners and administrators for every manager. Clearly, there is a need for more managers and fewer bureaucrats; that will be a painful transition.

In the initial stages the response to *perestroika* has been fear and skepticism. "Nobody feels the advantages of *perestroika*, and some feel the disadvantages. Some salaries have been lowered, and quality controls have been installed. The number of jobs in ministries has been cut back," explained a high-ranking journalist. "It will take two or three years for *perestroika* to begin to bear fruits."

The great paradox that our friends in the Soviet Union are struggling with today is that they were born to be Socialists, and it is the dream their parents dreamed for them. To abandon it because it does not feed them and because it has tied their economy into immobility and stagnation is to reject the reason for the revolution. If it has not worked, somehow, they feel it is their fault, which for them is a greater guilt than the crime of accepting Stalin's repression. Their modern, technological, educated minds tell them that they must be practical and that what does not work must be abandoned for changes in the system that may indeed create a Western-style market economy. Their emotions, however, are as strong as their rational pragmatism. They ask themselves, "If we are not Socialists, then who are we?"

What Gorbachev has created is an identity crisis for Soviet idealists, the elite who cared and believed the system could be made to work for the working class. For whom does the revolution exist if not the workers? It is their lives that will be most dislocated by rising prices, profits for middlemen, and the closing of inefficient factories. The Socialist dream is that the Soviet Union presents the vision of a working-class society for the rest of the world. Young Soviets are asking if socialism must be abandoned for the country to move forward. We heard less praise of socialism under Gorbachev than we heard twenty years ago, but socialism is still what the Soviet Union is about, and it remains the dominating psychology of its citizens. They are looking for an answer in Sweden or Western Europe or any of the other variations of socialism that the twentieth century has attempted. In every country that embraced the same ideal—Italy, Great Britain, France, Israel—socialism has become discredited because lack of incentive created a smaller economic pie for the workers to share. The same guilt for not making the dream work infects the Socialists of the West. Socialism is in crisis everywhere.

The Literary Scene

Over tea and cakes I asked each of our Soviet friends what were the best-selling books of the last year. "We don't have best-sellers here in the same sense that you have in America. Here an important book first appears in a literary journal such as *Novy Mir* ('New World') or *Znamya* ('Banner'), which publishes the whole story, filling one or more editions of the magazine. There are not enough copies to satisfy all the readers who want to buy it, so one journal is passed around to a large group of acquaintances. Then the next year, after perhaps a hundred thousand people have read it, the demand is still very great so it is published in book form. There are never enough copies. A printing of half a million copies for a popular book is quickly bought up."

There was general agreement that the most sought-after literature of the past year was Anatoly Rybakov's *Children of the Arbat*, which recalls the political purges of the 1930s; Vladimir Dudintsev's *White Coats*, about the Soviet geneticist Trofim Lysenko's perversion of science to support Marxist theory; and Anatoli Pristavkin's *When the Golden Cloud Spent the Night*, a story of two orphans and the extermination of the Chechen people. All of these novels recalled the Stalin regime's repressions and distortions of reality. By invoking the authority of the Central Committee of the Communist party for his view that inheritable changes can be brought about by environmental influences, Lysenko became the dictator of biological sciences. His repudiation of the generally accepted chromosome theory of heredity set back Soviet agricultural science by decades.

Soviet readers love dramatic historical novels on village life, nationalistic stories of prerevolutionary Russia, and novels that warn of the danger of human intervention into nature's processes. Science fiction is a popular genre, as is light adventure stories. Readers prefer moral tales, and in recent years there has been a return to religious themes; the appearance of the Virgin Mary and Pontius Pilate in novels has stirred ideological controversy in the officially atheist state.

There have always been satirists in Russia to test the limits of society's ability to laugh at itself. In the bright light of *glasnost* it is hard to tell the difference between criticism and laughter. The most popular satirist writing today is Mikhail Zhvanetski, whose biting humor fills the recital halls. "When I leave the theater I think there will be soldiers outside to arrest the audience," said a sympathetic critic. Zhvanetski writes for a team of two comedians, Ilchenko and Kartsev, and also has published a book of short stories that broke through the sugar coating on official descriptions of problems. For years his routines were taped and distributed like *samizdat*, but now they are printed in book form by a state publishing house. One of his comments: "Can you imagine taking a tank and driving up to the central market, looking through the slot with guns pointed, and saying, 'How much do you want for those tomatoes?' It might also be a good idea to drive the tank up to a state food store and ask, 'What's this line all about?' " Soviet audiences roar with laughter at the idea of using force against the Soviet state.

In another routine, Zhvanetski says, "It's okay to take Swiss drugs from the pharmacy. They kill the bugs. Soviet drugs feed them." Then he tells the audience: "I like movie critics, they are highly sophisticated. They can write about movies they have never seen, especially those in the West. Without seeing or thinking they know that Western movies are cruel, violent, and filled with gangsters."

Andrei Voznesensky invited us to an evening of poetry reading sponsored by *Yunost* ("Youth") magazine at the Oktyabr Theater on Kalinin Prospekt. The program included a satirist from Leningrad, Mikhail Zadanov, who read an apocryphal letter addressed to "the esteemed general secretary," supposedly from the residents of a town recently visited by Gorbachev. With three days' notice, the town party officials "managed to do more for our city than they had in all the years of Soviet power." The houses were all painted on the side that Gorbachev would see as he rode by. Roads were vacuumed clean and statues were washed with Yugoslav shampoo. Party officials gave up their *dachas*, which were turned into kindergartens, and the first secretary's country house became an airport. The audience was falling from its seats, doubled over with laughter. In the comic exaggeration they recognized scenes from their own lives.

The letter continued: There was food in the stores again that they thought no longer existed, so they stocked up for three years. They got back phone lines that had been cut during the German invasion in World War II but they still did not have hot water. The satirist said that his poor old mother would like to take a bath. The letter recalled a Gorbachev-style speech: "You told our leaders they should have individual personalities, but you neglected to tell them how to go about this . . . you are forever telling them to go forward but you never explain to them which way is forward. They themselves have no idea." The letter asks the general secretary to come back in three years—or tell the town's leaders he will visit—so the party officials will be moved to do something again. The letter was later printed in the popular Soviet magazine *Theater*.

I called a friend of Jerry, formerly an editor at *Izvestia*, who is now a high official of the Writers' Union, to talk about publishing. Mike Sagatelyan speaks nearly perfect English and welcomed my call with effusive greetings to Jerry. When I arrived at his office, however, he had taken the precaution of having two other men, one a "consultant" to the union, and another officer join the conversation. They asked me about my work, and I began to explain what a literary agent in the States does in the publishing process. They listened with stone faces, so I explained further. "No, no. You don't have to explain, we know what it is you do," the consultant assured me. They were bored by my introductory questions about the structure of the Writers' Union, and patiently explained to me that it includes novelists, critics, poets, nonfiction writers (but not journalists), and translators, the last of whom are not least in their eyes because of the necessity of translating the literature that is written in the native languages of the Soviet republics into Russian.

To join the Writers' Union, an aspiring writer who has had some luck getting published applies to the local chapter of the union with recommendations from three members. Then he or she must be passed by a committee at the national level who are not officers of the union. There are great advantages to becoming a member: The union has the resources, partially supplied by the government, to give stipends on which the writer can live while he completes a work. The union makes contributions to a medical fund for special ambulances and hospitals far superior to standard medical services. It also offers rest houses where a writer can live for two months and work quietly, paying only forty rubles ($64) a month, including meals. The union gives legal help in making publishing contracts or in a case where a writer feels he or she has been plagiarized. The Writers' Union has five publishing houses of its own that can choose to publish books by its members. The union has about 10,000 members, 2,500 of whom live in and around Moscow. Of these, about 25 are stars. The union also conducts seminars where young writers are tutored by established figures, who then promote the most promising and help them get published.

"There are plenty of members who got in on the basis of one essay and haven't written anything worthwhile since," said Sagatelyan.

He referred obliquely to the battle that has been raging within the Writers' Union during the past two years and was becoming more heated. The front pages of *Literaturnaya Gazeta* burned with accusations by the old guard, who charged their foes—the "new thinkers," Gorbachev's supporters—with ideological laxity and "religio-nationalism," because they had reintroduced Christ and Pontius Pilate into Russian literature. The struggle for control of the Writers' Union had left the conservatives still dominant. The pro-Gorbachev faction—Voznesensky, Yevtushenko, Pristavkin, Rybakov and their followers—were unable to round up sufficient votes to unseat them.

Sagatelyan and his co-workers laughed when he told me that critics are on the low end of esteem in the union. "There are lots of them but only a few good ones," he said. "When the Literature Institute here in Moscow starts a new class, twenty sign up to be poets, ten to be critics, and five to be prose writers. At the end of the course there are two poets, two writers, and the rest become critics."

Book publishing is one of the few industries in the Soviet Union that pays its own way. The demand for books is so great and the print runs, even when huge by U.S. standards, are insufficient for the demand. Almost every one of the 80,000 titles published each year, twice the number of U.S. titles, sells out. Publishers make a profit despite the low prices. Only children's books are directly subsidized.

Soviet book publishing contracts are different from most of the ones I arrange for my writing clients in the United States. American writers usually receive half of the advance on signing the contract and half when the book is finished and accepted for publication; Soviet writers receive 25 percent on signing, 35 percent when the book is sent to the printer, and then must wait until the book is circulated by the publisher to receive the final 40 percent. The author is given a flat payment for the first printing rather than an advance against royalties as in the United States. The payment is based on how many signatures (sixteen-page sections) the book contains. If the book goes into a second printing the author receives only 60 percent of the original prices. The percentage diminishes, down to 25 percent for additional printings. This creates a game in which the authors try to provide new versions of their books that will be considered first printings rather than second or third reprintings. Novels are usually printed first in literary journals that have circulations around 300,000, and authors receive 2,000 to 3,000 rubles ($3,200 to $4,800). A novel of 30 signatures, 480 pages, could pay 300 rubles ($480) per signature, or 9,000 rubles ($14,400) for the first printing. Two items appear in every contract: one, that the material has not been plagiarized; and two, that the book will not be circulated if the content becomes suddenly obsolete.

"Does that mean a change in the party line?" I asked.

"No, no," Sagatelyan said, turning to the other men for corroboration. "Have you heard of it happening to any writer?" he asked them, and they both shook their heads. "It means that if you do sign to do a book on a murder case and by the time the book comes out new evidence emerges that the supposed killer is not guilty, the book becomes obsolete."

From other sources I learned that the warehouses were spilling over with books on the Soviet economy and U.S.–Soviet relations that had become obsolete as soon as they were published because they did not correspond with the new line of *glasnost* and *perestroika* laid down by Gorbachev and his appointed deputies. The poor publishing officials who had signed off on them and paid the authors the final 40 percent of their contracts were left with unsalable stock when the Gorbachev changes began, an official at the Literary Rights Agency (VAAP) told me.

"We need *perestroika* in the publishing industry and it will happen soon," Sagatelyan said ruefully. He described "press equipment so ancient it could have printed Napoleon's memoirs when he was still alive. It takes a year to print a book." He complained that the number of books printed in a press run is arbitrary and has no relationship to the demand for the book. "My first book, on the American military-industrial complex, *Washington Merry-Go-Round*, sold five hundred thousand copies and the publisher has an equal number of orders for my new book on John F. Kennedy. However, we have been allotted a press run for only one hundred thousand copies. The publisher sends out catalog copy to the book distribution organizations, who use this advance description of the book to get orders from the booksellers. These orders from all over the Soviet Union are put together and are supposed to be the basis of the print run. But, in fact, it isn't the last word on how many they will print. Sometimes there are orders for thirty thousand for a book, but on the say-so of an official in the publishing ministry fifty thousand are printed and twenty thousand sit on the shelves; nobody wants them. With *perestroika* we hope to get a more rational system."

Sagatelyan said that under *glasnost* it was now possible to print anything, but practically speaking there is a limit. "We will not print anti-Communist books any more than your mainstream publishers will print books in favor of communism." He explained that the Soviet Union was now in the process of opening up historical papers that are of intense interest to Soviet citizens but not to Western readers, such as the deliberations for the Brest-Litovsk treaty that took the Russians out of World War I. "We know that you in the West are focused on revealing Stalin, but we have many gaps in our history that don't concern him." He explained that in the past it was only possible to write of historical persons in a black-or-white, evil-or-good approach.

He was anxious to write a study of a White general in their own civil war who had fought the Reds, lost, and went into exile. Once out of the fighting he was approached to work against the new Soviet state, but he refused, saying that he was still a Russian and did not want to do anything to harm his country. "In the past you could not write about him because he was not on our side, but in fact he was a patriot in his own way."

Sagatelyan thinks that John F. Kennedy was our Gorbachev. Without speaking the words, he implied his fear that Gorbachev might meet the same end. He believes that the United States is dominated by the "military-industrial complex." "We are not a mirror of you. Our generals are servants of the party, not independents." He analyzed a long conservative trend in the United States that had begun with Dulles and culminated in Ronald Reagan. "Watergate had deep roots. It was a cabal against Nixon because he was conducting his own *perestroika*." When I cautioned against his conclusions, he told me I was blindsided by seeing the world through American eyes.

Back at the hotel, Jerry was waiting for me to join him for lunch, and I breathed a sigh of relief when I saw him. "It finally got interesting, but they started out looking down their noses at me. They were so condescending, I had to work hard to get them into anything substantive."

"Join the club," Jerry laughed.

In the final minutes of the meeting with Sagatelyan his aides gave me what I had come for: the home telephone number of Anatoli Pristavkin, member of the Writers' Union and author of *When the Golden Cloud Spent the Night*.

It was that simple, a phone call, and when I called him, Pristavkin insisted on coming in his car to fetch Katie and me. He asserted, and I later learned he was right, that it is difficult to find his apartment from the metro stop nearest the writers' cooperative building where he lives. He came well dressed in sport clothes, and he liked driving. "My wife, who is pregnant, and who is an editor at a publishing house, goes to work on the metro and she comes home exhausted from the ride. It's better to ride in a car if you can," he said with obvious pleasure. It was an ingenuous statement, but in the short time it took to hear of his past life the words took on a new meaning. Pristavkin, a man of medium build with a mid-fifties paunch and the face of an aging cherub, savors the rewards of his success without forgetting the hard past that is the inspiration for his writing.

Anatoli was born near Moscow, but when the Germans attacked the Soviet Union he and his little sister were sent to a children's home beyond the Urals for the duration of the war. The two children were put in separate dormitories and were able to meet once a week. His sister told him of her terrible hunger, because the bread that was available, doled out in small pieces, was often stolen by bigger children. At night she crept out of her bed and caught live goldfish, which she ate on the spot, out of the school aquarium. After a few nights she was caught and beaten.

At their weekly meetings he showed her pictures of their mother, working in Moscow, and their father, fighting at the front, and of herself and himself as younger children. Then their mother died. "So each week I pointed at father, sister, and me. Then we heard that father was killed, so I could only point to her and to me. We contacted an aunt, but she could not take us in." At the end of the war Anatoli, by then a young teenager, left the children's home and worked his way back to Moscow. At times he lived in a hole in the ground and chewed on his own hands when he was hungry. He learned to do a knife trick in which he spread his hand, palm down on a table, and brought the dagger down between each of his fingers in a fast rhythm, a display that was useful for betting with other men. They stared transfixed, waiting for his steely nerve to slip so that the dagger would come down in the wrong place and he would draw his own blood. He always won his dare, and they paid off in hunks of bread.

Anatoli still has the dagger, and he insisted on showing us the trick, which, he lovingly remembers, fed him when he was hungry. The knife danced between the splayed fingers of his left hand laying flat on the table, beating a tattoo as the speed increased. Nobody breathed as he moved the knife back and forth, faster and faster. He did not miss, but he could have.

Through chance contacts Pristavkin learned that his father was alive; he showed us the first letter he received from his father at the front, containing fifty rubles to buy fruit and meat, none of which was available for money. His father had no idea how the children had suffered. When they were reunited, his father told them of a dream in which his mother's ghost came to him when he was asleep in a foxhole, urging him to move to another place. No sooner had he settled down in the place to which she had directed him than a shell landed where he had lain before, killing his comrades. "Father was sure that mother saved him to take care of us."

Anatoli described the time at the end of the war as the period of greatest hope. His father was from Smolensk and longed to have his own house and land, "but every time he got a little bit ahead he was hit again. My father was a self-sufficient person. If we had more workers like him we could do something with this country. My father wanted to build communism on his own private plot." Anatoli laughed.

Anatoli trained to be an airplane mechanic and read everything in the town library. He applied to the Literary Institute in Moscow, for which he was ill prepared, but the admitting officer listened to him recite poetry and decided he could catch up with the others after he entered the school. (Hearing the story today, Soviets are amazed at this leap he accomplished; one professor of literature told me it was equivalent to a young trade student in Chicago being accepted to the Harvard writing program.) He thrived there for two years, but then he had to find a job. He had no place to live in Moscow, which meant that by law he had to leave the city. He sold his first book, and with the three hundred rubles he received for it began to build a house in his native town of Lyubertsy, a working class suburb of Moscow. He could find only enough wood for the sides. It was cold without a roof. His friend said, "Let's go to Siberia, it will be warmer there. We'll have a roof." He took a construction job in Siberia, where he lived in tents, and felled trees. From there he began to write short stories of the lives of the workers, and he became the regular correspondent for Moscow's *Literaturnaya Gazeta*. He married and had a son. He submitted longer manuscripts, but for years they were not accepted. Then one was retrieved from the wastebasket by Georgi Radov, a new editor at *Literaturnaya Gazeta*, and he suddenly found his stories about the harsh reality of the lives of workers to be in style. Radov advised him to apply for membership in the Writers' Union, where he was accepted, and a short time later he moved to Moscow, when he was thirty years old. To achieve membership in the Writers' Union and be invited back to Moscow at such a young age meant that he had been taken into the literary establishment and had reached spectacular success. His tales about his life as an orphan during the war became well known, so well known that when he traveled around the country strangers asked after his sister as if they knew her.

Pristavkin's writing has been described as a mixture of literature, magic, and salvation. He is a storyteller who writes with artless freshness and authenticity. He told Katie and me that at first he resented the extensive editing he received from his publishers, but now he welcomes the detailed suggestions he receives from his wife, Marina, who is a professional editor. The recital of poems by Tvardovsky that got him into the literature institute were narrative picaresque yarns about the soldier's life that were popular during the war. The title of his most famous novel, *When the Golden Cloud Spent the Night*, is the first line of a poem by Lermontov, one of a dozen poems that all Soviet students memorize as part of their schooling to evoke patriotism and love of the motherland.

In the early 1980s Anatoli began to write about the Soviet Union's troubled past under Stalin. He, like other writers who could not publish works that criticized government policies, believes that "the past demands words." His novel *When the Golden Cloud Spent the Night* is about a Sunni Muslim minority group of the Northern Caucasus, the Chechens, whose men were used as cannon fodder by Stalin at the German front lines. These mountain horsemen were slaughtered by German tanks. When the Chechen rebelled against Soviet army conscription, their land in the Caucasus Mountains was taken away from them by Stalin in 1943. They were deported to western Siberia and Kazakhstan, but many of them escaped to the hills and could not be found. The Russians killed whatever children they could find and burned the houses of the exiles. The story centers around Russian twin brothers who have been evacuated to an orphanage in the Chechen region of the Caucasus and their elementary school literature teacher, the wife of a pilot, who has also been sent there. The orphanage is attacked by Chechen, forcing the boys and their teacher to go into hiding in a mountain village. The teacher is courted by a man from the village. It is a sparse landscape, with a few cattle and sheep; a little corn grows in the dry wind, but there is practically nothing to eat. They are again attacked by a band of renegade Chechens; the village man and one of the twins are killed. The survivors find a lost Chechen boy, who joins them. The Soviet army sweeps the area again, and the two boys, one Russian and one Chechen, claim they are brothers even though one is blonde and one black-haired. The boys and the teacher are sent to a central orphanage. The KGB questions the teacher to find out if the boys are really brothers. She says yes, but both the Russian and the Muslim boy are declared Chechens and are sent to Siberia. In an afterword of the novel, KGB officers are heard receiving rewards for putting down the Chechen rebellion. The surviving Chechen can only hope that their time of freedom will come again.

In 1981 and 1982 Pristavkin read a chapter of the novel to a few writer friends who came to his apartment. They asked him to read another chapter, and then another, until he had read them the whole book. "Hide it," they advised him. "Who needs this? Why did you write this? Nobody needs it. No one will print it, and you'll only make trouble for yourself," they cautioned him. Other people heard about the reading and came to read the book for themselves. One woman came from Leningrad and spent all night reading it. The book lay "between the linens," dispersed between his bureau drawers and those of his friends, until Gorbachev came to power and the new literary thaw began. In 1985 Anatoli brought his novel to the Writers' Union, where he hoped to get support from the other members to have the book published. The union delayed having a group discussion of the novel for a year, and then held the meeting in a small room to avoid a large gathering. In 1987 it was published in *Znamya* and he became a celebrity of *glasnost*. "Nobody in the union supported me but now they all claim they did," Anatoli said, and showed us the proposed cover for the hardback edition, which in the Soviet Union is published after the book has appeared in a literary journal.

As a result of the fame of *When the Golden Cloud Spent the Night*, Pristavkin has received thousands of letters from other minority peoples whose lands were confiscated by Stalin and are still trying to reclaim their homes. The letters tell of their personal suffering and plead with him to become a spokesman for their cause. He answers each letter personally with the help of his wife Marina, but he knows he will not be able to help them. "I am a writer, not an activist. I live a quiet life. I don't know how to be a public advocate," he said.

The American rights to his book have been bought by Knopf for a substantial advance, but Anatoli and Marina, who gave birth to their daughter while we were in Moscow, will receive only a small portion, between 7 and 20 percent, of the dollars from the American publisher. The rest goes to the state. Anatoli and Marina will not receive the dollars from his foreign rights in Moscow; they can only spend the money when they travel abroad. "Will you come to America for a visit?" we asked. Anatoli wasn't sure, and he couldn't predict whether or not he would be sent on an American tour to promote the English translation of his book. "I have been offered a trip to Cuba. Is there anything to buy there?" he asked.

At first Anatoli and his wife showed us the changes taking place in their apartment to make room for the baby that was almost due. Katie and I looked at his icon collection, which he has put together during the past twenty years and which covers most of the wall space in the foyer, bedroom, and sitting room. "Hold your hands a little way from the Madonna," he offered, "and you will feel the heat coming from her," which we did feel. One plate on the wall, not an icon, has a carved relief scene of a church and monastery. Anatoli and Marina told us that it dates from the thirteenth century and is their most valuable piece, but they would never consider selling it. The kitchen was fitted with white shelves, all put up by Anatoli, covered with perfectly neat rows of decorative canisters labeled in Hungarian lettering. He had rigged an automatic light to indicate when the electric stove was on, to avoid cooking accidents. Near the window was a special meter designed by Anatoli to control the temperature in a built-on root cellar where he stored homemade pickles, preserved tomatoes, and cabbage slaw, and quickly boiled berry jams. "I learned that when I was an airplane mechanic," he said proudly.

They described to us an uninhabited island where they go for their vacations. "We take nothing with us and live off the land. We have a tent and camping utensils hidden in a hole in the ground, waiting for us whenever we come again."

Anatoli took out scrapbooks of his youth and photographs of himself with writer friends we might recognize. He wasn't sure what we had come to see him about, so he was laying his life and his art before us to take what we wanted. Then we sat down for tea at his writing table in the dimly lit living room, and I asked what direction Soviet literature would take after its current introspection that delves into the Stalinist past. He answered and I took notes, but he stopped me. "You don't have to write anything down. I will explain it to you so you don't forget anything."

He was in Moscow in the early 1960s, when there was another literary thaw, another time of hope that the country would become democratized and writers could print the truth as they saw it. In October 1964 Khrushchev was overthrown and the party conservatives took over. In September 1965 the writers Daniel and Sinyavsky were put on trial and sent to a labor camp for publishing anti-Soviet literature in the West under pseudonyms. That was the end of the time of hope. How had this watershed, as it appears in retrospect, affected the lives of writers at the time? "It became evident very quickly that the best people were being passed over. Stupid people without talent became managers. Everything in the stores got worse. All direction came from the top down, nothing from the bottom up. Inferior people were becoming the editors of important journals. No one dared to print the truth. The little bit of light that had come through with *One Day in the Life of Ivan Denisovich* by Solzhenitsyn was shut off again. A lot of people read *Doctor Zhivago* in *samizdat* then, but it wasn't published. In the sixties and seventies many good writers left the country or stopped writing. The rest of us stayed to fight." Anatoli said he could never leave because he is rooted to the land. "It is in my nature to be a farmer."

From 1965, when the first thaw ended, until 1985, when Gorbachev began to assert an era of new thinking and openness, there was virtually nothing printed in the Soviet Union that filled in the blank pages of the history of the country under Stalin. The great measure of *glasnost* is that the nation's conscience, its novelists, were able to once again describe real people and their real suffering under the forced collectivization of the 1920s and 1930s. The Communist party purges of that period, in which Stalin eliminated his enemies and his supposed enemies, and which had been taboo in Soviet literature, sprang to life in novels saved in the drawer for years by leading writers. Later, while Soviet publishers are still finding space and paper for this backlog of social history written as fiction, there will be a series of memoirs by high-ranking party members, led by longtime foreign minister Andrei Gromyko, that will describe their experiences during the Stalin era. The late 1980s in Soviet writing is a period of self-examination about the past and a time of atonement for the sins of the fathers of the nation. What about the future? What about young writers who were only coming into the world just as Stalin was leaving it? They are not wrapped in the guilt they lay on their parents for accepting and loving Stalin. What raw material and what identity will they have when this period of breast-beating has run its course? What happened to Pristavkin from one thaw to the next?

Pristavkin did not take offense at my questions. He listened thoughtfully, now at ease because he was no longer in doubt about what to do with us. We could sit and talk as Russians always talk, drinking and refilling their cups and staring into the tea leaves looking for just the right way to say what is in their hearts. "In the early 1960s we thought we could write everything, and then suddenly we couldn't. We had to take a long, deep breath and could let it out only after twenty years. We have begun to breathe again, but the tragedy is that the new generation of writers"—he hesitated, looking up from his cup and straight into my eyes with a mournful irony— "was born asphyxiated."

Pristavkin's image of Gorbachev is of a leader who is trying to stir up Soviet society and bring back to life what is dead with one hand, while with the other he fights off the bureaucracy. "For the process [of *perestroika*] to work the people have to believe that it won't turn back on them. So far people don't believe that. We came out of oppression seventy years ago but we lived in spiritual slavery under Stalin. The nineteenth century was a silver age for writers—there was little censorship—and the most freethinking time in the Soviet Union was in the 1920s, before Stalin consolidated his power." He smiled at his pregnant wife and mused that in a time of hope more children are born.

Before we left Pristavkin's apartment the first time we asked him if he would be willing to be interviewed on camera. He readily assented and asked when we would like to film him. He had to think about timing because of the expected baby. "We start shooting the end of September. Will you be here then?" I asked.

"If Gorbachev is here, I'll be here," he said, laughing. "If Gorbachev is gone by then, I'll be finished, too," he said, indicating the demise of *glasnost* and of himself with a slice of his hand across his throat.

Young Writers: Struggling for Breath

Pristavkin's image of a generation born without breath, a literary tradition, and continuity, stunned me. The first question on my mind when I later went to meet Sergei Pavlovich Zalygin, seventy-three, editor of *Novy Mir*, was "What about young writers today?" After all the novels that have "laid between the linens" for the last twenty years are pulled out and published, what will come next? After Soviet writers have unburdened their souls of sad memories, suffering, and their ambiguous guilt for the Stalin era and the dry dust of the Brezhnev years, what is the direction that Soviet identity will take in the new literature?

The offices of *Novy Mir*, behind Pushkin Square, are modest but comfortable. Zalygin, who has written about village life in *After the Storm*, parts of which could not be published until Gorbachev came to power, has a full head of white wavy hair and the smooth features of a man who knows his own mind. Zalygin was forthright in telling us that "it is a hard time for young writers." Zalygin admitted that young writers are not being published in Soviet journals now because there is such a large backlog of novels and memoirs waiting to be printed. There is a deep split among writers between the conservatives and the supporters of Mikhail Gorbachev, but there is an even greater difference between the young writers and those with established reputations, he said.

The novels of the past agonize over what was right and wrong in the building of socialism, Zalygin told us. Soviets agonize over the question of how much should be forgiven Stalin because he was forced to make hard decisions that caused great suffering in the process of industrializing the country. The older generation's view of right and wrong is shaded with subtlety and self-doubt, Zalygin explained. The new generation sees the past in primary colors. They think they know what was right and wrong because they only know the past as an abstraction and "did not have to live through it," he said. I nodded as he spoke because young people told me that they do not need to be restructured; they were born with less baggage of the past to carry and weigh down their judgments.

"I have spent a lot of time with the younger editors helping them. They have a more radical view of the past than we have, a very negative view of the past, more so than the older generation. They are more decisive. Their way of being negative is standard, like one surface. It is not deep," said Zalygin, who went on to describe his encounter with a young writer:

"You are like a prince," taunted the young writer.

"Why?" asked Zalygin.

"You are not giving us young people a chance."

"Bring me a novel I can publish," Zalygin said.

"You get out and I'll write it," taunted the young man. Zalygin complained that "until now I have not seen one novel that is good enough to print. We have published one that is beautiful aesthetic prose by a new writer, but he is sixty years old and the story has nothing to do with today's issues."

Zalygin's gentle humor sees the ironies of literary fashion, which puts in the forefront today what was taboo fifteen years ago. The poet Josef Brodsky was forced to leave the Soviet Union in 1972 because the regime would not allow him to write on purely apolitical themes that, they said, did not serve the cause of socialism. Only weeks before Brodsky was awarded the 1987 Nobel Prize for Literature, Zalygin told us that he had sent an emissary to Brodsky in New York to discuss the publication of his poems in *Novy Mir*. A selection of his poems was published in December 1987. "It is hard for me to understand now why we could not publish aesthetic literature in the Soviet Union before this. It was simply stupid. I can understand not publishing poems that disagreed with the policy of our country, but it makes no sense to push a man into exile when his writing has nothing to do with policy and only speaks for the human heart," said Zalygin.

The novels most loved by Russian readers are human stories set in an historical event. Russians learn their history from literature. Russians can cry, suffer, and be angry at events that occurred four hundred years ago because historical memory is tied to the romantic figures in novels who transmit this national lore. The revolution and the civil war, the crimes of Stalin, the tragedies of collectivization, the anguish of World War II, the distortions of Lysenko's genetics, will all be understood through the prisms of Boris Pasternak's *Doctor Zhivago*, Zalygin's own novel of the twenties, *After the Storm*, Anatoly Rybakov's *Children of the Arbat*, Mozhaev's *The Muzhik and the Peasant Woman*, Vladimir Dudintsev's *White Coats*, and Daniil Granin's *The Bison*. A few articles have appeared recounting Stalin's mismanagement of the early days of the fighting, but a blockbuster novel, which will describe how the great leader was tricked by the Germans into executing his top generals in 1937, awaits the present leadership's decision to further demolish Stalin's image. The novels appearing in 1986, 1987, and 1988 reflect the party's decision on how much of the truth can be told. Soviet historian Arseny Roginsky gave me the collective, official view of Soviet history, summarized by decades:

In the late 1920s and early 1930s, collectivization of agriculture was a good policy but poorly carried out. The 1930s purges were bad, but the rapid, forced industrialization carried out by Stalin was good. Stalin's executions of the best marshals and generals in the Red Army was bad and he was a bad leader at the start of the Great Patriotic War. The years 1945 to 1955 are a blank page and nothing can safely be written about them. Khrushchev was a "voluntarist," meaning that he did what he wanted and did not heed the guidance of the Politburo in his years of power from 1953 to 1964. He is now being given credit for his accomplishments, erasing his earlier image as a fool. Khrushchev's greatest achievement was de-Stalinization, launched by his secret speech revealing Stalin's crimes at the Twentieth Party Congress in 1956. Under Khrushchev hundreds of thousands were released from forced labor camps. His flawed but sincere attempt to reform the economy and encourage at least a partial intellectual thaw is recognized as inspiration for the present *glasnost* and *perestroika*.

From 1965 to 1983 Brezhnev sat dead still in the water, and nobody dared to make waves. He had the soul of a bureaucrat and caused the economic and spiritual stagnation from which the country is now painfully trying to extricate itself. The Soviet people had great hopes for change under Andropov, the stern disciplinarian father, but he died too soon to accomplish much. His successor, Konstantin Chernenko, is forgotten, a fallen eyelash of history.

Gorbachev became general secretary in 1985 and up to now he has accomplished very little in real economic terms, but he has generated a fierce power struggle among intellectuals and in the arts, the historian said. He describes the two dangerous courses that Gorbachev must avoid: to do as he pleases and get ousted like Khrushchev—and Soviet citizens remember that it took only a vote of the Central Committee for the usurpers to remove him—or behave like a traditional leader, making some changes, but basically keeping things the way they were, with power centralized in the party and the police organs. Gorbachev personally is way ahead of the rest of the Politburo in his aspirations for *perestroika*: it is only because of his rising stature as a world leader that he can indulge some of his ideas.

Roginsky's quick list of the good and the unacceptable subjects of Soviet history prepared us for Gorbachev's speech at the seventieth anniversary of the Great October Revolution, which opened the way for rehabilitation of such figures as Nikolai Bukharin but maintained Trotsky's role as an arch enemy of the Soviet state. Three months later, in February 1988, Bukharin was fully restored as a close associate of Lenin whose advocacy of incentives, small-scale market economics, and gradualism toward industrialization provide historical rationalizations for *perestroika*. Khrushchev got a mild nod of recognition from Gorbachev. Khrushchev's name appeared in public again, but he remains a quarrelsome figure in the official iconography of Soviet leaders.

Most instructive to me and least understood of Gorbachev's oratory at the self-congratulatory anniversary spectacle was his treatment of Stalin's memory. For the first time he spoke of Stalin's crimes and declared that Stalin was fully aware of the gravity and scale of his repressions. By referring to a "range of views, convictions, and assessments, which require consideration and comparison" Gorbachev opened the way for an historical reality that is not imposed from the top, by the Communist party, but emerges from a pluralistic discussion among individuals and unofficial groups. Gorbachev is neither a cowboy moving ahead by himself nor a traditional leader imposing his will through the party. Rather, he is gradually removing the taboos and opening up for argument subjects of history and social life that until now have been kept out of the press and in limbo, about which it was dangerous to express opinions. He has not removed the party's instruments of control, but he has made a giant step toward democratization. He is taking a giant risk, because he is giving as much freedom to the enemies of change as to his supporters. In some cultural areas, such as film and in the literary journals, the old guard has been replaced by Gorbachev supporters such as Zalygin, Pristavkin, Voznesensky, Yevtushenko, and Grigory Baklanov, editor of *Znamya*, the journal that published *When the Golden Cloud Spent the Night*. However, the powerful conservatives who lead the Writers' Union have been able to hold their ground against attacks by these *Gorbachevtsy*.

The official Soviet view of its history remains unclear. The academic leaders who have to give their stamp of approval are leery of sticking their necks out. As a result, no serious historical writing is being published. Novels lead the way.

Jerry, Steve, and I went to meet Grigory Baklanov at the offices of *Znamya*. The conversation was unemotional until I asked him what he expected the future relationship would be between the Soviet Union and its writers forced into exile during the Brezhnev era. Baklanov's eyes narrowed coldly. "That depends on what their relationship will be to us," he said. I learned what it meant when forty books brought to the Moscow Book Fair by English and American publishers were seized by censors and banned from the fair. The American books were mainly novels written by émigrés such as Vladimir Voinovich and Vassily Aksyonov in Russian-language editions and published in the United States by Ardis Publishers. Also banned were George Orwell's *1984* and works by Alexander Solzhenitsyn.[1] When we talked to our friends about this blatant action nobody wanted to acknowledge that censorship was an official policy under Gorbachev. They blamed the ban on overzealous customs officials, indicating it was not likely to happen again. In fact, a line has been drawn: writers who have been forced into exile and whose works were seized are considered "enemies of the country."

Pristavkin and Zalygin painted a gasping and grim portrait of the young writer coming of age under *glasnost*. I had to seek them out

---

1. In May 1988 the Soviets announced that they will publish *1984* in an official Russian-language edition.

for myself. Since the older generation had no suggestions, I took our younger generation's suggestion to see Tatyana Shcherbina, a writer in her early thirties whose poems have appeared in the journal *Druzhba Narodov* ("Friendship of Peoples"), and who has published one book of verse in the Soviet Union. Doveen warned me that Tanya was cold and hard to talk to, but when Steve called her she readily agreed to meet with me. Steve and I climbed the steps to her apartment in central Moscow because the elevator was under *remont* (repair).

I was struck by her strong, well-formed features and the contrast of stark black bangs and straight hair against her white skin. We stood in the doorway of her sparse living room furnished with a backless couch, a table, and five chairs, some made of wood, the others of metal with plastic seats. She raised her face from her tea to say hello and then went back to her conversation with three male friends. Steve and I could fend for ourselves.

After an awkward wait, the men removed themselves from the table and made a place for us. She busily smoked a cigarette and looked at me, waiting to see what would happen. It was clear I had to help her. So I began by asking if she had yet received the contract from the American publisher who was considering a volume of her poetry. She was still waiting for it, she replied, but was eager to talk about the problems of publishing. She gave me the names of some Americans who were translating her work and showed me a poem in English by an American poet written about her. She again looked at me, waiting. I told her that I had not come to talk to her as a literary agent but that I was interested in knowing more about young Soviet writers today. Her expression was intense and unsmiling, but she was sincerely trying to find a way to begin describing the situation of writers in their twenties and thirties in the age of Gorbachev.

Then she threw up her hands and seemed like a bird taking off in frightened flight. She simply could not speak her thoughts, but was willing for Boris, her male roommate, to speak for her. He is a dark-haired young man with glistening brown eyes and full sensuous lips. He spoke clear and elegant Russian so that Steve had no trouble translating him thought by thought, as she nodded to affirm her agreement. Through Boris she wanted me to understand the difficulties that nonconformist writers in the 1970s faced in dealing with the socialist realist limitations that the authorities placed on Soviet writers. She called their writing "Conceptualism," and I had to keep probing to find out what she meant by it. As he talked she pulled out art magazines to demonstrate to me conceptualism in art that paralleled the same period in writing. A painting of Greek muses visiting Stalin in his office was an example of the absurdity of the regime the artist was mocking. The writers of the late 1960s, 1970s, and early 1980s played with the clichés of Communist party doctrine, manipulating familiar phrases into grotesqueries and satire. Yet no matter how hard they tried to distance themselves from the chaos of Soviet official language and socialist consciousness, their revolt never allowed them to rise above the objects of their scorn. They were caught in a game where their literature tied them to their oppressors. Many of them were still painting Andropov and Gorbachev bestiaries, still skirmishing in the mud with distortions of socialist realism. Tanya had put that period behind her. "She is the only Soviet writer working in the realm of universal culture," Boris said. Tanya now joined with him to tell us in slow, halting phrases that she represented a return to a depth of ideas totally unattached to Soviet symbols. She worked hard to connect herself to prerevolutionary Russian tradition. Her interest was the subtlety and play of ideas, expressed in humanistic themes that dealt with individuals rather than society in the abstract. She strives for the understanding of personality that would again enter into the nation's culture. I asked her where she placed Josef Brodsky in this literary landscape. Had he not been writing "pure" poetry in the 1960s and 1970s? "Yes," she said, "he never passed through conceptualism and never had to shake it off as the new writers are gradually doing. Nor is he in the Russian tradition, in which I find myself. Brodsky, early on, embraced a totally different tradition. He took his inspiration from John Donne and the British seventeenth-century writers who also wrote of the human spiritual condition."

In 1986 and 1987 Soviet writers have come to a crisis in which they are attempting to reenter the mainstream of world culture. They are attempting "a clearer higher relationship to reality. They must choose now between eternal themes and the conceptual toys they have been playing with for the last twenty years. They are again dealing with the uniqueness of individual personality," she said.

Tanya had only one copy of her poems and so she gave me the names of people in America from whom I could get a translation to illustrate her reaching out beyond the borders of socialist realism. One of her works follows:

An Address

Oh, Zero, Zero, you are not a quantity
but a whip of numbers no matter what I multiply—
you stand alone. Yes I am involved
and look with interest where you lie.
Your touch is like a bruise,
you're an exterminator of numbers, a fuse
and only the bronze-skinned monument to Peter
will not be sucked into your black hole.
I, the kitchen stool rider,
see the approaching dawn,
as the Reichstag shows pink in a gray haze,
it seems that all poetry's but a trace,
and people are all artificial like Golem.
You're the medium between the number and the volume
which lies beyond the borders of the scale,
you're the feature of the world where voices have no volume,
from where the zeroes are cascading only.
You are an apparition with no face, no foolish features,
oh God, to solve, invent this creature.
To you, oh, Zero, as an introvert I'm drawn,
and this attraction is a tumble.
I, therefore, conclude my poem lying down.

—Translated by Nadya Peterson

Tanya and Boris said they believe that the new writers created Gorbachev's image, rather than that he created the new atmosphere for them. She said that she is a fatalist and cannot depend on Gorbachev's survival. If he does not succeed, whoever follows him will be different from what preceded him. "Now that we have passed into this period of liberalization where for the first time there is no despot at the top and where a form of democracy is being handed down from above, the conditions have been created for the forces of conservatism and progress to fight for the soul of Russia. Gorbachev has made the fight possible, but only within the bounds of the system," she said.

For Tanya, Gorbachev's reforms have changed the relationship of the people to the system. "In the 1970s it became clear that the Soviet Union was a locked house that began to fall apart from within. The role that the dissidents played was to make the KGB aware that the house was falling apart. The crumbling of the house forced the system to change. In a crisis everyone in the family thinks about survival and focuses only on necessary actions."

Like others we met, Tanya and Boris told us that the Soviets have lost their capacity to do anything well. "They cannot write good poems. They cannot make a good thing," she said sadly.

Tanya told us she yearns for access to world literature, to be able to read whatever she wants and to write for a universal audience. She strives to enter the pantheon of Pushkin, Tolstoy, and Lermontov. Her generation never lived under Stalin. For other young writers the task is to expose the guilt of complicity in the crimes of the past, even if they include their own parents. These themes are appearing in plays and films such as Tengiz Abuladze's *Pokayanie* ("Repentance").

Other critics with whom I spoke believe that the literary scene is now overcrowded with novels that negate the past. They plead for a literature that does not discard what was good in the past. They hope that within a few years Soviet writers will strike a balance "between critical and constructive novels." They look forward to a literature that provides examples for a morality better than the corruption of life under Stalin and Brezhnev. A new literature is emerging that depicts moral conflict in families and between individuals. For the first time since the temporary thaw under Khrushchev, Soviet leaders recognize that socialism has the everyday human problems that exist in every society and are willing to let them be aired publicly.

Instead of looking at society as a whole, the new writing examines the problems of "small cells of society." Now the writers who for years railed against censorship have to show their talent or be silent. The general consensus is that it is a painful and slow process to develop good writers, especially in a genre that is continually breaking new ground. There is freedom to write about individual morality rather than socialist state morality, but there are not yet writers with the experience to produce works of meaning. The experience is too new. It will take time for the fires of conflict to cool and the new stars to rise and be recognized.

Andrei Voznesensky

The poet Andrei Voznesensky was in motion. "He has already left for Moscow for a meeting at the Writers' Union," explained his wife, the writer Zoya Boguslavskaya, when I called their home in Peredelkino. "Then he will go to the airport to meet Mrs. Chagall, who is coming for the opening of the exhibit at the Pushkin on Thursday. He will be at home late in the evening. Call then. I know he wants to talk to you." Andrei appears as a knight errant of *glasnost*, jousting with the conservatives in the Writers' Union, meeting with foreign poets, and lobbying for his causes with journalists and editors.

Over the years Voznesensky has been the object of scorn and praise. In 1963 Nikita Khrushchev attacked him at a meeting in the Kremlin, accusing him of attempting to bring about a Hungarian Revolution in Russia. "Clear out of the country," Khrushchev shouted at him. The Khrushchev order came directly from the top down and Voznesensky's career remained frozen until after Khrushchev was ousted in October 1964. Voznesensky's poems attacked Stalin and his abuses of power. They lamented the human condition, mocked long lines and shortages of consumer goods while testing carefully the limits of criticism. His critics charged that he never fully came to grips with the more terrible realities of Soviet life.

In the spring of 1970 we attended the premiere of Voznesensky's *Save Your Faces* ("*Beregite Vashi Litsa*"), a sweeping poetic review at the Taganka Theater. It was the time for celebrating the hundredth anniversary of the birth of Lenin. In the midst of somber, boring tracts on the importance of Lenin, Andrei's fanciful, free-wheeling imagery was fresh and even slightly unorthodox. The evening was a delight and I wrote:

Around the rich frame of Voznesensky's poems, with songs by a popular balladeer, Vladimir Vysotsky, director Lyubimov wove an elaborate theatrical tapestry of music, pantomine, dance, light show, and shadow play. Nothing like it had been seen in Moscow since the dazzling Meyerhold productions of the 1930s ... Voznesensky also represents a tradition. He is a disciple of Boris Pasternak, yet he has developed his own style of soaring imagery that rings clean, his own voice.

He speaks for a generation that was reared after World War II. His lines do not have the staid ring of propaganda, his ideas are subtle and richly timbered. There are complex levels of meaning. In daring to deal with the problems of a superpower in poetic form Voznesensky courted controversy. Always he comes back to his main theme: the shame of man and the need for the poet to expose sham. The young rebel has become the maturing prophet who questions even as he tries to believe that

The truth is in the asking
Poets are the questions.

Dissenters on the stage with posters that read "I Love Kennedy," "Make Love Not War," and "Exploiters, Serve Yourselves" outraged the censors, even though it was pointed out that the dissenters were American—"theirs, of course, not ours." The overriding theme of the evening was the need to preserve one's individuality. The Vysotsky ballad, "The Wolf Hunting Song," which described a pack of dogs hunting a brave, lone wolf, had an obvious symbolism: contemporary society crushed the individual no matter what his social and political affinities. It could apply to the Soviet Union as well as America. The wolf as predator, justifying the state's repressive policies, was not mentioned in the lyrics, but such an interpretation could always be salvaged and used as an explanation with the censors.

Voznesensky's poem, "And the Moon Disappears," a plaint that the moon has lost its mystery because man "had trod on her soul," was interpreted as an unwarranted reminder of the Soviet Union's failure to land a man on the moon before the United States. Even worse, the dancers wore flesh-colored tights and created the appearance of nudity to the socialist realists in the Ministry of Culture. Lyubimov and Voznesensky could not have their play and save their faces. The show was canceled. Lyubimov struggled with the authorities until 1984. While touring Britain he was stripped of his Soviet passport and was unable to return home. Lyubimov remained in the

West staging highly acclaimed productions from the Taganka repertory until the spring of 1988. Under a new Gorbachev policy to welcome back Soviet artists who defected or were forced to remain in the West, Lyubimov returned to Moscow for a visit. He was guest director for a Taganka production.

In the Brezhnev years poets were an endangered species. Words were weapons that had to be licensed by censors and culture ministers. Josef Brodsky, who won the Nobel Prize in 1987, was forced to leave the Soviet Union in 1972 or face imprisonment as a "parasite." Andrei Voznesensky and Yevgeny Yevtushenko became a new breed of literary entrepreneurs traveling to the West in the days of détente, reading their poetry, and then returning home. They became extensions of the establishment, their visits a weather vane of the political climate. Unlike Brodsky, who refused to be manipulated, Voznesensky and Yevtushenko legitimized the regime by their visits. Andrei was fascinated with the new technology he saw in America and wrote about its challenge to the individual. He never made a frontal attack on the abuses of power in Soviet society, but he fought quietly for the publication of the works of his mentor, Boris Pasternak. He supported *Metropol*, the anthology of writing brought out in Moscow in 1979 by a group in the Writers' Union after they failed to win official approval for its publication.

After the beginning of Gorbachev's *glasnost* policy Voznesensky began a new effort to get Pasternak published with official approval. *Dr. Zhivago* appeared in full in *Novy Mir* in 1988, and a complete edition of Pasternak's works is planned. Voznesensky is working to get Pasternak's *dacha* in Peredelkino designated as a state-supported museum. It sits silent in the autumn mist resembling, as Voznesensky has written, "a wooden version of a Scottish tower. Like an old chess castle it stood in a row of other *dachas* on the edge of the enormous square Peredelkino field, lined with furrows. From the other side of the field, beyond the cemetery, like figures from a different chess set, the sixteenth-century church and bell tower shone, like a carved king and queen, painted toys, dwarf relatives of St. Basil's."

Andrei gave his first poetry readings in the wooden house at age fourteen. The *dacha* was filled with the expansive laughter and excited voices of poets, critics, artists, and musicians who graced the giant dining room table while Pasternak's huge black dog lay beneath it. Today the house sits empty, with only a caretaker. A small, neatly lettered sign on the white gate outside reads: MUSEUM TO BE.

In the brutal world of Soviet literary politics, Voznesensky is being challenged as the heir to Pasternak. Does Pasternak need a museum to become an official Soviet writer after being ostracized and harassed in his lifetime? Who will benefit, the critics ask, Pasternak or Voznesensky? Such is the Soviet poet's lot. Base motives are imputed to generous behavior; enemies appear like ghosts.

Andrei has also encouraged official recognition in the Soviet Union of Marc Chagall as a great painter. He even tried to convince the local city authorities in Vitebsk, Chagall's hometown, three hundred miles west of Moscow, to turn the house where Chagall lived into a museum. The result has been a fierce battle between Voznesensky and his allies and the anti-Semitic group *Pamyat*.

Ostensibly formed in 1985 to preserve Russian architecture and cultural values, *Pamyat* did not attract attention until May of 1987, when several hundred of its followers demonstrated in the Manezh Square demanding they meet with Boris Yeltsin, then secretary of the Moscow City Committee of the Communist party, to discuss cultural preservation. No anti-Semitic or racist themes were voiced, and Yeltsin agreed to meet with the group at the Moscow Soviet. This set an unusual precedent because demonstrations are usually handled by the KGB or the police and rarely result in negotiations or such meetings. Since then *Pamyat* has become the most controversial of the new informal organizations, *neformalnyye obyedineniya*. The full extent of its membership is unknown. It has gathered sincere believers in the preservation of Great Russian culture along with extremists who preach anti-Semitism and virulent nationalism. Its leadership includes anti-Semitic writers, artists, and academics who warn against the dangers of a Jewish conspiracy and the disproportionate role Jews play in Soviet society when compared to their percentage of the population, which is less than 2 percent.

Pamyat has challenged Chagall's genius and derided him as a Zionist. Voznesensky has been attacked as "a Jew lover" and seen the reverse side of *glasnost*. Those who criticize the new openness and would return to a Russian nationalist past now have a right to speak out for their reactionary causes.

It all came to a head on the evening that Andrei appeared in a program for *Ogonyok*, the weekly magazine, which has led the fight for openness. Andrei strode onto the stage of the Oktyabr Theater and read his poem "The Driver," about a truck driver who kept a picture of Caesar (Stalin) on his windshield. The poem recounts Stalin's abuses ("The ones that you killed cry hail to thee") and is a bitter comment on the homage to Stalin that still lingers.

Then Andrei described to the audience his efforts to establish a museum in Vitebsk in the house where Marc Chagall was born, and the extremist backlash directed at him because of it. The Pushkin Museum in Moscow was host to a major retrospective show of Chagall's paintings and graphics. The show finally recognized Chagall as a Russian even though he had emigrated to France in the 1920s in frustration with the limitations placed on artists by the revolutionary regime. During his lifetime Chagall had tried to make peace with the Soviet authorities, but not until Gorbachev was there a willingness to welcome him back as a Russian-born, world-class artist. One result of Andrei's efforts was that *Pamyat* publicly attacked him for elevating Chagall, a Jew, to the pantheon of Russian artists.

Andrei celebrated Chagall by reading a poem in praise of Chagall's lovers soaring over village rooftops and the color of cornflowers that appears repeatedly like a signature in his paintings. When the Chagall exhibit at the Pushkin opened people sent fresh cornflowers from all over the country. In its attacks on Chagall *Pamyat* linked the blue of the cornflowers with the blue color of the Star of David in Israel's flag. Chagall created the stained-glass windows of the Israeli Knesset (Parliament) at a time when Israel was being attacked by the Soviet Union for its victories over the Arabs. Andrei was, by association with Chagall, a Zionist in the minds of the *Pamyat* members.

At the meeting held by *Ogonyok* magazine Andrei was addressed in notes sent up to the stage that included drawings of swastikas dripping with blood and a penis with the words "Why don't you suck on a dead rabbi's member? Good appetite."

"It was a shock for me. You know I have been on the stage for many years and I thought I knew everything. I was reading my poems through all of Russia and this is the first time such a thing happened to me. Somebody said to us that in the audience of four thousand there were about two hundred members of a chauvinistic organization named *Pamyat*. They came and took places near the stage. For them *Ogonyok* is the leader of *glasnost* and is a Jewish organization because it is for freedom, and against repression. *Ogonyok* is for a modern and open society. For them it is Jewish, against one Holy Russia. I wrote a long poem this year about twelve thousand Jewish people in the Crimea killed by the Nazis. Now people begin to open their graves and take the gold teeth from the skulls. I saw this myself, the broken bones and skulls. It was not in a book, but along the roadside where I was standing. I was so shocked. It was very difficult to get the poem published, but now there is a monument for the twelve thousand people. On these letters from the audience the *Pamyat* people put one line from my poem, and after it they said dirty things to me. I was referring not only to a dead rabbi, but a rabbi killed by the Nazis. They wanted to attack the stage and take the mike. I said my poems against Stalin and then I showed this ugly picture of the Star of David and a man's sexual organ. I said I am sorry that women in the audience had to see this. I said, 'It is *glasnost*. Nobody will arrest you. You risk nothing. Please stand up and tell us what you think.' Nobody stood up. I waited for half a minute. I said, 'You are cowards.' They were afraid to stand up and attack us. The audience of four thousand people applauded. I was so happy. It was a Russian audience, a Moscow audience, and they were against this anti-Semitism.

"It is a paradox. You know I am for Russian architecture. I have saved a lot of ancient buildings in Moscow. I have dedicated my life to Russian art. They are not interested in Russian history. They are interested only in anti-Semitism. It is terrible. After this a not-so-pretty woman jumped on the stage and said to me, 'We are not cowards.' She gave me a manifesto which was very anti-Semitic, but without the dirty words.

"I am sure that when this organization was started the majority of them were only for preserving our history. Really, many monuments were ruined with our barbarism. It is terrible. That is why people's sympathy is with these people. The leaders of this organization are not leaders and they were not elected. They have to have seven generations of Russian blood. I can't be a member; in seven generations I have one drop of Georgian blood," Voznesensky said.

There has been official criticism of *Pamyat*'s anti-Semitism in *Pravda* and on television, but the organization remains vocal and the government is loathe to crack down on any of the informal organizations, even those with anti-democratic programs. Open debate and tolerance of dissenting views are still to be accepted as part of political life in the Soviet Union and *glasnost* has forced the Soviet Union to come to grips with the practical realities of democracy.

Andrei continued: "I am so sorry that at this moment of our revolution, this moment of our changing of history, and the time of our freedom we have to speak about this ugly thing. I was waiting for this moment but I did not expect such a terrible thing. It is the price for freedom.

"I am so happy the majority of four thousand people were against this. Now it is the first time that we have a great exhibition of Chagall, maybe the greatest in the world because some French people came from Paris and some from America. His widow came. It is one hundred years of Chagall. In his own native land there were several anti-Semitic articles against him. They said he was a Zionist. But I'm so happy that the majority of our newspapers were for Chagall. A new magazine, *Political Conversations*, attacked Chagall. They attacked me as the organizer of a noisy campaign for Chagall. We did not expect that democracy would bring this. We thought it would be paradise.

"All this year I spent helping to organize the Chagall exhibit, to organize for Pasternak, to help young poets, to help rock stars to fight for this kind of democracy. The paradox is that during this kind of crazy business I must stop my travels abroad. You have to be here because the resistance against democracy is terrible and you have to fight, step by step. Anyway, when your nerves are burning with such a fire it is good for poetry. I wrote some poems that were good for me.

"Nobody knows how poetry is born. Sometimes you are sleeping all day long, and resting and nothing happens. Sometimes there is electricity from God. Now we become more and more modern and more part of the world. Now with Chernobyl it is impossible to be isolated. We have suffered from acid rain from Germany. We have no borders. I feel there are no borders at all. When I met Allen Ginsberg, Robert Lowell, and William Jay Smith there were no borders. There was an iron curtain but now the world has become more and more together. When you lose freedom in one part of the world you are losing freedom everywhere. For example, we have freedom in our country and we fight for this. Freedom in the whole world is coming up. Everything has a connection now. The ivory tower is not a Russian tradition. The Russian poet is like a prophet who takes part in political life. Only to write something fine does not make me happy. I would be happy if people trust me."

We talked about the problems of filling the "blank pages of history" and how to come to grips with the search for the past, no matter what it reveals.

Andrei said: "We have two hot areas, the economy and history. History for us is not history because it is very much alive. We do not want these things to be repeated. That is why we spoke a lot about Stalin, maybe too much about Stalin, about that old man, that dead body. It is not about a dead body but about a live person inside us. For example, the mistake of Khrushchev was that even when he

opened the prisons inside himself he was a little bit of the product
of Stalin's history. It was his tragedy. He opened prisons but he did
not allow people to have democracy. It is a tragedy and it stopped
his revolution. Freedom did not succeed. Now for the first time in
our history we want to have democracy with democratic ways. Maybe
we will have a victory, maybe not, but we must try.

"It is a fantastic time and a dangerous time. There is no alternative
for the best people. Reactionary people are starving, hungry for their
antidemocracy. Some of them form a silent resistance. Some of them
are like the *Pamyat* society. They are primitive people, but somebody
is behind them. They are dangerous because they are losing all their
privileges, all their power.

"In our country we have to learn democracy because we have no
habit of it in our history. In the Czar's time we had no democracy.
In Stalin's time we had no democracy. In Brezhnev's it was, I don't
know, not democracy, but corruption. I hope it will become democracy."

For Andrei hope springs from the younger generation.

"Today's youth is the first generation free from fear. They are not
afraid to be arrested or killed, and they don't know what fear means.
They are the first generation that can read everything: all the documents against Stalin, all our classics like Bulgakov and Mandelstam.
For our generation this was underground. I am sure they will save
the country because they are a free generation, a pure generation,
sincere, and some of them are very political. The majority are more
engaged in rock and roll music. What does it mean, rock and roll?
It is international, it is the generation of information. If they have
truth inside they will go in the true direction. I hope."

For many young people Andrei is no longer an idol. The golden
glow of the 1960s, when audiences as large as fourteen thousand
listened to his poetry—as they listen to rock music today—has faded.
The youth ask why he did not go to jail with the other poets or did
not flee into exile. They cannot accept his struggle to survive as a
poet within the Soviet system. "Andrei and Zhenya [Yevtushenko]
are the call girls of Soviet poetry," said a young artist sadly.

In early 1987 Voznesensky was at the Manezh to introduce a young
poet and rock musician, Boris Gribenshchikov, taking part in an
evening of theater, poetry, and rock. When Voznesensky came on to
introduce the Aquarium rock group he criticized as "grotesque" the
work of an avant-garde, anti-art theater group that had just performed. Some young people in the audience were enraged and shouted

at him. One youth said, "You performed here twenty years ago, but all the people who were with you then went to the camps. Why didn't you go?" Voznesensky was shocked. He introduced Gribenshchikov and left.

Poets in the Soviet Union are moral exemplars who express the collective conscience of the nation in their words. Audiences come to hear them evoke the spirit of their times and the voice of eternal truths. Voznesensky was a cult figure in the 1960s, but as his fame grew and he traveled to the West his critics also increased and questioned his bona fides. In August of 1979 Clive James, in *The New York Review of Books*, harshly attacked Voznesensky, arguing that since he could not tell the direct political truth about the Soviet Union he could not tell the truth about anything. He could operate only by hints and evasions.

In January 1988 the Lithuanian émigré writer Tomas Venclova criticized Voznesensky in a review of *An Arrow in the Wall*, his latest book of poetry and prose.[1] The main charge: Voznesensky is a good, but not a great Russian poet. "The legitimate heir of the great tradition is not Voznesensky, but Brodsky," wrote Venclova. He derided Voznesensky's poetry as "the art of the Moscow yuppies" and attacked his efforts on behalf of Chagall and Pasternak as tinged with show business and cheap publicity. Because Voznesensky was not forced into exile or labor camps, as was Brodsky, his critics argue, he cannot be a great Russian poet.

Voznesensky gets it from both ends. The exiles and the pure at heart insist he has defiled the great tradition, while the reactionaries say he is a heretic, "Jew lover," and Zionist who should be dismissed without serious consideration.

If these slurs prove anything it is that to be a poet in the Soviet Union is the most difficult and risky of occupations. The poet lives in a political habitat of assault and invective in which he struggles to keep his hold on the muse. Famous poets each have a personal following that borders on a cult.[2] Voznesensky's words no longer convey prophecy, magic, and charismatic fire to a new generation; but he continues to write and to publish. Although his followers are older and fewer than in the 1960s, they cheer and applaud his recitals. In the Soviet Union that is no mean accomplishment. Whether he or

---

1. *The New Republic*, January 25, 1988, pp. 37–40.
2. See Gregory Freidin's study of the poet Osip Mandelstam, *A Coat of Many Colors* (Berkeley, Calif.: University of California Press, 1988), pp. 11–19.

Brodsky is the greater poet is not the issue being discussed here. Those who disparage Voznesensky have yet to learn to live with pluralism. They are products of the Soviet system in which truth, beauty, justice, and cultural policy come in one package with only one truth and one heir. Poets are not prophets anymore. The truths they possess and dispense are frayed, as is the society they mirror. The fire of the 1960s has burned out and the sounds of rock are the new language of Soviet youth.

Voznesensky is being judged by the standards set for Pasternak and Osip Mandelstam, poet-martyrs, who are seen in the West not only as great writers but also as expressions of the suffering of their times. Mandelstam died in a labor camp in 1938. Pasternak's epic novel, *Dr. Zhivago*, was not published in the Soviet Union and he was forbidden to travel to Stockholm to accept the Nobel Prize for Literature. Voznesensky has not suffered in the same ways they did. He has made compromises, but now he is alive and well, fighting the last good fight for *glasnost*. Voznesensky is an activist and literary entrepreneur who works the gray area between highbrow culture and pop. His accomplishments as a poet place him in a world class, well ahead of many; but held to the standards by which Pasternak and Mandelstam are judged he emerges wanting, without the aura of a martyr. In an era of transition the poet's lot is not pure or happy.

Making a Movie (Continued)

From the time we arrived in Moscow in August we let all our friends know that we needed an apartment sublet for September and October. In addition to the housing shortage, there are stringent laws about allowing outsiders to stay in temporarily vacant apartments that inhibit citizens from moving in with their relatives and making room for you. We heard about a foreign diplomat's wife living in a large apartment by herself because her son was in jail for murdering his father; she could use the money, but it would have been illegal to take it and she didn't need any more trouble. Jerry asked Gosteleradio to help us find an apartment; we heard that the Writers' Union has empty apartments for visiting foreign writers, but they said it wasn't so, they had to put their people up in hotels, the same as we were doing. The new international trade center has luxury apartments for businessmen who come for a few months, but there we would have been at the end of a long waiting list. We knew of other apartments whose occupants were out of town on long business trips, but no one wanted to draw attention to themselves and risk having their apartments taken away from them. We were willing to pay rent equivalent to the cost of an apartment in the West; for a Moscow apartment, for which the citizen pays only a small monthly fee, our offer would have been a huge windfall profit. Real estate speculation, like other forms of profit, is illegal and considered immoral in the U.S.S.R. All apartments belong to the state, and the low rents are a form of subsidy. Charging us a normal rent would abuse the system. Our only hope was a lapsed period between the departure of a foreign correspondent and the arrival of his or her successor; such apartments belong to the news organization, which pays rent similar to what it would cost in a European capital, even while the apartment is waiting to be occupied by a newly assigned journalist. It was such a situation that we heard about, in which the London *Sunday Times* would have a vacancy of about six weeks, after Louise Branson left for her new post in China, before the new bureau chief would arrive in late October. A perfect fit. No sooner had she left than Steve and Suprabha moved into the apartment, letting Doveen and Barney fold away their cots and sleep in real beds in the hotel until Kate and Ari, Evelind and Michael returned for the shooting.

Within a week after their departure, Nancy Sloss, who we had known for years in Washington, arrived to pinch-hit for Sherry while she was away and act as assistant producer when she returned. Gosteleradio said they would have someone at the airport to meet Nancy, but since their man didn't know what she looked like it was necessary for one of us to accompany him. We decided it was generally a good idea to have a familiar face waiting when any of us was arriving in case the chaos of going through customs at Sheremetievo was more daunting than usual. Dima, the young assistant assigned to us by Gosteleradio, called to tell me how I would find him, since he and I had never met. "You'll know who I am," Dima said. "I'll be wearing a gray coat, I have a blond mustache, and I'm good-looking." I took it as a good-natured joke until we met. He greeted me on a first-name basis, but I sensed immediate danger in this high-strung, chain-smoking, unsmiling *apparatchik* in his mid-twenties who pretended to speak in American slang but had only a Marxist-Leninist vocabulary.

The wait is always too long in the disorderly reception hall outside the customs area at the airport, and the discomfort is increased by the fogged window barrier that makes it difficult to see and wave to the person you are meeting. The crowds waiting for friends are bigger now, because whole families of Russians and Georgians come to greet their relatives returning for visits for the first time since they emigrated in the seventies and early eighties. Greeters from various ministries wait with handwritten placards for delegations from the East European satellites and Marxist allies from Africa. Radio Moscow runs continual contests for the best essays on communism, for which the prize is an expenses-paid trip to the Soviet Union; there are whole sports teams, young scout troops, and union delegations.

Nancy came out smiling, and Dima had an Intourist car waiting to take us to her hotel. In the car Dima sat between us and explained the difficulties Gosteleradio was having in its search for a factory in the Moscow area that would agree to be interviewed on camera. Evelind works for a camera manufacturing company, so it seemed logical to us that she should visit a Soviet camera factory. Dima said that there are only three camera factories in the Soviet Union, and each of them has departments that are defense related, therefore the whole factory is out of bounds for foreign visitors. Perhaps she could see a watch factory, but the only one available was the Number One Watch Kombinat, a showplace that the Soviets display to all foreign camera crews, not very interesting. "We have written to all the places on your list, but we have not yet received any replies," Dima said.

"None of them, after three weeks? Doesn't that worry you?" Nancy asked Dima.

"Not particularly. Everyone does things at the last minute. It usually works out in the end," Dima said.

Nancy kept smiling, but her worrying had begun. Nancy is a worrier; that's how an assistant producer gets his or her job done. She knew she had to change the subject. "What is your most important impression since you've been here?" she asked me.

It was the perfect opening. "The Russian people are really close to nature," I said. "Everywhere I go the kitchen stoves are filled with pots of black currants boiling to be made into jams and syrups. It's mushroom-gathering time now. It's wonderful watching men and women in boots carrying baskets of morels and huge wild mushrooms, having such a good time."

"Yes, it's true about Russian people. My friends and I like to go far into the woods on horseback, with only a sleeping bag and a bow and arrow. No prepared food, no pots or pans, no guns. We really live off the land," Dima said. That moment was about as close as Dima and I ever got to becoming friends.

Dima was to be our daily hand-holder and our watchdog. He is tall and flaxen haired, with an unruly mustache that only half covers a permanently sullen expression around his full, well-sculptured mouth. He is in his mid-twenties, so age might be the cause of his constant hunger for food, drink, and sweets. His ostensible job was to be present at all film shootings, in order to pave the way for the crew, respond to our special needs, and make sure we did not go off on our own to film anything for which we had not received permission. For all of these functions he showed a surly boredom most of the time. He did make himself useful when the crew was interrupted by a militiaman when they were filming a street scene by reassuring the cop that we had permission to be there. His English was good and he occasionally helped with translating a difficult part of an interview, but even then he had heard it all before, he said in his somnolent manner. He only woke up to perform the job he saw as his true one, which was to take down the telephone numbers and addresses of our friends, ask them intimidating questions, look through their books and papers, and once out of our earshot, to threaten them with reprisals if they voiced any opinion critical of the motherland.

Doveen, Barney, and Suprabha arrived on September 1, and began calling their own lists of phone numbers, given to them by friends in Washington and New York. Barney began to make a plan to see every art show in the city, and the first and nearest was an official retrospective called Workers and Art. It was at the Manezh, the huge equestrian hall that faces on Red Square, an easy walk from the hotel. Four of us, Barney, Doveen, Suprabha, and I, decided to see it together. While we were preparing lunch in the hotel room, Lyokha called looking for Steve, so we invited him to eat with us on the off chance Steve would show up. At lunch we told Lyokha that we were all going to see the giant art show at the Manege, and he nodded approvingly. He seemed to be glad that we would get an overall picture of what his socialist heritage was about, and offered to walk us there to make sure we got tickets.

We had no trouble getting in, and soon lost each other in the rooms of bronze tractor drivers, heroines of the lathe dressed in blue overalls, Afghan and Palestinian partisan fighters, posters celebrating the revolution and Gorbachev's reforms. Not far into the exhibit I entered a room where a crowd stood staring at one painting, a vase of fresh flowers on the floor in front of it. They were not a band of friends who had come to the show together who stood mute and mournful, looking at the painting, but rather each person was lost and alone in his own thoughts. In a realistic, academic style, the painting portrayed a shocking scene in which the police were arresting a man in the middle of the night. The frightened citizen stood barelegged in his knee-length nightshirt; his wife and children and a grandmother pulled their bathrobes tighter around their shivering bodies. One jackbooted militiaman stood guard at the door while a second leafed through the man's papers and books. The painting, dated 1985, evoked the sudden terror of the purge years nearly fifty years ago as if they were yesterday, and warned with a power close to physical revulsion that it could happen again tomorrow. The top border of the painting was an elaborate illumination in Slavonic lettering: "In the Time of Lawlessness and Repression, 1937," and at the bottom was the replica of a *spravka*, a bureaucratic pass, dated 1957, that restored the dead prisoner's good name, which was Zhilinsky, the same as the name of the artist. A fitting memorial to the painter's father, and now the centerpiece of *glasnost*.

Everyone who saw the painting knew that it could never have been shown publicly before Gorbachev. Its appearance in an officially sanctioned art show was a promise that slowly but surely the crimes of Stalin will be brought to light and discussed. In the autumn of 1987 the leadership was still not in agreement that the Stalin era should be opened to such a harsh light; there were still strong constituencies who believed that the nation should not rush pell-mell into telling the whole truth of its history and thereby destroying its heroes. This painting was as far as anyone could go. It did not raise the question of heroes, but at least it was a compassionate nod to the victims that said they were remembered collectively, not only in the misery of each family's sorrow.

Two nights later we went to Ben and Yadviga Charny's apartment for cakes and tea, a party both of pain and joy. After a wait of eight years from the time they first applied for emigration to the United States, during which time they could not work at their jobs and their children could not be admitted to graduate schools, the children, at least, had received permission to leave. Ben and his wife would have to stay behind because he was deemed to hold "state secrets" from when he worked on early rocketry in the 1960s, which means that his children may never see him again because he is suffering from a heart condition and cancer that cannot be treated in the Soviet Union.

At the party were other refuseniks in the same category, forbidden to leave because they worked on military projects years before. Marina, the wife of mathematician Felix, sat in a chair to my right in the crowded room and looked for a way to open a conversation with me. "Have you seen much of Moscow since you came?" she asked. "There's a big art show at the Manezh." I asked if she had been there and seen the Zhilinsky painting, but she had not gotten there yet, so I described it to her. Before I could finish the details she jumped up from her seat, reached across me and grabbed her husband's arm. He listened with downcast eyes while she repeated what I had told her, then turned to me to explain: "I lived through that scene. I was eight years old in 1938 when they came for my father

190

in the middle of the night. I cried and tried to hold on to him, but he patted my head and told me it was a mistake, not to worry, he would soon be back. We never saw him again, and he died in the prison camp in 1943."

In the next week everyone I met who had been to the show was discussing the Zhilinsky painting. "It says everything that must be said," one Soviet journalist told me.

The four of us who had been to the show alerted the rest of the family to make time to see it. I told Nancy to be sure and see the show, because we would certainly want to include the Zhilinsky painting in the film.

"I'm not so sure Sherry will want it in the film," Nancy said. "That's not her style, to film a picture on a wall. She likes people, discussion, action."

"Go and see it," I urged her, feeling rebuffed but confident that she would understand the painting's importance once she had seen it. "You'll see the faces of the people looking at it, and I'm sure Felix will talk about it on camera."

"You don't understand about filmmaking," she said with a smile. "It has to be natural."

Nancy did not try to accompany us to our daily appointments around Moscow. Sherry had already gotten a sense of Moscow through our eyes and she now had to think about how she would shape a film out of that kaleidoscope. It was Nancy's task to arrange the logistics so that all the subjects were in town and in place when Foster Wiley, Sherry's cameraman, and his two assistants, Hans Roland and Hugh Walsh, started shooting during the last few days of September. They had twenty-one shooting days, minus three days off, a lot to fill but also a short time to cover the activities of ten people.

There was plenty for Nancy to worry about. Day after day there was no answer when I called Pristavkin to set a date for filming. Had Marina gone to the hospital to have their baby? Had they gone on vacation and forgotten about us? Jerry ran into a correspondent friend who gave him Pristavkin's new phone number, which had been changed without warning, and which Anatoli had asked the friend to give us. Our phone number had been summarily changed, too, so he couldn't call us, either. (Moscow telephone information usually doesn't answer and is always out of date.) We planned to film a group of former dissidents at the apartment of Larisa Bogoraz, but we didn't have a firm date and time before she went to the hospital for a long-planned thyroid operation. "Just leave a message with Pavel," Larisa said, but after she left home Pavel, her fifteen-year-old son, was rarely there to answer the phone. No one in Moscow, it seems, has a phone answering machine. We had already begun shooting the film when Steve reached Pavel, who turned the project over to his older brother, Sanya Daniel, who put together a strongly articulate group that was ready and waiting for us at Larisa's apartment on the appointed Sunday afternoon.

Nancy wanted firm dates for my women friends to appear on camera to shop with me, once for a street line to buy vegetables, once to visit a department store. Sherry and I had walked the neighborhood together and decided we should look at ladies' winter coats in TSUM department store, a smaller version of GUM, situated only a block away from the hotel. The prices ran from three hundred to seven hundred rubles ($480 to $1,120) for a stylish wool coat with a fur collar, a month and a half to three and a half months' pay for an average worker. Elena agreed to shop with me on film, and since she doesn't go to work at an office she was flexible about the time. That was fortunate, because Nancy shifted the time for the shoot back and forth from Friday to Monday and then to Thursday, leaving it for a time when she had nothing else.

But would there ever be a shooting? After a week of frustration in which Nancy changed the calendar so many times it looked like a chicken's scratchpad, she announced to us at breakfast, "Sherry isn't sure she's coming to make the film. Nothing, but nothing, is firm. You can't reach Pristavkin, you don't know if the dissidents will show up, the producer of *Repentance* [a film critical of Stalin] is out of town, Voznesensky might or might not get back from his trip in time for us, Doveen's designer hasn't agreed to do the show, I can't pin Lyokha down to a date, and Gosteleradio hasn't gotten answers from anyone. All they have is a no from the fruit-and-vegetable bases, just as everyone predicted. We don't have a factory, a collective farm, or a *dacha*. How can we make a movie?" She wasn't all wrong.

We received a letter from our cousins Lynne and Harold Mayer, who are filmmakers: "If you think your producers were a little edgy now, wait 'til you see them with the cameras rolling and the budget rolling at the same time. Expect the pressure to be intense. But no matter what, YOU be relaxed and at ease on camera—like it didn't exist. That's easier to say than to do, we know, but practice filming with Steve before they come."

A few days before shooting was to start Steve bravely tried the Berlin Hotel barber. It was a good haircut, so Jerry made an appointment. Then I followed, but I got a woman instead of the barber. I held my breath until she finished, but I came out with a fine, blow-dried pageboy. The bill was five dollars. When I came out of the beauty salon I found that I hadn't been the only nervous one. The hotel manager was waiting to see how my haircut came out, and she was glad that I was satisfied. "*Normalno*" ("No problem"), she said, looking me over with a smile of relief.

Just as Dima predicted, everything fell into place at the last minute. Permission to visit a factory in Leningrad came so late Evelind nearly missed the chance to meet with the factory manager before the day of the shooting. But they did meet, and were able to communicate both an immediate friendship and an understanding of production problems that managers face on the factory floor in the United States as well as in the U.S.S.R. Only a couple of days before the filming was to begin, Gosteleradio called to say that Gorbachev's chief economic advisor, Abel Aganbegyan, would receive us for an interview on the first morning of shooting. This was their usual method of operation: the visiting interviewer meets the subject only moments before they go on camera. There is no preinterview meeting, and strict formality is preserved. We had asked to meet him or his associate, Tatyana Zaslavskaya, nearly two months earlier and had been given no encouragement that either one would see us.

Katie had gone to New York to enroll for the fall term at Columbia; she arrived back in Moscow on September 29, the night before the interview, but she was ready to participate with Jerry and me and to interpret for us.

It was a clear and sunny morning as we drove out Leninski Prospekt to the glass-and-steel offices of the Institute for Production Forces and National Resources, the economic think tank headed by Aganbegyan under auspices of the U.S.S.R. Academy of Sciences. The six-story headquarters is the command center for the planning of *perestroika*. Aganbegyan's role has been compared to that of the chairman of the President's Council of Economic Advisors in America; but he is more powerful because he works directly and closely with Gorbachev.

Aganbegyan developed his economic ideas in Novosibirsk in Siberia where he was director of the Institute of Economics and Organization of Industrial Production, a branch of the U.S.S.R. Academy of Sciences. Together with Tatyana Zaslavskaya, Aganbegyan is the leader of the Novosibirsk School, which led the fight for economic reform and decentralization of planning. His group's studies and papers blazed the trail for *perestroika*. Aganbegyan was brought to Moscow in 1985 by Gorbachev. Under Gorbachev's patronage, Aganbegyan and Zaslavskaya are the leading architects and advocates of restructuring the economy.

Aganbegyan is a handsome, heavyset man with a lavish wave of graying hair. He was busy when we arrived, and finished assigning tasks to his subordinates while Hugh and Hans set up the lights. It seemed as if he barely saw us during the time we talked with him; he gave rote answers, smiling all the while, finishing with us so he could get ready for the next interviewer. He sat up straighter and his face grew dark with defensiveness at questions that pointed up the difficulties the Soviet Union is experiencing in feeding its population or producing exportable products. His answers remained smoothly patient, so that he seemed not to notice what an extraordinary thing he was saying when he promised that price rises for food would be gradual and would be discussed in the press. "If the majority say no we will not raise prices," he said. "We will never repeat the experiences of the Polish riots." (He was referring to the 1981 Polish food riots after the government raised prices as much as 80 percent. To admit that the Soviet Union faced such a risk was indeed *glasnost*.)

Aganbegyan's basic thrust was that *perestroika* could be measured by improvement in the living standard of individuals. He put housing and construction first, food second, and health third, in terms of urgent needs.

We had recently read an article in which he advocated letting Soviet citizens buy more living space than the standard square footage the state allots per person. Such a market-oriented idea would provide the funds to build bigger apartments, it would reward talented people who earn more money and give them an incentive to increase their incomes, and it would soak up and thereby return to the economy some of the funds now sitting in savings accounts. In our interview with him, however, he carefully steered away from the discussion of whether or not *perestroika* meant that the Soviet Union would become a market economy. He had been accommodating and charming, but very careful not to embarrass himself or his patron.

The adrenaline that gets you up for the camera does not disappear the minute the interview is over. Still high, I asked Sherry, "How did it go?"

"It was okay. It was fine," she said reassuringly. "The first interview is always stiffer than the rest. It takes a little time to get used to the camera and break the ice."

Dima said he had heard it all before. "I have been chosen to attend classes in Marxist-Leninist economics. Everything he said I heard in my classes."

The formality and lack of personal connection in the Aganbegyan interview did not occur again. The only other segment of the film that Gosteleradio set up for us was a factory; there the filming was with subjects with whom we were able to establish a warm rapport ahead of time. Sherry wanted to include a collective farm; Jerry suggested we visit a farm family who had made one of the new contracts by which they could operate more independently than farmers who were part of the collective, a first step in the effort to restructure agriculture with more incentives. After many delays Gosteleradio found a collective farm near Moscow that would receive us, but they would not allow Sherry to meet the people there ahead of time. Sherry told Gosteleradio thanks but no thanks. She didn't want another formal interview in which the subjects would be total strangers meeting us for the first time, in which Gosteleradio controlled the scene to such an extent that there was no room for the accidental truths that emerge in a free-flowing conversation. We all applauded Sherry's decision.

The tensions that had built up between our family and the filmmakers in the last difficult weeks of scheduling receded once the shooting began. Sherry and Nancy were occupied from morning to night filming one or a few of the family or all of us together meeting artists, writers, journalists, refuseniks, visiting galleries or theaters, watching a movie, seeing a factory, joining a doctor on her rounds, or jogging at daybreak. Foster Wiley kept his camera on us riding the metro, dancing at the Berlin restaurant, visiting Leningrad, and traveling back on the train.

Once the shooting began, the pressure on Sherry and her crew was much greater than on us. Individually we appeared in one or two episodes a day, but they were on their toes all day and into the night. Once Foster spoke up to suggest we make our questions shorter, to avoid voicing part of the answer in the question. Otherwise he was a silent eye; at first meeting in the morning he often gave me a warm hug, cheek to cheek, wordlessly.

There were no children to look after in this venture; all of us, both crew and subjects, were professionals who took care of themselves.

Most days I waited to see who showed up for lunch at the Berlin hotel suite. I hoped that the ones who were late had taken granola bars to tide them over. "How did it go?" was my invariable greeting as they came in the door from a shoot. "Fine," was the usual answer. Once in a while somebody froze on camera, or a meeting had gone particularly well and the subject being interviewed had outdone himself or herself, or Foster had to change the tape right at a crucial moment, or the filming had ended just as the discussion was heating up.

At our filming of the writer Anatoli Pristavkin, his pregnant wife held her breath while he performed his knife trick on camera. Faster and faster he brought the dagger down between his fingers splayed wide on the dining table. At any moment she expected red blood against white linen. Just as he finished Sherry said quietly, "We'll have to do that over. It was the end of the tape." Marina Pristavkin gasped. Anatoli calmly agreed to do it again. His wife bolted out of her chair and waited in the kitchen until he had done the trick again and the camera had gotten it.

More than once the family and crew returned from a shoot fuming over Dima's behavior. "First of all, he's lazy. He's supposed to be helping, but he doesn't lift a finger. We have to serve him. He doesn't even say thank you," Steve said.

"The only time he makes himself useful is when we get stopped by the militia. He tells the cops that we have permission from Gosteleradio to shoot," Katie acknowledged. She had been mortified, however, when he yelled at her in front of the doctor she was interviewing because she told him they were late for their next appointment and had to leave, and he hadn't finished eating.

"The party went fine. A lot of artists from the Hermitage exhibition came, Ari played his guitar, we had a good time. Then, as soon as the camera stopped, Dima went around asking people their addresses and phone numbers. The next time he does that we should turn the camera on him. The Russian kids all expected it. They just shrugged. They know who the guy is that comes along from Gosteleradio," Doveen said angrily.

Sherry said, "He's outrageous, but we won't turn the camera on him. He's part of the deal. We have to live with him."

Sherry had to be constantly concerned that she did not violate her agreement with Gosteleradio. To have the freedom we had to interview anyone willing to be filmed, so long as we listed the event with Gosteleradio and allowed Dima to accompany us, was an unusual mode of operation for the Soviets. They were used to setting up the interviews and controlling them. Sherry probed to find out how they would respond to our putting dissidents and refuseniks on the list. "You can go anyplace you are invited," replied Valentin Yegorov, Dima's boss. He even agreed that in such sensitive situations Dima would remain outside so our subjects would not feel uncomfortable.

The next morning Dima arrived for work with a swollen jaw. He could barely open his mouth to describe the pain of his toothache. He was so pathetic I had to feel sorry for him, but we were all relieved the next two days when he stayed home in bed.

Valentin accompanied us in Dima's absence. It was a Saturday morning, and first on the schedule was a filmed private tour of the Chagall exhibition at the Pushkin Museum. We were supposed to leave before the regular Soviet museumgoers arrived, but here was a gray area in which Sherry and the crew could push their luck just a little and get shots of the populace, lucky enough to get tickets, arriving to see the paintings. Valentin was aware of what they were doing; he tried to herd us out in time but he remained equable when Foster continued shooting.

From there we went to the weekend Bird Market, which had been a favorite excursion when the kids were small. Jammed into a large yard between apartment houses are tanks full of goldfish and snails for sale, dog breeders with puppies and the mother bitch covered with medals like a Russian general, kittens, mud-covered nutria unhappily piled on each other, tropical birds, and rabbits.

In the entrance to the market the crowd pushes around children and old ladies standing with one or two mongrel kittens to sell for a ruble ($1.60) or to give away. There I spotted an old man, obviously a pensioner, offering a handmade reed basket, still green, the sort I had coveted in my friends' houses but didn't know where to buy. He wanted three rubles ($4.80). I frowned dubiously about the price and kept walking. Then I reached into my purse, and there was a three-ruble bill. I quickly reconsidered the price, decided it was fair, and went back to look for the man with the basket. I found him in a minute and held out the three-ruble bill. He looked at me blankly. "Didn't you say you wanted three rubles? I've decided to pay your asking price," I said in Russian with a smile. Slowly, he handed me the basket and took the money, but his reluctant expression showed that he had also reconsidered, and wondered if it was worth parting with his handiwork for a few rubles, soon spent.

We had to form a line and hold on to each other so we would not get lost in the crowd. We snaked our way through, calling excitedly to Foster to film the animals each one would have liked to take home, and miraculously all of us gathered under Sherry's wing at the far end of the market. However, we had lost Valentin. We waited nearly twenty minutes, hoping he would show up, and then left the pet market, because we didn't want to be late for the next meeting on the schedule. The next shoot was a kitchen table seminar of former dissidents, on the other end of Moscow. Valentin, of course, was sure we had purposely shaken him because we didn't want him to go there with us. Poor Sherry had a hard time the next day explaining what had happened, and Valentin was furious.

Then Dima's tooth infection healed and he came back. He stayed in the background during an interview that afternoon; he was still there when I left. Kate and Ari remained for tea and heard Dima threaten the subject of the interview with reprisals because he had criticized the Brezhnev years while praising Gorbachev on camera. During the filming Dima had been busy rifling the man's private papers.

On one of our free nights Jerry and I went with Vadim and Natasha, who had become close friends of Steve, to see Bulgakov's *Heart of a Dog* in a stage production at the Theater for Young Audiences. In the play, which was written in the 1920s, a famous professor transplants the brain of a Soviet citizen into the head of his pet dog. In this satire about the revolutionary regime's attempt to create the New Soviet Man, the humanized dog becomes a swaggering commissar who tyrannizes the professor's household. The actor who played the dog was energetic and skillful; there was something familiar about this misogynist as he stomped around the stage apartment in his brand-new leather suit, terrorizing the Pygmalion-like benefactor who had created him. Of whom did Sharik the dog remind me? Was he a *golem* of East European folklore? Was he a male Eliza Doolittle? No, no, no. He was Dima, and all the New Soviet Men like him.

A week into filming I asked Sherry what she had decided to do about the Zhilinsky painting at the Manezh. She sighed with exhaustion. "I'll walk over and have a look at it," she said, and later in the day informed me that the exhibition was closed. "Too late, we missed it," she said.

"Let me know in the next day or so if you want to go to his studio to see it and talk with him about it on camera. I have a friend who may be able to arrange it," I offered, but that was the last time we talked about Zhilinsky.

Halfway through the shooting, the crew and family—except for Steve, Jerry, and I—all went to Leningrad for a few days. Gosteleradio finally came through with a factory, and Evelind found the woman in the Leningrad office of Gosteleradio intelligent and easy to work with. In addition to the Proletarsky Trud factory, they filmed street scenes, met refuseniks, and were invited by sailors to visit their ship in harbor. Barney and Suprabha spent their time at the Hermitage and the Russian State Museum. They never did find the plumber for whom Doveen had an introduction from a friend in New York because the phone number she had for him was so old it had only six digits; Leningrad has been modernized with seven-digit telephone numbers.

We spent evenings with our friends Pyotr, Natasha, Yuri, and Nadya whenever we could find time. We gathered for dinner and inexhaustible talk. So much had changed and yet so much was the same. We never tired of exploring the years between the hard past and the hopeful present.

Evelind, thirty-three, had been fourteen when Yuri took her on a leisurely walk on a spring afternoon in 1969 and pointed out the courtroom where he had first met Jerry during the 1968 trial of Pavel Litvinov and Larisa Bogoraz for their protest against the Soviet invasion of Czechoslovakia. After twenty years Evelind remembered a gentle, warm person who had explained Russian history as they walked in the soft sunshine. Now they greeted each other as two adults with shared professional interests.

Yuri has a job on a state commission, where he is developing a new program for guidance counseling in Soviet high schools. For the Soviet Union the idea was revolutionary. It was the first time in the seventy years of Soviet power that students would be consulted and their aptitudes and interests matched, on a scientific basis, to careers. His project aimed to improve motivation, decrease job turnover, and reduce young workers' alienation.

When we first met him in 1968, Yuri had moved from the law department at Moscow University to psychology. The psychology department, established in 1966, was a new discipline fraught with difficulties because psychology is often in conflict with orthodox Marxist-Leninist ideology. During this time he fell in love with Nadya. Through their friendships with prominent dissidents they became politically active. One of the dissidents had grown up in the same apartment house with Yuri and had been just ahead of him in school. Yuri and Nadya signed a series of letters protesting the imprisonment of dissidents. Some of the letters were circulated in the world press and the signers of the letters were punished by loss of their jobs and expulsion from the Communist party. Yuri and Nadya were expelled from the Komsomol organization where Yuri was an active leader. If they could not find suitable work they would be forced to take whatever jobs the government offered them, which could be menial labor such as a watchman or cleaning worker. If they remained unemployed they could be prosecuted for "parasitism" and sent to a labor camp or into internal exile. They earned money translating scientific articles from English to Russian and found other jobs through friends. Until Gorbachev took power the jobs were always below their abilities.

Pyotr had found a job to match his intellectual curiosity and drive. He works at the ministry that prepares and publishes all the school textbooks published in the Soviet Union. Pyotr is in charge of developing new texts. Natasha now teaches music in an elementary school. I asked Pyotr how Gorbachev's rise to power had affected him and Yuri. "It is the time of our own quest to do something," Pyotr explained. "It does not depend so much on the external conditions. There is a time in one's life when you wish to do something. Of course there can be conditions which prevent that, but nowadays conditions are not like that."

At the end of the evening at Pyotr and Natasha's apartment, a friend of Pyotr, an engineer named Mark, stopped by to meet us. Mark and his wife are both Jewish and they are part of the majority of Soviet Jews who have made no move to emigrate to Israel or the United States. Like a Russian Jewish woman we met who had visited her relatives in the United States and complained that "their letters from retirement in Florida are filled with news of their houses, their clothes, and their dishes—nothing about culture," Mark is content in Moscow. For the first time in their lives they have seen and heard Soviet officials on television denouncing anti-Semitism. They believe that life for Jews is getting better under Gorbachev. Mark's family came to Moscow from an area close to the Polish border, but they had lived in the capital long enough to be a part of its life. Mark is an engineer. We could see by the warmth between them that he and Pyotr are close friends. When he invited us to a party for his son's sixteenth birthday we asked how many of us could come. "You are all welcome."

Mark lives in an apartment house from which there is a spectacular view of Novodevichiy (Convent of the Maidens). Mark's wife, Svetlana, and their son, Grisha, greeted us warmly and took us to their eighth-floor window to see the convent. The golden domes of its cathedral and the heavy wall with towers and battlements are reminders of the history it hides. Peter the Great's first wife is buried there, as is Stalin's wife. Nikita Khrushchev rests in its cemetery waiting to be rehabilitated and transferred to an honored place in the Kremlin wall.

Mark had seats for the five of us around two dining room tables placed together and laden with food and drink. We joined a dozen of his friends who knew we were coming and introduced themselves to us eagerly.

"These are all my students," Pyotr explained. "I bet you didn't know that I was once a teacher of physics. I was a graduate student, only a few years older than they were. They have stayed physicists but I left the field."

"Why is it that there are so many physicists? It seems that ninety percent of the Russians I know are physicists," I asked.

"Yes, that's curious. But there's a reason. In the late forties and throughout the fifties the government poured its resources into creating a body of scientists who would develop rocketry and nuclear power. Those were the days of *Sputniks* and Khrushchev's claims that we would overtake the United States. Our economy and the rate of technological development never absorbed all the physicists that we trained, so many of them went off into other fields. I personally was not suited for physics and much prefer my work in education," Pyotr explained.

I said, "Jewish mathematicians and physicists I have met tell me that those were the few fields they could enter without prejudice."

"Yes, everybody who was qualified could go to graduate school in those days," recalled Pyotr.

In the Archipova Street synagogue on Yom Kippur a handsome young Soviet Jew told us that he desperately wanted to emigrate to America. "Can you imagine," he said, "being a computer expert in a country without computers?" There was nothing he could do about his frustration because his parents would not sign the permission papers for him to leave the Soviet Union. No matter how old he was he must have their permission to emigrate, and "they are crazy Communists who really believe in the system. They will never let me go."

Pyotr's voice brought me back to the party. With a look of amusement in his eyes he turned to his sister, a lively and attractive brunette who had been laughing at a joke told by her companion sitting next to her. "Leona told me that in her life she has worked and raised children," Pyotr said, taunting her, "and she thinks raising children was better. What do you think?"

She replied deliberately, but without hesitation: "I think the best thing"—and her eyes sparkled as she prepared us for her answer—"is not to work and not to have children." The table roared with laughter.

"And have a big credit card so you can go shopping all day," I offered, still laughing.

"*Nyet*," she said, dismissing the idea with a wave of her hand. "There is nothing to buy here."

Mark had an array of homemade vodkas and wines flavored with a variety of berries and fruits. We tasted the wines and I liked one made with a melon. The one Jerry liked best was a rose-colored wine made from *kalina* berries, a Siberian red berry also common in the Moscow region, that tastes slightly tart and lighter than raspberries. We had seen baskets of them in our friends' kitchens to be used for syrup, jam, and wine.

"This wine is marvelous. It's a new taste for me. We should go into business and export it to America. It will sell better than vodka and we'll become millionaires," Jerry joked.

Mark turned around sharply in mock anger. "I don't want to sell it in America. I wouldn't give up my secret recipe for anything. Is that what all Americans think about, becoming millionaires? I don't want to be a millionaire. I have enough." He turned to his wife and son, smiling at them.

Then the group encouraged Natasha to sing, and she began an a capella folksong with two others at the table. The brooding, repetitive melody changed the mood of the evening and made everyone thoughtful as they listened and stared into their wineglasses. When the song was over, we had to leave to take Barney and Suprabha to the Leningrad station. Pyotr kept saying "It's still early, it only takes ten minutes to get there on the metro." Now we knew why he was always late for our meetings with him. We dashed for the station and found the sleeping car that the camera crew and Sherry had already boarded.

As the train departed, we looked at the other tracks. Men with bedrolls and camping equipment on their backs were boarding a train for Murmansk. They reminded us of how big the Soviet Union is and that the cold September midnight air was like a spring breeze compared to the frozen northern climate to which the train was headed.

The great hall of the Leningrad station was crowded with people coming to and leaving Moscow. Travel requires permits and passes. Our fellow travelers carried their life's history on their faces. As we left the station there was shouting in the corner, and a squad of militia moved in to break up a fight. The station was alive even though it was past midnight.

The Art World

The midnight train to Leningrad was cozy and quiet as we sat in the Moscow station, waiting to pull out. Suprabha and I were joining Evelind, Doveen, Katie, and Ari, who had gone the day before. Our wagon was nearly empty until a gaggle of eleven Japanese women in their early twenties boarded the train, chatting excitedly as they paired off into their cabins. I could not help grinning from ear to ear as I stood in the passageway and greeted them in Japanese. My sense of time and place dissolved happily and I did not try to resist. In the midst of trying to revive some memories of my two years in Russia, the four years my family spent in Tokyo paraded in the door.

I had just settled back into my cabin when the conductor came in to ask for my help. She was a stern-looking woman in her sixties who seemed completely in charge, but she could not budge the Japanese women out of the passageway. They did not understand a word of Russian. I went out and spoke with them in English, and their leader explained that they filled five cabins and had one woman left over. Couldn't the two men in the remaining cabins be put together so that she would not have to sleep next to a strange man? I translated into Russian, but the conductor said that one of the men was already asleep and it could not be arranged. The bewildered man who was awake sat quietly with his newspaper, his beret, and his chest of war medals as the women peered in at him.

I was about to offer to move in with the man when the women paired off again, and all along the corridor cries of "Jan, Ken, Poi" rang out. In a moment they had set up a solemn tournament of Stone, Paper, Scissors—a game of hand signals that would decide impartially who would be the odd woman out. The sight of this childhood game from Tokyo, which my family now uses to see who will clear the dinner table, sent me and Suprabha into fits of laughter that we barely concealed by retreating back into our cabin. Finally, the Japanese put three women into one cabin, and we all passed a peaceful night to Leningrad, warmed by tall glasses of tea in filligree holders served by the conductor.

In the morning Suprabha and I joined the others at the hotel and then set off for the Hermitage Museum like pilgrims to a holy shrine. Here we would see the great paintings we had only looked at in books for years.

I was also on the lookout for any canvases that might have risen from the depths of storage into the new atmosphere of *glasnost*. Ever since Stalin proclaimed Socialist Realism the official art form of the Soviet Union over sixty years ago, most abstract art has been hidden from public view. Just before the Bolshevik Revolution of 1917, the Russians were at the forefront of artistic innovation. Tatlin and Malevich, with Contructivism and Suprematism, had already achieved an aesthetic revolution in sculpture and painting. When the Soviets came to power, these artists embraced them, believing that pure abstract art would provide a visual language appropriate to the new social order. Stalin, however, wanted art to serve the propaganda needs of the state. He wanted art to depict familiar images and glorify the people's work, not provide abstract symbols for contemplation. Abstract art was labeled "bourgeois formalism," meaning that it was art for art's sake, without any social purpose. So, while the Russian avant-garde had an enormous influence on the development of modern art internationally, the development of abstract art came to a halt in the Soviet Union in the late 1920s.

But the Soviets are now taking advantage of the comparatively open political atmosphere to fill the gaps in their art history. We wandered through the enormous, ornate Hermitage Palace, repeatedly asking for directions and repeatedly getting lost in our search for the elusive staircase to the third floor, the home of the twentieth-century masterpieces. It was worth the search. The string of rooms with stunning works by Dégas, Cézanne, Matisse, and Picasso would have been enough. But these have been on display for years. The surprise was an alcove at the end of this string with half a dozen brightly colored abstract compositions by Kandinsky. At last the Soviets were letting their own modern masters take their place beside those of the "bourgeois West."

On the way out we bought some postcards before heading back

to the hotel. I went straight to the café for a quick sugar fix. However, I forgot that it would not be like grabbing a sandwich or a slice of pizza on Manhattan's 57th Street and rushing off to the next gallery. I found a crowd and a line in the hotel's café, but I decided to wait, thinking it would only take five to ten minutes. After a few minutes I had reached the counter, but the woman serving cakes and coffee cut me off before I could blurt out my order.

"Here we have a coat check and you had better go use it if you want to get served," she said with icy reproof. Suddenly my scarf and jacket weighed one hundred pounds and reminded me with a jolt how easily I could get out of step with this culture. I felt like a first-grader again, reprimanded by the *babushkas* for eating buns with my gloves on in the bread store. The threshold of what is considered rudeness is set by a slower clock, which says you don't rush in and out. And if you do, any member of the collective may reproach you for this antisocial behavior. The woman in the café was deaf to my rebuttal, so I had to stand in line all over again after hiding my coat at one of the tables.

I took my hard-won cakes and coffee to the table and examined the astonishing pack of oversized postcards I had just bought, entitled "Art of the October Revolution." The gorgeous reproductions included Malevich, Filonov, Chagall, Lissitsky, and Tatlin, grouping them with the more moderate experimental artists of the 1910s and 1920s. The text included with the postcards began by asserting the supremacy of realism, just in case anyone should interpret these images as anything more than historical curiosities:

> Art of the Early Soviet Period was marked by a new revolutionary approach to all life phenomena, a passionate search for new artistic forms. It was a path set about with possibilities of error, a hard beginning in the struggle for the realism of a Socialist epoch.

While the writer claims a monopoly on the truth for Socialist Realism, he wants to have his cake and eat it too: "And indeed, the painters of young revolutionary Russia were far from backward, they originated ideas much in advance of their own time and influenced the progress of world art in many respects."

I finished my cake and went over to the State Russian Museum across the park. Much of the museum was closed for the expansion project that will bring even more avant-garde work out of storage in December 1988. In the single room of twentieth-century paintings, a token Kandinsky seemed a harbinger of things to come.

The ambivalent and contradictory text in the postcard package seemed to sum up the paradoxes of *glasnost* and *perestroika*. The new policy of openness and restructuring is an opportunity to restructure the historical record. It is a chance to fill in the "blank pages" and assert the seminal role of the Russian avant-garde in the evolution of Modernism, to establish the Soviets as world players in the cultural realm. At the same time, the authorities would like to rehabilitate the avant-garde with the clear message that these experiments belong to a closed episode in the past. They are not an invitation to renewed experimentation rife with "possibilities of error."

This points to another paradox. In Moscow I saw that *glasnost* means unprecedented freedom and public exposure for unofficial artists. By refusing to make "socially useful" art, they demand a greater sphere of autonomy from the state, and thus approach a model of the creative individual more familiar to us in the West. The example of art illustrates the challenge of *perestroika*: can this society dedicated to collective values encourage free, critical expression and individual initiative while maintaining its socialist identity?

In Moscow I also saw the warm, protective side of that socialist spirit that had made me stand in line twice in Leningrad. During our first week in Moscow, Doveen and I stuck together a great deal, pooling our language abilities and going on walks despite the incessant rain. The whole family was sick, and eventually my chest cold drove us, dictionary in hand, to the pharmacy in search of eucalyptus extract to use in a steam treatment. Our first sally at the counter was repulsed by a new bit of vocabulary. We looked up the offending word to discover we needed a prescription. Incredulous, we stood there for a few minutes, soaked with rain, looking rather pitiful, I imagine. Then Doveen said, "Let me try something." She consulted the dictionary briefly and then approached the counter. "My brother is sick," she said, her hand pressed flat on her upper respiratory tract. In a moment the woman had filled out the receipt and we were off to the cashier.

Doveen and I liked to browse in Children's World on these walks, finding again the school supplies and toys that were the texture of our lives twenty years ago. One of my most ardent desires in Soviet first grade was to get a box of children's plastilene. The oily sticks of modelling clay came in assorted colors, eight in a box. Extruded like cake decorations from some kind of grooved mill, these bars were my gold. At first I needed them because they were required for the art lesson. But I soon found this unrewarding, because success in all the drawing and modelling exercises depended on how closely one copied the given model: a flowerpot, a figurine. At home I had free rein and fashioned a menagerie of multicolored monsters. I kept my drawings and creatures at home a secret from my teacher and classmates. It was clear to me that art in school did not mean "do your own thing."

On a higher, adult level I was also getting an inkling, from my parents' collecting, that there were different and conflicting categories of art in the Soviet Union. They brought home a canvas by Oskar Rabin, and it exuded its somber vision through layers of crusted black paint, oily images of a fish, a samovar, a newspaper. Even a six-year-old could see that this was of another order and spirit from the vigorously optimistic "realism" in textbooks, on postage stamps, and on the ubiquitous Soviet posters.

When we returned to the Soviet Union seventeen years later, I was a Master of Fine Arts candidate in sculpture. Rabin and many of his contemporaries had emigrated to Europe and a new generation of artists had come of age. As my father and I shouldered our way through the crowd at the opening of a retrospective exhibition of thirty years of unofficial art, organized by the newly formed Hermitage Group, it was clear that the art world had developed dramatically. The existence of this show and the faces of the young artists mingled with the old revealed that the rules had changed and so had the personalities.

We ran into Volodya Nemukhin, who my father knew in the late 1960s and who is now, for many, one of the patriarchs of the struggle for unofficial art. For my father, Nemukhin was a point of reference in an art world that had changed beyond his recognition in almost twenty years. I could feel the urgency with which my father wanted to bridge that gap, to introduce me to a man of his own generation so I might judge the current situation with some historical perspective. Nemukhin said I should visit him at his studio, and eventually I did so with Steve and Suprabha.

The visit with Nemukhin provided a cornerstone for my understanding of the Moscow art world. I built on this foundation with visits to painters, sculptors, and photographers, both official and unofficial, trying to get a picture of the life-styles they had chosen, of their artistic and political ideas, and of the political climate in Moscow as it determines what art is being shown.

Most painters who produce unofficial art have completed the required six years of academic training and are members of the Artists' Union. By joining the union they gain access to studio space and exclusive art supply stores. Most important, union membership gives them an official status and function in society. Those artists who live completely outside this system can be accused of parasitism by the state and must work at other professions with breaks of no more than four months at a time in order to keep the militia at bay. Union members can find more time for their unofficial work by simply doing fewer official commissions and making up the lost income in sales to foreigners. Inside the union there is no norm or quota to fill. On the contrary, there are more than enough thoroughly official painters competing for the government commissions.

By keeping one's ear to the grapevine—there is no advertising or Gallery Guide for such shows—one can see that public exhibitions of unofficial art are now much more frequent and their content less restricted than before the advent of *glasnost* and *perestroika* in 1985. There is general agreement that conditions are better for unofficial artists. "We can breathe now," said Tanya Kolodzei, an art collector who introduced me to several of the painters whose works are in her collection.

Tanya had me, Katie, and Doveen over for tea and bite-sized grilled-cheese-and-tomato sandwiches served by her thirteen-year-old daughter, Natasha. When the table was cleared, we sat on one side of the tiny room and from an armoire in the corner Tanya brought out, one by one, the highlights of her thousand-piece collection of paintings, drawings, and sculpture by 120 contemporary Soviet artists. Most of these works were gifts from the artists.

The state does not officially recognize her activity as a collector, so Tanya organizes official art exhibits for the government on a part-time, contract basis, a job she did full-time for thirteen years. This work keeps her employment record up to date, but how she maintains her unusual status, both financially and politically, remains a mystery. During the past twenty years Tanya and her collection have served as an entrée to the unofficial art community for foreigners looking to buy Soviet art. Tanya also hopes that her collection and a book she plans to write on one hundred Soviet artists will help to create some historical record of unofficial Soviet art.

Tanya set up a meeting with the painter Sergei Gorokhovsky, and as the three of us sipped coffee in his studio, I found them both very guarded in their assessment of what the new political conditions mean and what they bode for the future. They cautioned me against an overly simplistic appraisal of the situation and urged me to analyze it in the context of the ups and downs of the last twenty-five years.

"Past experience shows that for every permission we have received, another hand was taking something away," Tanya told me. "Rather than a steadily rising curve, a more accurate picture of artistic life here is the roller coastering line on an electrocardiograph screen."

Gorokhovsky explained further: "The shows of unofficial art you see here and there in Moscow are not the result of a single, monolithic policy of liberalization at the highest levels of government. There is division there, and in the local party bureaucracies for the various regions of the city, where conservative forces are even more entrenched."

He stressed that the two major groups of artists, official and unofficial, are divided internally by numerous factions. Not everyone's fortunes change at the same time in the same way.

In the struggle for unofficial art, Gorokhovsky and Kolodzei identified the 1962 Manezh exhibit as the first confrontation. The abstract painter Belyutin and members of his school, including Yankilevsky, Sooster, and the sculptor Neisvestny, were lured into showing their work at the central exhibition hall. The show was a deliberate provocation designed to identify the nonconformists in the union. Khrushchev visited the show and made scathing remarks, publicly condemning the work. These artists went underground for the next twelve years.

In 1974 another major confrontation broke the dozen years of relative silence: the authorities used a bulldozer to disperse an open-air exhibit by unofficial artists. It was the first evidence in twelve years that abstract and surrealist art had not been completely snuffed out. Gorokhovsky said this came as a shock to the authorities. But the violence of the reaction had the positive result of focusing world opinion on the plight of unofficial Soviet artists.

This crisis made it clear that the government had to renegotiate its relationship with the unofficial art community, if only to gain firmer control over it. Two weeks after the bulldozer incident, the authorities allowed a four-hour outdoor show at Izmailova Park, which went down in Moscow lore as the "Four Hours of Freedom." Larger and longer exhibits soon followed. In 1975, 20 painters were given a show at the Bee Keeping Pavilion of the Exposition of Economic Achievements. But the authorities realized that outdoor shows were too sensational and hard to regulate, so they began moving them indoors. Later in 1975 Kolodzei helped organize a show of 546 works by 146 painters, which was mounted indoors at the Economic Exposition. This was the first art exhibition in the Soviet Union without a jury, Kolodzei told me.

But I also learned, from my conversations with a young photographer, that the exhibit's achievements had been marred by KGB censorship, which exacerbated the divisions within the art community. Four pictures were removed from the exhibit, and some of the artists were detained by police for fifteen days, the photographer told me. Seated on the floor, he had watched in awe as Rabin stood up on a trash can and exhorted the group to shut down the entire show in protest against censorship of any kind. But Rabin's words fell on a divided group. The struggling young painters did not want to give up this rare opportunity to show their work. They felt that Rabin and his faction were acting on principle because they could afford to. They were older and more established. Granted, they had been underground for twelve years, but they had contacts and outlets in the West.

When the show closed, some of the artists, including Rabin, did emigrate. For those who remained, the government formed a special section of the Graphics Trade Union for painters and gave them gallery space on Malaya Gruzinskaya Street. With this official status these artists could now live as painters, selling their work legally and receiving benefits from the government. Kolodzei and Gorokhovsky pointed out that the creation of this group was motivated less by goodwill than by the need to keep tabs on a troublesome, disenfranchised group that would have liked to join the already swollen ranks of the regular Artists' Union. By giving them a gallery of their own, the government ensured that they would fight more among themselves than with the government.

Despite the vicissitudes of the last twenty-five years and the internecine rivalries, some artists I talked to were openly optimistic. They framed the problem in terms of developing connoisseurship among the Soviet public. There can never be fundamental change in the Soviet art world until there is a market for contemporary, unofficial art within the Soviet Union itself, they said. Expanding opportunities for public exhibits in 1987 were a means, a beginning, of exposing the public to a different kind of art. This would be a long and difficult process, but perhaps it had begun. Lyonya Bazhanov, an art critic and one of the Hermitage Group organizers, said, "Maybe like the works of Chagall, the contemporary art which is now flowing out of our borders in fifty years will be recognized and reclaimed for the Soviet cultural heritage."

For other artists, the Soviet cultural heritage still means portraits of Lenin, Gorky, and Pushkin. For the official artists I met, the need for radical change through *perestroika* was not in increased tolerance of free expression. Rather, they hoped for a restructuring of the Artists' Union bureaucracy and a fair allocation of government funding to artists by what they called, in Russian, the "mafia" that controls the union.

Within this official world the artists I met are generally contented. They paint and sculpt realistic portraits and scenes for public buildings, plazas, and collective farms, filling commissions disbursed by the union. The socialist system enables them to live on their artwork and have a regular, secure life-style like anyone else's. Some were cramped for studio space and needed more supplies. Change might mean improved material conditions. On the other hand, I found some official sculptors and painters, who execute large monuments and portraits of high-ranking officials, to be among the wealthiest Russians, and I glimpsed some of their studios, too.

In part, *perestroika* is an exhortation from the Soviet leadership to the people, urging them to work harder and to take initiative on the job. Criticism of inefficiency and corruption is now encouraged. So how can the artist respond? In addition to attacking the union bureaucracy, the official artist may drink less vodka and spend more time on his government commissions. But what about the unofficial artist, who joins the union to stay alive and keep working but whose individualism has already put him at the fringes of the system? He benefits from the government's attempt to unleash new economic energy through an atmosphere of relative political openness. But the exhortation does not stir him to revamp his work habits and his contribution to society. The painter Petr Belenok said, "We have always been ourselves, pursuing our own visions as artists." Nemukhin expressed it succinctly when he said of artists, "We have always been restructured."

Nemukhin met me, Steve, and Suprabha at Mayakovsky Square in front of the Sofia Restaurant. He looked older than when I had seen him in the gallery two days earlier, because his beret and glasses concealed his keen, deepset eyes and the shocks of silver-white hair that spray forward in cowlicks. He took us to his studio, which he shares with another artist. It was in an old building, seven stories high, and they were on the top floor with the lowest ceiling. We put our coats on the couch in a tiny sitting room. On one wall were paintings and prints given to him by other artists: Kabakof, Yankilevsky, Shteinberg. On the opposite wall were old photographs and posters. The desk and chest of drawers were cluttered with sculpture-objects, including a fish tank filled with "useless" still life items such as bottles, thimbles, and silverware, all turned into bronze.

He led us out of this room down the hall to his work space, which was no more than a small area partitioned off from the other artist's space. He explained that most of his works had gone abroad so there was not much to see. A Belgian multimillionaire was his most recent buyer and had alone taken a large number of paintings. We discussed the various routes for getting art out of the country and how prices had increased over the years.

"One option is for the buyer to pay a customs tax of one hundred percent on the value of the painting, as determined by the government, but this is a ludicrous process," Nemukhin said. "The customs office is in Chekhov's house, and it's like a theater. The Jews are lining up with their heirlooms, brass samovars, and other antiques to see whether they can take them out or not when they emigrate. This is where our paintings are assigned a ruble value. It's a ridiculous scene, like a Chekhov play. Imagine if they did that in Mark Twain's house in America."

A second option is to sell the work through a government art gallery, of which there are two in Moscow. The gallery acts as the intermediary between the artist and the buyer, taking an enormous commission. This leaves the artist with about one eighth of the purchase price. But many artists prefer this route because it increases sales and because payment is in hard-currency coupons, which can be spent on imported goods and the best food available. The government does not mind selling abstract art because it is leaving the country. "You should stop in at one of these salons," Nemukhin urged us. "It's a very slick operation. They'll give you a whole sales pitch and try to sell you something.

"Diplomatic circles are another means of getting work out, but we generally don't discuss that in any detail because they have their own methods and channels," he concluded.

The works left behind were representative of his main motif: playing cards. The paintings are ghostly and elegant. Several playing cards or rows of them in a grid are barely visible through a wash of white oil paint. Not a thick impasto, but layer after thin layer of paint was applied until the cards became part of the painting, not simply applied to the surface. Some of the paintings had a green background, like the felt of a card table with a few cards strewn across it as if by a dealer. Some had neatly made slashes in the surface.

"The slashes remind me of works by the Italian artist Luccio Fontana," I said.

"That is a common response," Nemukhin replied, "but my idea is completely different." My comment had stirred him up, so to illustrate his point he picked up a scrap of paper from the desk and, with a pocketknife, made a slit in it and held it open to us. "You see, Fontana's was a spatial idea about piercing through the canvas to the other side. My paintings are meant to be card tables. The slashes are literary references to the novels of the nineteenth century in which officers, upon losing at cards, would draw their swords and slash the tables." This conceptual transformation of the pictorial surface into a horizontal plane carrying real objects might be related to Rauschenberg's innovations of the 1950s, I thought. Rauschenberg challenged the conventional, vertical orientation of the picture to the viewer by treating the surface as a literal plane to which he attached solid objects such as ladders, clocks, and chairs. His pictures hang on the wall, but they refer to the horizontal planes (floor, bed, table) on which we perform various activities.

As the conversation progressed, the 1950s indeed appeared to be Nemukhin's frame of reference, at least for American art. He spoke of the hunger in the Soviet Union for Western art and information and referred to a major exhibit in Moscow in 1959 of American painting, which was a milestone in opening up Western artistic ideas to Russians. But simultaneously, Nemukhin defended his countrymen against the charge of provincialism. "You Americans have your gods: Pollock, Motherwell, Rauschenberg. But that is only one of the many schools of painting around the world. Russians may be accused of being isolated, but really they are developing their own school. Chuikov and Kabakov are very bright, and are developing their own idioms."

The point was well taken. America is obviously not the only center of influence. Nemukhin also spoke admiringly of the German conceptual artist Joseph Beuys and of his enormous influence on younger Soviet artists, especially in the area of sculpture objects and installations. This I already knew from going to the final evening of an earlier Hermitage Group exhibit at which many of the artists were gathered around a television, avidly watching videotapes of Joseph Beuys.

We moved back into the sitting room and sat on the couch facing him. He is heavily set, with a strong, clear voice and small, intense eyes that both scanned the horizon for his broad ideas and then focused sharply on us when he addressed us. "The main periods of contemporary Soviet art are prebulldozer and postbulldozer." He spoke in Russian but pronounced the word *bulldozer* in English, as do all Russians when speaking about the 1974 art exhibit that was shut down when the authorities sent police dressed as workers, doing volunteer Sunday work, to trample the art. The artists were roughed up by plainclothesmen and chased by the bulldozer when they tried to rescue their paintings from its plow.

"Before this, all unofficial art had been shown in apartments, privately. This was the first confrontation with the authorities, and it began a new period of speaking out, of developing a new relationship with the authorities," Nemukhin continued. "I would have to say that Malaya Gruzinskaya gallery is perhaps the single most significant development in the postbulldozer period. Yes, the work there tends to be very kitsch and commercial now, but the gallery has been operating for over a decade and has given so many people an opportunity to show their work. Every major contemporary artist has shown there."

I had seen the current exhibit at Mala Gruzinskaya entitled "Grotesques," which illustrated Nemukhin's point. The entire category of grotesque art, with its surrealistic or satirical distortions, is a blatant subversion of Socialist Realism. So the subject matter of the show was a measure of the new political climate. The satirical painter Sosoyev, who had spent two years in a labor camp for his "anti-Soviet" caricatures, had several pictures in the show. One entitled *Triceratops* was a portrait of a high military official in full uniform, but he had the head of a dinosaur with horns and a parrot's beak. His medals were claws and skulls. This kind of satirical humor with some macabre surrealism and some nudity thrown in made the gallery very popular in the late 1970s. The public wanted a break from academic realism. But the quality of the work was at best uneven, and when the crowds stopped coming, the titillating, cartoonlike pictures left the gallery with a tainted reputation.

"What about more recent developments like the formation of the Hermitage Group this year and their gallery space out at Belyaevo?"

I asked. This group is one of the societies or clubs that have been formed in the last year with permission from a new law. It is a loose confederation of about one hundred artists who have a large gallery space in what used to be a library in the ground-floor rooms of an apartment building in the southwest corner of Moscow. Eventually they hope to move into a larger permanent space and establish a museum of contemporary art.

"Compared to Malaya Gruzinskaya, the Belyaevo group has a more disciplined approach," Nemukhin said. "They have more of a political idea in the way they structure their shows." The retrospective exhibit where I had met Nemukhin was a good example. This show marked the first time that contemporary works by émigré artists were publicly displayed in the Soviet Union. "But the group has capitalistic motives in its organization," he continued. "Because the gallery takes fifteen percent on sales of the art, profitability can become a motive for selecting works for display. Another factor which makes its significance as an independent alternative space questionable is that the local council for that region of Moscow retains a key to the hall and can close a show if they decide it is politically unsuitable."

From Nemukhin's criticisms I gathered that some things at least would never change: loyalties, factions, and rivalries were permanent elements of the scene. But when I asked him about the government's exclusion of Rabin from the retrospective and if he saw any parallels to the censorship at the Second Economic Exposition in 1975, he closed ranks with the Hermitage Group.

"I don't see any parallels. The only one censored was Rabin this time. It's a pity he couldn't be in it, but this was a very important historical show because it gives the sweep and development of unofficial art. Rabin was kept out because he was a vocal leader of the unofficial painters before he emigrated, and now that he has gone he does not exist for the authorities who took away his citizenship. But to close the show for Rabin would be to say that it's a show about him, which it is not. And it's remarkable that about one half of the artists in the show are émigrés and are being shown here. We will have some separate evenings to honor Rabin."

Rabin made some powerful enemies who apparently still hold grudges against him. Perhaps there is more to be gained now by compromise with the censor than in confrontation. Bazhanov and his team, it was rumored, had succeeded in whittling down the censor's list from seven names to just one (Rabin) during the three days in which the opening was delayed. The Hermitage people plan to remain in Moscow for the long haul, so they have a different strategy than their irate predecessors of a dozen years ago. Nonetheless, with all the new freedoms, the government's tactics haven't changed all that much. On the night of the opening, the organizers had to dash halfway across the city to control a flood in a small gallery on Niglinaya Street where they had a show of prints. They were convinced it was no accident.

Nemukhin concluded his panorama of Soviet art history by mentioning the revolution as a kind of afterthought. "Of course there is also the revolutionary art of Malevich and his contemporaries; this is another separate period." This remark brought home how important the 1974 bulldozer incident was in his mind as a milestone. He was not claiming that unofficial Soviet art of the last decade is of the same stature as that of the revolutionary period, but his vision of history was in terms of breathing periods in which artists broke through the suffocation of academic Socialist Realism.

I wanted to pursue this revolutionary period, this piece of their heritage from which Soviet artists have been cut off by almost seventy years of suppression. "Have you seen the show at the Manege?" I asked. "The Artist and Time" was an enormous, overstuffed panorama of Soviet art from 1917 to 1987, celebrating the seventieth anniversary of the revolution. The Manezh is proportioned and styled like a Greek temple, and the single vast gallery inside holds enough art for several hours of viewing. I visited the show twice to hunt for treasures hidden in the dizzying procession of paintings, sculpture, graphics, pottery, and folk crafts. Like several others I had asked in the unofficial art community, Nemukhin had not seen the show. Like the others, he seemed to know what he might expect from such an official jubilee show.

"There were some surprising pieces," I said. "Beginning in the 1910s with theater and costume designs by Exter and Tischler, then photographs of Tatlin's proposed *Monument to the Third International* in the architecture section, and a couple of paintings each of Malevich, Filonov, Altman, and Shterenberg." Nemukhin nodded as I ticked off the names. He knew the argument, but it seemed to depress him, rather than herald a new era of openness.

"Granted, these pieces were not the best examples of these artists' work and they were blended as inconspicuously as possible into the soup of hacks and academics who comprised the bulk of the show." My tone was growing less enthusiastic and more conciliatory by the minute. By his air of disapproval, I knew Nemukhin was about to destroy my hypothesis. "But isn't this part of *glasnost* and *pere-*

stroika, this acknowledgment that Socialist Realism did not begin right after Impressionism and continue uninterrupted until the present?"

"But it's a false approach, a false idea, to present all of this as one culture. They are not trying to show the breaks in the chronology but rather to unify culture in a false way."

I said that the wonderful, comprehensive Chagall show then on display at the Pushkin Museum for the centenary of the artist's; birth seemed to me another example of the art establishment using the new political climate to make up for great losses in the Soviet cultural heritage incurred by decades of repression.

Chagall, who spent most of his life as an expatriate in France and whose work for decades could not be found on display in the Soviet Union, could now, after his death, come home and be embraced as a truly Russian artist. He did return in 1973 for a show of his work at the Tretyakov Gallery in Moscow, and in 1982 he was included in the Pushkin's "Moscow-Paris" show. But the 1987 show was unprecedented in size and scope. And the Russian people welcomed it enthusiastically, with lines that wrapped around the outside of the museum hours before the ticket booth opened. A young curator told me with a straight face that the show simply confirmed the facts: Chagall was always above all a Russian. And the administrators at the Pushkin downplayed the novelty of the event, pointing to a long record of showing modern masters. But Kolodzei was repulsed by the hypocrisy. She said the elite would visit the show on the first day and *ooh* and *ahh* about "our Chagall" when they had hated him for decades. Similarly, a young teacher told me she felt a wave of embarrassment when she saw the marvelous paintings: the gorgeous show made the stupidity of all those years of suppression all the more glaring.

Nemukhin responded with an ancedote that he said might apply to Chagall. It summed up the situation and lightened our mood. "There was an international conference on elephants which the Soviets, the Americans, the Germans, and the French attended. Each country responded according to its true nature. The French submitted a paper titled 'The Love of Elephants.' The Germans submitted six scientific tomes containing facts about elephants. The Americans contributed a paper titled 'Things You Need to Know About Elephants.' It was a very short paper. The Russian report was called 'Russia, the Motherland of Elephants.' So you can see that the official line on Chagall is that if he was born here he's our bastard and we're going to love him more than we hate him."

The conversation with Nemukhin went on for hours, but we hardly noticed the time passing. Warm hospitality and time for conversation, I learned, were never in short supply in Moscow.

Since Nemukhin had identified Kabakov and Chuikov as practitioners of a self-sufficient, indigenous idiom in painting, I was especially anxious to see their work. The old guard Modernist had turned over the stage to these postmodern conceptualists.

A Russian friend set up a meeting with Chuikov and took me and Steve to his studio overlooking the old Arbat, a street, sealed off from all but pedestrian traffic, where artists draw portraits and folk singers play on their guitars. People stroll and have their pictures taken by photographers peddling their wares. It's the most commonplace sight in the world until you remember you're in Moscow and that it's a phenomenon born with the new atmosphere of *glasnost.*

We turned into one of the old carriage tunnels that cut through the buildings lining the Arbat, and left the crowd behind. We came through to the vast courtyard and found the stairwell at the back of the building. It was a long ascent, past urine and rotting fruit on a couple of the landings. But the studio at the top was a bright aerie commanding a view down the length of the bustling old street. The two rooms were not enormous, but it was a very good studio by Moscow standards. It was quiet and there was plenty of natural light. Chuikov, a tall, thin man in his early fifties, greeted us with a warm smile. He exuded informality in his blue jeans and leather boots, his abundant corkscrew curls of gray hair halfway down to his shoulders.

"Vanya, how long have you been in this studio?" I asked.

"I have only been here for five years. It's very nice, isn't it? For the first two years here I couldn't really produce anything. I couldn't get used to having so much room." He laughed. "For eight years before I got this place I only had about twenty square meters of studio space. Before that I was in my father's studio."

"That must have been rather difficult, too," I said.

"Well, yes. My father was a well-respected painter, and when he saw the kind of work I was doing he said I was wasting the talent and the promise I had shown during my six years at the academy. Despite our differences I am still very grateful to my father. He introduced me to the Impressionists, the post-Impressionists, and the avant-garde through books when their work could not be seen in the museums."

"Aside from your father's disapproval, what is it like trying to paint as you please and be a member of the Union of Artists at the same time?" I asked.

"When I first joined the union I would submit paintings to the juried shows, but when they were repeatedly rejected, I contented myself with small discussion groups and apartment shows with like-minded painters. When foreigners came to buy my work of course I sold to them. Now, with the gallery at Belyaevo, I can show some work publicly in Moscow. I used to show at Malaya Gruzinskaya, but that gallery is tainted by commercialism. Belyaevo is an important alternative space. Actually, it's not an alternative space, it's the only space for art of this kind."

The opportunity to show his work publicly in Moscow brings Chuikov tremendous satisfaction because he sees it as a step to a more open society. He does not expect Soviets to buy his work yet because they have no experience in viewing and collecting contemporary art. In the meantime he must sell his work to foreigners.

We began a tour of his paintings in the back room with a canvas that had just been refused by the export salon when he tried to sell it to a client in the West. At the last minute an official had deciphered what at first seemed to be just some brushy yellow paint in the upper lefthand corner: it was actually the bottom half of Lenin's face in profile. This piecemeal deployment of the hallowed image was enough to assure the painting's status as contraband. The painting was an assemblage of fragments, and the red piece of Soviet flag with Lenin's beard sticking into it also contained the last letter and exclamation mark in the Russian words for "Communist Party," "С!" Any Russian, however, would recognize the fragment from billboards and posters.

By pulling these bits of familiar visual and verbal language out of context, Chuikov was trying to expose the complete images and words as empty conventional symbols, to drain from them all the political meaning Russians have been conditioned to fill them with. In less political ways the rest of Chuikov's art pursues the same project: to examine the assumptions and conditioned responses that constitute how we make art and look at it.

The series of wave paintings Vanya pulled out next are a good example. The series consists of twelve canvases, each with the same black-and-white photo of the surf printed onto it, and each with different painted images over it. He pulled out the paintings one by one and lined them up against the walls until they surrounded us like a low fence. "We're trapped," I said.

"That's the idea," he said, laughing. "The first canvas over there is a demonstration of the problem and the materials. Just a photo and seven colors." Seven bright, unmixed blobs of paint were lined up horizontally across the middle of the photo. In the second, he had simply put the canvas on the floor and started painting squiggly lines with the colors. The few bright lines across the dull photo set up a reasonant contrast.

"As the series progresses, the colors become more and more organized. Here in the fourth one the overlapping grids painted over the photo are a convention from technical drawing to represent the meeting of two planes, in this case the sky and the land." In others he painted foliage over patches of the photograph. Near the end of the series he began to paint waves with black and white paint onto the black-and-white photo of waves. "This one is a complete tautology," he said, grinning broadly at this bit of satire. "You see, in the art academy we were taught to paint from nature, to imitate. So this seems to me the purest way to paint from nature."

In the last painting all of the different approaches are brought together. "By putting several conventions together you show that each one is not adequate to the reality. They are just different ways of depicting something. The photo, taken with one eye from a fixed point of view, like all the ways of painting and drawing is a conditioned and limited system of representation."

Having examined the problem from every angle, Chuikov then disclaimed the whole process with the exuberance of an artist who simply loves to paint. "I didn't want to do all this analyzing. I had a few of the panels visualized before I started and so this gave me a pretext to paint."

Chuikov's paintings and ideas, far from being provincial, would be right at home in the postmodern discourse of the New York scene. Americans often assume that the Russians are twenty years behind the rest of the world artistically because they are so cut off from information. And most of them are. But the most advanced Russian artists, while naturally hungry for outside news, don't agree that it's a game of follow the leader.

"Ideas are in the air," Chuikov said to me. "When you are seriously involved in this activity, you can't help but feel what's going on around the world."

"Unless the government prevents you," I said.

"The most fundamental ideas are the same," he continued. "But they are different in each country, in each society. Artists use different cultural materials. For example, in Ilya Kabakov's earliest work he can be called a Pop artist. But obviously it's different from American or European Pop Art. He is reacting to different surroundings. If Pop Art in America is about consumer goods, advertising, and glamour magazines, it's about something else in Russia. But both kinds of Pop Art are fundamentally the same: they are about language. The Soviet artist of this trend reacts to Socialist Realism, to traditional, conservative painting. Certain localities hand print their own community newspapers, which have evolved a very specific kind of language which is familiar to everyone here: this is another source for Pop Art. So the color and flavor may be different but the idea of involving nonart language from popular culture in a high art context is the same."

"Isn't this called 'Sots Art,' " Steve asked. "Like 'Socialist Art'?"

"That's the name that the émigré artists Komar and Melamid and their followers came up with to describe this Russian Pop Art," Chuikov said. "But Kabakov is really a conceptual artist I would say, especially in the way he has used verbal elements, texts in his paintings.

"My own work as a whole refers to our Soviet reality and culture, but not in this particular wave series, which is a pure landscape idea, about the different languages or ways of depicting anything." The series he showed us next, however, made some very imaginative use of Russian elements.

From a desk drawer in the next room Chuikov pulled out a series of pastel drawings in which real postcards of Moscow were blended seamlessly into incongruous, invented scenes. In one drawing the Kremlin inhabited the same landscape with Egyptian pyramids and Islamic mosques. In another, monumental sculptures from around Moscow lined the banks of the Taj Mahal's reflecting pool.

After looking at more paintings and drawings we sat down to tea and apple cake in a cozy alcove. As Chuikov poured tea I looked through some of his German art magazines and copies of A–Z, a magazine about contemporary Soviet art that is published in Paris.

"That tall building there with the tower is the new Ministry of Culture, I hear," Chuikov said, looking out the window.

"Is there much talk about the new minister, Zakharov," I asked.

"There is not a great deal, but he is known to have said that we can no longer ban anything. Those days are over."

"But we still see censorship all around," I said. "Do you really think things have changed in the last couple of years?"

"In the last year, yes. The granting of the exhibition space at Belyayevo and the Hermitage Group's first show there in May 1987 was a major development. Also, a show of young, nonrealist painters here in Moscow in November and December of 1986 was another unprecedented event.

"The main thing about these shows is that people are finally seeing our work in the Soviet Union. It will be a long process to develop an audience and a market for this work here. For example, one woman came in off the street at Belyaevo, liked a painting, and thought it might cost about fifteen rubles [$24]. She was shocked to find out the price was four hundred rubles [$640]. But at least she had bothered to come into the gallery. And the opportunity to show here may mean that fewer artists will emigrate. This will also build continuity in the art community."

The conversation at Chuikov's went on for hours, and even after we had all put on our coats to leave we stood and talked some more. Our friendship with Chuikov grew during our stay in Moscow, through subsequent visits to the studio and dinners at each other's apartments. When we parted I promised Chuikov that I would get him pictures of my next sculpture show. We hugged each other and he grinned. "Don't forget to send those pictures," he said.

The other artist with whom I developed a warm friendship was an official sculptor, a man at the opposite end of the artistic spectrum from Chuikov. Doveen contacted Sasha Chichkin through a mutual friend, and he invited us over for tea at his studio in the basement of an old building off Kolkhoznaya Square. Steve, Suprabha, Doveen, and I went and chatted with him. Sasha is thirty six years old, short and stocky, with brown hair and a beard and mustache. He is handsome and energetic, and his eyes sparkle when he smiles.

He explained that the studio was small, but the building would soon be torn down and the union would be obliged to give him another studio that would probably be better. "Getting a studio can be a real problem, but fortunately I have an older brother who is a painter and he passed this place on to me." The telephone punctuated our conversation, as Sasha let it ring for neighbors on the same line. A neighbor dropped in to take a bath; Sasha was the only one in the moribund building with any hot water.

I said it was hard to get studio space in America, too, and very expensive, especially if you wanted to be in New York, where I was now in school. Sasha looked over my portfolio, which included a number of portrait busts, and then made his proposal. "Your work looks very professional to me. If it's so hard to work in America why don't you spend some time in my studio while you're here? We can do busts of each other, and you can take a plaster cast of your work home to America with you."

Over the next several weeks I went to Sasha's studio half a dozen times, and we modelled clay portrait busts of each other and preserved them in plaster. At our first meeting Steve was there to translate for me and for Sasha, who spoke no English. But for the rest of our project I communicated with Sasha in Russian. I found Sasha to be a very skillful artist. He had received a thorough training at Moscow's elite Surikov Institute, which we visited together and which he told me admits only six sculptors a year from all over the Soviet Union.

In his studio he had double-life-size busts of Lenin and Gorky in progress for which he used photographs and smaller busts as models. For Lenin's likeness he also used a plaster death mask, which hung unceremoniously from a nail in the wall. Not that Sasha was irreverent. It was just that by now the mask was standard issue for Socialist Realist sculptors.

In fact, Sasha was very enthusiastic about his government commissions. When he had completed a study for a ten-foot-tall monument of a soldier scanning the horizon with his cape blowing behind him, he brought the twelve-inch figure off the shelf with evident pride. "After I model the full-size figure, it will be realized in hammered copper." His eyes sparkled with excitement at the thought of such an impressive product.

Clearly the state was his partner, and enabled him to participate in its artistic life on a grand scale. Even with a small studio, he pointed out, he could produce a ten-foot-tall figure by using a recess in the floor to gain vertical clearance. The state factory would then dispatch mold makers to his studio to take an impression of the piece in plaster. The mold could easily be brought to the factory, where it would give birth to the final sculpture. If an even taller sculpture was required, Sasha explained, he would be given unlimited space to work at the factory. (In addition to hammering copper and making molds, this factory, or *kombinat*, produces bronze, marble, and ceramic sculpture for the state.)

Despite his enthusiasm for the grandeur of these technical possibilities, Sasha clearly found special satisfaction in working one on one with me to produce what he called a "creative work." This portrait of me he could call his own and put in an exhibit. It was this kind of work that set him apart, he explained, from sculptors who worked only for money.

"In such a portrait, strict imitation is not necessary, but rather you should select some characteristic features and exaggerate them to express your particular vision." Sasha offered these thoughts during our breaks, when we would step back and examine the clay heads. He was twelve years older than I and could not resist taking on the teacher's role. And I let him go, fascinated to see his other side emerge, the side that yearned, however conservatively, to unhitch the harness of social purpose and create pure, expressive forms. I was amazed, for example, when he invoked the seminal modernist works of Brancusi.

"Concentrate more on the simple volume of the head instead of on the features," he urged. (Sasha's busy beard and mustache were giving me some trouble.) "Think about the simple egg-shaped heads of Brancusi, with the features just barely scratched in." He gestured softly with his fingers.

We worked only a few feet from each other, sculpting and posing simultaneously, circling each other, stalking profiles and three-quarter views. As the sculptures progressed, I saw that Sasha had emphasized the bridge of my nose and the forward thrust of my lips in his portrait. The forms were bold and artful distillations of anatomy.

The plaster casts of classical sculpture around the studio, heads and torsos from statues of antiquity, were further evidence of the depth of Sasha's artistic training. Soviet academies still have students make drawings from these casts as part of their regular curriculum. Sasha was incredulous when I told him that this European tradition had fallen out of fashion in America with the birth of modernism, and was confined to a handful of art schools. He presented me with the better part of his cast collection to take home with me to start my own school. I eagerly accepted the casts for my own study of their sculptural forms.

The casts gave the studio the aura of a chapel in the late Roman Empire or the Italian Renaissance, where elements of classical and Christian culture were often blended incongruously. On one wall of the den were Russian icons, and on the other, casts of the heads from the Greek statues of Antinoüs and Apollo. Above the studio door was a sort of diorama set up in a box. A reproduction of Botticelli's *Allegory of Spring* was the backdrop for little plaster casts of a madonna and a Venus de Milo amid plastic foliage.

Sasha had made some plaster horses styled after the Italian Marino Marini and a head in the manner of Modigliani. On the shelf was a book of another Italian sculptor, Giacomo Manzu. While Sasha admired these expressivie twentieth-century figure sculptors, they ultimately remained extraneous to his work and to his enthusiasm for the grandeur of Socialist Realism.

Through the prolonged study of each other's faces, the hours together in the studio, and Sasha's patience with my Russian, we had developed a warm camaraderie. The object had been for each of us to produce a sculpture we could add to our body of work. Sasha said he would put the portrait of me in his next show and call it *American Sculptor*. With my plaster portrait of him wrapped in brown paper and tucked under my arm, I said good-bye to Sasha. "Come on, Barney," he said, casting aside all formality with his open arms. I put the portrait down and he gave me a big Russian bear hug and a kiss. I had only seen men embrace like this in Soviet paintings and epic war movies, so I was glad our friendship merited such a grand gesture.

I did not meet Kabakov, of whom Nemukhin and Chuikov had spoken so highly, but I was able to see his work at a show of the Hermitage Group in early September. He was showing a series of recent oil paintings that placed familiar images of Soviet life in an ambiguous context. Apparently copied from photographs, the paintings showed scenes of families posing or playing at their *dachas*—doctors with children, scientists and farmers at work, all smiling. But stuck onto these sentimental images of Soviet life, in a regular grid pattern over the whole surface of the canvas, were bits of tin foil, colored crepe paper, and cloth. The ambiguous juxtaposition seemed to subvert these optimistic images. I read the bits of material as bon bons or flowers, which expose the packaged artificiality of the pictures.

At the same show I saw paintings by one of the few women artists I met in Moscow. (Kolodzei estimates that women make up 30 percent of the Moscow section of the Artists' Union. The republic of Estonia has closer to 50 percent women painters in the union, she said.) Alyona Kirtsova, thirty-two, takes doorways, window frames, and corners of rooms as her motifs, and draws them accurately. But her palette of bold purples and yellows, and the way she fragments the motif, makes the paintings look like geometric abstractions. She argues that they are not. "What I do is realism," Alyona said, pointing out that she works from observation. To interpret her personal vision of reality as abstraction, she implies, would be to miss the point of her work. In the Soviet context her argument has a political dimension, because it challenges the state's monopoly on the term *realism* through the official form of Socialist Realism.

Alyona talked to me about her work at the show on the final night, when many of the artists had gathered to close out the event as a group. The work ranged from paintings by Kabakov and Chuikov to installations and performance pieces by younger artists on the theme of "Abode." One piece was an inflated plastic bag about forty feet long and wide enough to crawl through with a television playing inside and a sleeping bag, a kettle, books, and other provisions. The twenty-year-old artist lounged in this environment for two hours during the opening of the show. He described the piece as an "ecological experiment" by which the layer of plastic created two discreet environments in the gallery.

There was a performance piece in a room full of chimes made from found objects hung from the ceiling. The twenty-nine-year-old artist turned out all the lights and lit some candles that floated in metal buckets of water. He also lit some fuel pellets in hanging wire baskets, which gave off smoke as well as light. All the while he beat a tambourine and danced with measured steps through his forest of chimes and gongs made from pots and pans, gears, silverware, and scraps of steel or aluminum.

He was dressed in baggy clothes and wore a thirties-style suit vest. On his completely bald head he wore a kerchief, like a pirate. For a lapel pin he had a dry leaf and a sardine preserved in clear plastic. As he danced about with the tambourine, he sounded some of the chimes with his head. He also set off a chain reaction of gongs with a kerosene-soaked cord, which released swinging strips of metal as it burned. With a bow made of string pulled taut around a piece of wood and two soda cans, he produced eerie sounds on a vibrating sheet of tin.

During the second two-week installment of the retrospective exhibit (covering 1977 to 1987) I also saw photos of happenings by the group called Collective Action, a title that takes on a great deal of irony in the Soviet Union, especially because it refers to a group of nonconformist artists whose actions are anything but "socially useful." One series of photographs from 1983 showed the group on a country road. One member wore a yoke on his shoulders and walked ahead of the others, who held up the strings that trailed from the yoke. This group of about a dozen people headed for a larger group that waited and then parted in two as the contingent with the yoke passed through their midst.

These private and group rituals in both shows and the excitement over happenings, performances, installations, and environments gave me the feeling that young Soviet artists are just beginning to explore ideas that were new in America in the 1960s and 1970s. The freedom to display these art forms in a public gallery is also new, and compounds the excitement of the experience.

The thrill over these events barely trickles down to the general public. There is no advertising or Soviet press coverage for the performances. Word of mouth spreads efficiently through the artistic community, which musters large audiences. The gallery, however, is a forty-five-minute subway ride from the center of Moscow. The nonartists who attended seemed to be those who dropped in from the neighborhood.

The restrospective exhibit received more attention because it included émigré works from the Soviet collections. A Soviet television crew attended the opening and filmed the artists and organizers, who held an impromptu press conference in the gallery.

While the first half of the retrospective (1957–77) was politically charged simply by its inclusion of émigré artists, the authorities allowed works of explicit political and social satire in the second half. Erik Bulatov, an artist in his mid-fifties and a contemporary of Kabakov, Yankilevsky, and Chuikov, submitted a canvas titled *Unanimous*, which shows a committee of bureaucrats in an assembly hall all raising their hands together. Over this image, which, like Kabakov's canvases, is painted in a rather indifferent copy-from-photo style, the artist has painted *YEDINOGLASNO* ("UNANIMOUS") in huge, neat, red letters. This single word nearly obscures the image underneath.

While I was studying the picture, a young man came up to me and began a conversation in English, saying he had learned English and practiced it with American exchange students at the Pushkin Institute, where he studied. He did not know much about this kind of art, but he lived nearby and had stopped in. I figured he was either an informer or he was exactly the kind of audience the organizers were trying to reach. He seemed genuinely interested in the show. He particularly enjoyed the Bulatov painting because it expressed the frustrating contradictions of Soviet life and how they are glossed over by outward conformity.

"You know, we say that there are six principles of life in the Soviet Union," he explained. "One, there is no unemployment; two, there is no unemployment, but nobody works; three, nobody works, but everyone has money; four, everyone has money, but there is nothing to buy; five, while there is nothing to buy, everyone has food, clothing, and housing; six, with all these things, no one is happy with their lot, but nonetheless, we all vote yes unanimously." He shook his head and laughed, very pleased with the painting.

In addition to the Hermitage Group's shows and the show of young painters that Chuikov mentioned, Kolodzei told me of other unprecedented shows in the past year. There was a show in December and January 1986–87 on Milionchikova Street of seventy painters, in the forty to sixty-five age range, which, according to Tanya, drew twenty thousand visitors in ten days. This, of course, without any advertising. Many of the artists were union members who had never been able to show their work before. This and another show at Avtozavodskaya (the name of the metro nearest the exhibit hall) of artists in the twenty to forty age group had events every evening: jazz performers, slide shows, and discussions.

"Even though we had permission," Tanya said, "we had conflicts with the local authorities along the way for these shows. But there is certainly more opportunity now. And the authorities are allowing work out of the country on a larger scale for shows." The painter Petr Belenok, for example, had his first gallery contract abroad in 1988. The Kostakis Gallery in Athens bought one hundred of his paintings through the official Soviet art salon. Before, he only had individual sales. Edward Shteinberg was allowed to make a similar contract with the Claude Bernard Gallery in Paris, Kolodzei told me.

I met Belenok twice, once at his studio and once at Kolodzei's. He says it's a coincidence that he was born near Chernobyl and that his work suggests man in an anxious flight from titanic forces that swirl around him. Kolodzei calls his work "panic realism." He cuts out tiny running or crouching figures from magazine photos and collages them into his "landscapes" of brush stokes and ink washes. The shift of scale turns a brush stoke into a tidal wave looming over a man running for his life. Belenok combines wit and imagination with existential angst.

Belenok, now fifty, is rather reticent about his work. Bearded, tall, and thin, with a big bald pate, he looks like a biblical prophet. Trained as a sculptor, he makes his living from government commissions out of a tiny basement studio. His paintings, now flowing out of the Soviet Union, have had little exposure there. In 1969 he was in a group show at the Bluebird Café, Moscow's main jazz club. Then a one-man show at a scientific institute in 1973. These were the underground years.

At Kolodzei's we had tea on a Sunday afternoon and he readily agreed that there were more opportunities for shows since Gorbachev came in. But on the subject of *perestroika* he did not have much to say. He picked up some newspapers from the couch and we flipped through them together. He pointed out the slogans about restructuring with bemused detachment. *Perestroika* for him was a phenomenon of the press that meant a few more art shows, for now.

One artist I met, a painter and ceramic sculptor named Matzumaro, seemed much more optimistic that a new era was at hand. He told me that Gorbachev had allowed individual enterprises, so he was going to make a cooperative gallery with several other artists. They had received permission to proceed and had gotten 120,000 rubles ($192,000) in loans from a state bank to remodel the space. They wanted to have artists come from abroad and work for a month at a time in their studios and then have group shows in the gallery. "With all the foreign interest in Soviet art generated by *perestroika* and *glasnost*," he said, "we should have no trouble selling the art. The government will be happy that we're bringing hard currency into the system." Matzumaro wanted to work the situation from both ends. He too thought the changes were a public relations phenomenon, but he welcomed them with open arms.

The artists who work completely outside the system, braving the rules about parasitism, do not see reforming the system as a possibility. These artists want to emigrate to the West. In some cases they have applied and been refused. Subsequently, they were expelled from their unions and forced to find other work. Unlike the artists of the Hermitage Group, who they put down as imitators of Western trends, these artists see the new freedoms as isolated concessions, not the first steps in a larger restructuring of the rules. One artist said to me, "I want to be introspective and do my work, but that is not possible in a collective society. I am crowded in mentally and physically. The system itself is the problem, not parts of it. For one thing the union system promotes mediocrity. There are just too many artists here, and they are all getting government support. And there are not enough supplies. And the quality of the supplies is poor. You live here and you try to solve each problem. First you change the light bulb. When that doesn't work you think it's the wiring. After you've tried to fix that, you realize that there is just no power source to begin with."

The painter Sergei Volokhov, a member of the Graphics Union, also used the metaphor of electrification in his criticism of the system. After showing me a number of paintings in the studio, Volokhov pulled back a curtain to reveal his magnum opus, an enormous painting about eight feet across and six feet tall, titled *Russia*. The central frame is bordered all around by smaller frames about one foot square that contain small paintings or relief constructions. "Like the inset images on the borders of an icon," he said. The central image is a pregnant woman writhing on the ground, her body a grotesque black hue like a corpse. Bare light bulbs hang over her like interrogation lamps, and a ghoulish hand reaches out to her from the edge of the frame. The ground beneath her is a shattered map of Russia on which the constitution is printed, along with passages from *The Brothers Karamazov*.

Sergei explained that the central image is a satire of Lenin's exclamation about the electrification of the Soviet Union: "All we need is communism and electricity." The smaller frames contain symbols and images in various painting styles and 1920s avant-garde lettering. These frames amplify his theme of ideals gone awry, of lawlessness breaking the bounds of government to oppress the people. One box shows a flowchart of the elements of society: "Law, Government, Progress, and Fear." Volokhov's grotesque poster-icon suggests that the system would work if its laws were observed.

In September I also saw a show of ten unofficial painters, members of the Graphics Union, and the Moscow Union of Cultural Workers (another union artists use as a means of official status so they can do their artwork) at one of the exhibition sites for the Economic Exposition. This one was across the river from Gorky Park and displayed building technology. It was a rather incongruous setting for these semiabstract, surrealist and satirical painters. They were given Pavilion 9, a good-sized gallery. They also had a sound and light show there with synthesizer music and laser graphics projected onto a huge sheet. These rebels of the 1970s no longer constitute the cutting edge, but to see them in such an official setting was an indication of change.

In the press, too, I found some signs that the limits of discussion were expanded. Half of the Literature and Arts page of *Moscow News* on August 30 was taken up with an editorial by the painter Boris Zhutovsky, a member of the abstract painter Belyutin's school in the late 1950s and early 1960s. Here a representative of the unofficial community was given space in an official forum to broach openly all the major issues in the art world.

With only a thin veil of satire, he mocked the idea of professional credentials in art and the reality that one must belong to the union to be recognized as an artist. He attacked the union for the secrecy

and inaction of its bureaucracy. He called for the tolerance of practicing artists of any school, for the preservation of the legacies of
those deceased who were suppressed, and for the recognition of émigrés.
Names that were driven out of public knowledge in the 1960s and
1970s—like Sidur, Zverev, Sooster, and Weisberg—were published
in the hope of cultivating their memory.

Zhutovsky also remembered the revolutionaries such as Rod-
chenko, Filonov, and Kandinsky. He criticized the Ministry of Culture for their late recognition and for sending their shows abroad
rather than to the Soviet people. (In Leningrad this grievance is now
being addressed with a series of shows at the State Russian Museum.)
The editorial began and ended on a personal note, expressing the
loneliness of an artist working for his whole life without any possibility of showing his work in his own country.

In addition to new artistic societies and unprecedented official
shows, there were shows during my stay of individual artists who
had experienced just the kind of loneliness Zhutovsky described. The
sculptor Vadim Sidur is an important example. When he died in 1986
at the age of sixty-two, Sidur had been sculpting in Moscow for thirty
years and was showing abroad, mostly in Germany. He had long
since left his academic training at the Strogonovsky Institute behind,
and was pursuing his dark vision of human existence. For his figures
composed of found objects and installed horizontally in crates on
the floor, he was known as the father of "Coffin Art." Human suffering and death were his central themes.

A Jewish couple who were friends of Sidur's son took me out to
see the show on a Saturday morning. Like most shows of unofficial
art, this one was a half hour from the center of the city by car. I was
introduced to Yulia Sidur, the sculptor's widow, and she greeted me
warmly. She is a short, robust woman with graying hair pulled back
in a bun, and very large, very round, eyes. She and her son had found
the gallery space through a filmmaker friend who had hoped to turn
it into a theater but had found a better spot. The local authorities
were willing to let her put on the show because they were wonderful
people, Yulia said. My friends pointed out that, in the end, these
authorities would benefit too. After she had remodeled the space and
had her show for a couple of months, their region of Moscow would
have the exhibition hall it lacked.

I had seen a few of Sidur's pieces at the retrospective exhibit at
Belyaevo, but they did not have the same impact as when I saw them
in the context of his entire body of work. Even this show took some

time to get into. The small aluminum pieces, about eight inches tall (studies for monumental works), are unprepossessing at first. Each one is like a three-dimensional pictogram, a simplified symbol of the human figure seemingly cut and folded from a single slab of metal. The more complex compositions seem vaguely informed by the cubism of Jacques Lipschitz and the surrealism of Henry Moore. The assembled sculptures echo Picasso's use of found objects, but with a grim twist.

These are the forms of an original and modern sensibility groping in the darkness of a closed society. Cut off from the achievements of twentieth-century sculpture, Sidur has nonetheless made a few points of contact with the major formal innovations of modernism. His tenacious pursuit of his vision, the gravity of his themes, and the depth of his commentary ultimately overcame my first reactions and I was moved by the work.

In *Treblinka* (1966) Sidur memorializes the Jews who perished at the death camp, incinerated in pyres made from alternating layers of human bodies and wood. The spaces between the stacked figures in his sculpture also read as the empty eye sockets of skulls.

In his *Memorial to the Victims of Force* (1966) the figure is again simplified, anonymous, a graphic symbol in solid form of universal human suffering. The kneeling figure's hands are bound behind its back and then thrust upward, forcing the stumplike head downward and the body to double over.

What at first seemed like bland generalization of form and features in individual pieces became, in the show as a whole, a relentless anonymity and dehumanization. This feeling pervades both his memorials to victims and his indictment of Soviet society. In a cycle of pieces called *Holidays* Sidur depicts the Soviet worker at leisure as a mindless, brawling drunk, pacified by songs on the accordion.

In a 1983 wall sculpture called *Faces from the Crowd*, the three faces are rusted shovels without handles capped with workers' hats. The wedge shape where the handle should insert makes a nose. The frame is an aluminum serving tray from a cafeteria—where one might well find a crowd standing on line. The shovel faces reminded me of Picasso turning a leather bicycle seat into a cow's head and the handlebars into horns. But here the humor is lacking. Here is the ultimate image of the alienated worker, the instrument of hard labor substituted for the human visage, the two combined into a sightless, inanimate artifact.

Conspiracy (1983) is a little more humorous. It consists of three pipes from toilets, each about eight inches in diameter and two feet tall, standing on end on a low table. Each is capped with a fedora and has a joint in the middle from which a second pipe points downward at an acute angle like a nose. The long "noses" are pointed toward each other, and it looks as if these intellectual toilet pipes are conspiring in the depths of some building, hiding out from the "Big Ear."

Since the show contained only the smallest sculptures along with his paintings and graphics, Yulia and I agreed to meet at Sidur's studio a few days later. She led me down a steep, narrow flight of cement steps into the basement of an apartment building. There was a fair amount of space, but the ceilings were low and the light was meager. Thirty years of sculpture filled the main room, several storage rooms, and an office. The main room was a graveyard of found objects that Sidur had transformed into his terrifying Coffin Art. Some of the figures were actually in coffinlike boxes—discarded car parts for faces, radiators for rib cages.

The six-foot-tall *Salome with the Head of John the Baptist* (1977) looks more like a menacing Darth Vader, the villain of *Star Wars*. Her veils are chain link fence, her hair and jewelry are rusted coils and springs. Her face appears to be part of an engine block with bolts for eyes, and she displays a platter with the crumpled metal head of her victim. These are not slapdash constructions. Sidur seems to have found just the right hunk of metal for each feature, and the result is chilling.

Yulia and I sat in the office and she showed me catalogs of his exhibitions in West Germany. "How was it possible to finally have a show of his work in Moscow after thirty years without one?" I asked.

"When Vadim died last year, the union followed their usual procedure and told me to clear out of the studio. We would have to give this large space to the next artist in line. But as you can see, this is not an ordinary situation. Only some of Vadim's work has gone abroad. I have thirty years of sculpture here. Where would I put it?

"We appealed to our friends in the artistic and scientific communities and they all wrote letters and made phone calls. The poet Yuna Moritz spoke out and the physicist Vitali Ginzburg wrote a piece in *Literaturnaya Gazeta* called "Sculptures We Don't See: The Art of Vadim Sidur." With this kind of publicity we were finally able to keep the studio. And Vadim was given his first show here in May and June of 1987 at the Soviet Committee for the Defense of Peace.

There were twenty-four sculptures shown. I am hoping to keep this larger show open for several months at least."

Yulia's story demonstrates that *glasnost* is not a simple and straightforward process of liberalization by which old barriers have been removed unconditionally. It seems rather that *glasnost* is a mood or a context in which people feel that democratic procedures and tactics, like the mobilization of public opinion to affect change, will prevail.

In the case of Javad Mirjavadov, a sixty-five-year-old painter from Baku, the year 1987 also meant his first show in the Soviet Union. His garishly colorful paintings of Azerbaidzhanis in traditional dress, of witch doctors, demons, and belly dancers, are executed in a primitivist style. The compositions dispense with traditional perspective and collapse figure and ground into flat, decorative patterns of red, yellow, blue, pink, and orange. Mirjavadov's work may not inspire admiration, but his story illustrates what can be attempted and accomplished in the atmosphere of *glasnost*.

Both in subject matter and style these works defy the limits of what is politically acceptable. In a canvas titled *Mafiosi*, a grotesque black demon sits enthroned on a donkey while three grinning sycophants wave in unison from a reviewing stand. A nude woman dances for the four of them. From a window of blue paint in the background, a startled face observes the scene. The word *mafiosi* is widely used in the Soviet Union to describe any corrupt and entrenched bureaucratic clique that dispenses and withholds privileges.

In Mirjavadov's case, he had to skirt the art union bureaucracy in order to get his work shown. He appealed to a friend on the Secretariat of the Writers' Union, the well-known author Chingiz Aitmatov. After much stalling by the Artists' Union, they were finally able to get a small show in Baku. The celebrations for the seventieth anniversary of the Revolution also worked in Mirjavadov's favor, in that each republic would have its turn for displays in the capital. Aitmatov was able to have a show of Mirjavadov's work at the House of Writers on Moscow's Gertsena Street. It was here that I met the painter and his wife through Kolodzei. We strolled with them out of the exhibit. Mirjavadov, a big teddy bear of a man, wore a large fur hat. He could not adjust to the northern climate, he said. He spoke softly and walked slowly, having just recovered from a heart attack. We chatted as dusk fell, and I couldn't help thinking that the hour was late for him to savor this token recognition in the capital.

For a thoroughly official painter, life is not such a continuous struggle. Boris, in his early thirties, is an official painter, whom I visited a number of times in his studio because he encouraged me to drop by anytime. In fact, there seemed to be a continuous party going on there, with friends drifting in and out throughout the day. Nonetheless he managed to get some work done on his realist portraits and scenes of factories and workers in the fields. He did not seem passionate about this work, but rather regarded it as a professional occupation that allowed him to lead a happy and very social existence. His studio became a kind of den where he, his friends, and their young women friends retreated from their families and from the pressures of the world.

When I arrived at Boris's the first time, he was slicing a huge round of pork into cubes and marinating them for shashlik. As he broke up some old crates and set them ablaze in the fireplace he explained that I must stay because some friends were coming over for a meal. Three in the afternoon seemed a strange time for a big meal, but I was already getting the picture that this was a life that existed in the pockets of time that might be gleaned out of the workday, before returning to the wife and kids at night.

Soon another artist showed up, and he had four women with him. They seemed a few years older than Boris and his friend, who was also in his early thirties. They were cheerful, but attractive in a rather matronly way, so the charged, flirtatious atmosphere had a humorous quality that everyone accepted and enjoyed. As Boris explained later, he and his friend entertained these women annually because they were helpful in acquiring art supplies, which are scarce. He didn't want to be too specific.

The women flitted around the studio admiring Boris's canvases or criticizing them in their motherly way. Meanwhile Boris was skewering the big chunks of meat as the fire died down into coals. He had also set out plates of pickled coleslaw, pickled red and green tomatoes, and pickled cucumbers, as well as plenty of vodka. Soon we were all gathered around the table eating as I answered a barrage of questions from the curious women. How big was my apartment in New York? Were there really a lot of cockroaches? What about AIDS?

The conversation lightened up a bit as the toasts grew closer and closer together, and we emptied the shot glasses for each one. Boris served the sizzling chunks of meat onto a platter in an endless supply. Lightheaded and laughing, we devoured the food with our fingers. It was a picnic. We tore clumps of coleslaw from the watery mass with thumb and forefinger and dropped them into our mouths from above.

At 5:30 P.M. one of the women excused herself. She had to pick up her little boy at kindergarten. At 6:30 P.M. the party disbanded and we all returned to our families.

On another occasion I arrived even earlier, around 11:00 A.M., and two Armenian friends of Boris showed up shortly after me to get the party rolling. They had flown in from the south for a few days and were using the studio as a sort of depot, so they threw the party. From their airline bags they produced bottle after bottle of cognac, each one neatly wrapped in newspaper and then disguised with numerous layers of Armenian flatbread. They ripped the bread off the bottles and set it on the table to be eaten with goat cheese, thin slices of raw peppered beef, and links of lamb sausage. The bread was supple and had taken on the form of the bottle, so the many unfolding layers around a hollow core at first looked like a bird's or wasp's nest. The food merely punctuated the flowing stream of toasts and amber cognac.

An hour later it was lunchtime, 12:30. Another artist friend of Boris—a married man—showed up with his girlfriend, and the party continued. The lovers sat close and kissed between sips of cognac, which they drank with arms looped together. Meanwhile the Armenians were testing me to see if I would change money with them, or take their money and buy them ten cartons of American cigarettes at the dollar store. Boris was trying to get them to knock it off, and I was pretending not to understand exactly what they wanted. The bottles of cognac were enough of a clue that they were speculators on the make.

The painter disentangled himself from his girlfriend long enough to discuss his life with me. He wanted to impress on me the positive aspects of the Soviet system and the Union of Artists. "In the Soviet Union there are eighteen thousand painters in the union. They are officially recognized and make their living from art. There are five thousand in Moscow, three thousand or so in Leningrad, two thousand in Kiev. Other smaller cities and towns have anywhere from a dozen to one hundred and fifty union artists. These are all people whose art is purchased by the government for schools, libraries, and other public buildings." He clearly felt these numbers were impressive.

I said that in New York City alone there were probably fifty thousand people who called themselves artists. But only a small fraction of those made a living from sales of their artwork. In America it's the marketplace and not the government that decides who will make a living from art and who will work at other jobs.

"I do not paint what I want," he said, "but I am able to live as a painter, and that is what is important to me. What I like is the plasticity, the light, the colors in a painting, so it doesn't matter what I happen to be depicting." Not ideology, but economics determined his official status.

He claimed that he could not paint as he pleased and make a living, but he could have pursued a double life, painting official commissions and making time for his own work. This, however, would entail rejection by Union of Artists juries. He would be forced to find foreign outlets and alternative galleries for his work. When I mentioned the Belyaevo Gallery to Boris and his friend, they quickly changed the subject. It was a separate realm they did not wish to enter.

When I asked about *perestroika*, he applied it to the structure of the union rather than to the possibility of free expression. His thoughts were geared to the bureaucratic battle. "I am doubtful that any change can really be accomplished in such a cutthroat situation as the union. There is so much badmouthing of competitors and self-promotion in order to get work. Among the administrators there is greed in allocating funds which are meant for all of us. I'm hopeful but not optimistic that *perestroika* can correct these problems, which are mainly in human psychology."

As the afternoon was winding down Boris and his painter friend asked me if I had met any Russian women. Did I like Russian women? Would I like them to introduce me to one? This offer seemed a little excessive, given that I had said yes enthusiastically to the first two questions. But thinking I had better not be an ingrate, and not knowing what I was getting into, I said, "Of course."

When I visited Boris the next time a young woman was with him in the studio. It was about 2:00 P.M., and he was setting out some lunch. I joined him for some sweetened tea with which he offered me sour farmer's cheese as a wonderful counterpoint. The young woman was pouting and rather listless. She sipped flat champagne dispensed from a nearly empty bottle. She was not unattractive but not pretty. She wore a good deal of makeup and her hair was almost punk. It shot up in big arcs. She asked me to drink champagne with her so she would not be the only one.

"Do you like Russian women?" she asked in faltering English with a heavy accent.

"Yes, of course."

"Which do you like better, Russian women or American women?"

Fearing where this line of questioning was leading, I started to blunder. "Well . . . it's hard to say . . ."

"Do you like me?" She had confirmed my fears. No choice but to go with the flow—for about five seconds.

"Yes, you're very nice."

"You are very nice, too. Do you want to come to my house?" I tried to look away as I said no. I had already met my share of truly beautiful Russian women and she was not one of them. Besides, she was so direct and so blunt, I suspected this just might be her profession, in which case I certainly was not interested. If I had been, the thought of incurring any debts, public or private, that would have to be paid in illegal hard currency would quickly have dampened my ardor. I trusted Boris implicitly, but she might be a provocation waiting to happen. She looked very offended.

"Did you understand the question?"

"Yes," I said. Boris had been busying himself in the next room during most of this conversation, and his English was even worse than hers. So when he returned he asked me if I wanted to leave with her. He smiled broadly, closing one hand down on top of the other, in case I had missed it in Russian.

"I already asked him, he said no," she interjected, annoyed.

"He's an American, what can you do?" He looked at her almost apologetically.

"How much money do you have in your pocket. One hundred dollars?" she asked.

I did not bother to answer. I was feeling rather uncomfortable at this point, as she was at least putting on a good show of being offended.

"The word in English is *to fuck*, isn't that right?" she said. I assured her the pronunciation was just fine. "What is wrong, you don't like me?"

"No, you're very nice, that's not it."

"My husband is at work, if that's what you're worried about."

"Well, not really, it's just not a good idea. I'm American, you're Russian. I have to be careful and so do you."

"So what if we are of different nationalities?"

"No, that's not it."

"I know, you're afraid of AIDS. I assure you I won't give it to you."

"No, no."

"Well, good-bye then," she said. "It's a pity, you are very nice."

I made my exit and Boris did not seem too upset that I had turned down his hospitality.

Boris and his friends seem to have found a comfortable niche in the system. They would like larger studios, but they are not stuggling economically. Boris acknowledged that there are privileged artists who live opulently because they have connections in high places. But he did not begrudge them their commissions and large studios. "They must have talent as well as connections," he reasoned, "or they would not continue to get work." Boris's painter friend had been more critical of the union situation, but was also fairly contented with his standard of living.

If Boris and his friends seem complacent it is because they are products of the system in which they live. It is a system that turns artists into government functionaries and does not require from them any exceptional drive or inspiration. They turn in their own work on time and ask only that no one question how they got it done in the privacy of the studio.

One evening I visited the studio of an obviously well-connected sculptor, and I saw that his life was more of a struggle than Boris's in some ways and less in others. He had more studio space and comforts than Boris or any other artist I met, but he had to work hard to sustain this life-style.

With an introduction to the sculptor's son from a Russian friend, I arrived one evening when the sculptor was out. I entered the studio through the garage, where a 1935 Mercedes was under perpetual repair and one of the sculptor's assistants was polishing a bronze bust of Lenin. In the main studio the sculptor's son and two more assistants were hammering and welding sheets of copper into a huge relief sculpture. This was the second in the edition, so I could see a completed one on the wall. The familiar trio of overlapping profiles of Lenin, Marx, and Engels stood out in high relief, each face about six feet tall. This studio looked more like a small factory. Large shelves going up to the ceilings were cluttered with plaster sculptures, often several versions of a single idea that had been submitted in competitions for monuments. One figure group was of Red Army cavalry in the uniforms of the revolution charging forward with swords drawn. The sculptor's son led me to a corner of the large room where he was working on his own sculptures. They were mostly elongated figures that looked as if they might belong in an Italian Mannerist drawing. The son seemed to be searching for an expressive alternative to strict realism, but without making a violent break from his academic training. He had finished the six-year course at the Strogonovsky Art Institute in Moscow a few years earlier, and was working out of his father's studio.

"I haven't joined the union yet. I'm putting it off because the paperwork involved is so daunting. I have a job in the *kombinat*, the government sculpture factory, so there's no rush."

Most artists are in a hurry to join the union when they get out of school so they get on the list for a studio. But the sculptor's son probably had more space here in his father's studio than the union would offer him fresh out of school.

"What was the institute like?" I asked. "Can you describe the teaching philosophy?"

"The philosophy, of course, was Socialist Realism."

"Yes, but that mostly prescribes the content of the work, doesn't it? What about the formal approach? Aren't there some stylistic options within realism?"

"I will tell you what the options are as we used to describe them in school. Suppose the task is to sculpt a war hero who has only one eye and only a stump just below the knee of his right leg. Romanticism says you make him look handsome and robust. Realism says you sculpt him just as he is with all his defects. Socialist Realism means you sculpt a man kneeling on his right leg and squinting with one eye as he aims his bow and arrow into the distance."

We laughed and then moved into the kitchen adjacent to the studio. We sat down at a large wooden table in front of the fireplace. "When a young person in America decides to be an artist," I said, "the question of economic survival looms very large."

"It's the same here," he said. "I would like to pursue my own ideas in sculpture, but who will buy such work? The Soviet public doesn't know what art is, much less collect it. So if you want to survive you have to compete for public commissions, and you have to work your connections. Sure, there is a system where work is disbursed every month at the factory. And the government is a huge consumer of art. But more often than not, a sculptor gets a commission because he knows someone at an institution who tells him they are planning to put a sculpture on the grounds. The sculptor then goes to the factory, tells them about the commission, and gets himself selected for the job. If it's a big job and the materials are scarce, the sculptor may clinch the deal by locating the materials himself through contacts in the construction industry."

His father was obviously doing well. Attached to this huge studio and cozy kitchen were a changing room, a swimming pool, and a sauna. I was given a tour of the cluster of wooden rooms. The pool was only long enough to swim a few strokes, but for cooling off after a sauna it was spacious. The only light came from the bulbs behind a stained-glass sunburst window in one of the walls, which filled the room with a soft orange glow.

In the Soviet Union money is not enough to buy such luxuries. One can't simply call the contractor. It was clear that the sculptor and his son had designed and built this place for themselves, and, of course, had located the materials.

If Boris exemplified the socialist guarantee of a median existence, this sculptor confirmed that a combination of social connections and individual initiative will produce an elite stratum in any society. His son is at a crossroads. He could easily enter the highest echelons of the system, but following his own ideas might put him at its farthest fringes. Like Chuikov when he was young, this son is reluctant to walk in his father's footsteps. Chuikov's daughter is also studying to be a painter. She has chosen the school she says has less prestige but gives her more freedom in her work. The work of this generation will need a new Soviet audience, an informed public that collects contemporary art. *Perestroika* has made contemporary art more available to the public, and this is perhaps a beginning. If *perestroika* is a sign at the crossroads, one wonders how many generations it will take to reach its promised land.

Taking leave of all the people who had been so hospitable, each in his or her own fashion, was harder than I expected. I packed my bags guiltily during our last three days. The warm weather, which had been like a gift to us during most of our stay, had suddenly ended. I felt like a thief sneaking out of Moscow just before the long winter. I felt guilty for the exuberance, the joy welling up in me upon leaving this difficult place for the conveniences of home. It was hard to leave my friends, and I had to take comfort in the fact that I would always know where to find them.

A Visit to Proletarsky Trud

After two months of waiting, Gosteleradio announced at 3:00 P.M. on Monday afternoon that, yes, we would be allowed to visit a factory. They "thought" it produced artificial leather. There was no further information, except that the factory was in Leningrad and we could only film on Thursday, since Wednesday was a holiday, Constitution Day.

We tumbled groggily off the night train in Leningrad at 7:30 A.M. on a chilly Tuesday morning and climbed into the Intourist bus for the old Yeuropeiskaya (European) Hotel. Centrally located off Nevsky Prospekt, the Fifth Avenue of Leningrad, the Yeuropeiskaya has the shabby charm of prewar Leningrad, with dark wood, faded carpets, and wide staircases. We could not have our room until noon, but the receptionist gave us a place to park our things in until then. With seven of us in an eight-by-ten-foot room, no one rushed to take a shower. Katie, Ari, and I left to get breakfast, before nine when we could make calls. The camera crew got to take showers.

The hotel buffet breakfast was a treat, and of particular importance to me, since I missed a number of meals over the next two days. For three dollars we ate our fill of hard-boiled eggs, porridge, farmer cheese pancakes, and sweet rolls, in addition to cold salads, cheeses, luncheon meats, and sausage. The best thing, however, was the coffee—real strong black coffee in normal-sized coffee cups, not the demitasse cups we found everywhere else.

After breakfast I was amazed to find I could dial Moscow directly on the rotary phone in the room and was delighted to reach Gosteleradio. Vadim told me to call the Leningrad office of Gosteleradio after noon. Perhaps we would get to see the factory before we filmed there, but we wouldn't know for three hours. We headed out to see Nevsky Prospekt.

Even in the rain the broad avenue was filled with people shopping in the food and department stores. It was the only street we saw on our visit, including Moscow, that had window displays that attempted to equal a Western city. Our first stop was a bookstore with ornate dark wood shelves and paneling. Upstairs in the poster room we updated our collection of brightly colored Soviet political posters, which now had the new themes of *perestroika* and *khozraschet* (self-accounting), the system where factories are now responsible for their own profits and losses. The promotion and spread of *khozraschet* is a blow to the power of central planning.

We continued on toward the river and found an art atelier. The studio had only a curtain in the window and a narrow doorway; in a small front room were a few simple watercolors. I walked around a corner and found another room with a large macramé wall hanging and glass display counters with attractive abstract jewelry. Ari, bored with the jewelry, walked off down a short flight of stairs. He called to us, "Hurry up and come look!" We were pleasantly surprised to find a long, high-ceilinged gallery hung from floor to ceiling with paintings by talented local artists. There were oils, watercolors, and lithographs in all sizes and styles. The prices were reasonable, from twenty to five hundred rubles ($35 to $800), but we left without buying anything after reminding each other that we did not want to go through the trouble of trying to get permits to take the artwork out of the country.

As soon as we got back to the hotel at twelve-thirty, I called Elena, our local contact for Gosteleradio. She had been trying to reach me because she had spoken to the plant manager and he was willing to meet with us that afternoon to discuss the arrangements for filming on Thursday. Since she had not been able to reach me, she had told him we would not be coming today. Everyone at the factory was leaving early because of the holiday on Wednesday. She was afraid we had missed our chance to see him. I implored her to call him back; without an advance visit to ask some probing questions the filming would only be a superficial look at the plant machinery and stereotyped answers. Since we had to catch a 12:45

P.M. train on Thursday, we would only have a couple of hours at the plant.

She called back five minutes later and told me she would pick me up in front of the hotel in five minutes. If we hurried, the plant manager would give us half an hour before he had to leave. I washed my face, tried to paint some color into my cheeks, and ran down the long hallways to meet her. We had been working to set up this meeting for more than two months, but nothing had been settled until this moment. Again, it was what the Russians, smiling, called *normalno*—"normal procedure" or "no problem"—but every Russian knows the word has taken on an ironic usage to convey the real confusion and discord that prevails beneath the exterior of order.

Elena greeted me with a bemused smile and ushered me into the backseat of the Gosteleradio van. She was in her early thirties, petite and pretty, dressed casually in slacks, with minimal makeup. She had not heard of the plant before this morning and knew nothing about it other than its address on Flower Street, an unlikely name for an industrial district.

The plant turned out to be in a working-class, industrial area that had developed along the railroad lines at the turn of the century. We passed a number of old brick factory buildings as we bounced along the narrow cobblestone streets.

We arrived in front of what appeared to be a five-story office building with ornate nineteenth-century window dressing. We walked through two sets of double glass doors into the main lobby. A large plaque proclaimed the name of the factory in traditional Russian script: THE PROLETARSKY TRUD [Proletarian Work] FACTORY FOR ARTIFICIAL LEATHER. Two older women in blue workers' coats hovered around a glass-enclosed receptionist's desk. They ushered us through a turnstile and up to the director's office on the second floor. After passing through a foyer with a secretary seated at a desk, we went through two sets of wooden doors, typical of the head administrator's office in other office buildings, either to keep in the heat or keep eavesdroppers away from the director's office.

We squeezed through the door into the director's office. My first impression was of a big, airy, red room. I later realized this was because, in addition to red curtains on all the windows of this corner office and red upholstery on all the chairs along a long conference table, one wall was filled by charts of plant statistics and the factory's plan on a red cloth background.

A tall, slender, youthful-looking man in his late forties greeted us and introduced himself as the plant director, Boris Aleksandrovich Pimenov. His lank brown hair was parted on the side and fell across his high forehead. He had high cheekbones and a wide smile that flashed a couple of gold teeth. He introduced us to a pretty, buxom woman with a magnificent bleached-blond chignon hairdo. She was the assistant director, Zinaida Georgiovna. We were shown to the far end of the conference table, which was set up with bottles of Pepsi, mineral water, and coffee cups. We arranged ourselves across the table from each other and Boris Aleksandrovich insisted on pouring us coffee.

Elena and I both perched nervously on our chairs, ready to ask all the questions we had prepared as advance work for the film crew. We expected to be rushed through a quick tour of the plant. Instead, Boris Aleksandrovich made sure we were comfortable and then launched into an introductory speech, explaining his intention "to be open and honest and show you anything you are interested in seeing." We smiled and listened.

"The Flower Street facility includes the original red-brick factory buildings, which are built around an interior courtyard, and a separate, newer building on the main street, which houses one production line and most of the workers' services. The original buildings are more than one hundred years old," he explained. "There are four production lines making artificial leather, synthetic chamois, and oilcloth. We have two thousand workers and our annual sales are one hundred million rubles [$160 million]."

At that point he looked at me and said, "You know, I want you to believe that what I am telling you is true and that this is a real factory." He explained that a group of American women had visited the factory and had been very friendly. Once they returned to America, they wrote him a letter saying that they did not believe the things they had been told; they had been shown a model factory that was not typical of true conditions in the Soviet Union. He was very hurt by this. Then he told me of a group of American teenagers who had visited the Soviet Union and announced their view that "the Russians are bears."

Boris Aleksandrovich explained that he was very supportive of the Soviet government because he had been orphaned in the war and had been raised by the state. "They always pulled me up by my bootstraps. They never let me be crushed," he said. He had been trained as an engineer and spent a number of years as a party official between various factory jobs.

He had been the director for only a few years, but Zinaida Georgiovna had worked in the factory for thirty-five years. She was now fifty and had started out when she was fifteen; her father had died, her mother was ill, and she had to have work. She convinced the plant manager to overlook the fact that she was not yet the legal age of sixteen, and he hired her. She requested work in one of the most difficult areas in the plant, where the cloth was coated with a protective film. Zinaida was a hard worker, and when her supervisor retired she was promoted to his job. She worked her way up to assistant plant manager, but had declined the offer to be the plant director. She was content to be responsible for all the social issues related to the plant and wanted to enjoy being a grandmother without the added headaches of being plant manager.

I tried to reassure Boris Aleksandrovich that I had a more open-minded and informed perspective on the Soviet Union than his prior guests. I told him that I had lived in Moscow for two years and attended a Soviet school. After studying the Soviet economy in college, I had finally understood the basic structure of the Soviet command economy and the problems it engendered. I admitted that my experience with the problems of the Soviet economy had led me to try to understand what made the American economy so successful and led to my career in business. I did not tell him, however, my favorite story, from our first visit to the Soviet Union, about the time we visited a cognac factory in Georgia and saw one after another of the bottles break on the conveyor belt as they were being capped. I did not tell him that in job interviews I used the stories of Soviet inefficiency to explain my interest in American business and why I had gone from being a Russian Studies major in college to a project engineer automating a computer assembly line.

I made it clear to Boris Aleksandrovich that I appreciated the opportunity to be a guest in his plant. "I am here to understand your job as a plant manager in the Soviet Union during *perestroika* and the complexities of operating a plant in this environment. I want to compare it to my experience working in American plants," I told him. Like Gorbachev, Boris Aleksandrovich was willing to admit that "the reforms had to take place because everyone had become complacent and the resulting problems are deep-rooted." I found that many of the problems of encouraging worker participation and developing incentives are similar to those encountered in American factories.

Over the course of the next few hours we became friends, giving each other examples of problems and solutions we encountered in factory management. We easily found a common language of management problems—how to motivate workers, how to develop leadership attuned to changing times, how to cut costs and make a profit, how to protect the environment.

The plant was profitable and had gradually added a number of services for the two thousand workers, the majority of whom were women. There were now twenty-six services provided by a number of organizations under contract to the plant. Their goal was to save time and give the workers more leisure with their families. They included:

Use of the telephone, along with those rare items, telephone directories for businesses and public organizations.

Repairs of clocks, photographic equipment, and household appliances.

Assistance in finding house-cleaning help.

An in-house hairdresser.

Masseuse treatment (with a doctor's prescription).

A tailor who remodels old clothes or sews from a pattern.

Dry cleaning of clothes.

A dry goods grocery with selections that change every few days, as supplies last. (There are also food items on a set list so workers can avoid standing on normal lines.)

A basic pharmacy that provides common remedies.

A mini "department store," run by representatives from the central department store, with top-quality selections of knit clothing from a local factory.

A coffee shop, in a narrow room next to the cafeteria, outfitted with an ornate espresso machine behind a wooden bar. Workers stood at a counter along the wall to drink their coffee. The shop was called Minutka ("a minute"), since it was used at break time for a quick cup of coffee or tea.

A small shop that sells fresh meat and prepared foods.

A buffet for serving free, government-required daily milk allotments given to workers to maintain their health on the job.

The main cafeteria, which serves hot meals to all shifts.

Eyeglasses are available at low cost.
A nearby polyclinic exclusively for the plant.

The little shops and buffets were tucked into rooms in both the main building and the new one. They were usually ten-by-twelve-foot rooms that had been allocated for their function and were simply equipped.

Between the two buildings was a small park with a statue of Lenin at the center. When we walked between the two buildings, I commented that the park was a nice touch amid the industrial buildings. Zinaida Georgiovna explained that this statue had been built because Lenin was the honorary director of the plant—at the time of the revolution the plant had been without a director and the workers asked Lenin to be the director. He had agreed, and had remained an honorary director.

We walked into the newer building, which was an industrial structure with bands of factory windows. On the first floor, a reception room, with a long counter cutting it in half, was comfortably furnished with wall-to-wall carpeting, curtains, and a sign on the wall listing the services the factory offered. This was where employees could use the telephone and drop off laundry.

We walked in as the bimonthly visit of the optometrist was in progress. The director noticed frames for eyeglasses that he liked and asked the attendant to order a pair for him. He proudly pointed out that eyeglasses only cost the employees three to seven rubles (about $5 to $11). I told them that I had paid more than one hundred dollars for my current pair of glasses and that was average for somewhat fashionable frames plus lenses. Boris and Zinaida were appalled, but by now we were good enough friends to agree that pricing and income were very different in both countries and it was hard to compare.

We moved on down a hallway that had all the service organizations listed on the wall to a long room decorated with paintings of fruits and vegetables. Along the counter were glass cases displaying the goods that could be ordered that day. The selection changed every few days based on what was available. The highlights were mayonnaise, dry baby food, instant coffee, tea, and smoked eel. Boris and I agreed that we did not really like smoked eel, although we did like other smoked fish.

We continued upstairs. On the second floor, next door to an employee locker room, was the hairdresser. A pretty young woman with bleached-blond hair was preparing a permanent on an older worker. The woman had come in early for her second shift job to get her hair done. Zinaida admitted that they would look the other way if a good employee took time off during the day to catch a hairdresser appointment. "It helps morale and the women will work harder to make up the time," she commented.

On the next floor were the masseuse, the mini department store, and the dressmaker. The masseuse had a long, narrow room with just enough space for her charts depicting all the key pressure points on the body and a chair and table for consulting. Her worktable, a flat examining room table, was set behind a curtained partition. Her patients were workers who required therapy and were given a prescription by the polyclinic. She was not trained in acupuncture, but she was trained in both Eastern and Western massage techniques. Since I did not have time for the full treatment, her demonstration was limited to showing me that she always started with the neck and then worked out to the affected areas.

In addition to these on-site services, the plant shared vacation facilities with other organizations and was examining the cost of sponsoring its own recreation area.

At every opportunity over the remainder of the trip I asked people if these extensive services were typical of other factories. Proletarsky Trud is a medium-sized factory with sales of about one hundred million rubles ($160 million) a year, representing a quarter of the output of the Soviet Union's oilcloth and artificial leather industry. While the services were certainly more extensive than in an average factory, the wealthier, larger factories had considerably more benefits to offer their workers. Smaller factories had less. Most enterprises try to provide their workers with extra benefits.

Just being able to order food through the cafeteria makes a large dent in the general waiting time required for daily survival in the Soviet economy. We could understand why productivity might be low if office workers try to do errands at lunch or leave early to stop at a store before it closes in the evening. There are long, time-consuming lines for almost everything except bread. A person has to stand in line ten to twenty hours a week to do the family's shopping through normal channels.

We walked through a heavy metal door into the loud noise of four large presses printing designs on the oilcloth material that would later be cut into tablecloths. The room was clean and well lit from walls of windows on two sides. A slight chemical smell from the inks permeated the room.

Modern, automated Italian equipment had been installed in 1982 and was running smoothly. The Soviet workers had been trained to maintain the equipment, and it required very little attention by the Italian vendor. Engineers visited Italy periodically for training or updates. Zinaida told us that all the printing lines had Italian equipment but that the gluing area, where the cloth was waterproofed, had not been modernized.

Work in this plant is considered difficult, and the environment hostile, as there is a large component of strenuous physical labor involved in many of the jobs. Workers have to contend with the noise of the heavy machinery and work with various chemicals. Workers who reach early retirement age—fifty for women and fifty-five for men—can retire if they have ten years of service in the plant. Normal retirement age for men is sixty, for women fifty-five. Earlier retirement is based on work in a "hazardous" occupation, which includes the Proletarsky Trud factory. The highest worker's pension is 120 rubles ($192) a month.

When I asked if there was an equivalent agency to our OSHA (Occupational Safety and Health Agency) to establish workplace standards, Boris Aleksandrovich said, "Of course, but I have to pull teeth to get the workers to use the required earplugs around the noisy machinery." I laughed and told him American plants often have the same problem.

The afternoon was waning by the time we walked back to Boris Aleksandrovich's office. We were in the middle of a discussion of the complexities of economic restructuring, and he invited us to sit down and poured us Pepsi. Boris Aleksandrovich started with the familiar argument that the Soviet Union had come a long way in its first seventy years. "First, it overcame the problem of educating one hundred and fifty million people. Then, in World War II the country had its major cities destroyed and lost twenty million people." He later showed me the plant memorial to the seventy-five people from the plant killed in the war.

That was hardly the issue. No longer could the horrors of World War II explain the failure of the Soviet economy to keep up with the rest of the developed world. After studying Soviet economics, I had begun to understand the structure that created the economy of lines and shortages that I had experienced while I lived there and had changed little in seventeen years. The existing system, in which prices, suppliers, and customers are all determined by central planning is rigid and inefficient. To cope with it plant managers rely on an informal system of the *tolkachi*, literally "pushers," or expediters, who can find, barter for, and deliver—for a price—critical parts when the state organization cannot. Incentive systems are tied to plant output, not to individual performance, so workers do not have to be productive to reap the basic benefits of wages, bonuses, and social services. Everyone is guaranteed employment, and alcoholism and sluggish performance are not causes for dismissal, particularly since such a large number of one's fellow workers display the same behavior.

To further aggravate the situation in the plant, the poor distribution system and problems at supplier plants lead to shortages and late shipments. Plants get into a cycle of starting the month with limited raw materials and pacing the work to fill time, producing whatever quantities are possible with what is available. By the time sufficient raw materials arrive to fulfill the month's quotas, 75 percent of the output has to be crammed into the last week or two of the month. This has led to major quality problems.

One example of this was television sets. We noticed that in our hotel room there was a sign next to the television set that said, "Dear Guest, Please unplug the TV set when not in the room." The quality of color television sets is so poor that a significant number of sets had exploded, causing fires and numerous deaths. During a five-year period ending in 1985, *Ogonyok* magazine reported that 927 people were killed and 512 seriously injured from exploding television sets that caused 18,400 fires and damages estimated at $24.8 million. "How could it happen that one of the greatest achievements of mankind can be turned into a bloodthirsty enemy of the people?" *Ogonyok* asked. The magazine urged an immediate halt in the production of color television sets, saying, "It would be fair to stop the production lines and confess in public that we do not have sophisticated enough techniques to ensure good quality or safety of television sets."[1] The organization for fire departments has started neighborhood campaigns to educate people to the hazards of leaving television sets plugged in when nobody is at home.

I asked Boris to describe the impact of *perestroika* on the Proletarsky Trud Factory. Boris said, "Under *perestroika* a portion of the

---

1. UPI dispatch from Moscow, Teledeaths 6-21, June 21, 1987.

profits remain with the plant and this facilitates the goals of further deepening *perestroika* and democracy." He said he thought that "the Soviet concept of democracy is probably different from yours since it guarantees jobs, food, housing, and education." He talked about democracy in an economic, not a political sense, meaning "democratic centralism," control through the Central Committee of the Communist party. He was arguing for a planned, central economy versus our market economy.

To me democracy means equality under the law and the ability to vote and participate in my government. If I don't like something I can work to change it. It means freedom of speech, assembly, and a free press. We didn't have time to argue about freedom of the individual and the merits of a market economy over central planning. I was there to listen, not to convince.

I asked Boris how important Gorbachev was, and he replied, "Mikhail Sergeyevich is very charismatic and he provides the impetus for making the reforms happen. It is high time for people to be shaken out of their complacency and become accountable. *Perestroika* is trying to get people to have a sense of ownership and pride in their work, to become the *khozyain*, the host or owner, again."

Later, when we came back to the question of the impact of *perestroika*, Boris Aleksandrovich became impatient. "Why are you Americans so interested in *perestroika*? This is our internal affair. People were getting lazy and complacent and these reforms are necessary. We want everyone to feel he or she is the *khozyain*."

"Americans are fascinated by the Soviet Union as a superpower rival and watch it very carefully. We do not yet understand the objectives of the reforms, and are trying to understand how the Soviet Union can apply what we perceive as free-market economy concepts to a command economy," I explained.

In January 1988 all factories and large and small enterprises had to implement the reforms. The restructuring of the economy began early in 1987 and additional programs are still being announced. In industry the basic principles are to install *khozraschet* ("cost accounting") and "self-financing." Compensation for workers will be tied to performance. This means that enterprises have to account for their costs and use profits to finance internal programs and growth plans. Consequently, the plants must be more conscious of cutting costs to increase profitability. Plants will be given more freedom to establish their own contracts with suppliers and for the sale of their products, once the government's plan has been fulfilled. Plants will be able to retain a portion of their profits for discretionary purposes, including a bonus fund and developing social services for their workers.

Government quality inspections (*gospriyomka*) are attempting to raise quality consciousness and improve the supply of products in the economy. In fact, much of the quality found by the government inspectors was so poor that often they had to reduce their standards to keep product supply flowing. One of our American friends on a tour told of sitting down to breakfast at his hotel and examining a plate full of individual packages of jam. Some were already open. He mentioned this to the Intourist guide, who smiled and replied, "*Gospriyomka*. The government quality inspectors must have gotten there first."

The reforms also encourage the formation of cooperative stores, restaurants, and professional services. Under the new rules individuals or small groups who receive state approval can set up their own businesses. The goal is to build a personal service industry that is now sorely lacking.

Boris Aleksandrovich gave me some examples of how *perestroika* had been implemented in the plant:

"Before, when the plant was fined for the shoddy product it produced, the fine came out of the general profits of the plant. Now it comes out of the bonus pool of the specific section responsible for the problem."

On the bulletin board in the main hallway, there was an announcement that a worker at another factory had been fined twenty-five rubles for poor workmanship. Boris Alexandrovich did not want us to see it and ushered us away.

"Much of the success of our plant is attributed to the use of a brigade system which has been in place since the 1970s. A work group of ten or so workers receives pay based on their final product. With *perestroika*, the *khozraschet* has been applied to the brigade, which is now responsible for assisting in cost cutting." Boris Aleksandrovich showed me an example of this at the printing presses. The brigade had decided that they did not need a separate person to run the forklift for moving the huge rolls of material because the machines were automated and running smoothly; one operator could both monitor the machine and keep it supplied with cloth. This resulted in the reassignment of one person to another position in the plant.

Boris Aleksandrovich said, "It makes my job easier and the workers seem to be accepting it. The plant has spent considerable time training the workers in the new methods and most have responded well. Resisters usually bow to group pressure and learn the new way. This plant is profitable and so there is a pool of profits to use for incentives." The workers we spoke to said their pay had been increased and they liked being able to make more money for better work. In addition, people were cross-trained so that if someone was out sick or on vacation the group could cover with minimal disruption.

Although much of the work was difficult, the numerous services made the plant attractive to workers and turnover was relatively low. Boris Aleksandrovich pointed out that there were always some workers "in transit," working while in school or not sure what they were looking for. This group stayed on the job for one to three years. Once workers had been there for five years they tended to stay permanently.

The new laws will make it easier to fire people for cause. Before, people were employed whether they worked hard or not; now they can be fired for alcoholism or poor work. A plant tribunal reviews all cases. An employee has a "work passport" or record that follows from job to job, so it is in his or her interest to keep a clean record.

The alcohol laws, which drastically reduced the production of vodka and do not permit liquor and wine sales until 2:00 P.M., have significantly reduced drinking on the job and made for safer, more productive factories. The government is scrambling to make up the lost revenues from alcohol sales, estimated at thirteen billion rubles ($20.8 billion dollars) in 1987. The reduction in lost time from accidents and improvements in quality is creating major savings in the industrial sector. Social costs are also lower, the government claims, as death and divorce rates drop with the decrease in drinking.

Ecology is another very visible subject. Proletarsky Trud had one wall filled with photos of the conservation and pollution control measures employed at the plant. Water pollution is a particularly sensitive issue in Leningrad because the drinking water has been tainted from pollution around the city. I noted, "The coffee in Leningrad is much better than in Moscow." Boris Aleksandrovich grinned and proudly told me, "The coffee is better tasting because of the water. The city's water used to be quite famous. The original Smirnoff vodka was produced in Leningrad, and after the revolution the exiled owner of the company imported the city's water to re-create the vodka's taste."

On that note, I pointed to the clock, which was now showing six o'clock. I thanked Boris Aleksandrovich and wished him a happy holiday the next day. We said good-bye, until Thursday.

As things turned out, Intourist mixed up our train reservations and there were not enough seats left on the return train to Moscow at 12:45 on Thursday. We were rescheduled on the 3:00 train, which still gave us an hour or so of daylight to film on the train. More important, for me, we did not have to rush through filming at the plant Thursday morning.

Filming in a factory is very difficult, as I knew from the experience of trying to film marketing tapes for my company. This shoot was no exception: the lighting was poor, the hallways were narrow, and Sherry reminded me that we could not just sit around the table and talk. I had to do my interview while walking through the various service offices and the factory. This resulted in a very frustrating morning for both the plant people and myself. Luckily, having established rapport with Boris Aleksandrovich and Zinaida Georgiovna two days before, we could joke with each other as we reentered a doorway together for the second or third time so the camera crew could get the color right.

During the interview on camera I learned more details of the reforms from Yevgeny Vladimirovich, a slight, pale blond man around forty, who is the plant economist and the official in charge of educating the workers on the reforms. We climbed up and down the narrow stairwells in the plant, with me holding my tape recorder as close as I politely could to Yevgeny's mouth because he spoke in a hoarse whisper.

The economics of the reforms allow the plant to keep 20 percent of its profits. This percentage was now an established figure, while in the past it had not been so and the plant could not plan on it. In 1986 this had amounted to around 3.5 million rubles ($5.4 million): 1 million rubles ($1.6 million) for the fund for payout as bonuses above base salaries, 1.7 million rubles ($2.7 million) for development of the enterprise, 500,000 rubles ($800,000) for housing for workers, and 300,000 rubles ($480,000) for technical research.

The plant is not large enough to fund its own construction unit to build apartments for its two thousand workers, so it pays the central construction organization for a set number of apartments in new construction projects.

The plant reports to the Ministry of Light Industry. It has a five-year plan and does annual updates to the plan. Quotas, prices, suppliers, and customers are established for the five-year period. With *perestroika* the plant has some latitude in developing additional suppliers and can sell production, above the amount it guarantees the state, to customers developed by the plant. It is the beginning of a market response to demand.

For any factory the supply of good quality raw materials is critical to the success of the product it manufactures. The government supply ministry designates specific suppliers whose plans are tied to the product they supply this plant. With the reforms, the plant is able to negotiate for some of its supplies of raw materials directly from other suppliers. As Boris Aleksandrovich explained, "Over the years, the plant has developed good relationships with its suppliers to ensure that the raw materials are of sufficient quality. In general, we do not have supply problems; we negotiate with suppliers to ensure good quality."

The customers for the plant's artificial leather, suede, and plastic-coated materials are other factories that make them into luggage, bedroom slippers, and tablecloths. The plant currently has one major buyer. Now it is also starting to sell directly to large department stores, which leads to feedback from the consumers on the most popular designs.

The patterns and colors are developed by an "artistic" advisory board in the plant. The design department attends annual trade fairs, primarily Soviet, to learn of trends in design.

As we wrapped up the filmed interview, I reminded Boris Aleksandrovich of his impatient response to my interest in the impact of *perestroika*. "Well," I asked, "what would you consider a more appropriate question? What are the three most critical issues facing you as plant manager?"

He smiled. "The most difficult problem is the requirement to keep reducing head count. This is an automated facility and so it's not labor-intensive, but still we must keep finding ways to cut costs. I know most of the workers and have to consider each one's personal situation." He admitted that the Soviets are just starting to deal with the issue of displaced workers. "In general, there is a shortage of workers in the major cities and displaced workers are assisted by their professional trade unions. In addition, I will try to find them work elsewhere.

"Next I worry about keeping my perspective. We must keep up with and anticipate new technology and styles. Also, the social problems are an ongoing issue, and Zinaida Georgiovna spends most of her time addressing them, ensuring that the workers' needs are met as far as housing and rest time, finding vacation locations and sanatoriums.

"And then there is the issue of the caliber of people who work here, their intellectual development, to keep them growing with the changing needs of the plant and the economy.

"Finding competent managers, particularly those with the ability to implement the reforms and function in a restructured economy, is difficult. This plant works with local institutes [the equivalent of two-year colleges in America] to develop students from the beginning of their training. We bring them to work at the plant for practical experience while they're in school and we're generally able to hire them once they graduate."

At that point the crew had to leave to finish some filming of the city. Boris Aleksandrovich exclaimed that he had hoped we would all stay to lunch. Katie, Ari, and I arranged to keep one of the cars. Boris asked Sherry to wait one more minute and Zinaida Georgiovna entered the room with her arms full. She presented us all with oilcloth tablecloths, and added plastic dolls for Katie and me. The crew thanked Boris Aleksandrovich and left.

The rest of us headed to the courtyard and then into a small, low-ceilinged room right off the cafeteria kitchen. This was the equivalent of the plant's executive dining room. Along one wall was a glass cupboard with brightly patterned dishes. A long table was set with a white tablecloth and covered with flowers and appetizers. Boris Aleksandrovich sat us down along one side of the table and insisted that we try all the appetizers. We started with smoked fish and a cucumber-and-tomato salad. Next, a grandmotherly woman appeared through a kitchen doorway with steaming bowls of beef soup. The main course was a meat cutlet with gravy and onions, accompanied by potatoes. As we were finishing and refusing seconds, Boris took tea and coffee orders. Katie commented, appreciatively, that the coffee cups in the cupboard had the pattern for which she had been looking all over. Boris Aleksandrovich insisted that she take a pair with her. No amount of resistance from us would sway him and the cups were carefully wrapped in newspaper. It was time for us to go, but there were still dessert cakes on the table. Earlier, I said poppy seed buns were my husband's favorite; now I, too, had to take a present—half a dozen buns.

We rushed back up to Boris Aleksandrovich's office to get our coats. Now it was time for good-byes. I pulled out a purple Le Clic camera from my company and offered it to Boris Aleksandrovich as my gift to him. I quickly loaded it with film and set him in front of his factory plan to take a picture. He took the camera, handed it to Katie, and put his arm around my shoulders. "Come, be in the picture," he said. Then we all hugged each other; Boris and Zinaida made sure Katie, Ari, and I each got a hug and a kiss on the cheek. As with so many of the people we met on the trip, Zinaida and Boris were now friends and it was hard to pull away and leave them, each of us going back to our normal daily life. I promised to send a copy of the film and to look for American equipment to modernize the plant.

Evelind Meets Limitchiki (Moscow Factory Workers)

One sunny cold afternoon, shortly after we returned from Leningrad, Michael and I went to see Yuri's new apartment. He was building shelves and had asked a couple of young friends to help him. He thought I would enjoy meeting them because they were "real" workers—factory workers—not intellectuals.

Yuri met us at the bus stop and we walked back to the apartment. Along the way he pointed out that he liked the area because it was near one of the many bends of the Moscow River and there was a nice park along the river. As we walked into the complex of apartment buildings the noise of the street receded. All the buildings were five-story *khrushchoby*, a play on the word *trushchoby* ("slums"). The *khrushchoby* were built with poor construction during Khrushchev's time as five-story walk-ups to meet the crushing need for living space. The *khrushchoby* grew around Moscow's outer rim, and in comparison to later apartment buildings with elevators they turned out to be somewhat larger.

It was autumn and most of the leaves had fallen off the trees. Children were playing on swings in one of the small parks formed between the buildings. A child had built a playhouse of boxes around the stoop of Yuri's building, and we climbed over it and up the stairs.

It was a corner apartment with large windows. It had a kitchen, a bathroom with both tub and toilet in the same room (unlike most

Moscow apartments, which have a separate small toilet room), a bedroom, a living room, and a hallway that already had been filled with shelves from floor to ceiling and packed with books and filing cards. The sunshine streaming in warmed the rooms. The apartment had a cheery feeling in spite of the fact that it was cramped.

One of Yuri's friends had already arrived and he greeted us with a shy smile. Sasha is a compact five feet six inches tall, trim, and obviously in good physical condition, with muscles bulging from under his T-shirt. He was in the middle of building a desktop for Yuri. We were all hungry and Yuri went off to make lunch. Sasha wanted us to translate a song he had recorded off the pop music radio station. It turned out to be called "You Are in the Army Now," a World War I and World War II popular song that became an anti-Vietnam war song. He liked the tune, but was not very interested in its politics.

This led to a discussion of mandatory military service in the Soviet Union. Both Sasha and his friend, Igor, had gone to military service after working for a year. They decided to put off applying to a university until they were out of the army. They had both been posted in the Soviet Union and did not know any Afghanistan veterans. They had met Yuri at a seminar for prospective students of psychology.

They did not get into Moscow University, but they got *propiski* ("permits") as *limitchiki* ("temporary workers"), since they were not Moscow residents. Having these permits is the only way they can legally stay in Moscow. Because of its better food and recreation facilities, Moscow attracts far more people than can be housed in the city. Therefore, the government has instituted residency requirements reminiscent of the guest worker system in Europe. As a concession to the shortage of factory labor, workers from outside the Moscow area are hired "over the limit" (hence the name *limitchiki*) and allowed to live in Moscow. After five years, provided they remain employed, they can apply for permanent residence. According to Sasha and Igor, the only other way to get permanent residence sooner is to marry a Muscovite—but she would already have to have sufficient apartment space for her husband. Both Igor and Sasha were continuing to try to get into an institute or technical school so they could live in Moscow as bona fide residents.

Awaiting such a find, or admission to a university, Sasha and Igor live in a dormitory for *limitchiki*, often three people to a room. They share bathrooms and cooking facilities with other boarders in the most basic of living conditions, without a refrigerator unless they get a group together to buy one. They can eat subsidized breakfast and lunch at the plant cafeteria and so they do minimal cooking in the overcrowded dormitory.

Sasha and Igor both agreed that, like guest workers in Europe, the *limitchiki* are treated like "second-class citizens." Sasha, for example, who works in an old factory, said he often felt "like a Jew"—left out of society with little opportunity for advancement, and stuck with the less pleasant jobs; Igor, who is a stone mason, said most of his fellow workers were or had been *limitchiki* and he did not experience any problems. In their personal lives, they admitted they generally stayed together and had few Muscovite friends.

Sasha worked as a grinding machine operator in one of the large automobile assembly plants. He had found the job by chance while waiting to hear from a "post box," the euphemism for an anonymous, military-related job. Sasha's factory sounded like the opposite side of the spectrum from the Leningrad plant I visited. He worked in an old plant that had not been remodeled. Special services for the workers were not nearly as extensive as at Proletarsky Trud. Sasha was hopeful about *perestroika*, which he had learned about through the media, and was interested in reforms just beginning to be implemented in his plant. Thus far, however, he said he had not seen any major changes or felt their benefits.

When pressed about the reforms, Sasha could think of only one example of *gospriyomka*, or quality control, a key element of Gorbachev's program. He told us a sad story that typifies the economic bureaucracy's response to the call for restructuring. In his area of the plant, Sasha explained, he and his fellow grinding machine operators regularly cut new grinding surfaces for their circular machines from large square sheets of abrasive paper, a process that leaves considerable waste in the form of the unused corner pieces. Some bright person had the idea to recut the excess grinding paper corners and make booklets of sandpaper. The plant sold these scrap booklets and made enough money for the revenues to show up in their budget. Then, with the introduction of *gospriyomka*, came government quality control inspectors. They inspected the booklets and complained that the corners were not even. The plant was now responsible for the income from the booklets, so workers cut up fresh sheets to make the booklets meet the quality control criteria and threw the once-recycled scraps away.

Soviet Education: The Michael Plan for Reform

After my wife, Evelind, returned from Leningrad we were invited to the apartment of Jerry and Leona's old friends Pyotr and Natasha to discuss the struggle for reform in Soviet education. Education was also coming under the scrutiny of *glasnost* and *perestroika*. Evelind and I took the metro to Pushkin Square, then waited for Pyotr to fetch us, because nobody had been able to give us detailed instructions for getting to his apartment. The problem resulted from one of Moscow's nicer features as a place to live. The city is criss-crossed by wide avenues heavy with truck, bus, and taxi traffic and lined with five- or six-story buildings. At intervals, however, these canyon walls are pierced by tall arches that lead to a maze of tiny streets lined by much smaller buildings and almost devoid of traffic. The arrangement creates intimate neighborhoods, safe from the bustle of the city beyond the protective walls of buildings lining the big avenues.

Pyotr appeared like a guardian angel, bundled against the cold, his hair disheveled by the wind and his gray-streaked beard tucked protectively into his scarf. He led us into the maze of apartment houses, and we wound our way into the neighborhood along streets still damp from their nightly cleaning by water trucks.

Finally, Pyotr turned into a dark backyard and entered an unlit door that gave the American urban dweller in us the willies but didn't concern him at all. He banged at a door padded on the outside for soundproofing, and his wife, Natasha, let us into an apartment full of the warm, rich smells of cooking and baking. I had never met them before but they were delighted to see Evelind for the first time in almost twenty years. We hugged and kissed in a tiny foyer crowded with hanging coats and sweaters, piles of boots, skates, and a boy's bike. Just above the level of the top of the door a makeshift shelf ran around the foyer's three walls, loaded to the ceiling with boxes, books, and more boots. Ahead was a tiny but brightly lit and well-organized kitchen in which every available bit of counter space was covered with serving dishes heaped with pickles and salads ready for the table. We were ushered into a room where any academic would feel at home. Bookshelves lined two walls, floor to ceiling, and another, freestanding, bookcase partially divided the room. The shelves were crammed with books ranging from George McDonald Fraser's comic, romantic *Flashman* to the *Oxford Dictionary of the Christian Church*. Separated by the freestanding bookcase stood two cluttered desks. Over Pyotr's hung a collection of church icons, while over Natasha's hung a single, simple, Japanese print of two courtesans sheltered from a light rain under an umbrella. Against the fourth wall stood Natasha's piano, a well-used black upright with brass holders for candles that once lit the sheet music.

The room spoke about its inhabitants. Pyotr is a deeply spiritual man with the look of a benign monk; he has dark, deep eyes and a soft, melodious voice. As his book collection indicated, he is interested in everything—politics, culture, philosophy, and education. He is a classic Russian intellectual, widely read and informed on social and political issues. He has the right background and personality for his job of producing new textbooks for primary and secondary schools. He works at the ministry that prepares and publishes all the textbooks used in the Soviet Union. His office, he explained, does not write textbooks, but does textbook-related research.

Pyotr is also a man with deeply held beliefs, a strong personal vision of right and wrong, of what human relations ought to be, of how society ought to function. As part of *glasnost* he is trying to start a new magazine to discuss educational reform. Like many Russians, Pyotr is not a liberal and has no time for arguments about a relativistic interaction of ideas. At issue for him is not whether there are truths that ought to be taught and enforced but rather simply whose truths should be taught. For example, in a later discussion, Pyotr admitted to finding our conception of free speech unacceptable. "How is it possible to think of free speech as giving the right to say or publish pornographic things my son might hear or see?" he wanted to know.

"How are we to distinguish between pornography and not pornography?" I countered. "And if we are to forbid pornographic utterances, what is to keep others from banning 'pornographic' political utterances, and so on?"

"Come on, Michael," he said, "you and I know what is acceptable and should be permitted."

We were waiting for Tolya, a young friend of Pyotr, active in the educational reform movement, the effort on the part of Soviet teachers and some government officials to shift the emphasis in education from rote memorization to critical thinking and analysis. Evelind and Natasha disappeared into the kitchen to arrange dinner while Pyotr drew me aside to talk. He went to the bookcase and pulled out a slim red volume.

"This is our annual," he said. "Each year we focus on a different topic; this year the subject is the evaluation of textbooks. I have two pieces in the collection. The first is about why it is important to study the history of textbooks and what their development can teach us, and the second is an annotated bibliography of books about textbook evaluation." As he flipped through the bibliography, I noticed that many of the citations were in English and stopped him to look at them. "Are these American?" I asked.

"Oh yes," Pyotr answered, "it is an international bibliography with entries from countries around the world, including all the Western powers."

"But are they available here?" I asked.

"Many of them are," he said. "You see these letters here at the end of each citation? They are the initials of different libraries and institutes in the Soviet Union which have this book in their collection. Of course, some are not available, so I've also given the initials of, for example, several American libraries which have the book if it's an American book."

"But how could you do that," I wanted to know, "and how were you able to write an annotation for a book that isn't available in the Soviet Union?"

"Easy," said Pyotr, smiling. "I found them by using the Union Catalog and the Library of Congress computerized bibliographic search system. After that, I ordered them from interlibrary loan at Lenin Library."

"Interlibrary loan?" I asked incredulously.

"Sure," he said. "I put in the request and the book comes from the United States in four to six weeks."

I couldn't believe it. At Rutgers it often takes me three to four weeks to get books on interlibrary loan from other American libraries—and I'd never even considered the possibility of requesting a book from the Soviet Union. For Pyotr, whose reading ability in English was even better than his spoken English, the Library of Congress was a regular source.

There was a burst of greetings from the foyer and a thin young man of medium height walked into the living room. He had a narrow, sharp face with a hatchet nose and pointed chin, and wore a gray-and-white zippered cardigan done up to the neck. He paused in the doorway and nodded briefly as Pyotr made the introduction. Tolya, he explained, is a physics teacher at a Moscow high school with double sessions because of overcrowding. I took Tolya's reticence for shyness, but soon learned otherwise. Tolya does not broadcast his feelings. He is a watcher; his gray eyes never leave yours while you talk, but his face is expressionless. Only when agitated by the need for educational reform does he come alive, leaning forward, jabbing with his cigarette or, if he's between cigarettes, with thin, nicotine-stained fingers. He is concerned with his students' apathy and the suppression of their natural curiosity by the prevailing educational system.

Natasha came in and broke up our conversation. She sat Evelind and me on a couch pushed up against one of the book-lined walls and pressed Tolya into helping her set up a folding wooden table in front of us. On it she, Pyotr, and Anton, their shy, beautiful son, set dishes of cabbage pickled in beet juice, sea kelp and egg salad, smoked fish, a potted meat, a basket of bread, and a plate of crackers, while Tolya looked on with a happy smile. When we were all settled, Evelind produced a liter of pepper vodka and announced that it had been prescribed by higher authorities as the official Soviet cure for her sore throat and cold. Everyone pronounced themselves willing to share in her cure.

In the confusion of passing plates, Pyotr asked me what I did. I said I was a college professor of politics, and that I was currently working on a textbook project. For a decade after the war in Vietnam, Americans tried to forget, but today we have an entire generation of high school and college students who have no memories of the war. They are fascinated by it because of its impact on all aspects of our lives. For the last two years, a group of colleagues at Rutgers and I have been exploring how to teach the legacy of Vietnam to our students, how to help them put Vietnam in the context of American history, and how to sort out the complex and contradictory messages they get about the war from Hollywood, television, politicians, and the media. Rather than attempting to give a single interpretation of the war, we want to expose them to a variety of viewpoints. We are not only talking about the war itself but the continuing conflict over the interpretations and lessons of the war. The role of the press and the treatment of Vietnam veterans are only two examples of such issues.

Pyotr was fascinated that as private citizens we could create a textbook, especially one that could offer conflicting views on such a critical political event. After dinner Pyotr asked me if I could send him some materials on our project. I had in Moscow a copy of a memo I had sent to Vietnam project members and gave it to him the next day. A week later Pyotr told me that he had included some of our ideas in a memo he had written suggesting the development of more "open" textbooks in the Soviet Union, which would challenge students to pursue their studies beyond the confines of the text and classroom.

"Who writes textbooks?" Pyotr wanted to know. "Who controls what goes in them? How do they get adopted? How can you prepare a text on such a specialized subject? How will schools fit it into the curriculum?" The more questions Tolya and Pyotr asked, the more clear it was that we came at education from radically different perspectives and sets of expectations. They, for example, found it inconceivable that something as important as the preparation of textbooks should be left in private hands. They found it hard to believe that the federal Department of Education exercised no control over textbooks or curriculum in American schools. Tolya was amazed. We compared our school systems and defined a common ground of shared concerns, which mirrored each other—we were each other's reverse images. The Soviet system is a highly centralized, standardized system in which each student gets the education the state believes he should have. The United States has a highly decentralized, unstandardized system of education that stresses local initiatives and the interests of the individual community.

Tolya, who despite his interest in Soviet education knew little about our system, led the way. "How does American education work?" he wanted to know. "What do you value most?"

"Our values," I responded, "reflect our historical legacy. Our country began from tiny communities of fiercely independent people who had fled to America to escape the dictates of kings and religious authorities with whom they disagreed. They brought with them a belief in the necessity for each individual to make his own relationship with God, a necessity which required an ability to read the Bible for themselves. So from the start Americans demanded community control over education and stressed the importance of individual self-realization through education. As our country developed, we built a national identity and the federal government replaced local and state government in many areas, but education is one area in which communities and states have resisted federal intervention. In fact, among the most contentious issues in American politics today are questions of the rights and limits of community and family control of the schools. All around the country communities are fighting about prayer in school, which textbooks to use in school and allow in the school library, and whether schools should teach sex education."

"Why do you say that this worries you?" Tolya wanted to know. "It sounds like what many of us would like to see here."

"Well," I said, "there are conflicts between community values and the Constitution. The Constitution mandates a separation of church and state. But in some communities there may be a Christian majority which would like to begin the school day with the Lord's Prayer. That would deeply offend Jewish, Muslim, and Buddhist families. Local control means that the quality of schools will vary tremendously from one community to the next and that it will be impossible for the national government to steer education in a direction beneficial to the country as a whole. The Department of Education is concerned that our students are not receiving enough mathematics and computer education to compete against Japanese students. The Department of Education, however, does not control school curriculums or school budgets. These depend on the community tax base and the willingness of voters to tax themselves to support education."

"What about individual students?" asked Tolya. "What is school like for them?"

"Again," I said, "we're caught in a dilemma. Historically, education's function is to help the individual discover his own talents. Now, many Americans are worried that we've pushed this too far, that we have a generation of students full of opinions but unable to read, write, and figure. They are completely ignorant of even the basic facts of their own history, to say nothing of that of the rest of the world."

Pyotr and Tolya looked at each other and laughed. "It's as if all your problems are our strengths," Tolya said, "and our problems are your strengths."

"How's that?" I asked. Then I raised the question of Stalin's purges and the failure of Soviet textbooks to mention them.

"You Americans are hung up on the issue of Stalin," replied Tolya. "The real problems of Soviet education go much deeper than that and affect physics as much as history. The real problem is state control of students' thinking and the stifling of individual expression, which is necessary for real education.

"The Soviet Union, too, began as a patchwork of communities, but the state has attempted to eliminate the distinctions. We have a national educational system in which the state determines what will be taught and how. It writes the textbooks, it defines the curriculum, and until very recently it has denied the legitimacy of any challenges to its control of education. The state was able to build a strong national identity and eliminate illiteracy very quickly after the revolution. Unlike you, we have a highly centralized educational system which offers every Russian child exactly the same education, at least in principle."

"In principle?" I asked.

"Yes, in principle," Tolya said, "because in fact there are great differences among schools. Big city elementary and secondary schools, Moscow or Leningrad schools, are much better than rural schools. They get the good teachers and new equipment. And even in Moscow there are huge differences among ordinary schools and the special schools and institutes. The ordinary or normal schools are overcrowded. Special schools and institutes teach foreign languages such as English and offer select courses in science, mathematics, and the arts. Admission to these schools is controlled by competitive examinations and political clout. It often requires some kind of party connection or pull to get your kids into one of the special schools. And it really makes a difference, since most normal schools are so crowded they are on double sessions, morning and afternoon—and they don't get the best teachers or the fancy equipment."

Evelind looked up from her salad and smoked fish and said, "I didn't really notice it when I was a kid, but when we went back to my old school, Special School 47, and Michael asked the kids in the class we visited what their fathers did, most were diplomats and government officials."

"What's the system like for the individual student?" I asked.

Tolya made a face. "Our students get a 'fixed menu.' They eat what is put on the table."

"Just like breakfast at the hotel," Evelind said, also making a face.

"We have a textbook for everything," continued Pyotr. "The system is built around students mastering what's in them. Our students are very good at that. They don't argue with the teacher or express their own opinions. But they also don't learn to think innovatively. The system is built on passive not active learning."

"So what is the alternative? What reforms do you see for the future?"

"The initial reform program," interrupted Pyotr, "was just more of the same. With the concern for improving economic productivity, and pressure from the bosses to do something, the Ministry of Education officials proposed adding more labor studies and labor arts to the curriculum [the equivalent of vocational education and shop classes in American schools]. We don't need more good followers; we need workers who can think for themselves and use computers and other modern technology, not welding torches and hammers."

"On the other hand," Tolya went on, "reform-minded teachers want to see education reoriented from molding students to helping them develop who they are. Our students are completely turned off by the current system. All my students are interested in is rock and roll. They're tired of old formulas and stuff that isn't relevant to their lives. School isn't reaching them now and can't achieve the new goals unless there are some big changes."

"But what exactly do you see happening?" I asked.

"First," said Tolya, "we need reforms in the way we teach in the classroom. We need to engage our students directly. We can't be content any longer with passive learning because it's not working. Second, we have to improve our teaching materials, our textbooks. Too many of them are false. They ignore Stalin's atrocities, ignore many important figures in our history, and don't give our students a correct understanding of the rest of the world. They don't introduce students to differing views of issues or alternative ways of solving problems."

"Who's the opposition?" I asked.

"The people you'd expect, the bureaucrats at the Ministry of Education. The reform movement inevitably points its finger at them and lays the blame for our problems at their door. They have completely controlled Soviet education for decades. Any decentralization of the educational system would reduce their power.

"Of course, not all teachers are interested in reform," said Tolya. "In fact, I'd bet a majority of them don't want anything to change. They want to go on doing exactly what they've been doing, because it's easy, because it doesn't require anything of them as teachers. All they have to do is come in and repeat the same stuff, year after year. They're lazy and they don't care."

At this Natasha made a face.

"What do you think your prospects are?" I asked Tolya. He made a face. Pyotr raised an eyebrow quizzically. "It's a very, very exciting time in Soviet education. The ministry has admitted that all is not well. The higher-ups are applying pressure. The press is publishing critical articles. A teachers' organization has been formed to pursue questions of educational reform. But who's to say? We are excited, but we are all scared. Who knows how far this can go? Who knows what will be permitted? Who knows if it will last? And then there are the tougher intellectual problems. Just what do we need? How do we want to reform the educational system?"

I turned to Natasha and asked, "If you don't like something about school, what do you do?"

"If you don't like your child's teacher," she said, "sometimes you can get him moved into a different class, and if you don't like the school, sometimes you can get him moved to a different school, but that's really hard."

As we talked, I realized an interesting opposition was developing between Tolya and Natasha. Both are committed teachers, both are deeply concerned about education, but there the similarities end. Tolya is the young Turk, an impatient, fervent believer in the need for educational reform. He's infuriated by the bureaucratic rigidity of the school system and by the plodding careerism of many teachers and school directors. (In his four-year career he has already changed schools three times and is still dissatisfied.) Natasha has none of Tolya's impatience; she exudes warmth and contentment. Like many American arts teachers, she wishes music and art did not get cut first when there are time or budgetary constraints. But she likes her fellow teachers and the school director, who she feels not only cares about education and the students but has made the school a better place.

It was after midnight and we were all beginning to fade, especially after the cumulative effect of heavy doses of Evelind's pepper vodka cold medicine. As we were collecting ourselves to go, Tolya said, "If you're really interested in educational reform, you ought to speak to my friend Marek. He's a correspondent for the *National Teachers'*

Newspaper and one of his assignments is to cover the activities of the Eureka Clubs."

Pyotr explained that Eureka Clubs were the new national organizations of reform-minded teachers. I accepted gladly, though I wondered out loud whether a correspondent for the official organ of the Ministry of Education would feel comfortable discussing such a sensitive subject with an American visitor. Tolya assured me that Marek would be happy to tell me anything I wanted to know. On that happy note, Evelind and I thanked our hosts and headed back to the Berlin Hotel.

Two days later, thoroughly chilled after a long family picture-taking session in Red Square—and nearly an hour late for our interview with Marek—Evelind and I ran down the street behind GUM, the state department store. We scanned the dozens of tiny signs posted by the doorways we passed, looking for the *National Teachers' Newspaper* offices. It took several trips up and down the block to find it. In the building's drab entryway we spotted two cleaning ladies drinking tea, their birch twig brooms leaning in the corner.

They directed us down a narrow corridor, cluttered with boxes stacked waist high, to a rickety elevator that took us to the third floor. We rushed down the dark hall, peering at the small nameplates until we found Marek's. Responding to our knock, a friendly fellow with unruly brown curls and an easy smile introduced himself as Marek and ushered us into a tiny, overcrowded office. In a space not more than twelve feet by eight feet were three desks, a small table, and a collection of stiff upright and broken-backed easy chairs. Slouched in one of them was Tolya. I apologized profusely for being late, but nobody seemed to notice and Evelind gave me a look that clearly said, "See, I told you people don't get as uptight about punctuality here as you do!"

We settled in with a cup of tea. Marek told me he was a journalist for the *Teachers' Newspaper*, the organ of the Ministry of Education and the Professional Union of Teachers. It covers general educational topics, issues concerning teacher-student relations, new ideas in teaching, and the activities of teachers' organizations. He smiled and said he was not a very senior person at the paper, just a general correspondent.

One junior person to another, I asked Marek why all the excitement about educational reform? Was it rooted in real problems, or just a reflection of the times?

"Both," he said. "If education doesn't reform, it will die. And without *glasnost* reform will be impossible."

"What are the problems?"

"For years the educational system has not served its social function. Students didn't learn anything and the system didn't demand that they learn anything. The day they left school was the day they got their diploma. Kids passed from primary to secondary school, and from there to university without learning anything. The dumbest then seemed to go into the Ministry [of Education] to tell us how to organize the schools. Parents and teachers—and many other people, too, I think—knew how bad things were, but nobody could do or say anything, and the bureaucrats were able to hide the problems with statistics. That has changed now."

"What has caused the change?"

"The people at the top began looking under the statistics and saw that the educational system could not support the reform program for decentralization and individual initiative that they envisioned."

"So the key to educational reform is top-level pressure?" I asked.

"No," replied Marek, "that's only the beginning. The key to successful reform is interest from teachers and parents who have been waiting for years for improvements in the system. The key to releasing that energy for reform has been *glasnost* and its invitation to discussion. That's why I think the Eureka Clubs are so important."

"Tolya mentioned them so casually the other night I simply assumed they were a regular part of the educational apparatus," I said.

Tolya laughed and shook his head. "We invented them, Marek and I, and we have spent years talking about education and educational reform, always trying to figure out a way to improve the system."

"In January 1986," continued Marek, "when an ordinance was passed allowing the formation of social organizations to discuss various issues, we saw an opportunity to tap the energy and interest of teachers, and to come up with innovative ideas for educational reform."

"Didn't this imply a criticism of the system? Wasn't it hard for you in your job to be involved in such a movement?" I asked.

"Not at all. This is precisely what the new thinking is all about. It is about tapping the innovative genius of the Soviet people. All through history we see the importance of individuals giving a creative push for change. We thought of the idea and the name, Eureka Club, right here in this office over a glass of tea. All I did was write a short

article for the newspaper, I think it was in Marc
suggesting such an organization of teachers and e
a good thing. Letters just poured in. At last coun'
382 Eureka Clubs across the country."

"Where's all this going?" I asked.

Again Tolya laughed. Marek said, "I haven't tl.
The whole thing got started overnight. We have no forma.
zation, no plan, and not even plans to have a plan. What's important
about the Eureka Clubs is that they provide an open forum for people
to discuss their needs and their interests and their ideas. And they
provide a way of spreading information, too."

"But this openness doesn't mean important things don't get discussed," added Tolya. "The people who come to Eureka Club meetings are influential—the motivated teachers, school principals, and
specialists from the institutes."

"With this open a structure," I asked, "is it possible to come to a
coherent position and actually influence the direction of educational
reform?"

"I think so," said Tolya. "We have many differences, but all these
people share one common concern—that is, reorienting the educational system toward the individual kid."

"This task isn't new," continued Marek. "It's been around since
the 1920s. There have been a lot of slogans, but nobody ever answered the question of how to do it. This is what we talk about most
at Eureka Club meetings."

"There are two basic positions," said Marek. "There are those
who focus on the content of what is taught and those who focus on
the relationship between student and teacher. The first group says
the textbooks set the learning environment and that until they are
improved the schools cannot be improved.

"People who take the second position think that the student develops through the learning process itself, through the classroom
experience. Right now the classroom is organized very
hierarchically—the teacher has all the authority and tells the students
what to do. There's no discussion. These people argue that if we are
going to move toward democracy, we need to educate democrats by
creating more democratic relationships in the classroom."

"Actually," added Tolya, "this is what concerns both groups. They
just have different views about the best way to get there."

"What are these Eureka Club meetings like?" I asked.

Marek and Tolya looked at each other quizzically. Tolya nodded

Marek shrugged. "Why don't you come see for yourself?" he
asked. "Tomorrow night the Moscow Eureka Club is meeting at six
P.M. to plan a national conference on educational reform."

The next day Pyotr agreed to come to the Eureka Club meeting
with us. By a quarter to six, however, it was clear that Evelind was
too sick with a sore throat to go out, so I left her to sip hot tea in
bed and went to the teachers' meeting alone. As I was putting on my
coat she urged me to eat something, but I declined, thinking I would
be back by 8:00 P.M., and did not want to keep Pyotr waiting. It
was a serious mistake.

I met Pyotr in front of Detski Mir, the huge children's department
store that stands next to KGB headquarters. Together we crossed the
underpass beneath Marksa Prospekt and walked down 25th of October Street toward Red Square, threading our way through the hur-
rying crowd, our coats pulled up to our ears against the wind. At
the offices of the *Teachers' Newspaper* we found Tolya and several
others standing in a group talking. Light from an office spilled into
the hallway, highlighting the gray haze of cigarette smoke, so thick
around their heads it barely moved as they waved their hands in
discussion.

No one paid any attention to my appearance, and Pyotr and I
slipped into corner seats in the meeting room. The room made me
feel right at home. Its high ceilings, beige walls, chipped paint, bat-
tered bookcases, mismatched chairs, and big, cluttered center table
looked like the teachers' room in an older American high school.
Only the portrait of Lenin staring down on us convinced me we were
in Moscow.

Tolya was engaged in three simultaneous conversations. To his left
sat Marek, who nodded a friendly hello before continuing his conversation. At the end of the table sat a silent young woman dressed
entirely in black, wearing huge earrings, who proved to be a tough
debater with an acid wit. Next to her, and facing Marek, sat Ivan,
a tall, handsome young English-language teacher who said little during the meeting but later invited Evelind and me to a wonderful
dinner at his apartment. Beside him sat a severe-looking woman in
a plum-colored suit who spoke to no one; later she harangued us all
about the necessity of a national educational system built on the total
moral development of each individual child. Behind Ivan and the lady
in plum were a tightly packed row of young teachers, all dressed in
sweaters and comfortable pants. Facing them across the room sat a
row of very distinguished-looking gray-haired gentlemen dressed in

suits. Pyotr translated for me and said, "They're from the institutes." It soon became clear that the practicing teachers and the theoreticians of education had different ideas on the subject of reform.

Marek called the meeting to order without ceremony. He announced that the national conference on educational reform scheduled for early November in Kharkhov had received responses from teachers as far away as Sakhalin Island in the Sea of Japan. Tonight's meeting, he said, had to decide how the conference was really going to be organized. A long silence followed during which Pyotr hunched over in his seat and translated quietly into my left ear. There was a lot of body English and gesturing; while I did not get all the words, Pyotr was good at giving me the general line and the fine points when necessary. People shifted uncomfortably in their seats and looked at their notepads. Finally one of the institute gentlemen, a craggy-faced fellow in a tweed suit, said, "I think we must organize the conference around the essential question—'What is knowledge?' Until we have understood that, and understood how the meaning of knowledge has changed today, we will not be able to proceed with a discussion of educational reform."

"And just what will we say about the subject for three days?" asked the woman in black, bringing a laugh all around.

"The issue isn't knowledge, per se," objected a tall, earnest, and uptight-looking young man who stood up. "Knowledge changes constantly. What matters is getting our students to engage knowledge in its historical context—to read the Greek classics in full translation or the original, for example, and enter into the Greek mind, to understand the development of human knowledge by re-creating it. Only this way will they be able to understand the present and the imperatives of future development." (Now such works as Plato's *Republic* are mentioned in textbooks but with a Marxist-Leninist interpretation of class struggle that pits slaves against masters. The full text or even excerpts are still not part of the curriculum.)

"No, you aren't looking deep enough," said a dapper, silver-haired gentleman from one of the institutes, later introduced to me as Boris. "Knowledge comes after. The problem with our educational system is that it is too focused on knowledge and doesn't take the child into account. Children progress through a series of stages in their cognitive development; our job as educators must be to design a curriculum which provides children with educational challenges appropriate to their stage of development, which will help them progress to the next stage."

Pyotr looked at me and asked, "Are you really interested in this?" I assured him I was.

The lady in plum leaned forward, pointing savagely at Boris, and asserted vehemently that he too was all wrong. "It's not a matter of cognitive development alone," she said. "It's not a matter of making children into little thinking machines. Education ought to address the whole child. It should promote the total moral development of a child. It should help each child develop himself fully."

At this the meeting fell apart as declarations and counterdeclarations flew back and forth across the table. None of the speakers could finish their sentences. Marek watched silently with a bemused expression on his face and finally sat down. Pyotr gave up trying to translate. I was amazed.

Here I was, in the offices of the *Teachers' Newspaper*, at a meeting of specialists to plan a major conference on educational reform in the Soviet Union, expecting a carefully orchestrated presentation of views followed by a unanimous vote. Instead, the chairman of the meeting, delegated by the Ministry of Education, sat quietly by while hard things were said about the state of Soviet education. The meeting seemed to be slipping into a shouting match.

"What is going on?" I asked Pyotr.

"The people here represent the different schools of thought on education in the Soviet Union," he said, "and each wants the conference to reflect their views on how education should be conducted."

While trying to keep me abreast of the ongoing battle, Pyotr gave me quick thumbnail sketches of the main schools of Soviet educational thought. As he talked I couldn't help thinking how very far all of them were from my preconceived notions of Soviet thinking on education. I had expected a "fixed menu," as Tolya had put it at dinner a couple of nights earlier, a stultifying conception of education as a mechanical process of stuffing kids full of the things the state thinks they ought to know. The menu for this meeting was strictly à la carte.

First, Pyotr told me, there are the "cognitive development" followers of Vasily V. Davidov, a psychologist, represented here by the silver-haired Boris. They believe the school system ought to be built around the stages of cognitive development through which all children progress—from the most concrete to the most abstract intellectual tasks.

Second, those such as Tolya believe that education ought to involve students in a "dialogue of cultures." Instead of comparing the past and other cultures to our own they should engage ancient and foreign cultures directly through primary source materials such as Plato's *Republic*. This way students will be able to "reenact" the development of human knowledge.

Third, are the proponents of a Montessori-like "school of the future." They see education modeled after the teachings of Maria Montessori (1870–1952), whose method of instruction emphasizes development of a child's initiative. The schools they envision would be without classes that separate children by ages and without the "cult of knowledge" that separates what children learn in school from their day-to-day lives outside of school.

Fourth, and perhaps most surprising, given the sensitivity of the subject, are the so-called Estonians, a group of teachers, psychologists, and educational authorities from that Baltic republic. They argue that it is essential to teach children not only a common national curriculum but also to ground them in the culture of their own community and to shape their education to the needs and interests of that community.

Finally, Pyotr explained, there are those who follow Shalva Amonashvili, a Soviet thinker whose work is closely related to that of Carl Rogers, the American educational psychologist. They believe in an open, gradeless primary school in which children can develop intellectually and socially at their own pace. Just as Pyotr was trying to explain Amonashvili to me all discussion stopped. We looked up to find everybody staring at us.

"Excuse me," said Marek, "everybody is wondering about our guest." Turning to me he shrugged his shoulders and said, "We've never done this before, so you'll have to forgive us for all the shouting." After Pyotr had translated, Marek asked for the benefit of the others there, "Who are you and do you think we're all mad?"

I explained who I was, why I was in Moscow, and concluded that no, I didn't think they were crazy, just very excited about a subject that made people raise their voices in America, too.

With that it was agreed we all needed a break. It was already 8:00 P.M., nothing had been decided, and people were starting to get hungry. As the others filed out, Pyotr turned to me and asked hopefully, "I think you've seen enough?" I said absolutely not, this was the best thing I had seen in Moscow. If I could, I would stay to the end. Out in the hallway, in the midst of a new cloud of cigarette smoke, Pyotr explained to Boris that he had to leave. Boris agreed to translate for me and to make sure I got home.

Pyotr disappeared down the hall, and I was immediately surrounded by teachers. Virtually everyone spoke enough English to understand me, and most spoke it well, if haltingly. They were all interested in American education and had heard of the damning 1983 report on the failure of American education, "A Nation at Risk." The report, prepared by the National Commission on Excellence in Education and presented to then secretary of education Terrell Bell, initiated the push for educational reform in the U.S.

I was the first American they had ever met. As in many such conversations during our stay in Moscow, they wanted me to make comparisons. Was the movement for educational reform in the United States like the one in the U.S.S.R.? Where is the pressure for reform coming from? How good are our students? Are they motivated? Do they like school? What's it like to be a teacher? How good are our teachers?

I threw up my hands and begged them to stop. How could I answer all their questions if I didn't know anything about Soviet education? "Okay," said a bearded teacher in a black leather jacket, "let's start with the reform movement here. There are two sources of educational reform and they have very different interests. On the one hand, there are the higher-ups. They are worried about education because it's failing, it's not producing the kind and the quality of workers necessary for a restructured economy. In the new economy, they need workers who can think for themselves, but our school system is turning out kids who just follow orders."

"No, we're not," said somebody from the back. "My students don't. They also can't read, can't write, and don't care."

"We declare them educated when they stop coming to school, not because they really know anything," said somebody else.

"That's an exaggeration," said Boris. He turned to me and smiled. "Just like you, we have a 'back to basics' movement."

"On the other hand," continued the teacher in the leather coat, "many teachers and parents are interested in reforms that would make the individual student the focus of attention—not because it would make him a better worker, but because it would make him a happier person."

"So what's the problem?" I asked.

"The bureaucracy," several of them said in unison.

"Have you seen *Is It Easy to Be Young?*," asked a physics teacher, referring to a critically acclaimed documentary film about young people in Latvia by Juris Podnieks. I nodded. "What did you think?

Do you have problems like that in America?" (The film begins with the trial of several teenage boys who vandalized a train on which they were returning from a rock concert. It features footage of young people talking about suicide and Soviet punk rockers—spiked hair, chains, and all. The film has been widely shown and commented upon in the Soviet Union since Gorbachev came to power. It has been seen in America at festivals featuring Soviet films.)

Again I nodded. "Of course we have problems like that—in fact, many of the young people in the film were imitating what they think American kids are like. But what I find interesting about the film is that it has caused such a stir. The film itself isn't surprising, what's surprising is that it should be viewed as such a breakthrough."

"*Glasnost,*" said somebody.

"That's what we're here for," said another. "To face up to our problems."

"What are they?" I asked.

"We haven't devoted enough attention to our students as individuals. That's why you see those kids in *Is It Easy to Be Young?* who lack any motivation or direction."

"Do you have problems with the quality of teachers?" asked a middle-aged woman, "and what is the position of women teachers in America?"

I laughed and told her that many Americans think the two questions go together. Before the 1970s, when the women's liberation movement began to win women the right to work in all jobs, smart women became elementary and high school teachers because it was one of the few careers open to them. It was a respectable profession, even if it didn't pay much. Then women could do anything they wanted if they were willing to struggle a bit. Suddenly, in the 1970s, smart women didn't have to be teachers anymore, so they went off to better-paid, more prestigious jobs and left teaching to those who had teaching in their blood or, more often, those unable to do anything else. Now, if you look at American elementary and high schools, you find a mix of extremely good, highly motivated teachers and barely qualified ones. Even more disturbing, those going into teaching are often from the bottom of the barrel.

Many teachers' colleges turn out certified teachers who cannot read or write proficiently and have only a tenuous grasp of their subjects. "That," I said, "doesn't do anything to improve teachers' already very low prestige."

Marek called us back to the meeting. As we were going in, the teacher in the leather coat said, "Now I know we are not so different after all."

Once seated again, it was clear Marek and Tolya had decided to try a new tack. Along one wall hung three big sheets of newsprint, one for each day of the conference, divided into three sections for morning, afternoon, and evening events. Again Marek asked, "How are we going to organize the conference?"

Again the meeting degenerated into a shouting match. One person wanted to have each school of thought present its program, one after another, but was told that would be too boring. Another suggested that arriving teachers be told to choose one school of thought and attend its sessions for all three days.

"This is supposed to be a marketplace of ideas," one of the teachers said. I asked Boris if the terminology was ideologically correct. He just smiled and kept translating. A third person suggested that each school give a sales pitch after which teachers would choose. A gentleman from the institute pointed out that this would mean there would be no sharing of ideas and no way for the different schools to interact and learn from each other. Soon the sheets of newsprint had been covered with scratched-out schedules and plans, and everybody was getting mad again.

As the battle proceeded, I only half listened to Boris's running translation while I reflected on the impassioned debate going on around me. At first glance the meeting seemed evidence of democracy's victory. Certainly, it was remarkably open by Soviet standards of even the recent past. It was also remarkable for what was not being said, and for how it revealed the limits of *glasnost*. There were no direct attacks on the school system, no references to history textbooks' silence on Stalin's atrocities, let alone a call for an end to censorship. Even in the heat of the moment, these apparently hotheaded teachers showed their cool political sophistication. They knew there was nothing to be gained by a frontal assault; it would merely result in their being silenced. *Glasnost* is not an invitation to American-style muckraking. It does, however, permit attack by indirection, and that is precisely what I heard all around me. By approaching educational reform in the most abstract, academic manner possible, the Eureka Club members could offer profound, often damning criticism. If accepted, their proposed reforms gave hope that equally profound changes in the Soviet system might be possible. The unstated subtext of the entire debate was their belief that children educated to think for themselves are the essential foundation on which a very different Soviet Union might be constructed.

Boris bent over and asked, "Are your meetings like this? Is this what democracy is like in America?"

I laughed and said, "Sometimes," but he was serious. If it were my meeting, he wanted to know, how would it be different? I thought for a minute and said, "Look, Boris, there are two problems with this meeting. First, everybody here is convinced they're right, that their approach is the answer to educational reform, and therefore none of them are willing to listen to the others or to do anything but push for the conference to be about their approach. Second, nobody here has done their homework. Nobody came to this meeting with a plan. Nobody took the time to ask themselves, 'What's the purpose of this conference? What do we want to achieve—as a group, not just as a school?' Nobody asked themselves, 'Who's the audience going to be? What are they coming for? What can we offer them? How can we organize this conference to give them the most?' "

"So what would you suggest?" Boris asked. "How would you organize our conference?"

I told him. He smiled and said, "I think that might work. Would you mind repeating it to everybody while I translate?"

"Wait a minute, Boris," I said. "I'm the American visitor here, I can't do that." But he insisted. "*Glasnost*," he said, and smiled. So, a few sentences at a time, I explained how I would organize their conference.

"This discussion," I began, "has been very interesting, and I have learned a great deal about Soviet education. The problem is that so far all you've done is to try to convince each other of the correctness of your views. What we've got to do is refocus our efforts to concentrate on the conference itself, not the ideas to be presented. Democracy requires that you respect each other and pay as much attention to the decision-making process as you do to what's being decided," I said.

Boris translated. Some people nodded, most people didn't even blink.

"Actually," I continued, "the discussion so far contains all the elements of a successful conference, especially a 'marketplace of ideas.' " Everybody smiled when Boris translated this. "The teachers coming to this conference are going to be in the same position as I am—

interested in education but ignorant of all the different approaches and systems of education. They need to be exposed to all the possibilities out there, all the different schools of thought." When Boris translated this, there were more nods and fewer blank stares.

"You're the specialists, and these teachers are coming a long way to learn from you. The conference has to really teach them something. As the gentleman in tweed pointed out earlier, there has got to be some interaction among the schools of thought and between the experts and the practitioners. The point of a conference is to gather new insights and ideas. The problem is how to organize the conference to achieve these ends." This time when Boris finished there were nods all around.

"Let me suggest one way of organizing this conference. First, I think the conference ought to begin with a 'marketplace of ideas' in the form of brief—fifteen-minute—presentations by each of the systems of education built around exactly the same set of major themes: What drives the reform movement? What's wrong with Soviet education? What's right? What should we be trying to achieve? How can we achieve it? Then, after the presentations, specialists advocating different methods of education can make themselves available to answer questions. This way teachers will be able to compare the varying schools of thought and make an informed choice about which approach suits them best. At the end of the afternoon, the teachers will choose which philosophy of education they want to attach themselves to.

"Then," I said, pointing to the newsprint schedule hanging on the wall, "the morning and afternoon sessions on the second and third days ought to be divided in half. In the first half, the teachers ought to meet with specialists from the school of thought they have chosen. This is where the real teaching will take place, where you will be able to introduce them to your ideas in some depth. But," I continued, "each of these sessions should be devoted to a common set of problems or questions. This way it will be possible for everybody to reconvene after a couple of hours of separate discussion and have an open meeting in which everybody can share their ideas on this common, limited set of issues. Otherwise, with this many people and so many different approaches, things will dissolve into confusion—like they did here." People laughed when Boris translated this.

"Running a conference this size takes a lot of work," I concluded. "If it's going to succeed, you are going to have to step back from your own positions to ask, 'What are the general problems we're all interested in?' If you don't coordinate among yourselves to provide a clear structure for this conference, it won't work. But I think with a bit of work you can come up with a common set of major and minor issues."

When I finished, there was a brief pause. Marek asked, "All in favor of the Michael plan?" Everybody voted yes; the Michael plan was approved unanimously. It was already 10:45 P.M., but everybody agreed that another break was in order before going any further. I was starving. I hadn't eaten breakfast, and lunch had been cut short. But I couldn't leave now.

Back out in the hall, someone asked me why, if I was a college professor, did I care about primary and secondary school education. I admitted that I had never thought about it until recently, but I was working on a project aimed, in part, at American high school teachers. As a result I had to learn about how our high schools worked. "What's the project?" they all wanted to know, so I told them briefly about the Vietnam project.

I stressed the connections with the discussion of educational reform. The cultural and political legacy of Vietnam is a critical issue for Americans to come to terms with, just as the legacy of Afghanistan will be in the Soviet Union; how will each country teach it?

We want a textbook that will not give students a single, pat understanding of the legacy of the Vietnam War. Instead, we want one that will force them to confront the contradictory and ambiguous "lessons" of the war and teach them how to think complex issues through for themselves. We want to attack what somebody in the meeting had called "the cult of knowledge" by creating a curriculum that will force students out of the classroom into their own communities to do research—to interview vets, for example, or investigate what people think of the war now.

When I finished nobody said anything. As we started back into the meeting room, the teacher in the leather coat said, "We'd settle for factually correct textbooks."

As we sat down, Boris came over and said he would have to be leaving soon because it was now after eleven, but that he would find me a new translator. She proved to be a middle-aged woman who had arrived late and had thus far been sitting perched on the corner of somebody else's seat in a corner. She gave me a nice smile when she sat down, and she spoke English very well with a British accent. But she smelled funny; in fact, she smelled distinctly fishy. I tried not to think about my stomach and concentrate on the meeting.

When everybody was settled, Marek turned to me and asked, "So what do we do now?"

"Time for everybody to do their homework," I replied.

"Each of the schools has to meet to decide the key issues. Then the group leaders have got to meet to prepare a common outline for the initial presentations and each of the working sessions. Next, each of the schools has to meet to work out its presentation and to prepare its lesson plan for each of the working sessions. That's a lot, but luckily it doesn't have to get done tonight."

As I talked the fishy smell got stronger. Finally, when I had finished, I glanced at my translator. Open on her lap was a greasy blue nylon knapsack in which she rummaged as she talked and from which she pulled forth fingers full of smoked fish, which she popped into her mouth between sentences. I was starving.

Marek looked at the others. "Agreed?" he asked. Everyone nodded and grabbed for their coats. It was nearly 11:30 P.M., and nobody but my final translator had eaten dinner. Marek, Ivan, and I walked out together. Twenty-fifth of October Street was empty. The three of us stood chatting a minute before Marek turned off toward Red Square. Ivan and I walked together for a couple of blocks. I asked him if I might come to his school; he said he would ask. Then he asked me shyly if Evelind and I would visit his wife and him. "We would love to," I told him. "We've been hoping to talk to a Russian couple our own age to see how the little things in life compare."

When I finally got back to the Berlin at almost midnight I went first to Leona and Jerry's room to see if I could find something to eat. When I knocked, however, Barney appeared and just looked at me around the door's edge. After weeks of living on top of each other, it was a look I immediately recognized. It said, "Just go away and don't even ask." I went.

Downstairs I tiptoed into our room thinking Evelind would be sound asleep and desperately hoping I'd be able to find something to eat without waking her up. Instead, all the lights were on and she was wide awake.

"Where have you been?" she demanded. "At ten o'clock I called Natasha to ask if she knew anything and she said Pyotr had been home for hours!"

"It's a long story," I said, "but I'll have to tell you about the Michael plan in the morning. Is there anything to eat?"

Comparing Life-styles with Ella and Ivan

Michael and I were delighted by the invitation to meet Ivan, a young high school teacher of English, and his wife Ella, who also teaches school. Since arriving in Moscow we had been hoping to find another young couple to talk to, a couple, like us, trying to balance the demands of two careers and family.

On the evening we were to go to Ivan's, we were delayed leaving the hotel due to an earlier meeting that ran late. We called ahead to make sure that it wouldn't be too late if we arrived at nine o'clock. He didn't mind at all, and in fact seemed amused that we were so concerned. Thinking about it afterward, we realized that Ivan and Ella, like all of our Russian friends, normally ate late and spent hours sitting up talking to friends. These late-night discussions, often passionate and complex arguments, seemed to be the social lifeblood of Moscow. We quickly adapted to these evenings of lively talk, good humor, smoked fish, and vodka, and we have sorely missed them since returning to the States.

As we left the hotel, we had a momentary panic when we could not find Ivan's station on our pocket metro map. When we arrived at the Marksa Prospekt station, however, we discovered it on the metro wall map and realized that we were on our way to one of the newer districts on the outskirts of the city. As we rode, all the stations were unique, each of a different modern design, constructed of tra-

287

ditional marble or exposed stainless steel columns with decorated chrome panels.

We stepped out of the subway station onto a desolate street lit by one streetlamp. We were in the midst of one of the huge housing developments I had watched sprouting up from our windows almost twenty years before. There were no shops, no cars, no street signs, and no people, but on either side of the road the tall, featureless apartment buildings stood rank upon rank like dominoes. Luckily, there was a telephone booth nearby and we called Ivan. He appeared from the shadows in less than five minutes, a tall, trim, and handsome young man with a clean-cut, boyish look.

Once off the main street we were in the familiar layout of a wide, winding, tree-lined street with apartment buildings and small play areas on both sides. We passed men chatting over a barrel of burning trash. After a couple of minutes' walk, we turned into a cluttered yard and entered a dark hallway. We climbed to the third floor and followed Ivan into his apartment.

Ivan and Ella share a two-bedroom apartment with their two-year-old daughter and Ivan's mother. The apartment is laid out along a central hallway: on one side, a kitchen, two bedrooms, and a bathroom; and on the other, a living room and a small balcony. This arrangement gives the impression of more space than in a typical, older Moscow apartment. They have a second bedroom because Ivan's mother lives with them. In fact, this family has just the allotted ten square meters per person (about eleven square yards) minimum decreed as the goal of the Soviet state. Ella and Ivan, like all our other married friends with a child, sleep in the living room and give the bedroom to the baby.

We were greeted at the door by Ivan's mother, a large-boned woman with a friendly smile, in her fifties. Ella appeared from the end of the hallway to greet us shyly, more hesitant than Ivan to use her English. Ella, beautiful in a very unassuming way, had her straight blond hair pulled back in a ponytail that exposed her pale, clear skin and large, penetrating eyes.

We settled onto the kelly green couch in the living room and the others pulled up chairs around the coffee table. There had been an attempt to decorate the small room; the kelly green couch and chairs matched metallic green wallpaper. The effort had succeeded in eliminating the eclectic effect we found in many of our friends' tiny apartments. Even though the living room was filled with furniture and books, the general clutter had been hidden.

Ivan's mother brought us some appetizers of smoked fish and bread, and we opened the bottle of vodka we had brought. Once Michael and Ivan had finished recounting the scene of the prior night's meeting, we started asking questions about their lives and tried to find analogous examples in our own lives in the States. We started with money.

Trying to compare household income and budgets reduced everyone first to shock and then to giggles. Our U.S. salaries and living costs were so much higher, using the Soviet exchange rate of $1.60 per ruble, that I found I had to divide my income and housing costs by ten to get to something we could at least discuss. Even then, however, getting a sense of how they actually spent their income took some doing.

The two of them teased each other that it would be a good idea to pay attention to a budget, but admitted that they found it almost impossible. Ivan has a weakness for buying books and Ella likes to buy sewing materials. But that wasn't the real problem. The scarcity of goods simply made it impossible to plan purchases. Often they used up their potential savings buying scarce goods whenever they found them. When it came to food, they did not even try to save. If they saw something they wanted and the line was not too long, they bought it. Clothing was also expensive and hard to find, so it fit the same rules. This was their way of compensating themselves for the long hours they worked.

Ella and Ivan are twenty-three and have been working for only a couple of years. They smiled when they recounted that teachers' salaries had been raised by 50 percent the month they started teaching. Their monthly incomes, after taxes of 13 percent, come close to the Soviet average of 200 rubles ($320) per month. Ivan makes 230 rubles ($368), Ella 200 ($320), and Ivan's mother about 300 ($480). Together, however, their combined household income of 730 rubles ($1,168) makes them quite well off by Soviet standards.

Ivan and Ella both work two jobs to make this income; Ivan teaches two sessions (they told us that most Moscow schools were on double sessions). Ella is head of her department and has a number of administrative duties in addition to teaching. Ivan's mother makes additional salary due to her tenure. (Ivan admitted that he did not know exactly how much she was saving for retirement, but was very happy she contributed to the household finances and glad she was putting some money away.)

After much discussion, Ivan and Ella managed to work out a rough outline of how they spent their income. As they talked, we were struck by how very different their budget is from ours. They spent their net household income of 730 rubles a month as follows:

Rent, telephone, electricity, gas	30 rubles
Food	300 rubles
Savings (not very successful), clothing, and weekly expenses	200 rubles
Mother's savings	200 rubles

I tried not to gasp at the cost of housing. "By comparison," I said, "we spend half our take-home pay on mortgage, utilities, and phone bill, and about ten percent on food; but we own our house."

"Don't you pay any type of insurance?" I asked, trying to find the Russian words to explain the homeowners', medical, life, disability, auto, and liability policies I consider a basic part of my financial life. They replied in the negative. They never quite understood the concept of liability insurance. "We don't own a house or car, the state pays for all medical expenses; if we're disabled, we will receive a pension. If someone drives into another person's car he pays for the damage, or finds a friend who can fix it. If he kills someone driving he goes to jail," Ivan answered.

Ella added, "You realize, don't you, that we pay all that money for the food we eat for breakfast, supper, and the weekends? We eat lunch, which is really dinner, at school, and you know that's subsidized." Food prices for good quality fresh meat and vegetables, which are hard to find in the state stores, are very high in the free markets when individual farmers bring goods from their private plots. For example, cucumbers are five rubles a kilo, more than six dollars a pound. A lean chicken is seven rubles, or eleven dollars, for two pounds.

"So how do you manage?" I asked. "Can you buy food through the school cafeteria? Some of our friends who are teachers said they can order through their school."

Ella replied, "Sometimes we can buy things through the school. Local vendors are supposed to help supply the schoolteachers, but you can't count on them. Sometimes I wait on line, but usually I buy whatever I can find where there is no line."

"Clothing prices are as expensive or more so than in the States," I commented, "and you don't have any discount stores where you can shop for special bargains." A winter coat with some style, comparable to good quality items in the United States, cost from 150 rubles ($240) up; a wool knit dress cost 80 rubles ($128). A pair of poor quality blue jeans made in a friendly country costs 100 rubles ($160) in the department store. Ella agreed that these prices were typical and added, "If the store has something you want, they probably don't have your size. My girlfriends and I know each other's sizes. At lunch we discuss what we are looking for. If one of them sees the pair of shoes I'm looking for in my size, she buys it. I do the same for the others.

"Our families are very important to our quality of life, as well," continued Ella. "We are lucky enough to have two *babushkas*. Both grandmothers help to make it possible for us to maintain two incomes and still have some time to ourselves. Ivan's mother helps keep the household running and this evening, for example, we can have some quiet time to have you over by taking the baby over to my mother's. During the day, when we are at work, we put the baby in nursery school. My mother is backup for baby-sitting when the baby is sick."

Unlike a number of other women we talked to, Ella studied at the teachers' institute through her pregnancy and the arrival of the baby. The baby was now two years old; which meant that she was born right around the time Ella was to start teaching. Ella admitted that she would have preferred to stay home with the baby for a while, but teaching jobs in a preferred school in a location relatively near home are not easy to find, so she took her job and started working.

The clock was inching toward 1:00 A.M., when the metro closes. We reluctantly gathered our coats, chatting all the way to the door. We promised to keep in touch, and Ivan took us to the metro stop.

We arrived just as the clock struck one, so Ivan came down on the platform to make sure we got on a train. The train arrived within minutes and we bid our good-byes, promising to keep in touch and see how our respective families and budgets turned out. As we settled onto the train for the long ride back to the center of the city, I commented to Michael that "their lives are very similar to ours in some ways and then almost the complete opposite of ours in others."

Soviet Medicine: House Calls and Hands-on Healing

When our family returned to the United States from Moscow in 1970, I was eleven years old. I was told that finally, after ten years overseas, we would stop moving and make Washington our home. Many of our expectations about America were quickly dashed in the first few weeks. It was a hot, muggy August in Washington when we first moved into our big house. As I walked through the empty rooms I couldn't imagine what it would be like to live in this three-story American house, where I had my own room. Initially, the cramped Moscow apartment where we had slept on bunk beds and had one bathroom for seven people seemed so much cosier and safer. I felt very foreign and suddenly afraid of the country I had longed to be a part of. That first night we all huddled together on rented chairs in the living room watching a rented . My father wasn't home, so all the kids sat close to my mother, each vying for her affection as we braved our first night in America. By chance, we watched a horrible murder show called "The House on Apple Tree Road." It opens with a scene in which a young girl comes home after school to find blood all over the refrigerator and her mother murdered in the bathtub. No one could sleep after that horror show, and we kept asking my mother for reassurance; that wasn't really what America was like, was it?

We had lived in the Soviet Union from the time I was nine till I was eleven. During those two years I had naively believed the slogan I was often told at school: "There is no crime in the U.S.S.R." Living under this assumption had made life very calm for me. At age eleven I had taken the metro alone (although I did get lost once), gone shopping alone, and frequently walked home alone in the dark. I had developed a sense of security and independence in Moscow that was suddenly invaded by American culture. I was rudely awakened by what we watched on television, the horror stories we read in the newspapers, my parents' cautions, and by what I was taught in school. Freedom of speech is wonderful and necessary, but it quickly destroys the cocoon of childhood that the Soviets have succeeded in prolonging.

I was also not prepared for my reception at school. I entered sixth grade at age eleven, and I assumed that kids would be open-minded and receptive to me when I told them about my adventures overseas. Adults at our home had been very curious and fascinated by our accounts of life in Russia. Unfortunately, the indoctrination process in Russia that had made my classmates wary of me because I was a *kapitalist* had worked its opposite charms on my classmates in the United States: my nickname immediately became Kate the Commie.

Shaken by these early warnings, I retreated into myself and my family. After the initial shock I adjusted to America, and gradually, as I got older, my feeling of foreignness dissipated as it became clear that we were here to stay. Nevertheless, those two years in Moscow left a strong mark on me and helped determine many choices I made. I was determined to study the Soviet Union more. Many contradictions about life in both the United States and the Soviet Union remained unresolved for me. Just as America had developed into an ideal during our many years overseas, now Russia had taken on an unreal image. I longed to go back, but somehow I always felt it was out of reach; a distant country, from a past that could never be recaptured.

My memories of Russia took on a dreamlike quality. I still wanted to return and make it a part of my adult life. Going back to Russia with my family was not only a chance to meet old friends, relive old memories, and see what had changed since we lived there, but it was also a chance to try to sort out some of the questions I had pondered after three years of Soviet studies in graduate school. I received a master's degree from Harvard's Russian Research Center in the spring of 1986 and started working on a Ph.D. in political science (with a specialty in Soviet studies) at Columbia University in the fall of that year. Those three years of study had generated many questions I hoped to explore.

I had been back to the U.S.S.R. on two trips before I returned with my family. On both trips I had been working, on one as a tour guide for a group of lawyers, on the other as a production manager for a PBS documentary. Both trips were so hectic I barely had a chance to appreciate the fact I was back in the U.S.S.R. Nevertheless, both times I returned to see our old house, the pond, and the forest. When I go back to that old neighborhood, I feel as if time has stood still. The old dirt path across the field is still there, and you can still see kids trudging to and from school on the well-packed earth. The pond sits peacefully and just as muddy as it always was. The cement fishing hole where Barney crashed his sled is still there, and every time I see it I relive that snowy day when I suggested Barney try the icy hill before me. He ended up smashing his head into the cement and breaking his leg.

Our apartment building still has that shoddy, gray, slapdash appearance that it had the day it was built twenty years ago. Barney's *detsky sad* ("kindergarten") is still exactly the same, and even though the trees in the forest near the apartment house have grown taller, it still has the appearance of a man-made forest. I looked forward to going back so all of us could relive these memories together, but I also had personal questions I wanted to answer.

When we got to Moscow one of my main goals was to interview a few doctors. I wanted to explore questions about Soviet health care that remain unresolved issues in Western scholarship. For example, everyone knows that the majority of doctors in the Soviet Union are women, but why is this so? Also, it is well known that Soviet medicine is less advanced than Western medicine and that the Soviets are talking about reforms to make health care more of a priority. Not only did health care seem to be in jeopardy, but I was also curious about the status of doctors. It is generally accepted in the West that the status and prestige of doctors in the Soviet Union is much lower than that of their Western counterparts. Much of my knowledge about Soviet medicine is based on historical writings and Western theories about the difficulties of a socialized health-care system. I wanted to hear what Soviet doctors had to say about these issues and whether or not they see Soviet medicine in crisis, as it has been characterized in the West.

At first it was very hard to find a doctor who was willing to talk to me. All our friends knew doctors, but none of them was willing to talk to a foreigner. I speculated that perhaps things were so bad in the field of medicine that these doctors simply couldn't risk revealing even the slightest criticism of the system in which they worked. Finally, we received the name of a doctor who was willing to talk to me, and if the polyclinic gave permission, we could film there as well. I called Larisa, the doctor, at home. After a short, friendly conversation, in which I assured her that we would just get together and talk and she didn't have to make any further commitment, she asked me to meet her outside of her polyclinic the next day. Just before she hung up she said, "Katia, are you sure you couldn't meet me somewhere else in the city, you know, maybe for coffee or something?" I understood her apprehension about me coming to the polyclinic. She didn't want to be seen talking to a foreigner, and she didn't want me to see the polyclinic, which was under *remont* ("repair"). I insisted that I wanted to see her at work, and the best place to meet would be the polyclinic.

Larisa is a "block doctor," which means that she ministers to a neighborhood or district (*uchastok*) that encompasses about twenty-five large apartment buildings. She is a warm, bright woman in her early thirties who is responsible for the health care of eight hundred children. Larisa has short, brown curly hair, a round, cheerful face, and looks younger than her age. When I met her that bright September morning, she was just setting off on her house calls, and she assured me it would be all right for me to come along. Larisa was the first physician I had met on our trip, and I was very curious to see how all my studies of Soviet health care would match up to reality.

I wandered through the polyclinic before I met Larisa, partly out of curiosity to see why she was so apprehensive. All I could see were crowded hallways with crying children and worried-looking parents. I saw a little *remont*, but for the most part the polyclinic reminded me of any children's clinic in the West. I was still a little early when I reached the front entrance where we had arranged to meet, so I sat and watched the parents bringing their children for treatment. One difference that struck me right away was how the parents left their prams out in the courtyard without a second thought. Parents left their children while they ran into the polyclinic to get some medicine or consult a doctor. No one came in a car. They all lived in the neighborhood and walked over, and no one worried about weirdos abducting their children or stealing their prams. There was a familiarity and ease in the way the parents came and went to the polyclinic, where everything is free of charge and there are always doctors on duty.

Larisa was friendlier and more easygoing than she had been on the phone. As we started to walk through the neighborhood, I sensed a mutual understanding between us that was never verbalized. Larisa was showing me her work. I knew I had to wait to ask any tough questions that would pry beneath the surface of what she was showing me. Strolling along the leaf-strewn streets, there were two conflicting thoughts battling in my mind. The devil's advocate in me thought: Beware of taking this doctor's word as a general example of what Soviet doctors think or feel. Remember she's just one person in a big city and she probably has privileges that many other doctors lack. On the other hand I thought: This polyclinic seems so wonderful and convenient, isn't it amazing that she makes house calls? She's so warm and kind, nothing like what I imagined. This conflict was never completely resolved. What I saw and heard with Larisa was mostly a very positive view of the Soviet health-care system, but I had to keep reminding myself that she was one of the few doctors I saw working.

I told Larisa that the practice of making house calls in urban areas in America is very rare now. She was bothered by this news and simply couldn't understand how a family doctor could really know a family and understand particular conditions if he or she had never been in their home. "Yes," I replied, "it is too bad that the practice died out." The only explanation I could give was that doctors had found the practice too costly and time-consuming. If a patient is too ill to leave home in the United States, the doctor will give advice over the phone, but the practice of house calls is almost unheard of. This is not so in Moscow, especially for families with small children. Three or four times a week Larisa spends most of her day making house calls. The two times I went with her she had a list of between seven and eleven families she would see that day. She spent fifteen minutes with some people and up to two hours with others. When a mother brings a newborn home Larisa visits every day for a week and a nurse makes follow-up visits the second week. Larisa explained: "This gives us a chance to make sure the mother and child are all right and help instruct the new parents how to care for an infant."

As we walked through the neighborhood everyone greeted Larisa using the respectful form of her name, Larisa Yevgeneyevna. One mother came up to Larisa and asked, "Doctor, my son is feeling better, is it all right if he goes to school?" Another mother we met along the way solicited advice about her toddler, and Larisa arranged a visit at the polyclinic for her. I realized that Larisa was far more than a pediatrician who took care of children's physical ailments. She knew every one of these families, their private joys and shames, their intimate family stories. The private problems of the parents and grandparents might only indirectly relate to their children, but Larisa was privy to them. She admitted she was not only the neighborhood pediatrician but much of her work involved psychology and therapy. At times, she confided, she was placed in a very difficult position. She had to not only help and teach adults how to care for their children but also explain to them that their living habits would have an effect on their whole family. She said she was not the kind of person who could separate herself from her work when she got home, and that it often intruded into her family life. Larisa admitted a little sadly, "I think my husband and daughter suffer most from my work. They're the ones who have been neglected at times."

Our first house call was at the home of a movie actress and a director who have a cute, chubby, seven-year-old son named Mitya. When we were being buzzed in at the door, the voice of the actress, Lyuba, asked who was there. "The doctor," Larisa answered. She sounded so official, so unlike herself. When we came into the apartment, Larisa tried to keep up that official facade, but Lyuba was a good friend of hers, and after ten minutes I lost track of the fact that we had come on official business. As soon as we stepped in the door Lyuba insisted that we take off our shoes and wear slippers. Then we went to wash our hands. Larisa hadn't told Lyuba and Mitya that I was coming with her, and they were very excited to have an American in their house, even though Lyuba had been to Europe and the Bloc many times. She kept saying, "All the way from America! You have come a very long way, Katinka. We'll have to give you something warm to eat and a hot drink. Imagine a girl from America who speaks Russian!"

We immediately went to the kitchen, where Lyuba made us coffee with a drop of cognac to warm us up. When we first came in, Larisa asked about Mitya's cold. But Mitya went off to play in another room while we chatted. I felt a little bad for Mitya that I had come and disrupted his checkup. Clearly there was no way to play "fly on the wall" and watch Larisa at work. I was too much of a novelty, and Lyuba wasn't going to let us get away with a quick house call. She also would never let us go with just one cup of coffee and cognac.

Little did I know what a huge feast she had in store for us. She took such pride in her cooking that there was no way to refuse. First she gave us a big bowl of borscht, then she piled a plate high with salads, sausages, and kasha. Finally, when I thought I might burst from so much food, she whipped out a huge homemade cake. With each course I tried politely to explain that I couldn't eat another bite, but there was no refusing this woman. Laughing, and a little overheated from all the food and cognac, I acquiesced. Larisa ate too. It seemed that she had been through this ritual a thousand times with Lyuba. No wonder Mitya was chubby. These people ate very well, and Lyuba had a knack for making even boring potatoes and cabbage taste unusual.

After I explained what I was doing in Moscow and why I was with Larisa, I felt that the atmosphere was so warm and friendly I could ask them some hard questions about Soviet medicine. I started by asking if they had ever thought about why there are so many women in medicine in the Soviet Union. Both of them were quiet. It seemed that no one had ever asked them that question. Then Larisa replied, "You know, it's strange, but I've never thought about that before. I think the main reason there are so many women in medicine is because women make better doctors." She went on to explain that she thought women are more nurturing than men, and therefore they make better general practitioners. Men, she felt, made better specialists such as cardiologists and surgeons. "You know, jobs where you need a lot of strength and stamina. Surgeons have to be on their feet for a long time, and they need big, strong hands, whereas women are much better with mothers and infants." Lyuba agreed completely. She too had never thought about it, but felt strongly that women were much better with children and other women and that men should handle the surgery and cardiac arrests.

Part of me wanted to protest and point out to these women that they had been socialized to believe that women are more nurturing than men. I wanted to tell them that our society has only begun to demystify the prestige of the male doctor who used to be considered so infallible. But I held back. I reminded myself that I was there to hear what they had to say, not to argue or try to convert. They believed what they were telling me, and I didn't want them to know how much I disagreed with them. There were many moments like this when we were in Moscow. We had come as observers, and even though I wanted to share and become involved with people I met, I often chose not to argue with them. We often expressed our opinions, and we had many discussions, but there were moments, like this one, when I chose to listen and not bring in my American viewpoint.

I was curious to hear what Larisa would tell me about infants and childbirth in the Soviet Union because I had heard so many harrowing stories. At Harvard I saw a film by a Swedish documentary filmmaker about Soviet women. One of the most unforgettable scenes was of three women giving birth on three bare tables lined up next to each other. There was one doctor for all three of them, and she had to keep running back and forth to help them. No one was allowed to be there to comfort them as they lay alone under bright lights panting and screaming. As soon as the babies were born they were whisked away from the mothers, swaddled tightly, and taken off to their cribs. I couldn't help wondering if there haven't been many mix-ups over the years among swaddled babies who look so similar all wrapped up together.

The story of a woman who had given birth three months ago was fresh in my mind when I saw Larisa. Anna Charny had told me that her baby, Sima, was taken away from her immediately after she gave birth, and she was not allowed to see her again for three days. During that period, both Anna and the baby were infected by a *Staphylococcus* epidemic that raged throughout the hospital. Anna was never able to nurse because of the infection, and the baby remained direly ill for two months, partly because she was not able to gain any immunity from her mother. When I first saw Sima she was still infected and her skin had a bluish palor. The first months of her life had been spent desperately trying to overcome the potentially fatal infection she had caught in the hospital.

Larisa told me that *Staphylococcus* is one of the biggest problems maternity hospitals face. The infection spreads rapidly and is particularly dangerous for newborns. American hospitals also had a problem with this highly infectious disease, but were able to control and practically eradicate the problem by the 1960s. Larisa claimed the Soviet hospitals are trying to discharge mothers with their babies as soon as possible so that they will have less exposure to the infection, but they have always had a traditional minimum of a week's stay after birth. This requirement prevails, and Anna was one of many women who still have their children whisked away, become infected, and then cannot breast-feed. Larisa told me they encourage breast-feeding, but the mother is often not allowed to see the child for the first few days and then only three times a day. In fact, the system discourages mothers from breast-feeding. Here was a good example of the Soviet health-care system battling diseases and problems that the West has overcome. Larisa acknowledged this by admitting her frustration with the whole maternity infection problem and confided, "I know you have taken care of this problem long ago in America." Larisa was very proud and satisfied with her job and the polyclinic. This was one of the few times she expressed any disappointment with the health-care system in which she worked.

In the United States childbirth does not have such rigid guidelines. If a pregnancy is going normally, women can choose various forms of birth and fathers are allowed to be with mothers throughout the experience. I have heard of numerous cases where mothers gave birth and went home the same day. This is simply forbidden in the Soviet Union.

A friend of ours, Tolya Pristavkin's wife, Marina, had a baby girl while we were in Moscow. The delivery was very difficult, and Marina lost a lot of blood. She was confined to the maternity ward, unable to get out of bed and isolated from her husband or any other visitors. Tolya was worried sick about her. All the other husbands were standing outside the hospital windows signaling to their wives, but Marina didn't come to the window the first day. On the second day she was able to stand up and signal to Tolya at the window. When we visited him he had just seen her and was trying to be cheerful, but he said that she was very weak and still in serious condition. Tolya told us the only way to communicate was either by sign language through the windows, by sending a note via the nurses, or by bribing a nurse to let him use a phone. He had sent a note through the nurse on duty, and after waiting half an hour for a reply, he inquired why it was taking so long. He was informed that the nurse who had taken his note had gone on her lunch break and he would have to wait another half hour for the note to be delivered. He had no alternative, so he waited.

These stories about Soviet medicine's inefficiencies are rampant. Natasha Zanegina told me that last year she was critically ill and had to call an ambulance to take her to a special hospital. The ambulance arrived but the medic on duty refused to take her to the hospital. The medic wouldn't say she wanted money, but she also wouldn't budge. Finally Vadim gave her a bribe (Natasha was too sick to talk) and off they went. I had read of corruption, inefficiency, primitive medical facilities, rising infant mortality, a lowering of life expectancy for males, and a general health-care crisis in the Soviet Union. Many stories I heard in Moscow confirmed these Western reports. Phenomena that we take for granted—such as disposable dishes, needles, and paper products—are simply not available in the Soviet Union. These disposable items allow hospitals and clinics to maintain a level of sanitation and sterility that the Soviets have never been able to achieve. Much of the spread of infection is due to this problem of having to reuse equipment.

The Soviet Union has about one quarter of the world's physicians and the ratio of doctors to patients is about twice that in the United States, yet despite these impressive numbers urban hospitals are overcrowded while rural hospitals are not fully utilized. One reason for this is poor distribution. The long lines and bureaucratic red tape that thwart the rest of the economy are just as prevalent in medicine. Also, because there is such an abundance of doctors and medical facilities, and no incentive either for the patient to be discharged quickly or for the doctor to discharge a patient as soon as possible, in 1980 the average hospital stay was ten days longer in the Soviet Union than in the United States.[1] This is just an example of oversupply that results in waste in some areas and overcrowdedness and extra demands in others. Nevertheless, my interest in Soviet health care goes beyond criticizing it for all its backwardness and its inability to keep up with the West, problems that have been acknowledged by Gorbachev and the Soviet medical establishment.

The Soviet experiment in socialism attempted to create a truly socialized health-care system for the first time in history. For all its inefficiencies, Soviet health care is accessible and basically free to everyone. There are a few private practices and paid clinics, but everyone has access to a free clinic. The elite have access to better care, but peasants in the far reaches of the Soviet Union who had never heard of medicine before the revolution now have doctors. Of course it is debatable whether health care is beneficial if it is of such poor quality, but one goal of the revolution has been achieved. Meeting Larisa and getting a chance to watch her with her patients gave me insight into some of the more positive aspects of this medical system that clearly has many problems.

My interest in the Soviet health-care system centers mainly on the role of doctors. Seventy percent of Soviet doctors are women, and this is a drop from a peak of 80 or 90 percent in the 1950s and 1960s. In addition to this extraordinary numerical domination of

---

1. William A. Knaus, M.D., *Inside Russian Medicine* (Boston: Beacon Press, 1981), p. 123.

women in medicine, the prestige of doctors in Soviet society is much lower than that of doctors in the West. One explanation for this difference in status stems from a stated desire on the part of the leadership right after the revolution to change the nature of health care and the high prestige of the prerevolutionary doctors. The Bolsheviks wanted to change the influential position and status of doctors and create a new type of medical system where doctors would be treated like other workers. Through structural changes to centralize and socialize the health-care system and limit the autonomy of doctors, a change in medical education, and compulsory rural duty, the role and status of doctors has changed dramatically over time. Along with the centralization and socialization of medicine, influential doctors' groups, which had developed a sense of corporate autonomy before the revolution, were crushed. Gradually doctors began to receive lower salaries; they became less specialized, less autonomous, and less revered in society. A process of deprofessionalization occurred, resulting in a denigration of the status of doctors.

There was also a conscious desire to channel women into medicine. Soviet statistics show a jump in the number of women who attended medical school after the revolution.[2] There are many reasons for this sharp increase. Men who were left after the wars and turmoil were mostly working to industrialize the country. Women were a great resource for a country desperately in need of medical personnel. Thus, through the massive induction of women into medicine, and a stated desire to change the whole medical system from a high-status profession to a low-status occupation without all the prestige that medicine has acquired in the West, the Soviet government created a socialized health-care system. Through these changes, the Soviet medical system has become a widespread organization, for the most part free and available to all. The drawbacks of these changes have been a denigration in the prestige of medicine and low-quality health care. As doctors were isolated from the rest of the world, paid low wages, and restricted in their research, the whole field of medicine suffered. Today the average salary of a doctor ranges from 150 rubles ($240) to 180 rubles ($288) per month, low even by Soviet standards.[3]

This theory helps account for the predominance of women in Soviet medicine and the low quality of health care, but it is not widely

---

2. *Zdravookhranenie v SSSR: Staticheskii Sbornik*, Moscow: GOSSTATIZDAT TSSU SSSR, 1960, p. 51.
3. Knaus, *Inside Russian Medicine*, p. 334.

accepted in the Soviet Union. My ideas about the role of doctors, women, and the history of Soviet medicine (all formulated while studying in the United States) brought various responses, depending on who I tested my theory with. Arseny Roginsky, a Leningrad historian, laughed at my ideas and immediately responded, "That's too rational! Your ideas are too rational for this society, Katia." Larisa did not find any humor in my ideas. Her response was first to seriously consider my theory, but then she thought I simply did not understand the Soviet Union. "No, I just think there is a majority of women because they make better doctors," she said. She did not comment on the issues of quality or prestige in medicine. One psychiatrist I talked to felt that the real cause of the denigration of prestige was because very early on (in the 1930s) medical schools were separated from other institutions of higher learning and acquired the status of vocational schools. This has certainly contributed to the denigration of the profession, but it does not account for the predominance of women in medicine.

One medical issue on the minds of many people to whom we spoke was how Gorbachev's reforms would affect the state of health care. Doctors and laypeople alike were discussing the government's plan to cut imports of all medicine, including imports from the socialist bloc countries. This cutback made people nervous. The shift is supposed to encourage the manufacturing of more and better pharmaceuticals within the Soviet Union, but one friend warned that this was an extremely idealistic goal. In a market where shortages are already pervasive, sick people were stocking up on basic drugs such as aspirin, vitamins, and cold pills. There was a sense of foreboding about this change, like people hoarding food before a war. This fear revealed not only how dependent the pharmaceutical industry is on imports from Europe but also how people recognize and face the drawbacks of the Soviet medical system.

Larisa, however, was not overly concerned with the proposed changes in the supply of pharmaceuticals. She said they had plenty of medicine, and indeed, the pharmacy at the polyclinic seemed well stocked.

After our large meal and a long talk about medicine and the two women's lives, Larisa checked Mitya and we prepared to leave. Mitya's cold was still serious enough to keep him home for another week. Also, his whole class was sick with colds so there was no point in his going back to school. His teacher came by or called every night with his assignment, and Mitya seemed content to spend another week in his doting mother's care. I asked Lyuba and Mitya if they would be willing to be in our film, and they agreed enthusiastically. I assured all of them that there would be no surprises and that they should do and say whatever they would normally.

Larisa wanted to take me on another house call, but we had been at Lyuba's so long that now I was late for a meeting at *Izvestia* and had to run. We parted in a hurry, but even though we were rushed, I left her with a sense that a strong tie had been made.

This was confirmed the next few times I saw Larisa. Even though we were both suspicious of each other's respective political systems and I had expressed my skepticism about what lay below the surface of what she claimed to be a well-functioning health-care system, Larisa and I battled out our differences amicably. I kept trying to probe below the veneer of official policy and dogma about Soviet health care, and Larisa tried to show me why she believed in the Soviet socialized system. When we filmed Larisa a week later she was nervous and kept a professional distance on camera. Larisa went through the filming perfunctorily. She checked children in the polyclinic and worked at a fast clip through the house calls. Lyuba had again prepared a spectacular meal, which we gobbled down quickly, but unlike my first visit, there was no cognac, and the focus of the visit was on the patient, Mitya. We did have a few moments of privacy though, and Larisa asked me to meet her alone the next day, Saturday. As the film crew was climbing into our van with the equipment, Larisa pulled me aside. Quietly she reminded me, "Outside the Krasnopresnenskaya Station, eight A.M., and remember, this is just between you and me, it's not for them to know about." I told Ari about our plans to rendezvous, but I knew if I told my parents they would veto it because by this time we were on such a tight schedule.

I met Larisa the next morning at the designated time. As we greeted each other on that cold, wet morning, we looked like two women who had been friends for years. We kissed on the cheek and immediately began to chatter about the filming the day before. Larisa suggested we go over to Lyuba's house for coffee. Lyuba's husband was out of town, and we would get a chance to talk without the pressure of the crew. Even though I only had one hour, I gladly acquiesced. Walking over to Lyuba's the secretive, mysterious side of Larisa began to unfold itself. Larisa seemed eager to explain why she had chosen to be a doctor, now that she knew a little about me and why I was interested in Soviet medicine.

She explained that much of her skill came naturally to her. "I work with my hands. Hands have a lot of strength and power. Through massage and warmth, hands can heal, and often make medication unnecessary." Indeed, I had watched Larisa massage each child she treated. Her hands seemed to take over the little torsos, kneading and feeling for any abnormalities. Most of the children had chest colds or winter flus. As soon as she massaged them, they began to breathe more easily, they relaxed and gave in to her touch. Even the most frightened ones untensed their shoulders and breathed quietly once Larisa had touched them. I had heard of faith healing and "laying on of hands" in America from a friend whose father practiced medicine and had been trained in these hand healing techniques, and after watching Larisa at work her comments did not come as much of a surprise.

"I saw how you massaged the children, it looked great," I replied. "But where do you get your strength from? Did you just sense it?"

"No, I developed much of it. It's a very spiritual thing, not something you learn in school. You have to feel it, you have to relax and let it come inside of you before you can give it to others," she said.

"I noticed that spiritual side of you. You seem so relaxed and at peace with yourself. I felt badly that the filming made you so tense, I could tell it interrupted the flow and pace of your work. Sometimes I long for the peacefulness you seem to have. I mean, we live such hectic lives in New York. We are always frantically trying to get all our work done, we often eat on the run, and there's little time for exploring our more spiritual sides."

Larisa agreed that she felt at peace, but that she too needed rejuvenation after a long week of work. "My husband, daughter, and I try to go out to the country on Sundays, especially in the spring and summer. Each one of us finds a tall strong tree in the forest and leans up against it. In Russia we believe that trees are one of the strongest, most powerful things alive. They reach up above all the chaos and dirt below them and draw the clean air and strength from what lies above us. When you lean on a tree and put your head against it, too, you can draw its strength into your body. The straight strong tree will give off its power if you wait and relax. Think about it. Trees live far longer than humans do. They hold many secrets within them. After a day in the country, and a peaceful time in a forest, I feel ready to deal with the city and my work."

Suddenly I became more aware of the trees around us. Most of them were scrawny, urban types that would have broken had we leaned on them, but it sounded like a good idea. It seemed strange that this Soviet woman, who had been brought up in such an anti-religious society, should be spiritually alert, but I was to find her belief in the power of nature among many other people we met. Later that day my family and the crew went back to our old apartment and took a walk through the forest. I told Doveen about the tree "cure" and we slipped away into the forest to find two big old trees. As we leaned up against two tall birch trees, we closed our eyes and breathed in deeply. We both felt a strange sensation. It was as if we were leaning against a tall strong person. Larisa was right, the sense of calm and tranquility was immediate. When we opened our eyes the film crew had found us and everyone was joking about how superstitious we were. The spell broke and we moved away from our trees, but both of us felt as if we had received a strong dose of strength and peace from our Russian tree "cure."

In the morning Lyuba and Mitya were waiting for Larisa and me with hot coffee, cake, and a strange sour berry pudding for breakfast. We chatted away about the filming. Even though Lyuba was an actress, she had never been in any kind of American production and found the event just as exciting as we all did. The hour slipped away, and before I knew it I had to leave. Both Larisa and Lyuba had brought beautiful presents. Larisa gave me a big book of prints from the Leningrad State Museum Russian art collection, with both classical and Soviet paintings. She had tucked into the book a beautiful photograph of her daughter in school. When we paged through the book, Larisa told me her favorite print was of an ancient icon, where Jesus is portrayed with dark, oval, almost Oriental eyes. It is a very simple icon with only one face painted in red, black, and gold. As we stared at the face, I could not help suspecting that Larisa was trying to tell me something. Our earlier discussion about spirituality seemed linked with her favorite painting. Without articulating it, Larisa wanted to let me know that things of the soul and spirit mattered and were part of their lives, even if the facade was an extreme, harsh Soviet exterior. I tried to let her know that she had reached me. Meeting Larisa helped explain a strange sense many foreigners carry with them when they leave Russia. There is a warmth and intensity to friendships in Russia that I have felt is inexplicable. People often try to explain it by the fact that life is tougher, so friends become essential in helping one another through day-to-day hardships. This is surely an important component of friendships in Russia, but my experience with Larisa made me think that there is much more. The spiritual element, the feeling of immediately connecting to and understanding another person, even though we are skeptical and suspicious of each other's political systems, played a large role in my friendship with Larisa.

Lyuba gave me a box of clay folk sculptures painted with bright colors. One of the sculptures was of a woman rocking a baby in a cradle. She told me she sensed I would have a baby in the next year, and this sculpture would bring me luck. She also gave me sculptures for Sherry, who had admired her collection.

Parting from this little group of friends was sad. We had liked each other immediately. In our talks we had opened up and reached each other as if we had been friends for many years. Once again I had to rush out to meet my family (I felt like the typical harried American who could not relax and forget about time), and after giving them small gifts in return, I left. Out on the street I heard them call my name and I waved back to them standing out on Lyuba's balcony. Lyuba was in her bathrobe in the cold as they blew kisses and shouted, "Bye, Katyusha. Remember to write us, take care, we'll see each other again."

I blew back kisses and yelled back "Bye" and "Thanks" as I ran to the bus stop laden with my gifts. On the bus and metro my mind was a jumble of thoughts about Larisa and Lyuba. I hated to leave them so abruptly and felt we could have spent many more hours discussing medicine, our two nations' systems, relationships, and religion. We had just started to get to know each other when I had to run. At the same time I worried about how to portray Larisa. Would I be able to claim that she was a typical Russian doctor? Should I reveal the spiritual side of her, or did she mean to keep that between her and me (as she had whispered the day before). Larisa had shown me her own world and what satisfied her about being a doctor, and I realized that all the books and scholarly research could not have exposed me to this side of medicine. Without ever saying it, Larisa had revealed an essential aspect of Russia to me. Sure, the medical field was backward, inefficient, lacking equipment and medicine, but she still loved what she did. She felt for each patient and gave of herself emotionally and spiritually. The pay was poor, the hours were long, but she embodied an idealism and sincerity that I have rarely encountered.

We met a few other doctors in Moscow, although Larisa was the only general practitioner who agreed to be interviewed and filmed. One psychiatrist Ari and I met was extremely paranoid about talking to us, and agreed to do so only on the condition that he remain anonymous. Ari and I took the metro and a bus to the outskirts of Moscow and found his building, "a green tower," as he described it, in a dry dirt field, isolated from any stores or other buildings. The doctor greeted us in his dark doorway and after we took off our shoes (as is customary) and coats, he led us into his apartment. It was spacious, three or four rooms plus a big kitchen. We went into his large study, lined on every wall with Russian psychology books. There was only one book in English and he did not speak any English. At first Ari was going to sit with us in the study while I conducted the interview, but after Ari asked if he could tape the conversation, the doctor became very nervous and asked Ari, with his tape recorder, to sit in another room.

After Ari left the room the doctor came up very close to me and whispered, "You realize, no one will tell you the truth in Russia. We are a country living in the Middle Ages, we have had little exposure to foreigners, and lead very secretive lives."

I could not help thinking this man was strange. He looked like a Russian version of Freud, with a bushy beard and dark, beady eyes. His proximity while he was whispering, and his paranoia, put me on edge. I reassured him that he should only talk about whatever he felt comfortable discussing and that I would not reveal his identity. *Glasnost* and "new thinking" seemed as far away as Siberia in this encounter. The way he whispered and looked at me as if I were an exotic creature from paradise, the West, I knew that it would be tough going.

Nevertheless, he told me revealing things about Soviet medicine. I knew the essentials of Soviet psychiatry from my graduate studies at Harvard and Columbia, and this helped me to carry on the conversation with him. In the Soviet Union psychotherapy has never had wide acceptance because these forms of therapy were considered to be too concerned with the individual and did not put enough emphasis on the collective. Also, they were not based on a biological approach. Dream analysis and free association were too far removed from concrete materialist science and were therefore considered a deviation from Marxism. By the 1930s both psychotherapy and all forms of Freudianism were abolished. Freud's orientation toward trying to find insights through talk therapy was considered inconsistent with Marxism.

There is a fundamental difference from the West in the way psychology is practiced in the Soviet Union. From its inception, psychology in the Soviet Union has been separated into two disciplines,

Barney, Steve, Evelind, Doveen, and Kate in front of their school, Special School 47. *(Didier Olivré)*

Doveen and her former teacher, Lyubov Matveyevna. *(Kate Schecter)*

Michael teaching English to a class at Special School 47. *(Didier Olivré)*

Sculptor Alexander Chichkin holds a head of Apollo with Barney. In the background is a bust of Lenin. On far left is Maksim Gorky behind Chichkin's head of Barney. On right is Barney's head of Chichkin. *(Aleksei Yushkin)*

Artist Ivan Chuikov, his daughter, Zhenya, and Steve. *(Didier Olivré)*

Artist Zhilinsky's painting of the arrest of his father "during the time of lawlessness and repression." Note flowers in front brought by viewers in memoriam. *(Yuri Korolov)*

The *spravka* or certificate announcing the rehabilitation of Zhilinsky's father. It reads: Military Board of the High Court of the Union of Soviet Socialist Republics   10 August 1957:   "In the matter of Zhilinsky, Dimitri Konstantinovich working until his arrest (20 October 1937) as a technical constructor at the steam turbine electric station of the Trust May Oil and confirmed by the Military Board of the High Court of the U.S.S.R. on 12 July 1957.

The verdict of the Military Board of 10 June 1938 in relation to D. K. Zhilinsky according to the newly opened conditions is repealed, due to lack of evidence of crime, this matter is closed.

D. K. Zhilinsky is posthumously rehabilitated."
(Yuri Korolov)

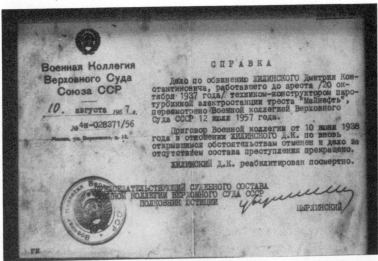

Steve with his friends: Lyokha, Steve, and Vadim. *(Didier Olivré)*

Vadim and Natasha *(Didier Olivré)*

Yevgeniy. *(Didier Olivré)*

Alyona Kirtsova and her son. *(Didier Olivré)*

Gosha, Doveen, Pavel, and creations. *(Didier Olivré)*

Designer Katya. *(Didier Olivré)*

Steve, Doveen in a Katya design, and Katya. *(Didier Olivré)*

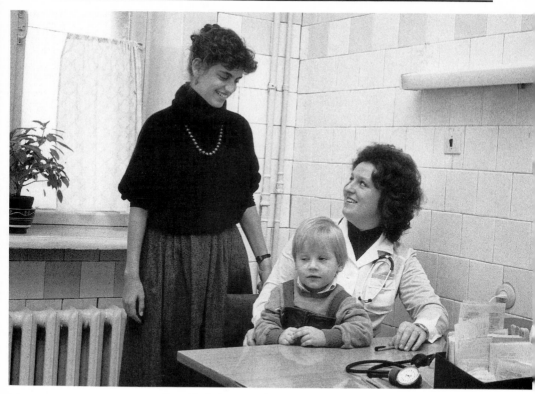

Kate, block doctor, and patient. *(Didier Olivré)*

Kate and children at Detsky Sad
in Yugo Zapad. *(Ari Roth)*

Kate and Yadviga Charny. *(Didier Olivré)*

Ari and Ben Charny. *(Didier Olivré)*

Ben Charny. *(Didier Olivré)*

Soundman Hans Roland and cameraman Foster Wiley follow Suprabha, Steve, and Jerry in Yugo Zapad, the Schecters' old neighborhood on the edge of Moscow. *(Didier Olivré)*

Foster Wiley shooting a day in the country with the local ladies enjoying the show. *(Doveen Schecter)*

psychology and psychophysiology, or the study of higher nervous activity. The latter of these two disciplines was founded by I. P. Pavlov, most famous for his experiments with dogs to test the relationship between the environment and conditioning reflexes. Pavlov was not actually a psychologist but rather a physiologist who believed in studying the reflexes of the brain to understand a person's psyche. Nevertheless, Pavlov has often been termed the father of Soviet psychology. Immediately following the revolution, Pavlov's theories were considered anti-Marxist, but under Stalin, Pavlov's theories enjoyed a renaissance. Stalin hailed the year 1950 as the hundredth anniversary of Pavlov's birth. Stalin saw Pavlov's theories as having direct relevance to Socialist theory. Stalin presumed that if psychologists could understand the laws of conditioning (through studying the brain's reflexes) the behavior of man could be controlled. Man could be molded to fit the image of the New Soviet Man. In a joint session of the U.S.S.R. Academy of Sciences and the U.S.S.R. Academy of Medical Sciences in 1950, an agreement was made to instill forced "Pavlovianization" on Soviet psychology.[4] Remnants of social psychology or methods that dealt with studying the conscious or the unconscious were prohibited. After Stalin's death in 1953, Pavlovianization was not as stringent, and it has gradually decreased as new theories and doctors have emerged. Centralization and old concepts about psychology restrict doctors from experimenting in psychology to the extent that they have in the West, but nevertheless, there has been an easing up on the type of experimental therapy that is allowed.

The doctor had been working in an urban general hospital for the past five years. In January of 1988, as part of the new reforms, he would be allowed to start a private practice after work hours. I asked him if medicine was still a prestigious field in the Soviet Union. "Oh, the prestige of medicine in this country has fallen. Before the revolution doctors and teachers were figures, people who were respected. Now they are like service personnel. I think this is mainly due to changing medical schools into vocational schools in 1936. People are not using their abilities. They are running for diplomas. The purges killed the best cadre and now there are many not-credible people working. Homeopathy has risen, and there are many quacks. There are some people who have the natural ability to do things like extrasensory therapy, but for the most part it is a fad. . . . Doctors make

4. Michael Cole and Irving Maltzman, eds., *The Handbook of Contemporary Soviet Psychology* (New York: Basic Books Inc., 1969), p. 7.

kopecks, now there is a huge shortage of janitors in hospitals—the situation in hospitals is terrible. January first we can expect our standard of living to go down overall when medicine will become scarce. Pensioners will be in a terrible position. . . . As it is, the fate of every sick person has to do with the doctor he gets," he replied.

He felt that women naturally tended to go into humanitarian fields such as pediatrics or teaching while men also naturally chose fields such as surgery or technology. The split between men in surgery or a specialization in medicine and women in other more general medical fields such as pediatrics seems to be a dichotomy that many Soviet doctors take for granted. When I asked about psychology, the doctor seemed bitter. "Only recently can psychologists do therapy. Pavlov destroyed psychology. Many people from the Pavlovian period are still in power, and there are many cosmetic changes. The political use of psychology was a reality, and leading psychologists took part. Now we are excluded from the World Federation [of Psychology] for this reason. The *spetshospitals* ['psychoprisons'] were horrible. They had a prison regime and prisoners wanted to be sent to the camps rather than there. A 'patient' was not given a sentence and had no idea how long he might be there. Everything depended on the doctor. People like Yesenin-Volpin and Petro Grigorenko[5] were lucky, they were protected by their doctors. There were many brave doctors in these hospitals, trying to protect the inmates. Many of these doctors were killed." Although he spoke of the *spetshospitals* in the past tense, his agitation and concern strongly suggested that these horrors are still present.

About science in general he also had bitter words, "There are still feudal relationships in science. Everything depends on the 'chef' [the chief scientist], and he will try to keep only his people around him. When a chef is gray, he surrounds himself with gray people. A whole generation has grown up this way."

Reticent at first, the doctor gradually relaxed after two hours of discussion, when he realized I was not going to attack him about the Soviet Union. As we talked he became more critical of the health-care system, complaining about the restrictions on private practice, the backward state of medicine and hospital facilities and the low

---

5. Major General Petro G. Grigorenko (1907–1987) was incarcerated in a *spetshospital* in 1964 and again in 1969 for five years for his opposition to government policies. He lived in exile in the United States from 1977 until his death. Mathematician-Poet Aleksandr Yesenin-Volpin, son of a popular folk poet, also emigrated to the United States. He is retired and lives in Boston, Massachusetts.

quality of young doctors entering the field. He seemed particularly angry about the state of Soviet psychiatry because only now, after seventy years, were the Soviets realizing the validity of individual therapy. Even though he was successful in his field, after working in various hospitals for twenty years, he gradually revealed an embittered, angry side of himself as he described these drawbacks of the system. Perhaps his well-entrenched position in the field added to his fear of us. As we left him, he sank back into his initial state of fear and paranoia. He wanted to hurry us out of his apartment, and he made sure we left no trail that we had met him. The only people who saw us come and go were his wife and an old man and woman who hung around the entrance of the building. (There is almost no building in Moscow that does not have its old perennial "spies" watching who goes in and out.)

Ari and I were famished after that encounter. When we reached the metro station we popped into a bread store for a roll and sweet cafe au lait. The lunchtime crowd stood at the counters eating their rolls, drinking their coffee, looking weary and more poorly dressed than the crowds in the center of Moscow. Even though our lunch had almost zero nutritional value we felt sated and relieved to be out of the "green tower." Ari was pleased that I had had such a long session with the doctor. On the phone the doctor had told me he could only spare forty-five minutes. Still I felt disappointed. Seeing such fear in a grown man, a sophisticated psychiatrist, was ironic and sad. The U.S.S.R. is supposed to be changing, shedding fear, and creating a new environment where people can speak freely and openly. Clearly that new world was a long way off for this doctor. Even in his own home he was constantly looking over his shoulder. Later I found out that he had applied to leave the Soviet Union nine years ago and had been refused. His fear of us may have also been mixed with bitterness about this refusal to let him emigrate. Resigned not to leave, he had taken a secure job in a hospital where he planned to stay until retirement. He was afraid of telling me too much, of being critical of a system into which he knew he was locked forever.

Our experience at the Moscow "hotline" was more hopeful. Although Steve and I only went there once to film, we had a fruitful conversation in the kitchen where the counselors took breaks. The hotline is located in a large old Moscow apartment in the center of town. It was established in 1982 by one woman, Professor Aina Ambrumova. There are six counselors working in small private rooms, answering callers all day long. Most of the calls come in the latter part of the day when people get off work. When we were there at 5:00 P.M., every phone was busy. The hotline receives five hundred to seven hundred calls a day, and one in every five callers mentions suicide.[6] The types of problems people call about vary, yet they sound much like the types of problems with which an American hotline might deal. The majority of calls come from women who need advice about their marriages and their husbands. Husbands call about their wives, but less frequently. Parents call to get advice about rebellious, rowdy children, and children call to complain about their parents. Depression and alcoholism are also common problems. The hotline counselors give advice over the phone and when appropriate give referrals. Each counselor is a trained psychologist or psychiatric social worker. The counselors we met were young, in their late twenties and early thirties. For most of them this was a job they did in conjunction with other work as a counselor elsewhere. Positions at the hotline were highly coveted even though they paid low wages. Counselors had to pass numerous tests and go through a competitive weeding-out process to obtain these posts. The jobs were so desirable because this was considered one of the most progressive mental health centers. The hotline was the only one of its kind in Moscow, and although another one had been set up in Leningrad following the success of the one in Moscow, there was still a great shortage of such hotlines and counseling centers in the Soviet Union. Therapeutic psychology for "normal" people is a recent phenomenon for the Soviet Union. The hotline is an example of this change in conceptualization about psychology and its uses.

The founder of the hotline, Professor Ambrumova, is an aggressive woman in her late sixties. She was domineering and did not want to let any of her "employees" talk when we first got there. Steve and I interviewed her for the facts about the hotline, but it soon became evident that she was not willing to tell us anything about the nature of the calls beyond a superficial explanation. She had fought so hard to create the center that she kept repeating the same story of how she singlehandedly fought the bureaucracy to create the hotline. "I was a very brave young woman. You see, at that time we were not as open about our social problems, so I had to blaze a trail through much criticism and bureaucracy. It was difficult, and for many years

---

6. *The Philadelphia Inquirer*, March 24, 1987.

I had a small operation with little support. But now, as you can see, we have grown and become the largest hotline in the country." We were told that there is another hotline in Leningrad, but it was unclear if there are any more on this scale in the U.S.S.R.

At first, when we asked to speak to some of the counselors, the director did not want anyone else to talk to us. She wanted to be the spokesperson, and kept asking us, "Why do you want to speak to them? I know the history of the hotline and can tell you anything you want to know."

Finally she agreed to let us speak with two counselors, a young man and a woman, but she insisted on observing our discussion. The young man and woman were very serious and unsure of how much to tell Americans. They told us the work was very draining and that many times it was difficult not to get emotionally involved with a caller. They never gave out their home numbers, and even if someone was suicidal, they could only help them over the phone or refer them to other kinds of help. Some people called repeatedly, wanting to create a relationship with a particular therapist. Although they tried to discourage this kind of relationship, they did encourage people to call back any time and to let them know how issues were resolved. I asked if they ever got calls about wife beating, and the young woman answered with a blush and a smile. "Actually, we have as many calls from husbands who have been beaten by their wives as we do from women." They told us they did not have a problem with unmarried teenage mothers, as we do in the United States, perhaps because people tend to marry young and start families early in the Soviet Union.

The kitchen was comfortable, but I could tell that neither of the counselors was able to open up to us. Out of the corners of their eyes they could see and feel the director watching them. Once again I felt as if *glasnost* was miles away. Although the people who called were open on the phone the therapists seemed uncomfortable discussing these social problems with us. The old Russian custom of creating a beautiful Potemkin village on the exterior for strangers to see, an illusion of perfect order, was hard at work. The hotline was supposed to destroy the habit, solidified during the Brezhnev era, of shunting all social ills aside and pretending they did not exist. It was clear to Steve and me, however, that it would take many years before the Soviets would be comfortable admitting they had the same problems as the rest of the world.

*   *   *

Both the psychiatrist and the hotline are part of an important trend in Soviet health care: a desire to deal with mental health beyond the borders of mental institutions. Although Soviet psychiatry still conjures up images of psychoprisons where sane dissidents are diagnosed as insane because they disagree with the Soviet system, these individual doctors represent the signs of change in Soviet psychiatry. Unfortunately, the signs are few and far between, and culturally it is still taboo to admit that social ills penetrate every layer of society. Nevertheless, there is a beginning.

Larisa's function in her neighborhood was not very different from these psychiatrists'. She knew every family and had been let in on all their family problems. Like the other doctors I met, she was reticent about the types of social problems her patients manifested. The doctors believed that these kinds of problems—alcoholism, family violence, drug abuse, depression—were domestic matters that should not be revealed to foreigners. They thought that perhaps if everyone refrained from talking to the foreign reporters we might leave thinking that these problems exist on a much lower level than in the United States. This kind of illusion is comforting (especially for children growing up in Moscow), but it cannot last much longer. Ever since *glasnost* penetrated the press there have been dozens of letters and articles published on these issues. Even AIDS is discussed in the press now. Although few figures have been released about the extent of AIDS, and the issue is carefully guarded, "SPID" (the Russian acronym for AIDS) was a topic discussed by many of our friends. Testing of foreigners is beginning to be implemented, and fears about AIDS have been expressed in the press.

In 1988 the Soviet Union reported 41 cases of AIDS among Soviet citizens and 150 cases among foreigners in the Soviet Union. These numbers are for people who tested positive to the AIDS virus. Murray Feshbach, an American demographer and statistician who specializes in Soviet health issues, told me: "I would not be surprised if the number were not up to 5,000 or perhaps more." Indeed, the Soviets are only beginning to address this major health problem.

I sensed that Larisa and the younger psychiatrists wanted to talk about these social ills more, but their training and cultural upbringing held them back. My experience with Larisa not only taught me about medicine but allowed me to see beyond the complicated facade that is only now beginning to unravel.

SASHA, NATASHA, and LIZA

We met Sasha and Natasha through an American friend, Laurie, from Columbia University, who told me I could reach her in Moscow in August. Laurie came to Moscow to marry a Russian, Slava, who she had met two years earlier when she was on an exchange program. Laurie and Slava had fallen in love, and after numerous visits they wed while we were in Moscow. When I called Laurie she invited Ari and me to dinner so we could meet her new husband and her friends. She instructed me how to take the metro to the suburb of Moscow where Sasha and Natasha lived.

I thought that Sasha would be meeting us, and I did not know he and Natasha had a daughter, so Ari and I looked for a man when we got off the metro. Natasha and Liza, her six-year-old daughter, walked up to us, immediately spotting the two lost foreigners, and Natasha said, "Katia? Hi, I'm Natasha, Laurie and Slava are busy at the embassy. They'll be coming later."

Both mother and daughter were dressed in colorful patchwork skirts. Natasha had dark straight hair, cut in a Dutch boy that was so austere she looked a little like an Egyptian. She was very pale and petite. Liza looked much like her mother, but not quite as frail.

Walking to their apartment, Natasha described Laurie and Slava's two weddings. The first, official one, took place at the Palace of Weddings. The woman who officiated the wedding had gone into a long speech about how their marriage symbolized the unity between two great nations and these young people were taking on a great responsibility. The next day, Sunday, they had a traditional church wedding. The day we came to see them, Monday, they were at the U.S. Embassy, trying to get permission for Slava to emigrate. (Slava received permission a few months later, and joined Laurie in New York.)

Liza was bored by all the talk about the weddings and longed to have my undivided attention: "Katia, did you bring me a present? Lara [Laurie's name in Russian] always brings me a present."

Natasha, embarrassed by her daughter's precociousness, tried to keep her quiet, but Liza had spotted my weakness for children.

"I'm sorry, Liza, nobody told me you would be here, but I promise you next time I'll bring two presents, okay?"

Liza knew she had me wrapped around her finger. "Okay, Katia. I can wait till next time. Have I told you about my cat family? They live under the stairs, a mother and three kittens, one is gray . . ." Natasha leaned over and whispered, "You understand, this is an imaginary cat family."

"No they're not, Mamma!" Liza shot back. "They just hide under the stairs. I see them every day."

As I translated for Ari (Natasha, Sasha, and Liza spoke no English) we both thought: What a curious child, she is so wild and rambunctious, far more like an American child than a Russian. Indeed, as we got to know this family, we discovered that Liza was different from the other Russian children we met. In Moscow I was struck by how well-behaved children were in public. In Detsky Mir we saw dozens of children being dragged around the crowded store. I think I saw only two crying children in public the whole time we were there. On the metros children sit quietly. They do not yell or scream in public, and we often saw them quietly waddling along (from so many layers of clothes) next to their parents.

One night the subject of children came up with Natasha and Nadya, my parents' old friends. They explained that children seemed well behaved to us in public, but this was not necessarily a positive phenomenon. "You see, we scare our children into obedience at a very early age. First we swaddle them, wrapping their legs so they cannot kick. Then we teach them from day one not to argue back. Children never raise their hands and disagree with a teacher. You know why? Because they are afraid of humiliation. They learn very early on to acquiesce. They are taught to go along with the group, and soon they become afraid of trying to break out. If a child acts up in public, everyone will scold him—his parents, the *babushki* around him, everyone feels they have the right to keep children in line. This creates well-behaved children, but it also thwarts creativity and individuality," Nadya explained.

I argued that perhaps some of this discipline was positive, and it was good that everyone was so concerned about children in Russia. "You don't see it, but we have child abuse and child neglect here, too. No, I would rather give them more freedom and risk having them be less well behaved," Nadya replied.

Liza was an exception to all these well-behaved children, and we soon found out why. Sasha and Natasha were not refuseniks, but they hoped to emigrate one day. Sasha called himself a "nonconformist." Sasha made a living as an artist, but the majority of his art was never sanctioned by the authorities. The couple lived on the fringe of society, planning to one day give it all up and start over in the West. When Liza was born, Sasha and Natasha decided to bring her up the way they wanted, not hand her over to the state day-care centers, as most Soviet children are while still infants. Although she played with the children in the neighborhood, Liza spent much of her time around adults. Her parents explained "doublethink" to her at an early age, and by six and a half Liza was clear about the distinction of what could be said at home and what to say in public. Sasha and Natasha were not anti-Soviet, they just wanted the freedom to live the way they chose. As long as Liza was below school age, they were able to bring her up without anyone interfering. This year, however, Liza started first grade, and she quickly encountered conflicts between what her parents had taught her and what she learned in school. The following week when I saw Liza she had just started school. She ran up to me, pulled my hand so I would bend down, and whispered, "In my class on the world today they taught us that America is our number-one enemy! What dummies! I knew it wasn't true, but I didn't say anything." She laughed nervously, waiting for my reaction.

I hugged her and replied, "You know that's not true, Liza, because you have American friends, but still it must be hard not to tell everyone what you know."

Liza was a bundle of confusion during the first few months of school. She kept coming home, telling her parents what she had learned, and having them tell her most of it was propaganda and incorrect. On the one hand Liza was very proud of the grown-up school uniform that she wore with her "Buster Brown" shoes someone had brought her from America. On the other hand, her allegiance to her parents was much stronger than to the school. Liza showed me her textbooks and, with a sophistication beyond her years, pointed out the contradiction of pictures of tanks, soldiers, and missiles in a textbook titled *World Peace*. Another time she got upset when her mother began to criticize her school. Jumping out of her mother's lap, she retorted, "That's not true, Mamma. Not everything is propaganda in school. I would know, I go there every day."

Natasha and Sasha were torn. They hated to see Liza suffer, but they also felt they had to be honest with her and try to explain why they did not believe in the system into which they were sending her. Liza was still too young to fully comprehend "doublethink" and why her family was different from her playmates' families, but gradually it was starting to take root. Also, now that Liza was getting bigger, her parents were becoming more strict with her. Their discipline tactics, such as a specific bedtime, not interrrupting others, and basic rules that every child needs to learn, were tough to enforce when Liza was going through so much sudden change. Liza was gradually learning the complicated reality of growing up, but it was a difficult transition. When we filmed her family, Liza confided to me that she was not going to tell anyone at school. "If they ask, I won't tell them you were Americans, just some foreigners came over, that's all," she told me.

When we entered their apartment the first time, we saw that Sasha's art was everywhere. The walls were painted with squiggly figures and hieroglyphics, the kitchen walls were painted with the profile of the Kremlin and the Kremlin walls, and the bathroom was covered with Sasha's cartoonlike antics. Liza's room had a painted rocking horse and a few brightly colored paintings on the wall. The apartment was Sasha's studio, and he had taken the liberty of painting most of the free wall space. In one doorway I spotted an icon with Reagan's face in the middle, and on a few shelves there were painted bottles with cutouts of Lenin and Marx peering from inside the bottles.

Sasha was a small, thin man in his early thirties, with a pale complexion and dirty blond hair. He always dressed in American T-shirts, tight jeans, and black Reebok sneakers. Sasha longed to be a part of the Soho art scene in New York. His art—large, modern paintings of heads and profiles of Lenin, Marx, Engels, Stalin, Brezhnev, and conglomerations of leaders—were painted on either canvas or long scrolls of bright silk. Some of these works had been taken out of the Soviet Union and shown in New York in Soho. Sasha dreamed of one day having his own show there. Many of his pieces revealed an Asian or Oriental influence. There were a few paintings of Lenin as a Buddha, and on many works Sasha had written a fake language that looked like Sanskrit. He did not like to talk about his paintings, or interpret them, but he loved to show them, and each time I went there he would show his collection to whomever I brought along.

The first night, Laurie and Slava never showed up, but we stayed late, eating, drinking tea, talking about their lives and why they had chosen this "fringe" existence. Sasha told us parts of his life story that night, and that helped to explain how they came to be living this way. Sasha explained: "About seven or eight years ago I was going to be drafted into the army, and I knew I'd probably get sent off to Afghanistan, so I decided to pretend I was crazy. I took some of my paintings and set up a spontaneous art show on the street. I was immediately arrested and taken to a psychiatric hospital. The hospital certified that I was crazy, which freed me from army service, but they kept me in the hospital for diagnosis. While I was there, Natasha sent me a letter, and even though it was written subtly, they understood that she had written something equivalent to, 'I know it must be hard to be there, but at least you are not in the army, where you would stand much more of a chance of being killed.'

"Well, as soon as they read this letter I was accused of faking being insane and brought before a committee of doctors. Luckily, a few of the doctors on the committee were good people, and they understood why I was pretending to be sick. They declared a different diagnosis for me, one less serious than the first, and I was able to stay on at the hospital.

"While I was in the hospital I painted every day. The hospital was decorated with my paintings, and the doctors vied with each other to take the paintings away from me so they could hang them in their offices. One day I decided to try to save some of my work, and I tossed a painting out the window to Natasha, who was waiting outside. A nurse ran out, grabbed the painting back from Natasha, and declared that none of my work was allowed to leave the premises of the hospital.

"I was released after a few months, but to this day I am officially an outpatient of the hospital and have to check back periodically. With this status of crazy person I don't have to have a job and can paint for a living."

Although Sasha's story sounded fantastic, his work made it more credible. Sasha was not completely isolated, however. He had been invited to be in a Hermitage show, had shown his less controversial paintings periodically in Moscow, and had been a part of the famous "bulldozer" art show of 1974. But for the most part he was a loner, working on his own, trying to get his work out to the West, and waiting for his friends in the West to help him and his family emigrate.

Every time we went to their house, Natasha prepared a delicious meal with beet salads, meat, rice, sardines, tea, and cakes for dessert. Laurie told me they were poor, so I tried to bring them useful gifts. They took great pleasure in the gifts (especially Liza), but it was unclear how they were able to always provide us with so much food. Wherever we went, even the poorest people always prepared these generous meals. With Sasha and Natasha I felt guilty, knowing how difficult their lives were, but without fail, no matter how much I protested, they always had a full table.

Despite their material poverty, Sasha, Natasha, and Liza were good examples of a family who had maintained their individuality and creativity under pressures to conform. Liza, at six and a half, was already her father's daughter, drawing constantly, presenting me with notebooks full of her masterpieces. Natasha sewed beautiful clothes and knit bright, unusual sweaters. Sasha, driven by his constant new ideas, could paint a huge canvas in a few hours. On the one hand it seemed as if they had chosen to live on the fringe of society, but once I got to know them I realized they had no choice—their own creativity forced them to break out of the molds into which society had tried to form them.

When we returned to the United States when I was eleven, for years I felt that Moscow and the world I had known there had been swept out from under me. We left so abruptly that I have longed for years to get that world back, to feel secure about its existence and that it could not be stolen from me. For some reason (maybe because it was my fourth trip back in two years) I now felt that I could go back and it would always be waiting, not changing very much even after seventeen years. There is a familiarity about the gray streets, the *kvas* stands, the *bulochnye* (bakeries), and the roly-poly children wrapped up for winter that I feel so at peace with. It feels like home. I still remember the pain I felt when I realized we would not be going back after the summer (of 1970) when I was eleven. My parents told us maybe we would go back to say good-bye, but in the end we left with no good-byes because we would see everyone again. Most of the people we never saw again. Only now do I feel that I have filled in some of the gaps. I still fear the possibility of being told we can never return to the Soviet Union. Like the Soviets who fear reprisals and backlashes, we Americans who are forever intrigued and drawn to the U.S.S.R. will always hope that greater personal freedom is truly coming to the Soviet Union, and with it the opportunity for us to return to be with our friends and the world we leave behind there.

The Curtain Rises on Glasnost

This was all to be new. Camera lights were shining brightly, a boom microphone hung over the dinner table, and I was often bringing a napkin to my perspiring upper lip. Our bon voyage meal was being filmed by Public Television, and the temperature in Washington had reached upwards of ninety-five degrees. Naturally, the conversation was somewhat strained. In my own family, I would know what to do: be the court jester and lighten the mood, or the angry young playwright making some outrageous statement; tempers would fly, a younger sister might squirm, and the cameras would have their "family scene." But sitting at this dinner table surrounded by mostly older Schecter in-laws, I was out of sorts and quiet. I didn't feel that I had much to add to the on-camera reveries. I had not been part of the original "American Family in Moscow." I had no tales of being lost in Soviet subways. I had never broken a leg sledding down some hill on the outskirts of Moscow. I'd never even been to Eastern Europe. So I had no recollections. I had no nostalgia. I had no idea what to expect.

Nor was I a great student of the Soviet Union. I didn't speak the language. That was Kate's domain. Mostly, I'd been reading magazines, the newspaper, and the occasional John Reed or Yuri Olyesha short story. I also love Chekhov, but he was before the revolution. Again, the feeling was one of humbleness: If only I'd have first read *War and Peace*. Then I'd be ready to go to Russia. But I had been studying a *Time* magazine with its recent Gorbachev cover and accompanying headline: IS THE COLD WAR FADING? I had taken a few notes. And during another pause in the dinner (or perhaps while the camera crew was switching tapes), I decided to enter the conversation.

"You know, Strobe's article really bugged me," I offered. Strobe Talbott is an old Schecter family friend, and even though I'd only met him once, at our wedding, I figured we were on a first-name basis. "It just proves to me that this *glasnost* hype is a product of Western narcissism. The media is going ga-ga because now the Soviets are beginning to look a little bit more like us. They're beginning to buy like us. Compete like us. Protest like us. And we like that. We like seeing Riga youths in Bruce Springsteen T-shirts. We feel vindicated. Strobe thinks the Leninist-Marxist experiment has been a failure. And *glasnost* proves we've been right all along! Don't you see the presumption? The hubris? This need to validate ourselves in such a specious manner?"

One by one, family members picked apart my broadside swipe. "Don't you understand?" Steve scolded in his mild manner. "*Glasnost* is being done by the Soviets, not by us. They are trying to revitalize their own society and their effort is going to affect us. That's why we have to take note."

"Then the media is missing the point," I said. "They make it sound like so much Westernization. It's not! There's still a Central Committee. There's still Lenin, and Marx, and a completely different conception of the individual and the state!"

It crossed my mind that I didn't need to be telling the Schecters any of this. But I was backed into a corner, and by the end of the evening we were arguing about worker inefficiency, Leona insisting that Russian workers "lacked incentive," when I pounded my fist on the table, shouting, "Incentive and inefficiency are Conservative party buzzwords whose sole purpose is to break the labor movement!" At that point the dinner table erupted with laughter as I had another glass of wine, all the while sweating from my upper lip. The cameras had their "family scene." It had been good television.

Our trip would wind up being quite a multimedia package. There would be the book, the TV show, Steve's own film, Barney's sculpture, Doveen's poetry, Kate's doctoral thesis; I would wind up with at least one play—and two songs, both written in room #316 of our beloved Berlin Hotel.

> On the first day of my trip to Russia
> I noticed that the crows

Had bigger, blacker beaks
Than any crows that I had known.
I noticed that the boulevards
Were ten lanes wide.
I noticed that about a dozen tanks
Could easily rumble by
And that an old train station
Could still mean poetry
And that the Kremlin walls were red and yellow
And a little bit of green.

"People are the same," was a first impression
People are the same . . .

We arrived at Sheremetevo Airport in a twilight that lasted well past nine o'clock in the evening. Riding in the backseat of our Intourist sedan, I craned my neck back and forth, for everywhere I looked was a reading lesson. *Pochta* (post office), *pectopah* (my favorite, that's restaurant), and countless *Apteka* (drugstore) signs lined Leningradskoye Chausée. The drabness of the large, modern apartment buildings was not surprising. What I had not expected was the complete lack of landscaping, or "beautification," along the sides of the road. For all the state ideology's alleged rigidity, grass here rarely grows in a straight line. It grows in cracks along the concrete banks of manmade ponds; in clumps on a tattered soccer field; it recedes from the roadway in sporadic washes of clay, stone, and weed. The closer one gets to the Kremlin, the more kempt the grass gets.

Our first meal in Moscow became a late-night ordeal at the renowned Berlin Hotel restaurant. Without reservations, we were told that it would be impossible for us to be seated. We explained that we had just arrived and would simply like a small meal, some caviar and vodka. But the hulking maître d' in his industrial blue jacket was clearly not the sympathizing type and informed us that the restaurant was closed. We walked out. With nowhere else to go at ten-thirty in the evening, we reentered. Quite luckily, the linebacker was no longer seated behind his desk at the entryway. A younger man in more formal attire gladly led us to a table near a gold fountain. Our hotel restaurant was quite an old-world European spectacle. Gilt marble pillars and fresco wall paintings of brilliant ballerinas, suspended angels, and other assorted cherubs surrounded us as a five-piece pop band played "Cha-cha-cha" and "We Are the World." Their musicianship was quite admirable, and the singers took pains to copy the vocal inflections of each of the twenty-four or so American stars who originally recorded the Aid for Africa anthem. A heavyset guitar player in beard and black tie did a pretty good Michael Jackson falsetto. The lead female vocal, however, all but destroyed the confection by mispronouncing the words in English. She had the Diana Ross nuance down pat, but couldn't say the word *making*. As a result, the chorus came out "There's a choice we're my-king," and the whole effect of verisimilitude was shot. The thought crossed my mind that night that young Soviets would do well not to imitate American originals, nor would Diana Ross be well advised to sing the "Cha-cha-cha."

Later that night I dreamed that I failed the literacy test in math. I scored only 2,000 out of a possible 23,000, and yet it was only a two-minute test. Apparently the stakes were high. I remember next that I was in the passenger seat of a stick-shift helicopter, navigating, Phil Donahue at the controls. We skimmed the tops of palm trees and then looked straight up at a giant building. Soon we crashed on a beach, and when I walked up the steps, I was arrested by the village police officer. I felt quite sure they were going to charge me with reckless navigation, but no. I was fined for having failed the literacy test. I remember this quite distinctly, that at the end of the dream, I wanted to call my father and have him straighten everything out with the village authorities.

The dream is a variation on a most conventional theme, but prophetic nonetheless. For during the course of our two months in Moscow, I continually felt illiterate and not entirely at the controls. Our many meetings with Jewish refuseniks made me fear that one day, perhaps quite suddenly, we would be charged with a crime that seemed quite nonsensical. And finally, that feeling, or that wish, that one quick call home to Daddy might set everything aright, that eternal American hope, or belief, never quite extinguished itself.

"Never give your name when making an introductory phone call. Just say 'I'm an American, a friend of so-and-so. Would you like to meet?'" We had received this instruction from two dear friends in Boston—Ronne and Bernard, who had twice been to Moscow and Leningrad—as well as from Misha Fuchs-Rabinovitz, and Katya and Volodya Apekin, recent émigrés who for years had been refuseniks in Moscow. They had provided us with a list of names and phone numbers, including refuseniks, artists, two writers, and a quasi-bohemian couple who knew a lot about theater. Misha explained that it would be best, when calling for the first time, to speak in English, as this would allay some of the refuseniks' fear. I assumed that by *fear*, Misha meant that a Soviet citizen always had to be on guard when meeting or speaking with a foreigner. One could never know if the stranger was truly foreign; perhaps refuseniks were afraid of being offered a present to be sold on the black market, only then to be entrapped by a KGB official.

Kate and I tried to explain that the purpose of our trip was not to politicize the plight of refuseniks. We were reluctant to bring in contraband goods. We were not going to bring in any Bibles, any Hebrew newspapers. We could not put our book or the film in jeopardy. Were it to be discovered that we were disseminating religious material, medical goods, or any items to be sold on the black market, our Soviet sponsor, Gosteleradio, might say that we were violating Soviet law and our preagreement with them. We could have been asked to leave the country. Furthermore, as a Soviet specialist with every intention of returning to the Soviet Union in the future, Kate did not want to put her career on the line. We felt the need to make that clear to our friends at Temple Israel. I imagine that we sounded a bit defensive.

The other man we met with on our late-July fact-finding mission was Leon Charny, an émigré now living in Needham, Massachusetts. Leon had left the Soviet Union eight years ago and had not seen his older brother or niece since. For the past two years Leon had been tirelessly devoting himself to promoting and politicizing his brother Ben's case. He had written countless letters, met with every member of the Massachusetts congressional delegation, and obtained the signatures and support of the entire U.S. Senate demanding that Ben and his wife Yadviga finally be given permission to leave the U.S.S.R. Ben was dying of cancer, Leon explained, but because of an acute heart condition, Soviet doctors were refusing to operate.

We had known of the Charny case for some time. Kate had appeared on a local Boston TV talk show with Leon, discussing health care in the Soviet Union. Again, we stressed our reluctance to get too involved. There seemed to be something provincial about our Boston friends' perspective on life in the Soviet Union. For them, it was only a place Jews could not leave; that was that. We did not share their sense of emergency. We stressed the point: We'll take phone numbers, no Bibles. Nevertheless, six hours later, after more stories, more addresses, and a screening of the "Donahue in Russia" series accompanied by macadamia nut cookies, we left Temple Israel with a Casio data bank wrist watch, Coca-Cola T-shirts, feminine hygiene products, personal letters, other gifts, and a Chicago Bears sports bag; all items to be given to the "friends" we were soon to be calling in Moscow.

The first call we made—from a pay phone, two blocks away from Red Square—was to Vadim and Natasha Zanegina. They were the quasi-bohemian intellectuals who, according to Katya Apekin, knew artists and liked theater. Kate called and spoke in English. There was quiet. Vadim, I assumed, was obviously uncomfortable. Soon, Kate began yaking away in fluent Russian, and I was beginning to get nervous. We had just violated our first instruction. Three minutes later, Kate was depositing more kopecks in the coin slot and being altogether too familiar.

"What is going on?" I asked.

"It's fine," she said, finally hanging up. "We're meeting them tomorrow in front of the Berlin at noon. He doesn't speak any English."

Oh, I thought. Great.

> On the second day of my trip to Russia
> I noticed that the men
> Would take you by the elbow
> Within minutes you were friends
> And that the women smile when they play tennis
> In their bathing suits
> And that the children cry when it's summer
> And their mothers make them wear their boots
>
> People are the same, I remember thinking
> People are the same.

Vadim and Natasha met Kate, Steve, and me exactly on time and knew exactly what to do with us. We went walking. Vadim sought out the Russian-speakers and assumed the role of tour guide and icon interpreter. He had a story for every statue, but I received little translation, for Vadim has a wonderful habit of taking hold and speaking directly into the listener's ear. Kate and Steve were gamely keeping up with his commentaries, and every so often turned to me, explaining that Vadim was very excited about all the changes taking place. I could see that he was excited. I asked Natasha why. Natasha had a fine command of English and, as I was to learn, could speak Chinese as well. Natasha explained that Vadim was especially excited by what was now coming out in the press. For years Vadim had never read the newspapers. He and Natasha consumed literature and poetry—their favorite author being Bulgakhov; their favorite poet, Akhmatova. Now, since moving back to Moscow from Zagorsk, where they spent the winter and spring in a rented *dacha*, Vadim and Natasha had been reading newspapers and literary journals exclusively. Vadim was staying up until three in the morning night after night, trying to catch up on the back issues of magazines he'd missed out on while away. Natasha mentioned a stinging review of a new experimental television show; the show was criticized for not being innovative or provocative enough. Well, I confess, I was not as impressed as Natasha, as one often reads this type of criticism from the average culture critic back home, but still the journalist in me took note: *glasnost* was being spearheaded by the press.

We walked past the Nikinski Gates when I suddenly realized that this was where Katya Apekin said we could find an excellent studio theater. "That's Mark Razovsky's theater," Natasha said, pointing, "on the second floor." Jerry had recently shown us a London *Times* review of a play Razovsky had directed at the Edinburgh Festival, Tolstoy's *Tale of a Horse*. I was excited to make the connection. Steve meanwhile was transfixed with the repertory movie house on the main floor. They were showing three films by Juris Podnieks and Steve was already planning out the rest of his week. We made a promise to return to that theater building and continued on our walk.

The weather up to this point had been beautiful. Moscow is very much like Boston or New York in that respect: When the sun is out, the city is gorgeous. You notice every tree, the buildings are brilliant, and it seems that there is never any traffic. Ever. There are some cities that can look beautiful in rain or under gray skies—Paris, Amsterdam—but not Moscow. When it's cloudy in Moscow, everyone scowls. There are no colors. The Intourist buses leave a trail of black soot, and all the kiosk stands selling Fanta orange soda are closed. Fortunately for us, on this, our third day, the afternoon was cloudless and I could not stop noticing the lushness of the tree-covered parks in the middle of the street as the occasional trolley car ambled past. "Enjoy this while it lasts," Natasha said.

An hour and a half later we were sitting under a sun umbrella outside a coffee shop watching a veritable monsoon of a downpour. The temperature had dropped fifteen degrees, Kate was coming down with the first signs of a terrible first-week cold, and I could not believe the metaphor I was sitting through. It was too obvious. "This is *glasnost*," we philosophized, as the sun slipped behind the clouds.

"Here today, and who knows about tomorrow?" We watched the sky turn from blue to green to gray and finally, almost black, as Vadim ran into the rain to make a call from a pay phone. All those who normally strolled through the Arbat on their way to Leninski Prospekt, or those who simply came to observe the crazy artists, were now huddled in a pharmacy, none of them buying, just waiting out the storm. From under our umbrella we could see a baby carriage and a very young girl with huge white bows in her hair standing watch, keeping dry under a canopy. The little girl was playing in a puddle, almost tap dancing, singing quietly to herself in the middle of the storm. "Where is her mother?" we wondered. "Why on earth is she so happy?"

Soon Vadim returned from his call. It was only lightly drizzling. The little girl and carriage were whisked away by a reprimanding woman. The pharmacy emptied out and people continued on their way. We walked down the Arbat until we came to the end of the block, where a huge puddle lay before us, too big to jump over, too wide to walk around. Someone had placed two wooden planks over the curb, extending just beyond the puddle. At first there was confusion, as people walked in opposite directions over the same plank, crashing into each other. Soon, however, a subway mentality asserted itself and separate lines of To and Fro began to form. Within seconds we were passing over the puddle in orderly fashion, as if this two-lane footbridge had existed for years. I wondered whether such order would ever be adhered to, much less conceived of, in New York.

We left Vadim and Natasha some four and a half hours later at a red-line metro (Soviets call the line by the name of the final stop, but it was easier for me to label them red-line, blue-line, green or purple). We made plans to meet the next day. Natasha promised to get tickets for the opening of a play in which her next-door neighbor was involved. On our walk, Natasha had asked me many questions about theater, but admitted to not being much of a theater-goer herself. In fact, she thought theater to be an inferior art form from a literary standpoint, vowing never to see the current production of *Heart of a Dog* because she loved Bulgakov's novel too much. She also wondered why I was not more interested in film. Echoes of Lenin (who claimed that the cinema was the true art form of the revolution) as well as every ex-playwright I'd ever known (who'd abandoned the stage for screenplays) were clanging in my ears. I had always assumed the Russian intelligentsia to be a passionate theater-going group, but I was discovering this not to be entirely true. Few of Vadim and

Natasha's friends ever went. So when Natasha asked me why I wanted to write for the stage, I feared all my earnest babblings about "live poetic moments" were falling on deaf ears. But Natasha was not cynical. She expressed real enthusiasm about her neighbor, Asya, and the new semiprofessional troupe with which she was associated. Natasha promised to meet us Monday night at the Sovremennik Theater for the opening performance of Mikhael Roschin's *The Seventh Labor of Hercules*.

We met Natasha and Asya in front of the white-columned entrance of the Sovremennik ("Contemporary Man"), a thirty-year-old "official" theater once headed by Oleg Yefremov, perhaps the most renowned actor/director still working in Moscow and currently artistic director of the Moscow Art Theater. The Sovremennik has long had a reputation for doing progressive, respected work. Earlier in 1987 they had staged an acclaimed production of Arthur Miller's *Incident at Vichy*, a play that twenty years before, under Galena Vocheck's direction, had been shut down by Soviet censors. I imagined the Sovremennik to be the equivalent of the Arena Stage in Washington or the Manhattan Theater Club in New York. But Natasha also informed us that we were not seeing the resident, or "senior," Sovremennik company tonight. We would be seeing the second professional production of Sovremennik II, a troupe of twenty-three young actors who all studied together at the Moscow Art Theater Institute. Only four months ago they had been invited in by the senior company and given rehearsal, performance, and administrative office space. "The play they will be performing tonight is a very controversial *glasnost* play," Natasha explained. "It's twenty-five years old, but has never been produced. I suppose this means it's also very new."

Written during "the thaw" of the Khrushchev era, Mikhail Roshchin's first play was actually submitted to the Sovremennik in 1963. As the playwright himself later told us, Oleg Yefremov was impressed by the work but said that it was "ahead of its time. Let's wait and see where these reforms are going." Within a year, Khrushchev had fallen from power and so too had the reforms and feelings of euphoria that had swept through artistic communities. Roschin's first play was never considered for production after that, although many of his subsequent plays have been well received in Moscow. Like many other writers in the Soviet Union, Roschin has seen his career flourish, even as earlier work still remains in the drawer. He now enjoys productions throughout Europe, and has attended American premieres of his work in San Francisco and Houston; even a workshop at the Eugene O'Neill Theater Center in Waterbury, Connecticut.

Tonight is opening night, which means that Asya is a welcoming, but very busy, hostess. Aisle seats are needed for the newspaper photographers, and ticket holders must be moved to make way for the "American delegation," meaning us. After receiving a quick tour of the modern, three-hundred-seat theater, Asya takes us to our seats, fifth-row center. She is literary manager of this new company, a title I once held for a brief time at the Circle Repertory Company in New York. We agree that we have much to talk about, although now she must return to the box office. We arrange to meet at intermission and again after the show.

No sooner does Asya leave than we begin to gossip. "What cheekbones," I observe, with less than a modicum of restraint. Natasha explains that Asya's finely chiseled features are attributable to the fact that she is Tatar. With her blond hair, green eyes, silver-framed glasses, and stylish corduroy pants, Asya hardly looks like a descendent of Mongolian Turks, but then neither does she look like a woman who's been through two marriages (one to the artist Kabakov), two divorces, all this at the age of twenty-five. Natasha whispers to us that Asya is now dating the artistic director of the young troupe, Misha Yefremov. Misha, all of twenty-five years old himself, is the son of Oleg. When *The Seventh Labor of Hercules* was first read by his father, Misha was exactly one and a half years old. Now he is co-producing and performing in the play's premiere, and going out with Asya. All this theater gossip, and we had not yet even seen the play.

As the house lights fade, we take in the striking central image of the set, a giant Rubik's Cube, seven feet high. To give it the mark of authenticity, there is a Rubik's Cube trademark in English embossed on the side of one red square. The cube is in a state of disassembly. Two squares from a side panel are missing, and spewing out from the bowels of the cube are the innards of elastic thread. Long white gauzy styrofoam tubes are strewn all over the stage, spilling over the proscenium. It's as if we are being shown the inside of the enigma. We are seeing the riddling, complex model of the Soviet Union broken open, and inside there is chaos. Indeed, one of the characters, when picking up a piece of foam, utters, "Shit! Look at all this shit!"

Sitting high atop the cube as the play opens is a slumbering Hercules, frozen in a Rodin-like *Thinker* pose. He has been asleep for thirty years, and, in his absence, the city of Elido has gone to seed. A menial laborer bemoans the stench of evil and stagnation that permeates the town. He implores Hercules to wake up, to stop being a memorial statue, and to start meaning, and doing, something. Much to this poor proletarian's surprise, Hercules responds. He descends from his pedestal and becomes repulsed by what he sees. "These people have grown used to their disgusting lives. I can't stand it. We're leaving." Within minutes, however, Hercules, ever the hero, commits himself to ridding the city of its filth. He picks up a fallen red ladder and holds it indomitably over his head. The laborer cheers the return of his hero, as Hercules presses forward, setting out to find his best friend and partner-in-valor, Tezei.

The Thirty Years of Sloth, however, have taken their toll on Tezei, who has become, without Hercules, considerably weaker of spirit. He is haplessly in love with a foreign "Amazon" woman, but is soon enticed by a long-haired prostitute in black fishnet stockings. Undermining any lingering sense of virtue Tezei might still have is the real "star" of the evening, Atta, the Goddess of Lies. Unseen by either of the young female objects of desire, Atta addresses Tezei matter-of-factly, suggesting that he indulge himself; that there is no such thing as loyalty, or a "right thing to do." It is Atta who rules the city of Elido. She knows that "nothing will ever change." Elido will always remain filthy because the "people are too lazy and unwilling to change." The play will become a major battle between Atta's cynicism and Hercules's anachronistic, heroic determination to clean up the town. It is a mark of the honesty and bitterness of this little allegory of a play that Atta should get the best lines, the longest speeches, and generally win the argument for most of the evening.

Soon we meet the farmers of Elido and learn that a new edict has been passed down ordering that "each cow must give birth to three calves." An aging farmer knows he will never be able to fulfill such an ambitious production quota, and grows morose. His son becomes angered. "All your life, all you've cared about are cows, nothing more! If the Czar told you to give birth to a calf yourself, would you do it?" "Yes!" is the father's immediate reply. Then, realizing the implication of his empty obedience, the father again concedes, " . . . yes."

In stark contrast to this barrenness of family farm futility, we are shown the evercheerful, menacing grin of state propaganda. A heavy-set Georgian actor with an unimpressive mustache (who we will later come to know as Genna) declares, "Welcome to Elido! We are the happiest people in the world. And the wealthiest!" A mad parody of Soviet pageantry and bluster quickly follows. Within minutes, the old farmer is arrested and imprisoned inside the cube, which has now become a jail cell. Atta arrives to devise a way of "getting around" the edict. She hypnotizes a prison official into granting the farmer a pardon, then instructs the old man to steal two calves from someone else and claim them to be his own. Corruption wins out in Elido once again.

Act One ends with the audience in a state of sidesplitting laughter. For the first time we meet a character who is a broadly satirical send-up of an easy political target: the Czar of Elido in the guise of a doting Leonid Brezhnev. The Czar and his assistant, Apparatchik, are having a good laugh over the most recent intelligence report. They read that "the slaves don't want to be slaves" (guffaw); "poets write subversive verse at night" (hysterical laughter); "the cows are clean and healthy—they're the cleanest things in town" (more knee-slapping uproar). The Czar asks that he be rewarded for his hard work with a medal, a nice big yellow one, and Apparatchik obliges, pinning yet another piece to the Czar's breast pocket. More bitter jokes bring more meaningless medals. With the audience clearly enjoying this routine, the Sovremennik production takes a bold turn. The Czar suddenly drops all feeble affect and states with solemn reserve, "Then kill the slaves. Make a public execution. Kill the poets." Minutes later the Czar is once again laughing, but a stunned audience has registered the message and walks into the fluorescent light of the lobby for intermission.

As we huddle against a wall during the break, piecing different translations and explanations together, the four of us and Natasha all agree that we are seeing something most extraordinary. "No wonder this play was repressed for so long," Kate says, clearly enthusiastic. Minutes later, Asya reports that "two people have walked out." Indeed, we saw a large white-haired man with medals on his jacket muttering as he walked up the aisle at the end of the first act.

Asya reports that the cast is very nervous, but it is hardly noticeable to us. The actors play as a true ensemble, full of energy, spinning the Rubik's Cube 360 degrees, leaping from place to place, occasionally smacking each other on the head as John Malkovich might do to his sidekick Gary Sinese in a Steppenwolf Theater production. All the actors seem to be in their twenties, all are attractive, athletic, and of fine voice. It is easy to conclude that we are watching a "cream of the crop" ensemble, and when Natasha tells us that the actor playing Hercules is none other than the son of Vladimir Vysotsky (the late and beloved pop singer and Taganka Theater star who died tragically in an airplane crash when his son was but a teenager) our impression is confirmed.

With attractive and privileged young performers such as Nikita Vysotsky and Misha Yefremov, the Sovremennik II troupe may, to some, appear to be the Soviet equivalent of our Hollywood Brat Pack. Even Natasha suggests that only the spoiled offspring of famous parents would feel comfortable and protected enough to present such cheeky material. Nevertheless, the Sovremennik performance has force and integrity. Such rugged American teen idols as Tom Cruise or Molly Ringwald have never quite thumbed their noses in the face of collective apathy and status quo authority the way Yefremov Junior and company are doing tonight.

As the second act begins we are led into the underworld, beneath the Augean stables. A black-faced slave practices voodoo, while a construction worker places bets on livestock quotes over the phone. It is not long before our hero, Hercules, comes crashing through the basement door, confronting the corrupted laborers. "Your life has turned you to cattle, but you're a human being! You need to have your nose stuck in manure so you'll understand!" But Hercules once again is challenged by Atta, the Goddess of Lies. "If you tell us to want more, we'll be unhappy with what we have now. We're used to what we have . . . [To get more] we'd have to restructure everything!" Atta actually uses the word *perestroika*, and the audience laughs in recognition. Hercules's response: "Okay, then that's what we'll do."

As the battle for the ear of the townspeople heats up, Atta delivers the first of two stunning monologues directly to the audience, demanding that the house lights be turned on. A silent assembly of townspeople and audience members listens to Atta chastise: "Yes, we live poorly. We're cowardly, crude. We're passive as cows. We're even lower than cattle . . . but you notice it doesn't bother us. We've gotten used to it. We like it! Even *were* Hercules to clean up this mess, he would never succeed. Things would get messy and disgusting all over again!" In her white laboratory coat, Medusa-like hair on end, devil-may-care delivery, and Mona Lisa–like smile, Atta is a dark, elusive temptress who speaks candor to the townfolk. But never does she claim her candor to be Truth. In fact, Atta, played by a beautiful young actress named Lyena, has no kind words about Truth at all. Standing high atop the cube, she tells the evening's final allegory: "Seven soldiers went out in search of the Truth. Six died. The seventh found Truth in the form of a lizard, slithering in the dirt. It turned out that the Truth was gruesome and horrible. The soldier asked what to do. The Goddess of Truth instructed him to return home and lie about the truth."

Two and a half months after the opening of *Hercules*, Atta's monologue to the audience with the house lights raised remained a stirring high point. On November 18, 1987, *The Washington Post*'s front-page lead story read:

> Three days after Moscow Communist party leader Boris Yeltsin was ousted from his job, a young actress stood on a Moscow stage and lectured her audience about their passivity in the "Yeltsin Affair." As spectators later recounted the remarkable outburst, the leading actress in *The Seventh Feat of Hercules* . . . departed from her script last Saturday and accused the audience of "standing by" while a new Hercules who had come to clean up the city was ridden out of town on a rail. The actress' bold accusation, which named Yeltsin by name, was greeted first by astonishment, then applause, according to people present . . . The next performances of the play, according to box office reports today, were sold out.

Mikhael Roschin's play reaches its ultimate crisis as Hercules threatens to kill the Czar. But he stops short of a violent overthrow because he knows that he cannot leave the people leaderless. Soon he and Tezei must be off to perform their last five remaining labors (according to the myth, Eurystheus imposed twelve labors on Hercules for having unintentionally killed his own wife, Megara, and children in a fit of madness). Hercules promises Tezei that they will enjoy a hearty feast once they have completed their remaining feats. "Let's skip the feats and just have the feast," Tezei wisecracks. But Hercules is in a bind. He knows that he is in no position to maintain his reforms in Elido. And so he concedes that Atta is right: people do not really want austere, radical change in their lives. He petitions the Oracle how to bring genuine reform to a cynical country. A red banner drops down from the ceiling, advising, "Clean the stables in one night. That way no one will know." This sardonic solution prescribes the perfect way for the citizens of Elido to have their status quo and clean it too.

The final scene is a euphoric cleansing party. Throwing off their overshirts, the actors grab buckets of water and begin splashing down the stage floor. The Rubik's Cube, stripped of all its colored panels, becomes a metal frame spinning out of control, and the actors howl and grin, dousing each other in a mad baptism. The cyclorama goes flying off as the naked brick wall of the stage is exposed. This final *coup de theatre* is quite excessive and, of course, has been done to death in college productions of *Spring Awakening*. But no one seems to care. The enthusiasm on stage is contagious. The entire space is cleared, the town has been cleaned, the actors are half-naked, and music rises to a triumphant crescendo, as all on stage assemble for a curtain call, styrofoam tubes having magically become transformed into, of all things, violins. The cast receives three curtain calls. The playwright, looking somewhat amazed and bewildered by this very wild interpretation of his text, comes up to receive the customary opening-night bouquet of flowers. My hands are red from clapping so long and so loud. Nevertheless, as the house lights come up and cast members rush off to congratulate each other, an ardent young spotlight operator standing in the balcony above us implores, "Comrades, you are not showing enough enthusiasm." Yes, we are still in the Soviet Union.

It wasn't always easy finding *glasnost* on the proscenium stages of Moscow. While we were able to see the work of several other progressive companies, including the Stanislavsky and Mossoviet Miniature theaters, I was disappointed to learn that both the Taganka and Moscow Art theaters would be dark throughout August and September and most of October. Their companies were touring and new seasons would not officially open until the day after we were to leave. I was hoping to catch a glimpse of the legacy left behind by Yuri Lyubimov, the Taganka Theater's legendary director, who had been dismissed from his duties in 1984, expelled from the Communist party, and ultimately stripped of his citizenship. In January 1987 we had been able to get two tickets to the opening of Lyubimov's breathtaking production of *Crime and Punishment* at the Arena Stage in Washington. One could see a true pioneer of the avant-garde at work, a pioneer who for the last twenty years had passionately committed himself to presenting antiauthoritarian interpretations of original and classical Russian plays. We were told that the Taganka company was embroiled in a wrenching process of soul-searching, having done battle with two artistic directors since Lyubimov's departure.

While the Taganka's hold on the center of the Moscow theater scene seemed to be slipping, *Moscow News* was whetting the appetites of theater goers by presenting an in-depth interview with Mikhail Shatrov, the well-known Soviet playwright and author of last season's *Prisoners of Conscience*. Shatrov was furiously writing to meet the deadline for a new play to be staged at the Moscow Art Theater by Oleg Yefremov that would coincide with celebrations for the seventieth anniversary of the October Revolution. The play was to be Shatrov's meditation on the Bolshevik Revolution as seen through the eyes of its participants, but from different periods of history. Shatrov promised that the play, to be titled *On . . . On . . . and On*, would be a revealing, complex portrait of Vladimir Lenin and his relationship to Joseph Stalin.

Months later we read that Shatrov had missed his deadline. Instead, an earlier Shatrov work, *The Peace at Brest*, received its premiere production. Like Mikhael Roschin's *Hercules*, the twenty-five-year-old *Peace at Brest* had been garnering an audacious reputation even as it gathered dust in its author's drawer. The play dramatizes the peace treaty signed by Lenin with Germany in 1918. Mikhail and Raisa Gorbachev were in attendance for the opening night performance one week before they left for Washington and the December 1987 summit. Gorbachev, according to press reports, felt that *The Peace at Brest* effectively depicted Lenin as a skillful negotiator who was able to give the young Soviet state the "breathing space" it needed so that socialism could take root throughout the land.[1] Perhaps in seeing Shatrov's Lenin, Gorbachev might have also been seeing himself: a skillful negotiator on the brink of signing a treaty that would give the Soviet state the economic "breathing space" it needed so that it might revitalize its moribund ways of thinking and doing business.

Shatrov, who enjoys productions in Moscow year after year the way Neil Simon usually does on Broadway, was finally able to make good on his promise to deliver a new "*glasnost* play for the holidays." *On . . . On . . . and On* was finished in late November 1987 and published in the magazine *Znamya* upon Gorbachev's return from Washington. It presents the most pointed, searing indictment of Stalin ever written for the Soviet stage. Lenin, at the end of his life, admits his guilt "before the workers of Russia" for failing to stop Stalin when he had the chance. In another scene, one of Stalin's deputies accuses him of ordering the murder of "hundreds of thousands of

---

1. *The New York Times*, January 15, 1988, p. A-4.

people."[2] Later Stalin is shown insulting Lenin's widow. He is accused of plotting the murder of rivals Sergei Kirov and Leon Trotsky and double-crossing fellow Bolshevik revolutionaries Lev Kamenev and Grigori Zinoviev. All of this material goes further in detailing Stalin's abuses than did Gorbachev's widely noted seventieth-anniversary speech.

Most striking to me is the stir created by Shatrov's play solely as a published work. Imagine people here lining up to buy the latest issue of *American Theater Magazine* so they can read what Arthur Miller has to say about Franklin Delano Roosevelt. Who cares? Who reads plays? In Russia, as the editors at *Znamya* know, people turn to their playwrights to hear a history that neither journalists nor general secretaries have seen fit to disclose.

At the Mossoviet Miniature Theater, the process of *glasnost* unfolds long before the play *Examples from Life* begins. Audience members are given pencils and asked to fill out questionnaires in the lobby. Steve, Lyokha, and I retire to the refreshments room to consume almond cookies and a Fanta. Steve translates the questions and I suggest that we put down ludicrous answers, just to mess things up a little. Lyokha laughs. Apparently questionnaires are a new development in the age of *glasnost* and are to be taken seriously.

> Question #1—Is your immediate supervisor competent? (Answer Yes, No, or another variant.) (Lyokha suggests we answer "Never.")
>
> Question #2—Could you change your boss or director? ("Sure, anytime," Steve chimes in. "Just quit!")
>
> Question #3—What is your field of work?" (We all put down "Filmmaker.")

Little do we know that our answers are to be tabulated and reported back to the audience by the play's director during the climax of this evening's performance.

Soon after we are seated, we are introduced to the evening's theme, "the Peter Principle," which purports that "the worse you are, the higher you'll rise" or "the dumber the bureaucrat, the more important he'll be." We then meet a cadre of incompetents, including a bureaucrat from the electrical ministry; a bumbling basketball coach;

---

2. *The Washington Post*, "The Cutting Edge of *Glasnost*," December 14, 1987, p. D-1.

a perky, idealistic, soon-to-be-crestfallen young schoolteacher; and a *dezhurnaya*, a nosy watch woman. The play is ultimately anchored by a frail old woman who sleeps on an upstage cot. She complains that there is a bomb under her bed. She tells of a time in World War II when planes flew overhead and her roof was ripped open; the bomb fell but never detonated. She complains to the local housing authority that she still hears the bomb ticking. A bomb squad is dispatched to the apartment, but the four men can find nothing. As the search for the bomb continues, the audience becomes aware that the actors are standing on the bomb itself. Lying flat upon the stage floor is an inflatable rubber dirigible core. Slowly, the floor begins to swell, but the hapless bomb squad pays no heed. They tell the housing authority that something must be wrong with the old lady; they can't find any bomb. The bureaucrat advises the woman to move rather than remove the bomb. By the end of the evening, the rubber balloon has inflated until it is twenty feet high, twenty feet wide, literally taking over the stage. The bureaucrats remain oblivious. We've certainly gotten the point about the Peter Principle in a striking, theatrical way.

Finally, the housing authority minister scales the heights of the huge bomb/balloon and deflates it. The show's director, who has played a young man with a broken arm receiving laughably poor medical treatment, stops the action of the play and reports, with the aid of a clipboard and hand-held microphone, that 61 percent of the audience feels it works for incompetent supervisors. But less than a third of the audience feels free to complain about such supervisors to ultimate superiors without threat of retribution. The director implores us to "call a spade a spade" and stand up for competence in the work force.

Another play that almost certainly could not have been presented a few short years ago is Mikhail Bulgakov's *Heart of a Dog*. Bulgakov's terse, acerbic novel, written in 1925 but not "officially" published until sixty years later, was now receiving two markedly different stagings within a six-week period. The first production, at the Theater for Young Audiences, was a highly impressionistic interpretation beginning with all the actors seated at the edge of the stage howling madly like dogs. The setting for Bulgakov's attack on the Soviet attempt to create a New Socialist Man is split between a 1920s Soviet kitchen, a laboratory, and a backdrop of ancient Egyptian pillars. Nefertiti and Tutankamen, wrapped as mummies, make brief cameo appearances and help reinforce the stage metaphor suggesting that man's struggle to conform to a prescribed political identity has been going on for centuries. The actors mournfully walk through a pile of ashes, as this highly anachronistic production effectively tells the story of Dr. Philip Philipovich's transplanting of a drunk Russian's brain and pituitary gland into the body of a mangy mutt.

Equally forceful is the Stanislavsky Theater's hyperrealistic interpretation of the rise and fall of Sharrik the Man/Dog. This production begins with a real dog on stage. The doctor, much like Pasternak's Zhivago, makes it quite clear that there is as much to be lost as gained during these early years of socialist fervor. Both productions of *Heart of a Dog* feature superb acting in the title role, a part that demands great athleticism—Sharrik must repeatedly go diving over couches in pursuit of wayward cats. The message of the piece rings clear: one can learn to spout rhetoric concerning "Good of Man/Will of Party," but it's much tougher to root out man's reckless will, no matter how powerful or scientific the socialist state dogma.

In between our visits to other local theaters we made sure to return to the fifth floor of the Sovremennik Theater building and touch base with the young company members who were fast becoming our friends. We attended rehearsals for three different plays that were to run in repertory alongside *Hercules*. The first piece, *Escarielle*, a one-act play by the Belgian playwright Michele de Ghelderode, shows a power struggle between a king, his wife, and their servant. This play was to be performed in tandem with a new Soviet play concerning the relationship between two men who share an *izba*, or log cabin, in Siberia. In the play, written by Alexander Obraztsov, an "angry young playwright" from Leningrad, one man looks for his vermicelli, the other quietly hums Russian folk songs. They are intruded upon by a young friend, fresh from the battlefront, and his eternally giggling girlfriend. A battle over the girl ensues. Nobody wins, least of all the girl, who spends the last fifteen minutes of the play crying and literally tearing her hair out.

Obraztsov's play is indeed angry and acrid, youthful mostly in its pervasive, monochromatic sense of despair. One character remarks, "The air is yellow, buttery, gross, and disgusting." The friend responds, "I've worked my whole life and gotten nothing . . ." Back to the vermicelli seeker: "A guy is sitting across from me, a regular Russian guy, and he's fat, disgusting. I instantly can't stand him. I look at this guy with such hate. What is there to live for with such torture?" Later he says of his sister: "She had nothing; no money; no brains. They wouldn't let her study or work. She would run wild. Nowhere to live. They threw her out. She died of hunger." Perhaps the play should have been about this destitute vagabond of a sister, who we only hear about, and whose tragic story might have unfolded dramatically before us. Instead we are presented with inert protagonists whose singular tragedy is eternal passivity (hmmm . . . strains of Chekhov?).

Misha Yefremov, the company's artistic director and production director of the two one-acts, was calling the evening "Theater Season."

"Why such a silly title?" I asked Misha.

He explained that the title for the evening was originally to be "Nightmare." Then Misha changed his mind. Last season, when they performed Yuri Olyesha's *The Slap*, the company was roundly criticized for presenting a bleak, cynical portrait of Soviet life. *The Slap* did not seem bleak to Misha, nor did Obraztsov's play.

"This is a play of the New Wave! A play with no message! No hope tacked on to the end. For us, this is exciting. We know we will be criticized for this. So we don't want to give our critics any more ammunition with a pretentious title. We just call it something dumb, like 'Theater Season.' "

Misha made the case for bleakness quite appealing, mostly because he smiled and did not seem to take himself all that seriously. At any given point in a rehearsal, Misha could be seen howling with laughter, rocking back and forth merrily, a perpetual cigarette in either hand or mouth, and always a line ahead of the actors. Misha knew both texts by heart. He and his actors had been rehearsing these one-act plays on and off for the past two years.

While I observed that not all of the work at the Sovremennik was of a uniformly brilliant level, I was simultaneously aware of my being envious of their ensemble, of their commitment to their craft and each other. Each of the twenty-three troupe members was paid a monthly salary of 140 rubles ($220). Not a lot, but how many twenty-six-year-old actors in New York City are guaranteed half that much for being members of a repertory company? Not many. None of the Sovremennik II members had to teach five-year-olds during the day, or wait tables, or take temp jobs on Wall Street. These young company members were being paid to eat, drink, and sleep theater. They would soon be performing four different plays at the same time, with every member appearing in at least two, and usually three, of the productions.

The situation for playwrights in the Soviet Union was another source of envy. While the Sovremennik troupe did not have its own playwright in residence, I learned that even a young, infrequently produced playwright like Alexander Obraztsov could look forward to a modest but steady flow of income from his plays over a long period of time. Because of the repertory system, a play that premieres in Moscow in 1987 might still be running two or three years later, without necessarily having to be a breakaway box office smash. That same play might eventually wind up traveling to some two hundred different theaters throughout the Soviet Union and stay in repertory for years. A playwright with a play running anywhere in the Russian republic can look forward to receiving a guaranteed 4 percent of the box office. A play running in any one of the other Soviet republics will bring a playwright anywhere between 1 to 7 percent. According to the Soviet Writers' Union, the average playwright makes approximately 200 rubles ($320) a month. American playwrights will often hear from their cohorts in the Dramatists' Guild: "You can make a killing in the theater, but not a living." In the Soviet Union very few writers for the stage are making a Hollywood-style "killing," but they are living quite respectably and, like the Sovremennik actors, are being paid to continue the practice of their craft.

Each week at the Sovremennik there is a company meeting at which any and all issues concerning matters artistic as well as business are raised. The Sovremennik II is part of a newly created group of "self-financing" theaters—neither "amateur" (once called "underground") nor "state subsidized." Their agreement with the senior Sovremennik troupe stipulates that they may draw money from the senior troupe's budget if it is replenished with money collected from ticket sales. Asya, the literary manager, explained to us that recent company meetings have been particularly vociferous, because the topic has centered around which play to produce in January. Everyone has agreed on one point: that the play should have something to do with Stalin, preferably about Stalinist labor camps. Asya has been searching for exactly such a play for the past year. Although she has found several, none has been deemed stageworthy. Exactly such an argument has been made against Alexander Azarkh's *Nasha Radoslovnaya* ("Our Genealogy"). Asya showed the play to her neighbors Vadim and Natasha, and they both agreed that the play was slow, abstract, and not confrontational enough. Asya's opinion, however, was challenged by some members of the troupe who felt that it was their duty to breathe new life into a play that, like so many others, has been gathering dust for the past quarter of a century. By late September the group decided to proceed with plans to stage Azarkh's three-act labor camp drama, to be co-directed by Misha Yefremov and the play's chief proponent in the group, the heavyset Georgian actor with the unconvincing mustache, Genna.

Late after one rehearsal, Genna gave me his only copy of the Azarkh play and asked if I would like to read it. I explained that I had a hard enough time reading street signs; there was no way I could read a three-act play in Russian, nor could I expect Kate to sit down and translate it for me. So Genna asked if I wouldn't mind trying to get it copied for him somewhere; somewhere being the National Hotel or the *Time* magazine office. I told him I'd see what I could do and took the script. It became clear to me that Genna had other plans for this script. He knew that I had loved *Hercules* and that I had spoken to Misha about trying to figure out a way to bring the production to the United States, perhaps to the Lincoln Center Theater, where South African productions were being imported on an annual basis. Misha and I both knew that such a production could be terrifically exciting, but in the end agreed that such a tour would, undoubtedly, be expensive. Misha also worried about logistical and administrative complications. Because the Sovremennik II was not a fully subsidized "official" theater, it was not high in the pecking order of GosConcert, the state entertainment agency through which all cultural exchanges were arranged.

Genna was undaunted. He pointed out that "his Azarkh play" would be infinitely cheaper to produce; there were only four characters. He was also quick to add that, were producers reluctant to bring over the entire Sovremennik troupe for the production, he and Misha would be glad to direct American actors in *Nasha Radoslovnaya*—or in any other play, for that matter. I concluded my brief business meeting with Genna by saying that the best way I could present his troupe to American theater producers was by showing them photographs of the young company in performance. Perhaps Genna could arrange for me to get a few promotional photos from their productions, and I would see what I could do. Genna said obtaining pictures would be difficult, but he would try.

By this point Genna had appointed himself my personal chaperone at the Sovremennik, as he was only one of two people there who could speak bits of English. All other interaction at the theater was facilitated through Kate or Steve, but with Genna it was always one on one. The first time he introduced himself to me he said, "You are

Jewish, yes? You work for American Jewish Theater?" I answered yes, I was a playwright-in-residence there. He said, "I'm Jewish too. Would you like me to show you Moscow synagogue? After rehearsal?" I said fine, and thought this might be a great opportunity to become closer to a working actor and get a tour of Jewish Moscow while I was at it.

We walked in a light rain for ten blocks until we turned downhill onto a side street that led to a police station, and beyond that, the central synagogue. On our walk Genna asked me if I was a Zionist. The question did not come completely out of the blue. He had first asked, "Where did you meet your wife?" I answered, "Jerusalem, Hebrew University." Genna then explained that he himself was an anti-Zionist. What did this mean, I wondered, anti-Zionist? A self-proclaimed Georgian Jew is taking me on a tour of Jewish Moscow and announces that he is an anti-Zionist.

"Do you see a difference between being a non-Zionist, Genna, which is to say disinterested, and being an anti-Zionist, which is to say opposed to the very idea of Zionism for others?"

"No difference," he answered. I figured the problem was my question.

"Genna, do you oppose the idea of a Jewish state?" I asked.

"Yes, for me."

"But what about for others?"

"I can only know for me. For me, I am anti-Zionist."

"Not non . . . ?" I said, holding out the olive branch.

"Anti."

We stood in front of the synagogue steps. I was reminded of the Kane Street Synagogue in Brooklyn, the borough's oldest, where I had once taught kindergarten on Sundays. There was a bizarre familiarity to this modest, solid structure. I read aloud the Hebrew words that welcomed worshippers. Genna said he was impressed. We walked up the steps and entered the narrow foyer. We peered into a side chapel where three people—one very old man seated behind a table, and two somewhat younger men in winter coats—waited for the early evening *minyan*, the gathering of ten men to begin the prayers. Genna motioned to another door and we walked to it, past the absent, oblivious men, and into a dark, scaffolded, towering cathedral of a synagogue. Genna told me I could not walk to the center of the room without a head covering, and he patted his head. I took a Kleenex from my pocket, put it on my head, and stared up at the balcony that extended the length of both side walls. The vaulted ceiling was obscured to me by the crisscrossing of metal, but a stained-glass Jewish star in violet and gray shone through high atop the rear balcony. Six weeks later I would reenter this synagogue on Kol Nidre night, along with fifteen hundred other Jews, huddled into wooden pews, resting my prayer book on a hand-carved phylactery box, gazing up at that same vaulted ceiling, now brightly lit and newly tiled with interlocking diagonals of white, green, copper, and blue. I would come to feel very comfortable in this Old World syn- agogue during the High Holidays. But on this cold, rainy late after- noon with Genna the anti-Zionist, ever-mindful that I not let the Kleenex fall off my head, I was anxious to be on my way, and soon said good-bye and thank you to the three oblivious men, and after descending the steps, asked Genna the way to the nearest metro.

There would be more incidents with Genna. One day he offered to be "our guide" if we, in exchange, could get him into the opening of the Chagall exhibit at the Pushkin Museum. We explained that we were not invited to the opening and had no idea when we might be going. Genna said that nothing was going to stop him from giving Vava, Chagall's widow, a kiss on the cheek. Genna wound up using other channels to get himself into the opening, and did indeed give Vava Chagall a kiss on the cheek. He had pictures of himself in a white three-piece suit to prove it.

We did do one favor for Genna. We agreed to deliver a Russian children's book to his three-year-old niece in Pennsylvania. Genna never gave an indication that he himself was interested in moving to America; he just wanted to direct at Lincoln Center.

Our interludes came to a close as we returned to the Sovremennik one last time, to interview the playwright Mikhail Roshchin on cam- era before the crew filmed a live performance of the play. We had been told that someone would meet us after the show with the pho- tographs for us to take back to America. Sure enough, as the theater was clearing out after a rousing performance and enthusiastic re- sponse from the audience (I'm sure the spotlight operator was more pleased), Asya took us into the administrative office, where we met a burly, bearded fellow in a tan corduroy sports jacket and photog- rapher's shoulder bag. He introduced himself as a friend of Genna and said that he had stayed up all night developing pictures for us. He didn't speak English. He didn't speak much at all. He glowered. Kate informed him that we were interested in helping the group become known to a wider audience and we had hoped that the theater would have a few pictures on hand for publicity purposes. We had never

344

intended that he stay up all night for such a small request. He said, "*Nichivo* ("It's nothing"),"" but then proceeded to show us over one hundred different 8½-by-11 black-and-white stills of the troupe in performance. "All of these are for you," he said. "All of them." Apparently that was the agreement, as he understood it from Genna. Now the photographer wanted fair compensation.

"Maybe you have a camera you can give me?" the photographer said. "A Nikon."

"We don't have a Nikon," answered Kate.

"So you can send me one." The photographer was calm but resolute.

"I think there's been a misunderstanding," Kate offered, putting the photos back in their folder and returning the package to the burly, bearded, and may I add, much bigger man.

"What if we pay you for the photographs we like?" I proposed. The photographer shook his head. Kate refused to translate. She knew he'd never go for it; he wanted his camera. But I insisted. I had picked out four or five decent shots from the pile and thought they'd be nice to have.

"He won't take money," Kate reprimanded me. "He wants a Nikon."

She thanked him, apologizing for the misunderstanding. The photographer grew indignant. He had been up all night, after all. What was he going to do with all these photographs?

In order to extricate ourselves from this most unfortunate situation, I insisted that Kate make an offer of ten rubles for four pictures. He refused. Twenty rubles. Kate was furious at me. I was steadfast. The photographer closed the door to the office and said he could not accept money for the pictures; it was illegal. Furthermore, he was not affiliated with the theater in any way. This was a personal favor he was doing for Genna and he thought he at least deserved something, if not a Nikon, then a Canon, or if not a Canon, then an older, less fancy camera.

"Why don't you ever listen?" Kate sniped at me. "It's a setup. We've been set up." And she went to get her coat. The photographer shook his head, collected his package, stuffed it into his shoulder bag, and waited for his friend Genna to meet him.

I never had the chance to say good-bye to the man myself.

On the third day of my trip to Russia
I stood in line for bread

On the fourth I bought a watermelon
And then promptly went to bed.
On the fifth day of my trip to Russia
I met a man Refused
I did not expect to see him smile
So when he did I was confused.

"People are the same," it's a song or prayer
People are the same . . .

Meeting a Refusenik Family

"On August 16, 1987, I met my first *refusenik*." That I should have referred in my journal to any member of the Charny family with so generic a term is not surprising in that I had grown up with the word *refusenik* perfunctorily being bandied around the classroom—or the cabin bunk, depending on the season. I had even worn a "Save Soviet Jews" T-shirt to bed as pajamas (to this day, Kate wears this tattered heirloom from the early 1970s, mostly when she does aerobics in the house). *Refuseniks* and *Soviet Jewry* had permeated my preadolescent consciousness to such an extent that I could ascribe no physical image or reality to the terms. I can remember going to rainy rallies at the Chicago Civic Center, climbing up Picasso's horse, paying absolutely no attention to the drones emanating from the speaker's platform, keeping a lookout for camp friends from the North Side, and mumbling along with the men in blue trench coats when they sang "Let My People Go." An earlier memory is driving up to Lake Geneva, Wisconsin, with my father for a protest sponsored by the American Jewish Congress against a Soviet delegation of scientists staying at the Abbey Hotel. Again, it was a rain-drenched affair. I remember stainless steel outdoor oil lamps burning orange flame with black fumes while then Illinois Attorney General Paul Simon, in the same horn-rimmed glasses, bow tie, and brown trench coat, addressed the mob of fathers in a melifluous, righteous voice. We sang "If I Had a Hammer" and shook angry fists at these faceless Soviet scientists, calling for the freedom of our faceless Soviet kin.

347

As the 1970s progressed, the Save Soviet Jews bandwagon became less the "in" thing, as organizational focus shifted from rallies to bulk mailing. Soon I began to recognize a few names and faces from the same-looking brochures. But *refuseniks*, to me, did not mean people; it did not mean lives dangling in a dangerous wind. *Refusenik* had simply become an overworked cliché; a "Save the Whales" for liberal synagogues and Hadassa-minded social workers.

To begin again: "On August 16, 1987, I met my first refusenik." His name was Yuri Charny Blank. He had agreed to meet Steve, Kate, and me at the Izmailova Park Station. He told us he would be wearing a brown leather cap. We walked down the middle of the outdoor train platform on a brilliant, cloudless afternoon. Yuri was indeed wearing his cap, as well as a crimson Harvard sweatshirt given to him by our friends Ronne and Bernard. Yuri was not yet thirty years old, but his manner was much older, unsmiling and soft-spoken. In the spring, during the Passover season, he had been on a hunger strike for more than a month, as had his mother-in-law, Yadviga. On this crisp, Chicago-like afternoon, Yuri's handshake was still soft, his eyes more sensitive than piercing. He seemed fragile and strange. He led us through an older, more dilapidated neighborhood than any we had seen before in Moscow. I paid close attention to the way some of the old *babushkas* seated on benches stared at us as we passed. In his solemnity, Yuri could not have been more different from Vadim, our ebullient icon interpreter. Yuri politely answered the occasional question but initiated little. We asked about his summer, remarked that the sun seemed quite bright and cheering, and inquired as to the health of his and Anna's new two-month-old baby, Sima.

I was very excited to meet Anna. We had been briefed that she was a refusenik of eight and a half years, and an extremely bright mathematician, now unemployed. Anna spoke perfect English and was a voracious reader of contemporary fiction. Our friends in Boston told us that Anna was the type of woman who might have become a doctor in the United States, or a Ph.D. candidate in the Soviet Union, had she not chosen to apply for emigration and summarily been expelled from the technical institute in which she was enrolled at the age of nineteen. We ascended the two flights of steps to their apartment and shook hands at the door. Anna nodded demurely. She was wearing an oversized T-shirt with shoulder pads and a pink print of a beach umbrella on the front (obviously a gift from Filene's Basement). Both she and Yuri wore Russian blue jeans. Their baby daughter was wrapped in a plaid wool blanket, sleeping outside on their narrow balcony in a cut out cardboard box. The sun was shining down on her as she lay peacefully sucking on a pacifier. Kate was overwhelmed by the sight of this suspended cardboard cradle rocking gently on a sun-drenched porch. I imagined Kate to be thinking, We New Yorkers are always complaining we can't have a baby because we don't have enough room, or we don't make enough money.

We presented Anna and Yuri with several presents and medical goods we had brought over, including a brown paper bag filled with eight large tubes of Femstat for feminine hygiene. Kate assumed that Anna would know who would need these. Anna thanked us routinely. She had obviously received material goods from Westerners before, goods that provided sustenance but little joy. Kate then took from her purse several *chachkies*, or novelty items, including pens, markers, silly-looking erasers, and a key chain with a dangling globe. "Thank you," they both replied. My take on Anna and Yuri at this point was that they were very serious, very intense people, who didn't have much patience for frivolous Americans and their *chachkies*. I was dreading the last present we were to give them, which Kate had bought at Suprabha's gift shop. It was a floating plastic hippopotamus with a moveable jaw. Inside the hippo's mouth was a small turtle attached to a string. You could pull the turtle and string back and watch the hippo chomp up and down, reeling in the string until it opened its mouth wide one final time and devoured the turtle. This is the wrong present for Anna and Yuri, I thought to myself. Kate was less uptight. She presented the gift as a family item, to be enjoyed by one and all in the bathtub. Anna and Yuri were entranced. This couple, who ever-so-matter-of-factly accepted a $350 camera, looked at this plastic hippo as if it were a jewel. Kate showed them how to pull the turtle out of the hippo's mouth and they watched with bated breath as the hippo chomped on the string. When it finally snapped its plastic mouth shut they shrieked like schoolchildren and immediately pulled the string again.

"It's a two-dollar toy from Korea," I tried to explain.

"This is beautiful hippo!" laughed Yuri, shedding about twenty years of sorrow before us. Anna eventually explained that her father's nickname was Hippo and that she had given Ben a stuffed hippopotamus as a present when she was little and that it remained a running joke between them. Anna and Yuri pulled the turtle from the hippo's mouth over and over that afternoon, and couldn't wait to show it to Sima.

That hippo was an icebreaker. We soon got to see Anna and Yuri smile quite a bit. Their solemnity during our first half hour had seemed quite disingenuous to me, as if they were projecting a mood that we were supposed to pick up on and conduct an earnest interchange about the plight of "our people." They had been through that kind of encounter many times now with American friends of friends, or with emissaries from various political action committees. There seemed to exist an agenda of discussion topics in these types of encounters between refusenik and refusenik-sympathizer; I imagined that this dialogue might include news from Israel, Bible study, updates as to the condition of recent émigrés, and expressions of reassurance that "your time will come soon." Such was not the case, as Anna and Yuri now seemed genuinely interested in who we were.

They wanted to know whether we thought there were any "real changes" taking place in their country. Steve suggested that people seemed "more hopeful" now. Anna said she was not so sure. "People are mostly being deceived." Steve then said that people in Russia seventeen years ago seemed to be "a little more idealistic," which was to say, more ideologically oriented. Steve maintained, "Now people seem more materialistic." Anna disagreed. "Perhaps it was you who was idealistic seventeen years ago. People here have not been idealistic since the end of Stalin."

I thought it appropriate to echo Anna's pessimism by recounting our recent discussion with Andrei Voznesensky, where he talked about his attempts to dedicate a Chagall museum in the artist's birthplace of Vitebsk. At first there was support for the museum, but after visits and anti-Semitic speeches from the revisionist historian Valery Begun and other Byelorussian authorities, public opinion in Vitebsk had changed and the plans for a Chagall museum had been put on hold. Anna corrected me. "There is no public opinion in the Soviet Union. Merely a shift in the administration's public view."

Throughout the afternoon she and Yuri reacted skeptically to our observations about their changing country. We talked about the documentary *Is It Easy to Be Young?* We had been impressed with its candor, particularly during interviews with wounded soldiers returning from Afghanistan. Anna and Yuri had seen the movie but said it was incidental and did not signify much of a change. We talked about the excitement on the Arbat; folksingers, artists, Hare Krishna engaged in public debate with other questioning, questing Soviets. Anna and Yuri had not been to the Arbat in months.

Anna soon began to make the afternoon dinner. Steve was showing

Yuri some of the new features on his camera and Kate was holding Sima. Anna asked me to come into the kitchen, as she didn't like to cook alone. She was cutting bread and cheese, boiling potatoes, slicing zucchini, chopping fresh parsley, basil, and dill. I asked her about the aftermath of the fiasco involving Phil Donahue's recent attempt to interview refuseniks while in the Soviet Union for a week of live broadcasts. I had seen some of the Donahue shows on tape and had read articles criticizing his handling of the refusenik issue. I asked Anna to give me her version of the chronology of events as she understood them.

Donahue had proposed to do a segment for the "space bridge" wherein three hundred refuseniks would be assembled in one studio with Phil Donahue asking questions. Gosteleradio had approved of the interview with the caveat that Donahue also do a segment on the "Happy Jews" of Moscow and Biro-Bidzhan. Donahue readily agreed. The week of Donahue's live shoot, Gosteleradio began to change the terms. They claimed that they could not obtain a studio big enough for three hundred refuseniks. But if Donahue wanted to go ahead with the segment, he could do so with fifty refuseniks. Donahue readily agreed. The three hundred refuseniks, who were to be coming from Moscow as well as Leningrad, Odessa, and Kiev, did not agree to these terms quite as easily. They knew what Gosteleradio was up to. Ultimately, they as a group (albeit an ad hoc alliance, for no official refusenik group exists) came to the decision that wives of the Prisoners of Zion, longtime refuseniks, and certain refuseniks sick with diseases would be included in this group of fifty.

The day before the scheduled interview, Anna continued, Gosteleradio informed Donahue's staff that they could not locate a studio big enough for fifty. They would only be able to proceed with twenty-five refuseniks. Donahue agreed, but this time the refuseniks said no. "They are trying to divide and conquer. They want us to turn on each other," was the prevailing sentiment in the group. Donahue's twenty-minute segment was in jeopardy, and he wanted to pressure the refuseniks into a compromise. It was unclear, according to Anna, whether Donahue bothered to put any pressure on Gosteleradio. What could he do, after all? Probably a lot, she thought, but it would have meant an unseemly confrontation or the possibility of "going black" and not having any programming for twenty minutes, which is to say, in television talk, "not an option." The refuseniks were adamant in their refusal to capitulate. Besides which, or more to the point, who would decide which twenty-five would participate and which would not? There were at least a dozen wives of prisoners, a score of people in refusal for fifteen years or longer, and another dozen critically ill refuseniks. This group, rather hastily assembled to begin with, did not include Anna's father, Ben, who had helped to organize press conferences in the past for a small group of refuseniks with cancer. It was already getting to be an ugly scene among the refuseniks when Donahue proposed that he do an interview with twenty-five or so of the refuseniks in someone's apartment. The refuseniks said they could not agree to an interview, but they would discuss their reasons for not consenting to one. Donahue agreed to meet the refuseniks at the home of longtime refusenik Vladimir Slepak, and it was preagreed that no one from Gosteleradio would be present.

When Donahue showed up at Slepak's, he came with a cameraman and his ubiquitous hand-held microphone. Introductions were made between Donahue and the dozens assembled in Slepak's small apartment, but when Donahue asked his cameraman to start filming and then began asking questions of the group himself, he was shouted down.

"We will only tell you why we cannot consent to an interview!" "We will not be treated like puppets!" came the cries.

Donahue stepped back and solicited, "All right, then, why doesn't somebody here tell me why you won't agree to be interviewed?" It is this discussion that was carried into the homes of tens of millions of Americans on daytime television: angry, overemotional refuseniks explaining why they could not answer any of Phil Donahue's sensitive, probing questions.

At one point in the broadcast, Donahue can be seen putting his arm on the shoulder of a wife of a Prisoner of Zion. Soon he turns to her and asks, "May I interview you? Your husband is a prisoner . . ." And the woman, with pathos in her eyes, looks like she very much wants to have her husband's story be made known. But she is shouted down by the group. "This is not an interview!" they maintain. Donahue becomes incredulous, with his masterful made-for-TV devil's-advocacy demeanor. "Won't anybody here let me interview this wife of a Prisoner of Zion?" Indeed, the refuseniks come off looking quite stubborn and mean-spirited. Couldn't they have allowed Phil to get just one heart-wrenching story? That's all he really wanted. . . .

In answering my question about the aftermath of this episode, Anna shook her head and said, "You know, we Jews live in a ghetto.

352

It is a new kind of ghetto in that we feel very much alone, cut off. We do not even have each other. But during an incident like Donahue, it feels, I imagine, much like an old ghetto." She explained that pieces of the Donahue broadcast were aired in the Soviet Union, and that the section involving the refuseniks was presented in an especially wounding way. A Soviet broadcaster illuminated, "Here are the same people who have been complaining for years about their lack of freedom, and now Mr. Donahue gives them the opportunity to speak and they enforce a vow of silence." Within the refusenik community, the experience left both a bitter taste and private finger-pointing, each participant trying to assess the various levels of blame for this missed opportunity to bring their plight to the world.

Later in the kitchen, Anna asked me about my plays, what they were about. I told her a little bit about my family play, a comedy about children of survivors of the Holocaust. She asked me if it had been produced, and I told her it had won an award, had received several readings, but no productions.

"If it has won this award, then why no production?" she asked.

I said that it was a big, expensive, crazy play and that while people may have liked it, there were many artistic directors who were tired of presenting plays with Holocaust themes. Or perhaps my play just wasn't good enough yet. Anna asked if I thought people were indifferent to works about the Holocaust, and I said, "Yes, sometimes." She asked me how I felt about that. It began to dawn on me, for the very first time, that my play might have fallen victim to some cynical backlash.

"I suppose there could be some sort of anti-Semitism involved, I guess," I stammered. And it almost made sense to me, speculating aloud in this Moscow apartment. Conspiratorial theories filled the kitchen.

At the dinner table, the five of us made toasts as Sima drank her formula from a bottle. We spoke of Israel, and of my youngest sister, who would be making *aliyah*, or emigrating, next year to settle a new kibbutz. Kate described my sister's *garin*, or group, as being very progressive; they wanted to promote Arab-Israeli dialogue, create a bicultural school, keep a kosher kitchen to foster religious pluralism, and also espoused tolerance for homosexuals. Anna and Yuri could not conceive of such a group of young Jews, but they seemed intrigued. Yuri asked if I was religious. He said that he was. He wore a *kippa* while in the house and when outside, always a cap. He prayed with a *minyan* every Saturday morning, and did not travel on *Shabbat*. But he said he knew very little Hebrew. And in their *minyan*, they had no one who could be a cantor. I told them that I worked as a cantor on the High Holidays for several years—mostly for the money, I added. I explained that in America, someone like me might go to work at a place called the 92nd Street Y or the Hebrew Arts School, and then go out for shrimp tempura (which is to say, unkosher food). I explained that I had gone to an Orthodox day school, Conservative synagogue, Reform summer camp, and then entered the world of the theater. Kate described a different, parallel odyssey of religious pluralism, including her four trips to Israel. Anna stopped us with a smile and then a bewildered giggle. She mused with a tear in her eye, "I couldn't help but think while listening to you . . . This is like a starving person who hears a gourmet dinner being described. It is like a starving person before a beautiful table of food being told to look, but not eat."

Anna's incisiveness left me speechless. My defensiveness about my own religious freedoms shamed me. We stayed at her apartment for five and a half hours and then left, exchanging hugs, kisses, and plans to meet again within the week.

KATE

The first time we met Ben, we arranged to rendezvous at the Kropotkinskaya metro station. Steve, Ari, and I got off the train and looked around. A man in his late forties dressed in a denim jacket and jeans walked up to us. He had a childlike, friendly face, was a little overweight, and had a flushed look to him, as if he was overheated. Later we found out his permanent blush was due to his illness. We shook hands and began to walk. He asked us to walk slowly, and it was only then that I remembered that Ben had cancer and a serious heart condition. Ben's pleasant demeanor, his warm friendly appearance, and his mobility make it easy to forget that he is suffering from two deadly diseases. Unlike Anna and Yuri, at first Ben was extremely warm and treated us as if we were his children the moment we met him. Ben spoke English well and, walking to his apartment, said cheerfully, "Oh, I have some very good news. Anna and Yuri have received permission to emigrate, they just got the postcard from OVIR [State Visas and Registration Department] yesterday. They must leave in three weeks, so there is much to be done."

I was delighted for Anna and Yuri, but fearful for Ben. "That's great, but you must be very upset. I mean, if Anna leaves, won't your position be even more difficult?" I asked.

"Yes, I will miss her very much, but to tell you the truth, my first priority has always been to get Anna and my granddaughter out. After that we can worry about this sick old man."

By the way that Ben had answered me I realized I should not push the issue. He had understood my question, but what could he say? Without Anna there to lobby for him and cheer him up, his chances might diminish, but Ben chose to try to be cheerful about the new development.

As we walked through his neighborhood, Ben pointed out landmarks to remember for the next time we came. Ben sensed that we would be back to see him many times. He was right. Over the course of our trip we saw the Charnys more than a dozen times.

When we got to the apartment, Yadviga, Ben's wife, was waiting for us. In many ways Yadviga matches Ben in appearance. She too is a little overweight, has a warm, expressive face, and is very affectionate. One quickly forgets what a hard life she has led. Yadviga was excited to meet us because we were among their first American visitors who spoke Russian. Like a dam bursting to be released, Yadviga spoke to us about all they had been through in the last nine years, waiting to leave the Soviet Union. During our first visit, both Yadviga and Ben were so eager to talk that, even though we all sat in one small room, we had two conversations going, one in English and one in Russian.

We asked them about *glasnost* and *perestroika*. Yadviga said, "Perhaps there are signs of an opening up in Russia. It is hard for us to tell because we are not part of the mainstream anymore, we haven't been for many years. But this I do know: until the Soviet government opens the borders of this country, we can talk as much as you like, but there will never be true freedom here. Everything else is meaningless until they open the borders and allow free exit and entry into the Soviet Union." As Yadviga spoke, she became agitated. She had often wanted to tell visitors what she thought, but she had to sit by demurely while Ben spoke. He occasionally translated for her, but even a good translator tires from simultaneous translation.

Ben wanted to know about us. What did we do in America, what were we doing in Moscow? We told him about our friends who had given us their names, and we each told a little about ourselves. Ben and Yadviga were so interested in us, it was refreshing to feel this genuine mutual curiosity—so often we played the journalists, never talking about ourselves and what we did in America.

We asked them what it had been like to be refuseniks for nine years. They explained that they had held various jobs during those years, mostly as teachers in secondary schools. Now Ben was too ill to work and they could not both be out of work without being arrested for parasitism. One of the main dangers that all refuseniks risk is being arrested for being unemployed, and therefore being a parasite to the state. Refuseniks are frequently fired from their jobs once their employers find out they have applied to leave, but they are still expected to find work in order not to be arrested. The KGB warned the Charnys a few times that they were in danger of being arrested during periods of unemployment, but now they could rest easier because Ben was simply too sick to work. He became a pensioner.

Ben told us a recurring nightmare he had: "I dream I am walking back into my old office at the Institute of Mathematics. Everyone is glad to see me. They say, 'We are so glad you have given up this hopeless endeavor, welcome back!' I look like I look now, nine years older and ill. In the dream I realize that I have thrown these nine years away, I have given up, and given in to them."

In fact, Ben had been approached numerous times by his former employers at the institute to see if he wanted to come back to work, but always on the condition that he withdraw his application to emigrate. Waiting, isolated from his colleagues and his work, the psychological stress had taken its toll on Ben. When they first decided to emigrate nine years ago, Ben had been a healthy man. The cancer and heart problems developed a few years after they had been refused, and we wondered how much the stress had contributed to his illness.

Yadviga had prepared a big afternoon dinner of chicken, eggplant salad, tomato salad, potatoes, and apple cake for dessert. Before we began to eat I remembered it was Friday night and asked them if they wanted to say the Friday-night prayer. There was a moment of awkwardness when Ben and Yadviga looked at me, then they explained that they were not religious, but would be happy to hear the prayers. I realized that I had put them in a slightly embarrassing position, but it was too late to retreat. Ari came to the rescue. He asked for two candles and some wine. There was a little bustling around to find the wine, during which I felt terribly guilty for ever having made the prayer suggestion at all. We each got our little wineglasses and Ari and I sang the prayers by the candlelight. Yadviga and Ben looked on with sad bright eyes, and as we sang I stopped feeling guilty for my suggestion. We ended up singing that prayer with the Charnys a few times, and even though none of us is religious, the touch of ritual gave all of us a sense of peace and hope. We felt united on those serene Friday nights.

ARI

At our first dinner, I was anxious to ask Ben and Yadviga how the role of dissidents and refuseniks had changed under Gorbachev. Leona had observed that Gorbachev's battle cry of "openness" and "self-criticism" had rendered much of what the dissidents had to say as irrelevant. Ben explained in his friendly but exacting manner that refuseniks and dissidents were of two very distinct camps, united by their calls for justice and personal freedoms. By and large, however, refuseniks were much more monolithic in their agenda, seeking greater religious freedoms within the Soviet Union but primarily focusing upon their desire to leave. Refuseniks were, therefore, less concerned with Soviet policy matters that had no bearing upon their fate. The dissidents' agenda was lengthier, addressing issues as various as nuclear disarmament, political censorship, the war in Afghanistan, agricultural reform. It saddened me in some way to hear that refuseniks, whom I'd always imagined to be activists in the most vocal and heroic sense, were a more narrowly defined "special interest group." There seemed to be something un-Jewish about a narrowly defined human rights agenda that didn't grapple with the problems at home.

I would learn that any sense of "home" Ben and Anna might have felt for the Soviet Union had now slowly eroded. Later in the evening Steve added that refuseniks were forced to be single-minded in their concerns because they were denied most forms of religious and political expression; they could not fight for *all* human rights when they had none themselves. I recalled Anna's sad allegory about the starving man in front of the smorgasbord: he first must be able to feed himself and his family before he can politicize other notable, but less personally debilitating, injustices.

Even as our conversations grew weighty and, at times, perplexing, we were nourished by Ben and Yadviga's warmth and friendship, not to mention wonderful food. On Friday nights we sang traditional liturgical and Israeli folk songs as well as scores of American folk songs that took on an added richness and resonance for being sung in Moscow. A friend of Ben, Isaac, knew only three Hebrew songs, which he had learned from a "Songs of the 1967 Six-Day War" cassette. But what Isaac knew, he knew perfectly, as he sang the four lengthy verses of *Yerushalaim Shel Zahav* ("Jerusalem of Gold") in a rich baritone voice and perfect Hebrew accent. Another night, with Anna at the table, I suggested that we sing an American workers' song so that she could prepare for her new home. Neither Ben nor Anna had heard "If I Had a Hammer," which surprised me, considering the imagery. She laughed quite poignantly as we sang about a hammer of justice and a bell of freedom. After the song, she explained that the reason for her amusement concerned an old Russian joke on a related theme. "An international track-and-field competition is being held in Moscow and the crowd cheers as the Russian hammer thrower tosses the hammer for a new world's record. A frail, scruffy-looking man jumps out of the stands and grabs the hammer, spins, and throws it even farther, shattering the new record. The crowd gathers around the man and asks him how is it possible that an ordinary Russian could throw the hammer that far without any practice. The Russian answers, 'If you'd have given me the sickle, I'd have thrown it clear out of the stadium!' " We all laughed at the time, though Ben had tears in his eyes every time we sang.

KATE

Later that week, Ari and I met Anna at her parents' house. Ever since she and Yuri had received permission to emigrate, their lives had been turned upside down. They had two weeks to sell their belongings, turn in all their documents (the most time-consuming and difficult part of the process), and move out of their apartment. Anna and Yuri were taking their sick baby, Yuri's parents, and his eighty-five-year-old grandmother with them. They would have to go to Vienna and wait there for entry visas to the United States. The wait in Vienna was indeterminate. They could be there a few days or a few months. Everything depended on luck and Anna's uncle Leon's connections in the West.

As we sat drinking tea with Anna that night, we couldn't help being excited for her. Even though each one of us felt terrible for Ben and Yadviga, the prospect of Anna's leaving was so exciting that we kept discussing what life would be like in America. Anna had changed dramatically since our first meeting, before the news. Her spirits were lifted, she smiled a little more, and she was much more curious about life in the United States now that it was going to be available to her, too. Even though they were leaving Russia with enormous responsibilities and with heavy hearts, Anna was still young enough to dream of the possibilities that life in America would offer her. "Most of all I want to get a good education. If it's possible I would like to go to medical school," she told us.

They planned to move to Boston, so Anna and Leon could work together to get Ben and Yadviga out of the Soviet Union. Ari and I tried to describe what life was like in Boston. We talked about our close friends from our two years in Cambridge, and the complicated religious and political layers they would encounter in America. It was hard to explain the large and diverse Jewish community in America, why some Jews might be apathetic toward Ben's plight, why Anna should accept charity from those in the wealthy Boston Jewish community, and why she might be considered something of a celebrity when she emigrated. Anna's story about her father and her family's wait would move many people to help her, but she would also receive a lot of pity. Many were sure to see her as a strange Russian woman with an accent and plight beyond their comprehension. Anna smiled, "Yes, I understand, there is much I will encounter, much for me to learn. It will be hard for me to accept this charity, it is not my way."

I replied, "Just remember you are taking it for your parents' sake, maybe that will make it easier."

Yuri came home late that night, and out of breath. He too seemed rejuvenated. As we were leaving, he grasped both my hands as if to gain strength from me. I said, "Don't worry, Yuri. I know it seems like a huge responsibility to take Sima while she's still ill, and your sick grandmother, but I have a strong sense that Sima will bring her own luck. Look, already she's brought you luck." He smiled, and we left, planning to see them that weekend for a farewell dinner.

ARI

Seated in the back of my mind during many subsequent get-togethers with refuseniks was the nagging, self-imposed corrective: "We are not meeting a representative cross section of the Soviet people here . . . These are the bitter, the dispossessed, the disenfranchised." When Anna spoke of her father's perilous condition and cruel mistreatment suffered at the hands of Soviet bureaucrats, she did so with measured, unflinching anger. "They are committing murder. Doctors refuse to operate. OVIR officials refuse to let him go. They are killing my father." There was no mistaking Anna's personal pain. But for Anna, personal and political emotion had become intertwined. To her, the Soviet Union was indeed an Evil Empire, and not evil in the abstract, or as conjured by successive generations of American anti-Communists. While accepting the authenticity of Anna's indictment, I could not bring myself to share her rage against the state. In my own family, I had been privy to tales of suffering, but sheltered from the actual experience of it. In that same familiar way, I found myself unable to identify completely with the wounds the Charnys carried with them. We were all fortunate enough to see Ben in a stable physical condition. In the intimacy of his living room, with story-telling, singing, and warm good-bye hugs, the most palpable emotions we felt were of warmth and healing. Anger seemed very far away, even as I reminded myself that Soviet officials had only recently told Ben to "not even think of reapplying until 1995." There was so little bitterness in Ben, in spite of all he'd been through. Perhaps it was his calm lucidity to which I aspired.

Or perhaps Ben had been simply hiding his despair from us. Weeks later I would ask him, "Are you angry? Is there anger in you? Or is anger just a useless emotion for you because there's nobody in the country who would listen to it?" Ben replied with his customary precision.

> Well, how to say it? Of course, there are several feelings, not one, but a lot. I am angry. At the same time hopeful. Practically, I don't have any grounds for hope. That's just my nature. First of all, about what am I angry? About the fraud. Which is wrong. For example, they say one thing, then do quite the opposite. The refusenik problem; they deny it exists. And of course, when you deal with the Visa Office it's terrible. There you are lied to by practically each person you meet. But all the same, it's not their fault; there are superiors who are much more guilty. And the government, they manipulate us and keep us hostages. . . . The idea of Marxism has been exhausted. Maybe it was right, say, a hundred years ago, but now it's quite cruel. I am extremely glad about Anna's situation, in spite of the fact that it's very hard for me to part with her. This is the first positive thing concerning my family for all these years . . .

Ben was a difficult man to figure out. He seemed gentle, yet his sense of pride and refusal to capitulate had led him into many confrontations with people in positions of authority. His soul seemed to be that of a man with clear, decent values, yet he spoke in circuitous and often convoluted sentences. I found him warm and engaging, yet at the same time was aware that there was something about Ben, some essence, that often seemed at a remove. The more we talked, the more pronounced my need to understand this man became. I asked Ben if he would allow me to interview him, so that I might be able to fill in the missing pieces of his life.

I arrived on a cold afternoon and brought with me three ninety-minute cassettes. Ben and I spoke for four hours. The next day I returned for three more hours. At various points in the conversations Ben asked me to turn off the tape, as when we discussed his work on behalf of Jewish Hebrew teachers during the early years of his refusal. A transcript of the interview runs well over fifty pages.

"Last Friday night you started to tell us a story about applying to do postgraduate work," I began, with little sense of where I might wind up. "There was a file being kept on you that eventually was used against you." I asked Ben to explain.

So, I was lucky to enter Moscow University in 1954, and I graduated with excellent marks, which was a great achievement for a Jew, I can tell you. Not only for me, but for all Jews who entered in that year. These were years when the authorities made obstacles for Jews to enter privileged universities. It was really difficult for everybody, it was a great competition. So I was happy to enter the mechanical mathematical department at Moscow University, which you know is situated on Lenin Hills. . . . I first studied in the mechanical department but then moved to the department for computational mathematics, where I graduated. Upon graduating, the institute usually gives to the student a paper which directs him to some job, agreed to by the student. I, originally, was among some privileged ones to be recommended for postgraduate degree. To be recommended is only the first stage. Then the person should pass some examinations, very hard examinations. But because of something that was found in my file at that time, they made a formal obstacle for me, and kept me from taking examinations. Not just the mechanical department, but the highest authorities of the whole university, informed me that I was not allowed to take these exams.

And the reason was that I had had this reprimand paper in my file . . .

I had lost some book at the library in my third year. They reprimanded me, and I didn't know about it, which was a violation of their own orders. I learned about this reprimand just incidentally. A young person in the administration showed all students of our year their personal files, which was another violation. . . . When I saw the reprimand paper, I immediately wrote an official application to have this reprimand ignored because almost three years had passed since I had lost this book. They did release me from that. They didn't count it officially. But, all the same, the highest university authority decided not to allow me to take the postgraduate exams. "We won't come back to this matter. Once we decide you not to be allowed, we won't change our decision." So I found a job at the Scientific Research Institute of Automation and Instrument Making, where I remained almost twenty years with space research.

I entered at the lowest engineering position. My salary was exactly one hundred rubles [$160] a month. That was a low engineering position. My job was connected with designing algorithms for the navigation of guidance of space vehicles. Fortunately, my job all the time was connected with peaceful projects, like flight to the moon, to other planets, and to return. That job was extremely interesting for me . . .

"What did the idealistic young scientist believe in during the early 1960s?" I asked Ben.

Man's flight to the stars was an idealistic idea which attracted me. The fact that the job would be classified didn't stop me, because it was interesting work, professionally and humanly. Eventually, however, I had to leave that office, because of all the obstacles and incidents of anti-Semitism I regularly met with.

Ben had risen to the position of senior scientific scholar but was repeatedly forced to work with incompetent assistants. He tried to bring in better graduate students, but his superior would not accept students with Jewish-sounding last names. Ben often protested, but his superior, a Tatar, was a member of a repressed minority himself, unable, or unwilling, to take up the issue of discrimination with his superiors. Ben described how his decision to leave his classified job at the institute in 1971 came about.

> I had frictions with the administration. That's quite a common thing. Second, I had a lot of restrictions connected with being in a classified job. I had no right to meet foreigners. Not in my apartment. Not anywhere. I had no right to leave this country even temporarily.

The reason given Ben and Yadviga by Soviet authorities for the repeated refusals to allow them to emigrate concerns the time Ben spent at the Institute of Automation. They claim that he is still in possession of "state secrets." Ben has repeatedly called these charges ludicrous.

> All my findings were published in scientific journals, both here and in the United States. They are speaking of work done some sixteen years ago. It is hardly possible to talk seriously about scientific secrecy in work done so long ago, considering all the advances in recent technology. The information capacity of space capsule computers at that time was extremely limited because of computer dimensions and weight requirements. To squeeze an algorithm into the computer, one had to invent a special mathematical technique, which I did. Is it possible that this work could still be secret today? Of course not. It is only obsolete! Microprocessors used today in personal computers are infinitely smaller in dimension. The part of my work considered secret some sixteen years ago has long stopped being so. It stopped being so the day the first microprocessor appeared.

I asked Ben if he would talk about his childhood. Invariably the topic returned to anti-Semitism.

> During World War Two, I, like many others, was brought to somewhere in the east, to hide from the Germans. I was in the Ural Mountains with my grandmother. I came back in 1943. The war wasn't over but, all the same, the whole family returned. And just that day I was asked the question "Who are you? Jew or Russian?" And on answering "Jewish," I was hit. I was just five, so I didn't know what to do—it was the

first time I was hit. I came to my father, and asked him what to do. He answered, "You can hit also!"

Ben laughed sadly, and continued:

So it began, for all my later life. I decided I would fight these acts of personal anti-Semitism. There were a lot of them, but they were acts of traditional anti-Semitism which could be fought quite physically. Of course there are situations where it is physically impossible but, all the same, it was different; personal anti-Semitism as opposed to state anti-Semitism, when they openly say that all people are equal and then do such deeds. . . .

I came to understand that due to state anti-Semitism there is a wall before each Jew in this country. Before one Jew this wall is closer and lower and before the other one the wall is further and maybe higher. That was the major reason for me to decide to leave. I realized that my position of senior scientific scholar was the maximum I could achieve in this country. . . .

My first intention was to go to Israel, so when I applied, I wrote to go to Israel. And I must confess to you that I still want to go to Israel. But all the same, because how things have happened, first of all, I will go to my brother if I have the chance, and I'll see. If I have health enough and possibility, maybe I will go to Israel then too. Roots are roots . . .

One month after our taped conversations, I asked Ben some of the same questions on camera at the end of the afternoon on Yom Kippur. By our second time around, the questions had gotten shorter, as had the answers; we were learning about the dictates of television. Near the end of the televised session, our producer passed me a sheet of paper from her memo pad upon which she had scratched down several questions for me to ask Ben: "Think about dying—What if die w/out seeing daughter again? Also grandchild. How did it feel to see daughter leave?"

I couldn't quite bring myself to be so direct, though I tried, as I had tried a month earlier to bring out a man's pain from behind the morass of detail and events that described his life. Ben says he does not think about dying. He thinks about hope. He is the strongest, most vulnerable man I have ever met.

KATE

Leon was able to get entry visas for Anna and her family within two days of her landing in Vienna, and they arrived in America one day later, three days after they left Moscow. At Logan Airport they were met by a crowd of friends and by three television camera crews. Leon and Anna spoke at an impromptu press conference, and the report of Anna's arrival and separation from her father became the lead story that night on two of the three local 11:00 P.M. news broadcasts. Our friends in Boston set them up in a spacious house, where they have been quite comfortable. Anna admitted it took a while to get used to so much space after living in one-room or two-room apartments all their lives. Anna and Leon have been working day and night to get Ben out, and she has applied to graduate school. Sima is doing well and has recuperated from her early illness. Yuri has gotten a job as a computer programmer in a Boston suburb and he is learning to drive. Leon and Anna worked frantically during the 1987 summit in Washington, hoping their lobbying might lead to Ben's release, but so far they have not reached their goal.

By the sixth day of my trip to Russia
I'm comfortable with the vodka
And I'm mastering the alphabet
I'm reading street signs in MOCKBA.
By the seventh evening of my trip
I fall in love face flat
With a six and one half year old girl
And her imaginary cat.

People are the same, all over
People are the same.

By the thirty-fifth day of my trip to Russia
I'm noticing that I
Am stumbling into subways
I've grown impervious to lines.
And I'm noticing that the weather
Does not seem so awfully cold
And that a kitchen conversation
Beats a dining room of gold.

And I say, people are the same, all over
People are the same . . .

ARI

Taking leave of our Moscow flat and our Moscow friends was like bidding good-bye to a moment in time. For all of us in the family, the moment had been a heightened one. We had all been roving reporters brimming with curiosity, jotting down insights, theorizing, speculating, and sympathizing for hours with newfound (or long-lost) friends into the wee hours of the night. It was a heightened moment in time for the Russians as well. Steve's observation that "the people here are on fire! There's excitement in their eyes!" had stayed with me, hauntingly so. As a neophyte to the Soviet scene, I still found it difficult to share the exuberance everyone there experienced because they were "allowed" to read about dissension within the Politburo. Editorials railing against bureaucratic inefficiencies neither inspired nor impressed me. Nevertheless, I had been genuinely enthralled by the Sovremennik troupe's daring production of Mikhail Roshchin's long-suppressed play. I admired their unsentimental look at the past and present, and felt very much a part of their artistic ambition. Vadim and Natasha had taken us to their favorite out-of-the-way museums and had lovingly led us to the pond next to which Mikhail Bulgakov's cat in *The Master and Margarita* got a ride on a trolley car. I had met many wonderful Russians, like Lyokha, who were happy to live in the Soviet Union and felt tied to their friends, their family, and their country; a vast, rich, spiritual countryside that beckoned city dwellers to move backward in time, over bridges and through the mist, to embrace the elements of water, fire, earth, and all values eternal. I had met journalists from *The New York Times*, internationally renowned poets, American embassy negotiators and diplomats, and felt the surge of adrenaline, the urge to impress, the fullness of self-importance. And I had met the refuseniks. I had found a remnant from a people's ancient past, my people's, and perhaps a living link to my family's past as well.

I had written several songs over our two months in the Soviet Union. The first song, recalling our walks on the Arbat (where I eventually got up the nerve to sing, in English), suggested that *glasnost*, like the Russian weather, could be a very fickle friend: "I'm looking for the sun to shine in Moscow/Looking for the sun to shine/ And oo, there it goes, there it goes/In Moscow."

The second song, a sort of singing travelogue, was written for our farewell party, at which at least sixty friends showed up. A truly democratic affair, the party, held at the London *Times* flat we had come to call home, brought crazy artists to the same buffet table as a Tass reporter, an American embassy official, and an incredibly surprised Soviet social worker. Ben Charny spoke at length with CNN reporter Peter Arnett (who would be detained by Soviet officials two months later for his covering of a demonstration of Soviet Jews during the December summit). Yadviga listened to Nina Stevens tell stories of coming to America in 1938 with "literally five pennies in my pocket." There was something almost intoxicating about this hybrid of mixed company. I wondered if all these people would ever see each other again once we were gone. Would Sasha the nonconformist, or Vadim the excitable social critic, ever eat again from the same table as the party official?

Ben and Yadviga left relatively early in the evening. They had stayed three hours. Kate and I walked them to the elevator and then decided to ride down with them. We said good-bye at the foot of the steps of the front entrance, a cold winter wind rushing in as Ben opened the door. We all hugged and then Kate and I watched them leave, arm in arm. We rode the elevator up to the seventh floor. I felt like crying, but the tears did not come. I returned to the democratic party and eventually found the words to sing.

> By the last day of my trip to Russia
> I'm feeling somewhat overwrought
> And also pretty guilty
> About all the dumb matroshkas that I bought.
> Yeah, I still feel pretty critical
> On about a dozen different spheres
> But mostly I feel lonely
> For the friends that I leave here.
>
> People are the same, all over the world
> People are the same . . .

The party went on for four more hours before we dropped off to sleep. When we awoke, a blanket of fog covered Moscow. We rode to the airport as the sun rose, and looking out my window, I noticed that it had snowed.

The Man with the Video Camera

When I returned to Moscow with my wife, Suprabha, and the family, I brought a small video camera with which I planned to make a documentary about my Russian friends. The early Soviet filmmaker Dziga Vertov made a famous documentary in the 1920s called *The Man with the Movie Camera*, which I had studied, and from which I had drawn inspiration in college. On my return to Moscow I wanted to be "The Man with the Video Camera," and carry out some of the same goals Vertov had set for himself. Vertov coined the term *kino-pravda*, which is known to most of the world in the French translation—*cinema vérité*. He wrote that the bourgeois form of the acted cinema would be "slashed open on the reef of the revolution," and that film should be used with its ultimate potential of capturing reality to show the best side of man. He saw the editing process as a way to show the public what the ideal future Soviet man could be by drawing together the best elements of life captured on film.

I was inspired not so much by Vertov's ideological task as by his excitement at the possibility of "catching life unaware" at twenty-four frames per second (in video, thirty frames per second). This fascination with showing "life as it really is" is at the core of what makes documentaries work. Along with the capturing of reality comes the responsibility of presenting the material so that it tells a story but also preserves its original "ontological authenticity." For me the guiding principle here is to be true to the material, to follow where it leads. Beyond that is the question of one's intentions: do you have an axe to grind, or are you trying to tell what really happened as best as you could understand it? My goal in Moscow was to go back to the roots of the documentary form and to tell a personal story of my friendship with Russians. Through these friendships I hoped to see where the society was headed and to show the basic elements of Russian culture that would endure when all the revisions of history had finished washing away the idealized stereotypes of the past.

Lyokha was my old friend from childhood. We had been neighborhood pals in 1968, when he was sixteen and I was eleven. In those days we considered ourselves *khuligany*, or hooligans, as the Russians call young toughs. We drank wine in the stairwells of our apartment building and played the guitar around camp fires in the woods nearby. Many of the other guys got very drunk and were involved in gang fights, but Lyokha was different. He had always been more soft-spoken and sensitive than the rest. Now, after seventeen years, his gentleness brought us together in close rapport right away. The closeness and trust we had as boys sprang right back into place.

Lyokha had tried a number of professions: he had studied biology in university, gone on to become a chauffeur, and then a medical orderly in the ambulance service. About four years ago he decided to become a photographer. He went to a trade school and then got a job with the city photographers' organization, which runs all the photo studios in Moscow. Lyokha was happy with the work because he had friendly contact with people all day long and he could work long hours to earn extra money. For Lyokha, photography is an excellent service in which he takes artistic pride.

Lyokha is the kind of person who naturally tries to please others. At the same time that he is highly sensitive to the feelings of those around him, he is also effusive and outgoing. The combination makes him a lot of fun to be around, and he has many friends. In fact, he has a whole network of friends and acquaintances with whom he trades favors on an informal basis, and this is what makes his life as a consumer in Moscow bearable and even enjoyable.

From a friend who is married to a Bulgarian and travels there, Lyokha has gotten a jacket and shoes. From a bartender he gets soft drinks and beer; a waitress friend gets him into a restaurant where all the tables are supposedly full; and from a friend at a bakery he buys cakes without waiting on line. In return he fixes their cameras, develops their film, and photographs their family events. These favors are generally not done on a barter basis. Money changes hands in return for goods and services, but the point is that the maddening inefficiencies of the system are bypassed, and whatever one needs is obtained quickly and pleasantly.

Lyokha's wish to please me and my family eventually came into a minor conflict with our inquiry into the state of society and change in his country. Lyokha is a strong patriot, and he always tried to show us the best side of his country. Lyokha was never one to cover anything up, but he was very aware that we were collecting material for a book and television program, and he wanted our general outlook to be positive.

The topic that seemed to bother him the most was the question of Stalin's place in history. When we were boys, Lyokha told me that it was really the secret police chief Beria who was responsible for the purges and that Stalin hadn't really known what was going on. Seventeen years later, Lyokha still held on to that justification of events. He was uncomfortable when he heard us discussing the role of Stalin in a more directly condemning way.

Lyokha tried to put the best face on his country's problems. When I filmed us waiting in a long line for a watermelon at a produce market, Lyokha became visibly uncomfortable. Usually he was able to steer me into situations where he knew people and could get hold of goods with miraculous speed. Even in our watermelon quest, however, he displayed his street smarts. He decided to give up on the long line, and after strolling over to a few other stands, he found one with watermelon that was a bit more expensive but had no line. We were amazed, and he was relieved.

Lyokha works at a photo studio in a newer outlying district of Moscow called Tyoply Stan. It is a bedroom community from which the inhabitants commute into the city to work, and during the day it is deserted. It is an area where a new metro station is about to open, and in the meanwhile at rush hour the buses to and from there are unbearably crowded. Lyokha never invited me to the studio where he worked, and he wouldn't let me invite myself there, either. He said it was in the process of being fixed up; they were repainting and getting in some new equipment.

When we wanted to film a sequence of Lyokha working in the studio for the "Frontline" show, Lyokha set things up so that he could shoot portraits in the most modern and up-to-date studio of the photographers' association on Kalinina Prospekt in the center of Moscow. Lyokha seemed a little jealous of the fellow who was in charge of that studio. He was about our age, but Lyokha said, "He must know a lot of people to be able to get hold of all that equipment." The studio was equipped with German lights and a Japanese camera. Downstairs it had a Japanese instant film processing and printing machine that was being used on an experimental basis after it had been in a trade show in Moscow.

Soon after I arrived in Moscow, Lyokha told me that the photographers' association administration was trying to draft him to become the supervisor for his shop. Lyokha's primary interest is the aesthetic side of photography, and he felt the administrative job would tie him down in paperwork and meetings. In addition he was not satisfied with his co-workers at his studio. One fellow in particular there was a slouch, Lyokha said. This man paid no attention to quality and botched things up no matter how many times Lyokha tried to correct him.

I asked Lyokha outright if I could film him at his job and see what happened with his supervisor position, but he was clearly not interested and made up a few excuses about why it would not work. For one, the other people at work would not want to be on camera, he said. "And besides, it will just be someone talking on the phone and looking at papers," he said. I didn't pursue it, but I kept asking Lyokha about how things were going. It seemed that he was trying not to say no to the supervisor job for as long as possible so as not to alienate his superiors. At the same time, he was more and more sure that he didn't want to do it. "I won't have any time to shoot pictures anymore if I take that post," he said. "Then I'll have to be involved in all the politics of personnel and who is not doing satisfactory work."

About three weeks before we were to leave, Lyokha asked to borrow my little cassette tape recorder. He said he wanted to record an important meeting with the head of his section of the association. He had come up with a plan to work with two friends and colleagues who currently worked in the central processing and printing facility. They were proposing to work together and run the Tyoply Stan photo studio. Lyokha told me that the meeting went well and that all they needed were a couple of other signatures to have the venture officially accepted.

Lyokha's plan came at a time when all the studios of the photographers' association were in the process of transferring over to the new economic order. As of the first of the year in 1988, they all became self-accounting, self-sufficient entities, having a choice of contractual relationships with the association that confer varying degrees of independence. They can either pay a rental fee for the studio facilities or gradually buy the facilities to become completely independent. When I first discussed these economic changes with Lyokha, he complained of the competition he would be up against. The *patenshchiki* ("patent holders"), those who have purchased permits to take photographs on the street, were already stealing his work, Lyokha claimed. According to Lyokha, the quality of their work was poor, and it seemed unfair to him that anyone, even those who were not seriously educated in the field, could go out and take pictures for a fee.

I was interested in what would happen to the people currently employed at Tyoply Stan. There were only two others besides Lyokha: the incompetent fellow (who Lyokha couldn't stand) would be assigned to a different studio, and another woman there would work part-time for Lyokha as a bookkeeper. I asked Yuri Tarasov, the head of the photographers' association, what happened to workers who consistently performed unacceptable work. His attitude was philosophical: "In the end we have to employ them somehow, so we keep talking to them, explaining their shortcomings, and trying to get them to improve. But these are rare cases," he added.

I was excited for Lyokha, that he would be able to set up a shop, more or less of his own, and that he would be working with colleagues in an atmosphere of mutual respect. He said they had already had some detailed discussions, including projections of costs and profits based on frequency of orders at the current shop. I remembered a conversation Lyokha and I had had with my parents when he was dealing with the question of the supervisory position. My parents had told Lyokha about their own two-person company, and Lyokha had said: "Well, at least there you're all pulling in the same direction. You have the same goals." It seemed to me that he had created a similar situation for himself with his new plan.

Work does not seem to play a very important role in the life of my other best friend, Vadim, who is in his early forties. To him ideas, history, spirit, freedom, and culture are what matter. Vadim loves to talk and seems to be able to do it inexhaustibly. Some of his speech was quite repetitive, but it was almost always fascinating. Vadim has a clear sense of who he is and what he wants out of life. He knows that this will compel him to make some clear and hard choices in his conduct. But he has been through enough in his life to make those choices.

Part of what first attracted me to Vadim was his inherent realistic optimism. When I first got to Moscow I used to ask the intellectual types I met whether they thought the *glasnost* and *perestroika* reforms were there to stay. Invariably the replies were negative. "I think this will all last until next June," one poet said. "Two years at the most," an artist commented. But Vadim was the one who told me I was asking the wrong question: "Those questions are not important. The main thing now is to live for the moment and to make the most of what we have. Everyone knows that it won't last forever. In 1968 we all had a lot of hope for what was happening in Czechoslovakia. But these changes are a gradual process. Even when there is a swing back to repression, some gains have been made which will continue."

Soon after we met, on our way to a party after the opening of a modern art exhibit, Vadim sketched out for me his way of classifying people in the world. "I guess there are some people who are fools, completely meaningless. They're not even worth talking about," he said. "Then there are the professionals. People who work steadily at their jobs but are just trying to get by. There are also careerists: those who are real go-getters, trying to get to the top of the heap, and that's their primary concern in life. In a different vein, there are lovers of life, people who live to enjoy things and are more concerned with fulfilling the moment. Finally there are God-seekers. These are the most rare and precious kind of people because they are solely concerned with spiritual pursuits."

"And which category do you fit into?" I asked Vadim.

"Oh, I guess I vary back and forth," he said. "Right now, I'm probably a lover of life, but at times I become a God-seeker, too."

Vadim has a tremendous capacity for sensing others' feelings and inclinations, almost to the point of telepathy. His intuition is incisive and quick, and yet in a sense he is a phantom person. He is enchanted with the idea of being an outside observer, on the margin of society. Since young adulthood he has refused to take a profession and become "a member of society." He believes that this is what preserves his openness and freedom of inquiry. He knows that he probably values this freedom too highly, yet he remains somewhat selfish in this way. Vadim is fascinated with the underside of society, "the *déclassants*," as he calls them, and even fancies himself as a part-time member of this class. But his endless analysis and intellectualization of life, which he values above all, makes him forever separate from these people.

One afternoon when we were out shooting in the old neighborhoods of Moscow behind the Arbat, Vadim told me about one facet of "the other side" of city life: "There's this expression: 'green gold,' " he said. "It means bottles, because bottles cost twenty kopecks [32 cents] each. So you can save up these bottles, and when you don't have enough money between paychecks you can take the bottles and cash in. So it's like a whole little industry. Some old people collect these bottles from the parks; train conductors collect them in sacks and bring them in. This is the lower layer of city life: various former alcoholics, people from the underclass. And me, too, sometimes." At that we both laughed.

On the surface this all sounds remarkably similar to the poor of our own society collecting cans from the garbage to get by. But because bottles in the Soviet Union are often worth up to a third of the cost of the product (from 32 cents to $1.60), more people from different walks of life take advantage of the income from the recycling process. Vadim exaggerated slightly to dramatize his story of the urban poor.

One thing the Soviet bottle recycling clientele all have in common is that they get very annoyed waiting in long lines. "Usually you have to wait for half an hour in line," Vadim said. "But when I can, I go to my friend who runs one of the stations, and he takes me without a wait."

Vadim's friendship with Andrei, the bottle man, gave me my deepest look into the "new ways of thinking" that are starting to surface in Soviet society. Andrei runs a bottle-recycling station in a western district of Moscow, and our visit there turned into a reunion of old school pals. Valery, another friend of Vadim from grade school days, happened to show up on Vadim's doorstep that day, so we all went to visit Andrei together. There was a strange sense that all three of these men had remained apart from the mainstream of their society. They were on the margin, observers of themselves and the culture at large.

Valery was probably furthest on the edge. Vadim told me that he had always been a little withdrawn in school, sometimes hiding under his desk, but he had been the most daring prankster of the lot. For the last decade he had lived "on a pension," as he put it euphemistically at first. It turned out that he was a registered psychologically abnormal person, and all he had to do was check in a few times a year at a clinic. He received a very small stipend and was left alone. For a long time he hadn't worked at all. Now he was the groundskeeper at a kindergarten. Valery told me, "It's not that hard to be registered with this status. The tough thing is if you want to change and be considered normal again. That is rare, and takes a long time."

There are no published statistics on how many people in the Soviet Union have Valery's status. But judging by the similar experience of Kate's nonconformist artist friend, Sasha, who has the same kind of classification, the concept of psychological abnormality is a convenient way to deal with people who do not want to fit the rigid mold of Soviet life.

I was the first American with whom Valery had ever spoken. He was a bit hesitant and cautious at first, but I was able to draw him out, and then we conversed easily. It was clear that he was very interested in spiritual matters. Valery had read Russian mystics of whom I had never heard, and he had a strongly delineated metaphysical universe in which he moved. He said my camera took away life energy when it was pointed at people, and at the end of our visit to the bottle-recycling station he said he felt drained because that particular environment, a former beer hall, was also energy sapping.

Andrei, a man of medium height and build, with a stubby beard and mustache and thick glasses, had an easygoing and familiar way of dealing with people. A big old radio played classical music in his deserted beer hall filled with cases of bottles. Soon after we arrived it started to chime three o'clock, and Andrei said, "I'd better get going, or these people will make trouble." He slid back the cover that opened his counter to the outside just as the radio beeped the exact hour. Vadim remarked that he always did it that way: punctually.

Andrei and Vadim were in Moscow University at the same time. Vadim was in literature; Andrei studied law. To Vadim it seemed that Andrei had it made. Andrei married a pretty young woman who was also well connected through her relatives. He received a post in the Ministry of Justice and was on his way up the ladder. He was able to indulge in his penchant for collecting military memorabilia: old pistols, helmets, and mine fragments. After a few years, though, according to Vadim, Andrei became disillusioned. He realized that he would not be able to practice law as he saw fit or to follow his ideals. Andrei then went through a crisis in his life and began acting irrationally. During a minor dispute he got so upset that he took a shot at an acquaintance with a handgun. The man was not harmed, but Andrei was arrested and jailed. Then, because of his connections and his position, he was released.

Andrei left the law and started a new life. He divorced and remarried, and for the last ten years has run the bottle-recycling station. Vadim described it as a place where he can be his own master. It's a family business, which he runs with his wife. He resells the bottles back to the factories and makes a decent profit. He also has a substitute who comes in every other week, so that he works one week on, one week off.

A decade ago Andrei found a job where he could exercise his own initiative and control his work in much the way that Gorbachev is now calling upon the whole country to do. When Vadim and I visited him at his apartment, I was surprised and fascinated to hear the depth of his reflections on the current direction the country is taking. In their conversation, which I shot on video, Vadim was the skeptic, while Andrei advocated Gorbachev's position. They have such conversations periodically, and Andrei reminded Vadim of some previous predictions he had made. Vadim had laughed at the time, but these predictions had since come to pass.

"Yeah, I said that Gorbachev would make a market. I said there would be two big years, and that a market system would be set up. And you said, 'Impossible!' " Andrei rubbed it in.

"No, it was Sasha who was so pessimistic," Vadim protested. "You were the healthy optimist."

"Well, I just didn't see any other way for Gorbachev to deal with the reality we're facing. Here's a guy who completed his law degree at Moscow University. Sure, there's a lot of idle talk there, but he still came away with a respect for the law. He won't build anything without putting it into law, which sure is different from Andropov. If Gorbachev brings some new form into our social life, first he provides a basis with laws, and that already is a step forward."

"Yeah, I agree with you. You're right," replied Vadim.

"And you know what else? They've got to close down those useless Soviet factories. Well, actually they can't put all those people out of work, so they should open up recycling centers for all the faulty merchandise produced. You know, right next door; so you go through the same gates to the factory and to the recycling shop for everything it produces."

This novel theory of Andrei's drew a laugh from Vadim.

"Then they should buy factories in the West, and step-by-step change everything over. Of course that can't be done openly, but I think that's more or less the way to go."

"You're probably right," said Vadim.

"And what's more, as I said, he'll do anything necessary to make peace with the West; and above all with America. That's exactly what's happening now."

"So what's your prognosis?" asked Vadim. "What new actions does he need to take now?"

"Actions. I don't see any new actions he can take right now. Naturally this meeting coming up with Reagan will solve a lot of things, but that's foreign policy. Domestically, he won't take any new actions. Well, he'll have to raise prices, that's natural. I don't see any other way. Although many are already cursing him, I for example understand him, and I support him. I'm saying that seriously, too, not just to show off."

"Yeah, yeah, of course. I believe you," said Vadim, nodding.

"His most fundamental problem right now is to try to bring to life everything that he has projected theoretically. This is the most gigantic, most unthankful, and most difficult task. What kind of new programs? I thought that with the establishment of this new law about individual work activity things would really start to cook. It turned out that I thought a little too well of our people. People have become so degraded and lazy . . ."

"Do you know what I saw on TV?" Vadim chimed in. "In the whole country there are only four hundred and eighteen cooperatives."

"Yeah, there are very few. That's just a drop in the bucket. I thought things would really start getting wild and that right away everything would flower. You know, like during the NEP? Well, you want to know what the difference is now? People were unspoiled back then, with completely healthy instincts. Now they're all wimps. They're both afraid of everything and lazy at the same time. They don't want to do a damn thing. This is a very complex problem, to revive all this. I think only the young people can do it. And until the youth grows up . . ."

"And this generation is already fairly parasitical," Vadim responded.

"No, I'm not talking about that youth," said Andrei. "I mean the youth that's just two or three years old now. So, you see how long this is all going to drag out. It's really terrible. I consider our generation to be a complete loss. And even the people who are leaving the country, ninety percent of them won't be able to do anything in the States because they have lost the basic human feelings of initiative, for example. They won't survive there."

"Well, they can find some simple manual work," Vadim protested.

"They can do some rubbish, I guess. But they won't really be able to participate. . . . Maybe ten percent of those emigrants can really do something good, but I think that's a high figure. I'm paying them a compliment."

Vadim knew that I was fascinated with Andrei's change of professions, and he steered the conversation around to a more personal question. "I get the feeling that at some point you made a choice in your life, and I wonder whether you're satisfied with that choice."

"Well, what choice is it that I made?" Andrei asked.

"You know, you cut yourself off from those official ties," Vadim said delicately.

"Oh, those snares, you mean," said Andrei. "You know what the deal is with this, Vadim. If I felt some kind of dissatisfaction, I would just leave and find something that satisfied me. I'm completely happy with this work I have now. It's even hard for me to think of anything better . . . say, something out of a fairy tale: suppose the Soviet Foreign Ministry appointed me as some attaché to, let's say, Austria, you see? I just wouldn't agree to leave and go there. I can imagine the responsibilities and the burdens. It wouldn't just be a recreational trip, it would be work, and work that's a lot worse, in my view, than what I have now. That's all there is to it."

"I can see that," Vadim said. "It just seems that sometimes some dissatisfaction might arise."

"No. What I like first of all there, and we've talked about this, is that there is no collective to deal with. Me, my wife, and I'm going to bring Wolf, my German shepherd. That's it. What's more, I work for a week, and then I get a week off. That way I can make some plans for my free time."

"So the pull of independence is an important parameter in your thinking?" Vadim queried.

"Undoubtedly, undoubtedly. And at the same time . . . I'm somehow legal. I don't fall out of the general picture," Andrei replied, in reference to the laws on parasitism.

"You have some kind of foxhole of your own," commented Vadim.

"I don't attract any attention, and if someone is interested, please, here it is; I'm working, it's all clear. I'm also not accountable for all the petty details, shall we say. I have some freedom for creativity, even in connection with this strange work. I can make decisions. I can take some initiative if it's necessary for me. Furthermore, I can see that I'm directly bringing some benefit to people. You know what I mean? Maybe it's a downtrodden contingent." Here Vadim and Andrei both laughed sardonically.

Andrei continued, "But very often they say to me, 'Thank you, sonny. May Christ save you.' That kind of thing, you know. Real nice."

The conversation returned to what lay ahead with Gorbachev, and Vadim voiced his reservations: "Don't you think that the whole method of drafting party members hasn't changed over the years?" Vadim asked. "This cadre politics is at the root of it all; its parameters haven't changed. It's all designed to promote the people who accommodate themselves to the system, the careerists who want to use it for their own selfish goals. As long as this system of finding and promoting party members doesn't change, we're just going to spin our wheels, because these people are going to continue to recruit their own kind. Don't you agree?"

"No, I don't agree. First of all, they have started to have elections for directors at industrial enterprises. That's already taking place. The large majority of the nonparty posts, deputies and so forth. Those, too, are being elected. And as far as the party *nomenklatura*, I don't agree with you. They're throwing people out right and left, and they're either being pensioned off, if they're old enough, or else they're knocking them down to being porters almost," Andrei stated.

"Well, maybe you're right, maybe all that is going to happen," Vadim allowed.

"No, it's not going to happen. It already is happening," Andrei retorted. He brought up an example of a high party official in a Muslim republic who had recently been disgraced posthumously. "What about that imbecile Rashidov who was the head of the region in Uzbekistan?" Andrei asked. "They dug up his grave and almost reburied him at the dump."

"Oh, yeah?" said Vadim in surprise.

"Sure. At first he was buried right next to the Lenin monument in the center of town. Then they exhumed him with a big scandal. He almost became a public enemy, and in the papers they wrote that if he had been alive he would have stood trial as a criminal for his corruption."

"So you think that, in this sense, some small changes are taking place. But doesn't it seem to you that some more . . ." Vadim started to say.

"Vadim, look, excuse me, but you know that time you came with your friend Volodya in the car, I told you the same thing. You can't expect Gorbachev in his first two years to set up national committees to de-Communize the country."

Vadim smirked.

"Of course it's funny," said Andrei. "Naturally he's not going to do that. But you know the hardest thing for him is to find people who are in tune with what he's trying to do. Yeah, you know even with all these personnel changes he's still not putting people in he trusts one hundred percent because he simply can't find them anywhere. . . . It seems to me that with time, maybe in five years, and again this is my opinion, I can't certify it, but I think he's going to establish a parallel party."

"You mean within the bounds of a socialist system?" asked Vadim.

"Exactly right," said Andrei. "They'll provide a socialist alternative. It seems to me that he'll have to do that."

"Yeah, I think you're right," said Vadim.

"Otherwise it's going to be very hard to really breathe some fresh life into the system. You know, without making any pronouncements, to bring a fresh layer of people into public life. Without this it's going to be impossible. Of course this one-party system is totalitarian, and it puts the brakes on everything. So that's how things will start, and eventually the members of this parallel party, with time, can begin to replace members of the current monopolistic party in ruling posts. Maybe it will even get to the point where the head of the Supreme Soviet of the Ukraine or Byelorussia or Tadjikistan will be from the parallel party. You see how it could work?" asked Andrei.

"Yeah, yeah, clearly, maybe . . ." said Vadim. "But don't you think that process is going to be dragged out and slowed down by the current system of drafting party members? Doesn't it work against the reforms?" asked Vadim, returning to his earlier theme.

"Look, if he were to propose all that right now . . ." Andrei started to say.

"No, I'm talking about cadre politics," said Vadim. "The reason the current situation is so dragged out and bogged down is because there are no human resources to draw on. No one wants to take responsibility for the new situation, which is unclear and hard to understand. This careerist type is all there is to work with now."

"That's for sure," replied Andrei. "It's a very difficult situation, and I'm doubtful whether any substantive changes can be even made in his lifetime for us directly. The value of Gorbachev, in my opinion, is that he's the first one to give a push in the necessary direction. That in itself is a big deal, and seeing how he's a fairly energetic person, measuring by his strength, I think he'll do everything that he can from his end. Of that I'm confident."

"Yeah, me too," said Vadim.

"As soon as he feels that without any sudden jerks, somehow smoothly, he can establish this new structure, then of course he'll go for it. Here of course Lenin will be brought in, saying that the one-party system was only a measure necessary during the civil war and afterward for several years until the government was firmly in place. This will all be argued and formulated accordingly, but he'll go for it," concluded Andrei.

Listening to Vadim and Andrei solve the problems of their country was the only time I heard people in Moscow speak with such freedom of imagination and hope for the future.

Alyona Kirtsova is another free spirit I met through Vadim and his wife, Natasha. She is a bohemian type, and she defines herself as an artist. Alyona is a member of the Hermitage Arts Group. She is also a mother with a five-year-old son, David, and her life has become stabilized as a result. When I first met Alyona, I realized I had read about her before in David Shipler's book about Russia. Later, when we knew each other well, I asked her about the story Shipler recounts of her as a schoolgirl being mesmerized for hours by a Matisse paint-ing of goldfish while on a class trip to the Pushkin Art Museum. She said yes, it was true, and recently she had revisited the painting while taking her son, David, to an art class at the Pushkin. She had stood looking at the Matisse and thought: This is where it all began.

In the seventies Alyona was part of a different group of avant-garde artists, many of whom got into trouble with the authorities over the political content of their work. Most of these close friends emigrated to the United States, and Alyona tried to do the same, but she was in her mid-twenties and her father, a Soviet diplomat, refused to sign her documents. Alyona says she's not a refusenik but a no-answernik, because she never did get a response to her emigration request. At this turbulent time in her life, she experienced an unusual awakening.

"I was completely a city person, and around 1976 I went to a village; it was really the first time in my life. I got a house there and lived there for three months. It was a remote village in the northern Gorky region. You see it was really strange because just at the time they refused me, I suddenly felt all my Russian roots. Up until then it didn't really matter to me. I had heard that mass of words: *moth-erland, roots, citizenship, fatherland,* and so on. But it was only at that time that I was moved deeply inside."

Alyona now lives with David in half of a wonderful old wooden house in what used to be the merchants' quarter of Moscow. The rent she pays to sublet the house is exorbitant by Soviet state-owned housing standards, and her friends worry about how she will make ends meet. She has a boyfriend (not the father of her son), but they quarrel often, and they do not live together full-time.

In the 1970s Alyona painted hauntingly beautiful landscapes and still lifes with pastel colors and blurred edges. They sold well on the diplomatic market, and she was financially secure. In the 1980s her style shifted to the painting of large geometric shapes with sharp lines and brighter colors. She insists they are still realistic, and points out the different corners of her house from which they are painted, but the reality is nonetheless more abstracted. These newer paintings have not sold as well, and she now spends a lot of time retouching photographs for publications. She is tortured by this tedious work, which is painful for her eyes, but she feels driven to give her son a settled home and a good education. "No one would have believed that I would turn into the perfect Jewish mother," she laughs.

"I paint these new paintings fairly quickly," she says. "But it takes a lot of time to look at the objects first. I have to sit and look for hours, you see, to work out the colors inside myself, to spin everything through the meat grinder. Everything has to get properly mixed and brought to uniformity; that is, to clarity and proper proportion. So that I can quickly escape from this awful vacillation that I'm swimming in.

"In general, in life, as far as I understand it, I'm a very unsure person. I'm always in doubt. I even tell everyone the story of how when I was in school and the teacher called me to the board, I would say, I'll tell it this way, or you could look at it that way, or even this way. And the teacher said, sit down, Kirtsova, you get an F."

The walls of the main room in Alyona's home are hung with her bold geometric paintings. On one side between the bookshelves are paintings by other artists, given by them as gifts to her. A white canvas hangs in a corner, waiting to be painted. From midafternoon to well past midnight the round low table in the center of the room was covered with teacups, biscuits, and ashtrays full of butts. Young people, older artists, and intellectuals all flowed in and out, engaging in four conversations at once, showing off artwork or the latest controversial article in the press. Alyona presided, bringing out a fresh pot of tea every half hour, and playfully expounding her latest theories of history, art, and life.

The first time I met her, Alyona impressed me with her brazenness. She used the informal *ty* form of "you" (like *tu* in French) right off the bat, which no one else I met had ever done. She was not as attached to being "right" in her arguments as most Russians are, and she felt free to ridicule my point of view if she thought I was wrong. Alyona struck me as a cynical person in the beginning. Later on I was convinced it was a defense against the realities of life in Soviet Russia. Alyona has a free imagination, and her fantasies about how life could turn for the better show a strong hope and faith in herself.

When I told Alyona about my family's project at our first meeting, she expressed amazement to the other Russians who were there. "Can you imagine anything like that happening with a Russian family?" she asked. "For us the family is a fictitious unit," she continued. "It is simply a matter of convenience, and the family can be built up or destroyed as the necessities of life such as housing, food, or work demand." Later on, in a late-night conversation with Vadim and Suprabha, she told me about the transformation of the Russian family in modern times.

"The breakdown of morality which occurred in Stalin's time had a lot to do with it. It was the times when a son would go out and inform on his father as 'an enemy of the people.' You know it wasn't just neighbors informing on each other in our wonderful system of communal apartments where everyone lived on top of each other practically like relatives. No, it was also the situation of a daughter informing on her mother, a mother informing on her daughter: completely monstrous. Yet this was the normal order of the day. I heard a whole stack of stories from older people about how this all took place."

"So this wasn't an unusual occurrence?" I asked.

"No, this wasn't rare, it was simply everywhere, you see. There's this wonderful sixty-year-old gentleman whom I deeply respect who told me very honestly about himself. As a youth, born and raised in that society, he once thought to himself: What is my father up to; he's behaving so strangely. And he sincerely thought: Maybe he's 'an enemy of the people,' and I should go report him. Thank God, somehow it all got smoothed over, and later he simply remembered the occurrence. Later his brain returned to normal. He's a dear, honest, and intelligent person, so he told me about it. The horror people lived through!

"He also told me a story of when he was studying in university, the father of one of his fellow students was identified as 'an enemy of the people' and was either sent off or shot, I don't remember. So then it came time for the son to speak publicly at a meeting and renounce his father. And all of a sudden he got up and said no, his father was an honest and worthy person, and everything that had been said against him was lies and slander. The son said he would never believe these accusations, and would never denounce his father.

"There was total shock in the hall. Such an incident was very rare. You see, it was the other way around. Because it was so rare and everyone was so shocked, this young man was able to slip away, and nothing happened to him. Everyone approached these things formally, on a fictitious level, and they were just in shock when someone refused to go along. So you see what kind of effect this could have on the institution of the family."

Alyona's family tree, just two generations back, is rooted in the Czarist nobility. She told us how her grandfather didn't like to admit his blueblood background.

"My grandfather, who was in the *nomenklatura* during Stalin's time, always wrote in his papers and documents that he was from the family of a stablehand. But my grandmother said this: 'Hah, from the family of a stablehand. If you could have seen these stablehands.' My grandfather's family had a huge stable with many carriages and horses—and stablehands—and his father was the master. But grandfather wrote that he was from the family of a stablehand."

Although Alyona and Vadim were always very clear in their condemnation of Stalin's crimes, even they seemed to have a slight regret that history had dealt him such an unforgiving hand. Vadim once told me that as an American I would never understand the Russians' contradictory attitudes toward Stalin. Once when I condemned Stalin's crimes, Vadim told me that I wasn't taking into account the other side of the coin. "Those were exciting times for the country as a whole. There was a sense of mission in the air. The rapid industrialization gave people a sense of control and power."

Although I was surprised to hear that kind of attitude expressed by Vadim, I had already grown used to a sympathetic opinion of Stalin from Lyokha. As an adult, Lyokha tried to avoid discussing the subject with me, but eventually it came out that he still believed the "old history." In both Lyokha's and Vadim's attitudes, in different degrees, was the barely stated xenophobic premise that the Russians know Russian history best, and outsiders have no place telling them about their own heritage.

Lyokha's views were reflected by General Secretary Gorbachev's speech on the seventieth anniversary of the revolution:

> It is sometimes said that Stalin did not know of many instances of lawlessness. Documents at our disposal show that this is not so. The guilt of Stalin and his immediate entourage before the party and the people for the wholesale repressive measures and acts of lawlessness is enormous and unforgivable. This is a lesson for all generations.

And it is because so many Soviet citizens still believe in Stalin that Gorbachev, the shrewd pragmatist, softened the blow in his speech by mentioning thousands of victims rather than millions.

On the evening at Alyona's when she told the story about her grandfather, Vadim expounded further on the historical circumstances: "Stalin's intuition and quirks created this whole system. But I think that Stalin was, to a large extent, the victim of certain historical circumstances.

"There started to arise a huge class, a huge group of people who used power for their own goals, for their own personal goals. These were former peasants who moved to the city. Their traditional worldviews were destroyed, and they hadn't yet created a new urban conception of themselves. Stalin was a symbol for them; he was close to many of them because he, too, was the same kind of *lumpen* ["uprooted individual"]. He carried out an enormous destruction of everything that was connected with his past. These people, in order to succeed, also had to destroy their own past and forget about it. Thus they created a kind of monolith, a kind of single organism.

"All of the Gorbachev reforms also have their prehistory, because they depend on a specific group of the population, which for quite a while has been working in that direction beginning in Khrushchev's time, after Stalin. All these activities were of a fairly narrow but quite active group—that is, the intelligentsia.

"They were also in fact the only real allies of Khrushchev through all the changes of that period. But, ironically, Khrushchev himself couldn't work with them. Thus he ended up without defenses; he had no base, no rear guard, no allies. That's why he took a fall. Gorbachev, on the other hand, has learned from those mistakes. And what's more, it's easier for him. Psychologically he's closer, and it's natural for him to ally himself with the intelligentsia."

However, the experience of the past made Alyona rather fatalistic about the present. "Our history has given a lot of examples of how these young green seedlings are so easily reduced to nothing. Everyone is saying: 'Even if something happens to Mikhail Sergeyevich Gorbachev, that won't change anything because you can't take it back. This situation of being sheep, and the lack of freedom; it's so ingrained, it's in the genes already. It's genetic. Everything could all go back very easily."

In the meanwhile, Alyona and her friends in the Hermitage Group are taking advantage of the warm winds of *glasnost*. Going to a show of new young artists there was like taking a step back into the abandon of constraints during the sixties in America.

One young man in his early twenties had fashioned a forty-foot-long tube of translucent plastic, which he inflated with a vacuum cleaner. He installed a television, books, a teapot, and other amenities of life, and then climbed in himself. "At the opening of the show, for a period of two hours, I stayed in this tube," he told me. "And it was real interesting to communicate with people. . . . Those who recognized me inside, and those who didn't notice me at all in this tube. Children ran up and tried to communicate with me through the plastic. Everyone said hi to me . . ."

When I asked this fellow whether he was trying to communicate the constraint and boundaries inherent in his own existence, his face darkened, and he said, "No, there's no political message here at all. I am just trying to say something about one's environment and abode. I was inspired by the title of this show: 'Abode.' "

Lyokha came with us to the opening of one Hermitage show, a retrospective of Soviet modern art. He had no context or point of reference with which to appreciate the work, and seemed a little dubious about it all, but he certainly understood that it was an event that could not have even occurred in the recent past.

"Straight off I can say I've never seen a collection like this all in one place," he said. "I'm probably also surprised that it's possible to freely display things like this now, and that people can come here. Because earlier such exhibits were put on in closed buildings for a certain circle of people."

At a discussion in one corner of the gallery at the retrospective opening, a number of artists were patting each other on the back. It was the first time they had felt the combined energy of their works as a movement or school in art history, and they were exhilarated. The painter Yankilevsky said, "You know when a child is born, you can't say right away that it's a genius. First he has to live till he's fifty and die, and then you can say, since he was five he was a genius."

The crowd laughed, and then a man who had just come into the gallery off the street said, "This whole show, which is open to regular people, is true to the new times. Of course, thanks to Gorbachev that he is standing at the head now." The crowd nodded and murmured in agreement. The plain-spoken man continued: "I wish you would really advertise it, so that the regular people come. I'm a working stiff, and just the plain people should come here, too. It's for the first time, and it's really wonderful. You know that slogan: 'Art belongs to the people'? It should ring out, and not be rubbed out the way things are in the textbooks."

The artists were overjoyed, and told him, "It's very pleasant for us to hear that. Thank you. You spoke very well, and we're grateful. . . ."

Mixed in with the experimentation of the younger Hermitage artists was a return to spiritual values and roots, I discovered. Volodya, a thoughtful man in his mid-thirties, pointed to a rendition of a vertical line, among his drawings of a nude and containers of kefir, a type of yogurt. "I painted a simple vertical line because a vertical is also interesting," he began. "It's something to think about. Thanks to God and the established laws, we walk vertically, everything grows vertically; an apple falls from up to down . . ."

Even in someone as different from these avant-gardists as Lyokha, I discerned this same respect for "the order of things" and the Russian past. Lyokha took me on a walk through the no-longer-active Donskoy Monastery in Moscow one afternoon. The old peaceful graveyard with its ornate tombstones commemorating the nobility, merchants, and intelligentsia of Czarist times had been a favorite place for him to paint watercolors when he was in his twenties. We walked to the far wall of the monastery, where he showed me some magnificent plaster reliefs that had been transplanted there from the former Cathedral of Christ the Saviour.

"This is what I was telling you about," Lyokha said.

"Oh, from that church?" I asked.

"Yeah, from the Cathedral of Christ the Saviour on Kropotkinskaya which they blew up."

"You mean in Stalin's time?" I asked. But Lyokha didn't want to talk about it any further. Later on I learned that the reliefs had been rescued from the enormous cathedral, which was blown up by Stalin during an antireligion campaign in the 1930s. Stalin tried to build the Palace of Congresses at the same site, not far from the Kremlin, but during construction the foundation shifted, workers were killed, and the project was abandoned. Many believers now consider the site of the former cathedral to be cursed. Today there is a huge outdoor swimming pool there, but we heard that old ladies say you will get sick if you swim in it.

Lyokha pointed out to me the figure of Count Donskoy being blessed with a sacred icon that was held in outstretched arms by the patriarch of the church. At the feet of these figures were tassels of grain, a green tomato, shriveled flowers, and candies. "You see, I was telling you," Lyokha said. "The people who are believers still bring flowers, apples, and oats. The old ladies bring candies."

It was at that point that I asked Lyokha, "And what do you think about faith? How do you feel about religion?"

"Well, I guess I believe passively," Lyokha replied. "I believe because Russian culture is that way through the centuries. . . . Russian culture is directly connected to the church. Of course, all those old church rituals aren't foreign to us, and so to say that I'm a zealous believer wouldn't be right, but one can't be indifferent to beauty."

One Sunday morning we went to the active Laura Monastery in Zagorsk outside of Moscow to see believers practicing their faith. I had to hold my camera at my waist so that I wouldn't be prevented from filming, but I was still able to come away with some marvelous material.

The majority of the churchgoers are older women, but we saw plenty of younger women and men, too. On the paths of the monastery complex, which is surrounded by a huge medieval wall, the clergymen were constantly approached by the faithful requesting blessings. Inside the cathedral, all the women wore kerchiefs to show their faith.

Many people were lighting thin yellow candles they had bought there, in front of beautifully ornate icons of Mother and Child. There were also icons with many layers of tiny detailed figures, one row after the other, in front of which ladies lit candles. These seemed to be lineages of historical figures. Every direction you turned there were crowds of people crossing themselves endlessly or standing quietly in silent devotion.

After crossing themselves in front of the icons, the old women would lean forward and kiss the feet of the image. The priests conducting the service were dressed in magnificently rich robes of silver and gold thread, and the presiding clergyman wore an elaborate golden hat. After the communion many of the churchgoers queued up outside under a gazebo for holy water from the fountain there. The water was not flowing at first, and a large crowd had gathered by the time the line started to move. These jostling ladies with their bottles and plastic jugs seemed a stark contrast to the devotional atmosphere inside the cathedral.

Suprabha and I had gone to Zagorsk with Vadim and Natasha, and after we left the monastery grounds they took us a little farther out into the countryside nearby, where they own a log cabin. Although individuals cannot own land in the Soviet Union, ownership of homes still exists, especially in the country. As we walked away from the main road where the bus had dropped us off, we started to enter the vastness of the Russian countryside. Rolling fields stretched in all directions as far as the eye could see from the muddy road that led to Vadim and Natasha's village. The shadows of passing clouds skimmed over the green-and-yellow expanses. As larger clouds swept across the sun, they created a great band of light that flashed over the contours of the hills ahead of us. The beauty of the landscape reminded me of the meeting Vadim, Suprabha, and I had had a few days earlier with the folklorist, Dmitry Pokrovsky.

Pokrovsky's folklore ensemble sings authentic ancient folk songs that they gather themselves on field trips to remote villages. Not only do they learn the music but they also learn the life-style that goes along with these songs. The group's singing sounds as if it comes from the earth itself; there are dissonant harmonies and extraordinary nasal intonations. Dmitry described the background of some of the songs they sang at their rehearsal that day: "We found a very interesting area for ourselves," he began. "These are ancient Russian calendrical songs that are actually pagan spells. The peasants themselves believe that these songs actually influence the weather and the harvest. And one can consider this simply to be superstition, but one can try to see it from their point of view, and when we did that, we understood that they truly do have an influence.

"And what's more, for example, we were able to sing; that is, we found a place and a time when the plants were attracted to this singing. For example, when we sang near a forest or a field, we recorded it and heard sounds that weren't in our singing. You see, all of nature resonates, and it completely changes the behavior of everything live around you. And you begin to feel contact. . . . Well, I can't use any other word . . . you see, that which they call the spirit of the forest or the local deities, the village ones; they really do exist, and when contact with them arises, you begin to learn things that you can't find out any other way. . . ."

On the way to the village Vadim told me that most of the peasants who worked in the area had been heavy drinkers. Once when his car had been stuck in the mud, he could not get any help until he mentioned that he had a bottle of wine as a reward. The fellow he was talking to got so excited that he spewed mud all over the place with his tractor in his hurry to get the job done. All that has changed drastically since the new laws on alcohol distribution came into being last year. "You can't buy anything to drink out here anymore," Vadim said. "But it seems that the fields are being harvested in a more timely manner, too."

The village of twenty-five homes where Vadim and Natasha live is virtually deserted. The only other inhabitants are two Moscow families who have also bought themselves log cabins at a minimal price. The former owners have all moved to the towns and cities. The *izba*, or log cabin, here is a four-hour drive from Moscow, and so it is not really a *dacha*, or summer home, in the traditional sense because it is too far from the city. High government officials are assigned such *dachas* in exclusive enclaves near the city. Other upwardly mobile Russians are saving their money to either buy or build their own *dachas* as part of the trend toward consumerism. Vadim and Natasha's *izba* is a real peasant's dwelling, and it has a big Russian stove that makes up one whole wall of the main room. This stove is supposed to make the home inhabitable year-round. Natasha told me that she had tried to stay there during the winter, but after just a few days it was so white all around—and cold, and lonely— that she couldn't stand it anymore. The price of these *izbas* is often not more than a few hundred dollars, whereas *dachas* range into the thousands.

As we entered Vadim's compound he went straight for the vegetable patch and sampled some leaves of lettuce. He opened up the pod of a dried poppy and gave each of us a few of the seeds to taste. The walk through the fields had turned him philosophical.

"There are different theories about the Absolute or a higher reality," Vadim said. "There can be different images for that, but nature of course is one of the most wonderful images for eternity. The infinite possibilities of the world, its constant vibration, movement, pulsation, and one's interdependence, one's interconnection with this movement, is one of the most thrilling and important experiences.

Just remembering it is enough to help one recharge and return to equilibrium."

Once we had opened up the house, we found wood and started the stove. Then we put on rubber boots and warmer sweaters from the house's collection and went outside to pick rowanberries. A wall of berry bushes right outside the front door was black with fruit. After we had eaten and picked, and gorged ourselves on the semisweet fat berries, we went inside for a light lunch of salad, bread, and tea with red rowanberry preserves in it. Then it was time for a mushroom expedition to the white birch woods just beyond the village before the sun went down. The mushroom season seemed to be drawing to a close, and we barely covered the bottom of our basket, but the countryside at dusk was very peaceful.

Our trip to the *izba* had been spontaneous, and we had been unable to bring much food along, but Natasha borrowed some potatoes from the neighbor and, with a can of beans from the cupboard, our dinner was quite satisfying. After the tea was poured and the preserves stirred in, under the single bulb of the *izba*'s old lamp, Vadim began his colloquy on Russian poetry.

"You know that in Russia there were wonderful poets at the beginning of the century," he said. "Then for a long time they slowly died off. And I myself am convinced that Akhmatova was the last poet, I mean the last great major poet, because after she died a whole epoch, a poetic era, ended." Akhmatova published her first poem in 1911 and died in 1966, after suffering through the Stalin era. She is revered as one of the country's greatest poets. "So who was this Akhmatova?" Vadim continued. "What distinguished her from the generations that followed? First of all she sincerely believed inwardly in the power and significance of poetry as a truly magical action. And this magic transformed the poet into a priest. Internally she was convinced that it was a priestly function. You know, like in an ancient Greek cult, the priest was the mediator between God, transcendence, and man. But the more man became distanced from God, as it were, the less faith he had in such a mission or function. So in order to defend and save itself, our generation, to a large extent, took to using irony, a sense of humor, and alienation. It is a method of adaptation to reality. We couldn't take reality too seriously. It was too dramatic and independent of our will." Vadim was speaking of traits I recognized in him and his friends.

"Akhmatova, on the other hand, was too serious," Vadim continued. "She was a person who took her personality and the mission of the poet very seriously. Unfortunately something disappeared from the air or the society, I'm not sure which; but now no one takes himself as seriously. There are a few people who have continued this serious relationship to poetry, mostly women. Akhmadulina, for example. She has very intimate bounded themes and doesn't deal with the large scale. This is what saves her. This kind of position seems funny in a world where all is relative." Bella Akhmadulina, whom Vadim praised, is a contemporary of Yevtushenko and Voznesensky, but unlike them she has stayed away from political questions, and thus maintained her purity in Vadim's eyes.

Vadim then spoke of a friend to whom he had introduced me. "The satirical poet Prigov is becoming popular now because his worldview, and his view of people, is that nothing is absolute. Everything is conditional and relative. Poetry, life, death, everything. This kind of outlook is an adaptation to the life we have to deal with." I had seen Dmitry Prigov perform as part of avant-garde cultural events, and although he is well known in certain intellectual circles, he is outside the mainstream.

Vadim continued his history of poetry: "So Akhmatova, and other great poets from the first part of the century like Pasternak and Mandelstam, they all took themselves, their personalities, and life in general very seriously. They probably had too great a respect for themselves, and for life itself. But we have lost that respect for life altogether, you see. That's probably our greatest calamity. We may have some respect for ourselves left, but for life in general, nothing is absolute," said Vadim.

"So how about Brodsky and Voznesensky?" Vadim posed the question to himself as we refilled our teacups. "What distinguishes them? Brodsky, at first, wanted to continue the tradition of serious poetry. His early poems were written in the style of Petersburg Acmeism; that is, the same direction Akhmatova took. He felt that Akhmatova passed on the baton of poetry to him when she died. But for Brodsky it was just a game, a stylization, because the situation had changed. The historical and social circumstances had changed. Akhmatova was born, and formed, and lived in a time when there was still the feeling of some kind of order in the world. World War I destroyed this order. The social cataclysm destroyed these forms of order. But the memory of the order of the universe and society was still preserved by Akhmatova.

"Our post–World War II generation didn't have this," Vadim continued. "We were only able to reconstruct and fantasize about a world that felt unshakable, eternal, stable, and unchanging. Namely all those things which are still preserved to some extent in Western life, especially in Western Europe. The feeling that everything which exists now was there yesterday and will be there tomorrow. In Russia such a feeling doesn't exist. We know that yesterday there was a cataclysm, now we have a respite, but tomorrow may be yet another cataclysm, you see. We find ourselves in a destroyed, a fallen world." I felt that Vadim in his usual Russian way was exaggerating the point, but in the dimly lit *izba* in the middle of the silent countryside, it made sense.

"So this is why Voznesensky is interesting," Vadim went on. "He was the first major poet of the postwar generation who took to poetry as a game. The tradition of a surface, extroverted game. A play with words like blocks. You see one on top of the other. This is formalism, of course, but this is not poetry. There's no depth or transcendence, no lyricism. He's simply a person who made something out of words like a child's game of blocks. But he was also fooling himself, because he said, 'I am carrying on the tradition of the avant-garde and futurism in Russian poetry. I am a student of Mayakovsky . . .' But that wasn't the case, because for those writers poetry wasn't just a game." I felt this was an overly harsh assessment, but I had heard similar views expressed by a number of other Russian intellectuals.

Vadim tried to conclude on a positive note by speaking of a contemporary poet he likes. "Prigov is an example of someone who, having gone through this process of destruction of foundations and supports, realizes that by intensifying the destruction one can surmount it. He carries the demolition to the point of the absurd."

I did not agree with Vadim's patronizing views of Brodsky and Voznesensky. Although I did not feel qualified to judge their use of language, and I was not fully aware of their positions in the pantheon of Russian poets, I had read poems of both poets that had moved me strongly. Voznesensky has written poems that jump off the page with the power of their expression of raw emotion. Brodsky can fill the heart to the brim with his evocation of ineffable yearnings.

On another evening I got into a searing argument with our friend Dmitry Prigov about what, if anything, he actually did believe in. But most of the time I felt my role was more to listen and learn than pass judgment. Vadim's nostalgia for a world of order struck me as an anachronistic yearning for stasis, but it was his dynamic and flexible approach to living that had cemented our friendship from the beginning. Our relationship floated between the poles of an intimate meeting of the minds at one extreme, and, at the other, his feeling that I could not possibly plumb the complexities of the Russian soul.

My wife, Suprabha, and I have been disciples of Indian meditation master Sri Chinmoy for over ten years, and part of our daily practice of meditation is running. For us, running is a refreshing way to quiet the mind and purify the whole system. Running can also be a way to go beyond one's preconceived limits of strength and endurance. Suprabha has excelled at this aspect of self-transcendence in running, and has done very well in a number of ultramarathons, ranging from the twenty-four-hour event up to a seven-hundred-mile race. When Dad's friend Dmitri heard about this he suggested that she run in a big race coming up to celebrate Moscow Day. The two of us went down to the Olympic Stadium on a raw, drizzly morning, and found crowds of young people grouping themselves according to the districts of the city. When I inquired about getting a race number for Suprabha, they said you had to apply in advance to your neighborhood council. We tried to find the judges, but it was getting late, so she just ducked under the barrier and disappeared into the mass of runners forming on the street.

On our daily runs in the city—around the Kremlin, along the Moscow River, and in Gorky Park—we saw very few individual runners out for a jog. Almost all the Soviet runners we saw were part of a physical fitness group working out at a stadium or in a park. It was always in connection with a running club, a factory, a school group, or a neighborhood organization. They came and did their workout together according to plan and then dispersed; we rarely saw a lone runner pumping along the boulevards of Moscow. I found this to be yet another sign of the conservative and conformist nature of traditional Soviet society. The sweat and striving of running have no proper place in the zone of cultured people on the sidewalk of the capital.

With the start of the race a few minutes away, I pulled out my little video camera and waded into the throngs of runners to shoot some of them warming up. The people of Moscow have not yet become blasé to the microtechnology of mini video camcorders, and all the runners wanted to show off for TV. One fellow in his late forties, dressed in shorts and a singlet in spite of the chill, stood on the damp pavement barefoot. He had a thick mane of wavy hair that looked particularly Russian, and in each hand he held a small weight with a spring to strengthen his grip. He was dancing and singing in a big deep voice about how wonderful the weather was and what a good time everyone was going to have. He waved his arms up and down, and soon he had a dozen people singing and clapping along with him. Everyone was very excited before the race, and when I walked along in front of the starting line of runners with my camera the police were worried because the racers surged forward. With a cannon shot they were off for seventeen kilometers around the Sadovoye Koltso, or Garden Circle, a verdant boulevard circling the center of town. While we waited for the runners, I filmed a military band singing a patriotic song of love for Moscow and its various bridges and buildings. They kept playing in the rain for a while, but eventually they too took shelter under an overhang of the stadium wall until the runners came back.

At the finish, former sports champions and war heroes, with their scores of pins and medals on a swath of cloth draped over their shoulders, gave out certificates of completion to the finishers. The first man came in with a big smile in a very respectable time. He gave a quick interview to Moscow TV, saying he was a marathon runner and that the race had been run in a very friendly, comradely way. "I was lucky today," he said modestly. An older woman with a sash full of medals, a former marathon champion, who had gray hair but a youthful smile, kept repeating "*Molodtsy, molodtsy.*" ["Good kids, good kids"] as she handed out the certificates.

Suprabha came in around the middle of the pack, invigorated and with pink cheeks. "The rain cooled us off at the end," she said. "I want you to meet my friends," and she introduced me to a couple of young men running right behind her. Yevgeniy, it turned out, had come up to her a few miles into the race and, reading her T-shirt, had said in perfect English, "Sri Chinmoy. He is a great spiritual master, isn't he?" As we shook hands, he said, "I am very interested in meditation. I have practiced a little, and if possible I would like to find out more about it from you. Do you think we could exchange phone numbers?"

I soon learned that Yevgeniy is a devotee of Krishna and has been involved with the movement in the Soviet Union for about ten years. His wife, Marina, is an opera singer. She is also spiritually inclined, but more toward the Christian tradition. Unlike many members of both of their belief systems, they had a flexibility and tolerance for each other's predilections. Yevgeniy began his spiritual search by "questioning the material world." He joined the Baptists, but soon became dissatisfied because their doctrine could not answer many of his questions. Then he became enchanted with the Vedic philosophy, and felt that it provided satisfactory responses to his ultimate questions about life and God.

The Krishna Consciousness movement began in the Soviet Union with the visit of Swami Prabhupad in 1971, at the invitation of Professor Kotovsky of Moscow University. Swami Prabhupad, the venerable founder of the Hare Krishna movement, had one principal Soviet student, Anatoliy Pinyayev. For two years, Yevgeniy traveled around the country as Pinyayev's assistant, while he gave talks and started up groups of Krishna devotees. In the beginning, Yevgeniy recalled, it was all easy. They could advertise openly for lectures on Indian philosophy. But soon the authorities connected their activities to the worldwide movement and a campaign of disinformation in the press began. The Krishnaites were accused of everything from starving their children with a vegetarian diet to being agents of the CIA and cultist murderers. In 1980, Sri Vishnupad, or Robert Compagnola, an American who is Swami Prabhupad's primary disciple, came to Moscow to tend the now-numerous flocks of Krishna followers. In Riga he was taken into custody for two days and then expelled from the country. Two years later a wave of arrests began, and the Krishna followers were tried under the law against bringing harm to the population under the guise of religious services. Yevgeniy says that he was the first arrested, and he spent a year in jail, but it does not seem to have seriously affected his life. He now holds a good job as a translator and teacher of English in an institute. He and his wife have a large, comfortable apartment.

In the fall of 1987 the Krishnaites had a high profile in Moscow. The worldwide celebration of Indian culture, the Festival of India, was in town, and under its protection they were performing their chanting sessions on the Arbat every evening only a few blocks from the Kremlin. Foreign guests from the festival came to join them, and that is why they were not disturbed. They stood in a circle of a dozen devotees, keeping time with the mridanga drums, the small finger cymbals, and plastic tambourines. They were mostly young people, with a few older members, and some wore Krishna buttons, but otherwise they were dressed completely normally. They sang quite beautifully in full voices, and there was always a big crowd around them. The singers had a dedicated and soulful air; they seemed sure of themselves and committed to their cause. I remember when I first saw them there I had not yet met Yevgeniy, and looking at the faces of the Soviets observing them, I could not help thinking that this was a subversive activity in the eyes of the state. This was something totally new for the Russians on the street. They watched with serious, hard, closed faces, betraying no emotion or sympathy, which was strange to me because the music was infectious both in its peacefulness and its joy—and with its beat. I found myself tapping my fingers and smiling, but the Russians around me were more guarded. The only comment I heard was one woman asking her friend "They only know one song?" after we had been listening to the Hare Krishna chant for over ten minutes. Just then the song came to an end and they started another one with different words, but a similar beat.

At around the time that the Krishnaites were big on the Arbat, I met a young woman who worked for Moscow television at a party of modern artists. She told me that she was working on a story about the Krishnaites and that the KGB was very interested. In fact, they were so interested that she got to use one of the two latest model Betacam video cameras in the station to shoot on the Arbat, an honor she had never been accorded previously. The KGB told her that the Krishnaites were a health hazard and that they also worked for the CIA. She did not know what they meant by a health hazard, and as for the CIA, she was not sure if this was true or not. She believed they should have a right to practice their beliefs, but she had heard about their tithing methods and thought that they were wrong. This girl told me that the KGB provided her with a foreign documentary about the Krishna movement, which she signed out for and was free to use as long as she returned it. "Oh, it's amazing. They have everything over there at the Lubyanka," she told me.

The Krishnaites appear prominently in the controversial documentary on the current state of Soviet youth by Latvian director Juris Podnieks titled *Is It Easy to Be Young?* The feature-length film, shot primarily in Riga, is a hodgepodge of various rebellious young people who talk about a loss of meaning in life and a sharp break in values with the older generation. The film shocked the country and got wide circulation as part of the *glasnost* campaign, yet it is far from being a very satisfying piece of filmmaking. The technique of editing often seems to lapse into free association. There are at least half a dozen story lines at work, and all they seem to have in common is that the protagonists are dissatisfied with their conventional lives and want to try something new.

I asked many different people for their opinions on the film, because the responses tended to be strong one way or the other. On the whole, adults thought the film was a convincing piece of work. When we visited Andrei Sakharov at his apartment, he told me he thought the film truthfully uncovered the problem of the generation gap in his society. However, many young people I asked thought the film was sensationalistic and narrow-minded and that the situation it portrayed in Latvia was not at all typical for the rest of the country.

The Krishnaite shown in the film is a young postman who sees the material world as the play of illusion. His real world is his participation in devotional rituals for Lord Krishna, and the chanting of mantras, which purifies his existence. At the end of the segment, the filmmaker asks the fellow about the role of his guru in his life, and whether he is not concerned about his subservience to the guru. "Would you kill if you were ordered to?" the interviewer asks. The devotee answers that he would even kill if his guru told him to. Yevgeniy and his fellow devotees told me that the KGB went through all of Podnieks's material on the Krishnaites and selected the parts to be used. The KGB cut the postman's answer in the middle to make it look as if he is a potential killer, they claimed. The young devotee in the film goes on to say that of course this situation could never occur because their path is based on the principle of nonviolence. Yevgeniy told me that this part was cut out. "It's too bad, because he was young and inexperienced when he was used in that film," Yevgeniy said.

Soon the singing of the Krishnaites on the Arbat was shut down, too. In late August they were taken in by the police and charged with performing religious acts in public without a permit. The participants were fined thirty-five rubles each. The end of the Hare Krishna chanting on the street also seemed to signal the end of a period of flowering of personal and artistic expression in the public forum of the Arbat. It was a sign of the struggle at the highest levels of leadership, between then Moscow party chief, Boris Yeltsin, who favored allowing the Arbat to flourish, and Yegor Ligachev, the powerful, conservative party secretary, who wanted the free nightlife to be curbed.

This street culture of the Arbat had been a relatively new phenomenon. It had just started in the spring with the appearance of portrait sketchers offering their services to passers-by. When we strolled down the Arbat on a warm mid-August evening, in addition to the portraitists, there were various artists offering their works in miniexhibits tacked up along the sides of the street. Some of this art was highly abstract and prompted derisive comments from pedestrians, but on the whole the atmosphere was one of live and let live on the Arbat.

This was evident in the variety of music. Much of the singing was balladeer-style, in the tradition of Vysotsky, but we also heard prison songs, songs of the Whites from the civil war sung by a Ukrainian, and one fellow who claimed he was a "natural anarchist." Another young fellow sang a sarcastic song about going on a trip to Paris and Rome. He filled out all of his applications in triplicate, but the last line of the song gave it away—the only traveling he had done had been on paper. Most of the singers tried to collect change from the audience for their efforts, which is illegal, so they came up with a variety of novel containers. There were the usual guitar cases, boxes, and hats, but there were also umbrellas and shoes slipped off briefly to serve the purpose. I was impressed with the flexibility and tolerance of the police in controlling the Arbat. They often had their hands full.

One evening there was a long line of young men festooned with red-and-white scarves, carrying red flags with the letter S in white. As they paraded down the Arbat, they were yelling chants to celebrate the victory of their team, Spartak, in soccer. We were standing around and listening to Krishnaites explaining Vedic philosophy in small groups, and we wondered what these sports fans were going to do, but they passed through peaceably enough. On an adjacent cross street some teenage boys had a Soviet version of a boom box, which was pitifully weak, but it was playing electronic pop music to which the boys were break dancing. They wore jeans and white leather sports gloves, but they kept goofing around with each other instead of dancing so we did not stay long.

At dusk a gang of toughs, two abreast, about twenty of them in all, ran by us down the crowded street. Everyone turned to watch, but they just kept going down the block. My friend told me they were an imitation of the Lyubers, "a neo-fascist group" of body-builders from a town outside Moscow who have a reputation for beating up rock and rollers and others they consider to have fallen to decadent Western trends. Later in the evening a few of the tough kids from out of town charged at other teenage boys in the midst of the crowds on the Arbat. Fists and kicks flew, and the crowd was swept along with the action, trying to see what was going on. Within three minutes the militia had the fighting isolated onto a side street, and soon led the contestants away. Little bursts of conflict broke out for the next fifteen minutes, but the police quelled each of them quickly.

When we were walking home, I stopped and listened to an argument between a plainclothes cop and a few of the boys who had been in the fight. It turned out that the gang was from Tula, famous for brass samovars since before the revolution, and some 250 kilometers from Moscow. The Tula boys had picked a fight with some local Moscow kids. The cop, who was a handsome and strong, nicely dressed man in his late thirties, had been a principal in stopping the fight. He was telling these local boys: "You have to think for yourselves. You're eighteen years old. Educated, cultured, responsible. You can't go along with this crowd psychology. It's not like a collective, where ten to fifteen people band together to get something done. Here there were hundreds of people and there could have been a stampede."

When the boys argued that their comrade was being clamped in a grip around the neck, the cop argued that they should have surrounded their comrade defensively and taken him away from the fighting. The debate continued when a spectator asked the cop whether he had ever fought in his youth. The policeman replied that of course he had on occasion, but it had not been in the middle of a street full of people downtown.

At eleven o'clock we strolled down the Arbat toward home. A group of drunken teenagers, who did not sound like much, sang Beatles' songs with a go-go dancer in their midst. They were just having fun being rowdy, and one of their singers kept yelling "Oh, yeah!" in English at the top of his lungs every few stanzas. A police car slowly cruised down the street, stopping every few hundred yards for one of the policemen to get out and tell the kids still singing that it was time to go home. In one of these exchanges a young singer said to the policeman, "In Paris they play 'til midnight. Why do we have to stop at eleven here?"

Later in the month we were talking to a singer on the Arbat. He showed us a note he had received that warned him to be on the lookout for a provocation by the authorities that evening. He was trying to decide whether it was worth staying around. By mid-September there was still some warm weather, but there were very few musicians still playing on the Arbat.

Soon after we met, Yevgeniy invited me and Suprabha to come with him and Marina to a meeting of the Krishna followers. It was in a residential area of Moscow, and as we walked on the wooded side streets among the ten-story apartment blocks, we suddenly heard the sounds of cymbals clanging and voices singing in the same cadences that we were used to hearing on the streets of Washington,

D.C., or Boston. Yevgeniy told me that the Krishnaites had no problems performing services in their own apartments, as long as they finished at a reasonable hour so that the neighbors did not complain. When we came in, the chanting was still going at full volume. Everyone seemed to know that we were coming, and they were eager for me to document the proceedings with my video camera. In the front of the room was a shrine with pictures of Swami Prabhupad and Sri Vishnupad framed on the wall against a shiny cloth. On the small table underneath were candles, flowers, offerings of food, a conch shell, and other "auspicious" objects.

In the apartment living room were about twenty people, most of whom were men. A few were over fifty, but most were in their twenties. Some wore Indian wraparound dhotis with flowing kurta shirts. One fellow was bare-chested, with a long cotton scarf wrapped around his neck. Many of the women were in saris, and there were more of them in their fifties than the men. The women seemed light and joyful compared to the men, who had more serious expressions on their faces. Yevgeniy told me that for him the chanting and meditation were a way to go beyond his individual self. He felt that he was joining into a large family of all living beings through his chanting. It was a feeling of joy that was very intimate and very subtle, he said. The joy of *ananda*, or spiritual bliss, is indescribable with words, he told me.

Three of the men took turns leading the singing, and after a half hour they stopped and had a reading from the *Bhagavad-Gita*. They had a version with Swami Prabhupad's commentary translated into Russian. While the singing was still going on a half dozen young people knocked on the apartment door unexpectedly. They had heard the singing from the street and wanted to come in to see what was going on. A couple of them were drunk and were turned away, but four of them came in and stood watching with the same puzzled and closed look I had seen in the crowd on the Arbat. They slipped away after the singing.

Soon the devotees spread a cloth out on the floor and offered a simple vegetarian meal of *prasad*, or blessed food. The Krishnaites were eager to know who we were and how their movement was doing in America. I really did not know, but I made up an answer as best I could. They had held a demonstration recently in Moscow protesting the fate of twenty-five of their members still held in jails or psychiatric hospitals. They showed me the photographs of their fellow devotees they had held up on the street. The pictures had been trampled underfoot by the KGB men who broke up their march. They told me that the men who disrupted the demonstration had been brutally rough, even with the women and children who participated. Yevgeniy showed me a picture of Pinyayev, the first Russian devotee, with whom he had been very close. "He has been in a mental hospital for almost five years now," Yevgeniy said. "He just stays to himself among all the crazy people there and maintains his own faith. That is really something: to maintain Krishna consciousness in that kind of environment."

Yevgeniy now feels that there may soon be light at the end of the tunnel. "Now we feel that the attitude of the authorities is changing, step by step, very slowly. We met the representatives of the religious council in Moscow, and they said that all of our victims were in vain. All the articles in the press were foolish, and all the expert witnesses were false. We just need time to rehabilitate you, they said. So it was quite a new attitude to us.

"Now we have better hopes for the future. We are expecting that by Christmas our question of registration, the legalization of Hare Krishna in the Soviet Union, will be solved. That's what we were promised, at least. But one way or another, even if we are not registered, we're still believers, and we'll go on with it."

On our way out, our hostess was saying, "Allen Ginsberg called me from Paris last night to see how everything is going. . . ."

It is hard for me to imagine being friends with Yevgeniy in America. Our spiritual paths are different enough so that in a country of free religious choices we would probably not associate with one another. But under the unique conditions of life in the Soviet state, friendship between Russians and Americans always has special connotations and resonances that do not exist elsewhere.

I took for granted that my Russian friends were interested in me to some extent simply as an American, but that was merely one of the elements that began our relationship. There was always the element of possible danger or discomfort for them in associating with a foreigner. But these aspects of the friendship were just surface phenomena compared to the deepest feelings that seemed to develop so readily.

What is it about Russians that one can go and meet people, spend two months with them, and leave with an experience of friendship as close as one has ever had? In many ways friendship is the testing of the boundaries of what one has in common with another. True friendship is when one goes beyond these boundaries, when one accepts what is there, and the friends either respect or tolerate those differences. Russian-American relationships are often either an overly rosy glossing-over of differences in a peacenik atmosphere or a battle between entrenched stereotypes.

A Russian friend was involved in translating for meetings sponsored by a group called the Center for Soviet-American Dialogue. She told us of a forum with Soviet and American filmmakers, so one morning we went to the House of Film, the headquarters of the Filmmakers' Union near Mayakovsky Square, to hear their discussion. The Americans had been in Moscow for over a week, and the dialogue we heard had already been in progress for a few days. The group of producers was discussing joint projects, and one American, Joel Edelman, was saying, "I'm really getting the feeling of 'Alice in Wonderland' here. There is a sense of fantasy about doing projects together."

A younger American colleague interrupted to say that before Edelman came in they had all agreed to finally get into the specifics of budgets, logistics, and timetables, but Edelman wanted to finish his piece. "In order to get to know each other, first we have to find out each others' interests, proclivities, and ways of working. We can't launch right into the substance of projects without first knowing each others' methods of operating. If we want to have a lasting marriage, we have to get to know each other one step at a time," Edelman said.

A Soviet filmmaker promptly responded: "You know, I knew my future wife for twelve days, and on the thirteenth day we were married. We've been happily married for seventeen years." Everyone laughed, and then—for a little while, at least—they got down to business.

A Russian who spoke some English launched into a detailed description of how a Soviet feature film is made from conception to completion. The whole process on the average takes thirteen months, he said. From what the filmmaker had described, in broad terms, the procedures seemed rather similar between the American and Soviet industries. There were a few more collective decisions and submissions to commissions in the Soviet process, but filmmaking is a highly collaborative art, and one can find a correlation between the power of the commissions in the Soviet Union and the veto power of the studios in Hollywood.

The American producer Robert Chartoff took it all in from a

different perspective, however. "The process you have just described is incredibly tedious," he began. "With all that bureaucracy to contend with, all your creativity must be squelched from the outset. I don't see how it's possible to function creatively in such a system. My interest in filmmaking is to generate enthusiasm for the job and to find new solutions every day for the different challenges that arise. Your methods are so plodding and methodical that I think my approach would be impossible here." From the producer of *Rocky*, the biggest wig at the meeting, this was quite a blow to the Russians.

"We are masochists!" the director with the quick and lasting marriage said. Everyone chuckled, but in a more serious vein he said, "We are all very devoted to our craft. We love the movies so much that we are willing to put up with the process. We all come from different fields of expertise; one was a scientist, another a journalist, and another was an engineer. But we came to this field because we know what we want."

Chartoff's rejoinder dug his hole deeper still. "Well, you know what I say—for every good masochist there has got to be a good sadist. I think you guys should look into the source of your problems, and find out who is creating this system and why they are torturing you. That is the only way you will be able to improve things."

The Russian director who had just spent half an hour explaining the filmmaking process fairly exploded. "Don't you understand? This is what *perestroika* is all about! We are about to make some major changes in our system. First of all, we're looking for different sources of funding, other than the government. Our film union, different associations, *kolkhozes* ["collective farms"], anyone should be able to finance a film. We are starting to make this changeover, and next week we are having a meeting about starting a studio that will get rid of many of these bureaucratic obstacles."

Chartoff tried to save face: "Well, that's great," he said. "We would like to describe the American system of film production to you. It has its problems, too. But maybe you can learn something from it for your own reorganization." A young Russian woman who had been translating for the group for a week told me: "It's been like this all along. It keeps going around in circles. First everyone describes the stereotypes and how they want to get rid of them. Then they talk about a few relevant details of work or say they want to, and then they start right in with the stereotypes again." The Russian filmmakers seemed to see the Americans as an instant source of exotic projects for which they could travel to America. The Americans' stereotype was that the Russians were enslaved in a state bureaucracy that was crushing their creativity.

An American woman, who was an organizer of the conference and who had been in Moscow for longer than the main group, came in during Chartoff's exchange. She tried to gloss over the differences. "Oh, I'm sure with some more discussion over lunch we can come to an agreement on these issues," she said. I was not so sure.

My friendship with Soviets who could be considered antiestablishment—such as Vadim, Andrei, and Yevgeniy—brought tensions to my relationship with my old friend Lyokha. Lyokha thought that Vadim was overly intellectual and talked too much, which was hard to deny. But Lyokha was also suspicious of Vadim's open condemnation of the effects of Stalin's excesses on Soviet society. It all had a distinctly unpatriotic ring for Lyokha. When I described Andrei the bottle man to Lyokha, he was unsympathetic. "What a weak personality and what a waste of a higher education provided by the state," Lyokha said. I decided it wasn't worth discussing Yevgeniy's case in any detail with him.

Early one morning, around six o'clock, when all the others had gone to Leningrad, Lyokha called. He said he had been partying with friends all night and wanted to come over to talk. I said fine, and when he showed up I had my camera going to see what would happen. Lyokha told me to turn it off a few times, and when I wouldn't, he went out into the hall. I followed him, and he put his hands over the lens, telling me not to shoot because he was in a bad mood. I got him to come back into the apartment, and told him that the reason I was shooting was to capture some kind of authenticity.

"Steve, you're a filmmaker. I'm a photographer. I understand you perfectly, and you understand me perfectly," Lyokha said. "The deal is that there is also an individual relationship between you and me. So there's no need to expose with this thing what exists between us.

"There doesn't need to be a camera or a lens, you see? . . . It's simply a personal relationship. You have relationships with your wife, and your parents, and you're not going to expose those, because it would serve no purpose. It's personal, you see. You don't get it?"

"Of course I get it," I replied.

"Then turn it off, and everything will be fine. And you and I will talk," Lyokha concluded.

We had a marathon conversation until about noon that day, but I was mainly listening as Lyokha blew off steam from the tensions that had built up around the making of both my film and the "Front-line" documentary. Lyokha's complaints were not that specific. He simply felt under attack by our attitudes, which he saw as being hostile. I tried to reassure Lyokha, and from then on was more careful to accommodate his interests and needs.

Like the rest of the country, Lyokha was in the throes of restructuring. His long-cherished beliefs about the history of his country were gradually being uprooted. The security of his livelihood was threatened in a way he couldn't really put his finger on. It must have been hard for him to have us rooting around and trying to learn all the details of this painful process.

Toward the end of our stay, Lyokha introduced us to his friend Allan, a traveler and painter of distant landscapes. Allan's nonconformist personality was a bridge between Lyokha and me that helped us to reconcile our differences. Lyokha and Allan had met at Moscow University, where they were both studying biology. But Allan had already been captured by the muse of painting, and soon he gave up his studies to attend to his canvases full-time.

Allan's paintings are richly detailed landscapes of mountain ranges taken from life while hiking alone in the Pamirs and the Tien Shan range near China. He captures the early morning light on a mountain lake, and the initial swirls of snow in a gorge that will soon turn into a blizzard. Allan's paintings were hung in an informal club of artists and musicians, and after we got to know him he invited us to his studio apartment.

Over tea and slabs of cheese on bread, Allan and Lyokha talked about their generation. "Our generation is very complicated. We were born in between," said Allan. "I was born in 1958, and all of my conscious life has been during Brezhnev times. I don't know of anything else; everything else for me is simply fictional literature."

Lyokha laughed. "Fictional literature, eh?"

"So when they talk about *perestroika*," Allan continued, "I understand perfectly well that they are talking about restructuring all of the problems which have formed me as a person. My negative attitude toward certain things, say, is what they are trying to correct. And at the same time I know perfectly well that no one will be able to correct these things for me. They won't find any Czar or general secretary who will be able to give the command and have everything fixed up. These things will never be corrected unless I myself decide to take action and figure out what really needs to be done. And it's like that for each one of us really.

"We are a generation which has not experienced conditions of democracy as we were growing up, and then when it came time to join the work force, we needed to restructure ourselves in order to fit in and have long-term goals. Maybe those kids who are running around now with the punk haircuts and the metallic trappings, maybe they'll have gotten all their craziness out, and they'll settle down to being normal, calm, working people. Some of them, of course, will still be acting crazy until they're ninety.

"They often say that democracy means a time when the wolf and the lamb and the lion will all drink from the stream side by side. No, I think democracy first of all means truth. It's when the secrets in all the hidden corners will rise to the surface, and a visible struggle is taking place. It's not when someone shoots someone else from a hidden position and you don't know who it is. No, everything should be out in the open."

"What kind of truth are you talking about? About the past?" I asked.

"Yeah, without the past there's no future or present," Lyokha said. "The funniest thing is that everyone is saying, 'Democracy, democracy,' but no one knows what to do with this democracy. No one knows how to fit it in. Everyone knows that democracy is great, but how to find a place for it . . . ?"

"And what would you like democracy to do?" I asked.

Allan answered: "Well, I for one, and everyone, really, has always wanted freedom. I don't really know what freedom is. We learned in school that 'freedom is the realization of necessity.' Who knows what that means? I think freedom is a concept like love, like eternity, like time, which we cannot grasp with words. It's something which is felt inside. It's an ideal which a person strives toward.

"But in every epoch freedom has characteristics which relate to the social conditions of the time. I think at this stage, the most essential freedom for me is the freedom of information, movement, and the freedom of work. These three are the most meaningful now. Information is most essential, and movement is closely related: to know how, what, and where; and to be able to move freely even around the country. Freedom of work means to be able to work at the profession you choose, to do what you want to do. This is a problem everywhere. It's very rare that a person gets to do exactly what he wants in life.

"We read and hear, or even ourselves believe, like the Christians, that there is an afterlife, or like the Hindus and the Buddhists that there is reincarnation. But for the concrete, specific person, it still remains the same—that he has one given life, and in this life he's got to deal with some problems, and for this he needs a certain degree of freedom."

The prevalent feeling among my friends was that materialist ambitions had taken over the motivations of their society. Seventy years of Communist rule, for better or for worse, have produced a society where caring for the welfare of others is a common value of which everyone is proud. When I walked down the streets of Moscow as a child, I knew that any *babushka* would scold me just like my mother if I misbehaved. But as more and more consumer goods have become available to the population at large, the drive to acquire them has shaped the life-style away from the communal altruism their ideology espouses. On a political level this is manifested in the party patronage system. Vadim told me this has to change if Gorbachev's reforms are to take root.

The Russians are still afraid to talk about it openly, but they all acknowledge that the inordinate role of the KGB in the domestic life of the country continues to be a strangling influence. I told my friends that an important part of change in the sixties in America was the revelations about domestic spying by the CIA and the restrictions put on the agency as a result. *Glasnost* and *perestroika* seem to have penetrated everywhere except the KGB. Most of my friends accept the secret police as a negative fact of life, but they all agreed that only when the powers of the KGB are visibly curbed will the public begin to believe that *perestroika* is not just another passing campaign.

When Vadim asked Andrei about the moral condition of Russian society, Andrei replied, "Anguish and despair; it continues as it was." He lamented that people are so malicious and mean to each other. "If I could get hold of a suitcase full of pistols, like in the States, and if I threw them out on the ground where people are lined up at my recycling station, I would just have to duck behind my counter for a few minutes and when I stood up there wouldn't be any line left."

Andrei believes that the root cause of this animosity is the economic situation. "When people have to stand in line for three or four hours, what do you think? Things need to be improved in both production and distribution to have an effect on the quality of life. And trade from overseas, with the Japanese, with the West Germans, with anyone; it's got to increase," he said. But Andrei's personal ambitions are very limited. "Even when I was studying in university,

I didn't have any special hopes for building a career," he said. "I didn't try and I didn't want it because I understood very well that if you don't enter the party, things will be closed to you, and by my nature I could never fit in there."

When Vadim accused Andrei of having the same lack of energy to work for change as the others, he replied, "It's not so much a lack of energy as a feeling of uselessness. I'm not prepared to work for the generation of the next century, although that's what needs to be done now. You can't expect anything for our lifetime. Our generation can only try to give some kind of foundation for the future."

Vadim told me that every Soviet has his own personal story about how the government has done him wrong. "It's a kind of mythology which I don't even pay attention to anymore. In many older people it turns into a kind of mania and craziness," he said. "But to maintain one's individual sense of self is not easy here. In America one can be in the stream and go with the current, and still maintain one's sense of self; but here in order to maintain that individuality one must swim against the current."

One afternoon at their apartment, Natasha said to me, "As a rule when people say *freedom*, they use it in a narrow sociological sense, even a political one. They themselves restrict the domain of their own personal freedom. But clearly you and Vadim are convinced that your sense of freedom is larger than that. Your freedom is bigger."

Vadim said, "Of all the things we've talked about, the most important is the area of inner freedom, and I think that's your interest, too."

Russians have a remarkable capacity to sum up their lives for you in a paragraph or two, and in the heat of our discussion on freedom, this is what Allan said: "Dostoyevsky said, 'Beauty will save the world.' I think he was right. Many people think of beauty as mere prettiness. Something purely aesthetic, but beauty from my point of view is an understanding of some very large common harmony. And when a person connects with it, well, the more people who connect with it the better off they'll be.

"I work as a painter; I walk, I ride, I look, I read, and I see; all that I am is for painting. I think that these pictures of mine will play their role. I hope so. Every person has faith in what he's doing. If I had no faith in this, I wouldn't be doing it. Maybe it will be a very small role, maybe on ten, twenty, or a hundred people. Or even if it's just one person. If my paintings can make someone look at the world differently, then I will already think that I haven't lived in vain."

On the evening of our farewell party, Lyokha proudly told me a rather extraordinary story. He had been riding home in a taxi the night before, and he noticed that the driver had a portrait of Stalin on his dashboard. Lyokha asked the driver why he had the picture there, and the man replied that Stalin was a great leader. "We could use someone like him now," the driver said.

Lyokha said, "No, that's not right. Now is a time when we are moving toward democracy, and more responsibility is being given to the individual."

The man insisted that what was needed was a strong and strict leader to bring order into the society. But Lyokha continued to argue that there was no turning back to the past. The country had to make this step or it would never grow great, he said. Finally the driver agreed.

I was truly amazed by this story because Vadim had told me about a similar episode, but with a different ending. Just before I left, he too had been driving home with a friendly cabbie. They had been having an enjoyable discussion until the topic of politics arose. The driver said, "Yeah, what we really need now is someone with a strong hand like Stalin." But Vadim immediately felt alienated. He cut off the conversation and went up to his apartment feeling discouraged.

Vadim's response was the typical alienation of the intellectual from the blue collar. Lyokha's argument showed a remarkable transformation of his own thinking that was just then taking place. Many of the Russian intelligentsia are still not ready to give up their feelings of superiority at having been right during all those years of repression. The intellectuals will also need to go through some changes in order to build democracy into the Soviet system.

At our farewell party we mixed all of our friends together in a way that is very rarely done in Moscow. There were some moments of anxiety, but everyone seemed pleasantly surprised to see how "the other half" behaved. Many Russians meeting for the first time exchanged phone numbers.

Suprabha's Stories

THE SLAP

Barney, Nancy, and I went one evening to see a play at the Sovre-mennik II theater studio space. We managed to arrive at the theater ten minutes after the play was scheduled to start. There was a young man waiting in the entrance who scolded us for our tardiness. He took us up to the top floor in the elevator, and as we stepped out the full impact of our predicament hit. The scale of the studio theater is intimate; the only entrance lands you right in the front row. If it happens to be full, you would have to try to climb over the audience in search of a seat.

There was an actor waiting with his ear on the door, listening for his cue. He spoke with our friend, and then strode off purposefully in the opposite direction. When he returned moments later, he was clutching three mugs that had just been rinsed and were now half full of milk. We were given these mugs and instructed in Russian with supplemental sign language to enter at the beginning of the next act, to sit down, and to drink the milk.

When the door opened, one actor entered and announced: "And now our American friends!" We piled in the door and sat down quickly in the nearest corner, which was blessedly vacant. I raised my milk mug and realized that in center stage an actor was also drinking a mug full of milk. With this spontaneous milk-toasting improvisation, the actors had created a role for us in their play.

MOSCOW DAY RACE

On Moscow Day there was a seventeen-kilometer race around the Garden Circle road of the city. Early that morning, Sudakkha and I headed toward the Sports Arena; he with his video camera and I in my running gear. As we approached the stadium, we passed group after group of runners of all ages gathering to receive their numbers. We discovered that these numbers are distributed to teams by district—so we gave up the idea of my having one. Instead I climbed under the rope and joined the crowd of several thousand excited runners.

As we started to run the drizzle turned to real rain, which continued with varying intensity for the duration of the race. This did not dampen anyone's enthusiasm. The runners were very cheerful and would shout with glee while running under each bridge, enjoying the echo. I felt the rain was a good thing because there was no drinking water along the way. I tried to imagine searching for thousands and thousands of paper cups in Moscow, and so I forgave the race directors.

My pace was just over eight minutes, and it seemed as though everyone would pass me. I noted that if I got ahead of any male runners, before long they made an effort to pass me. Many runners stayed in team formation throughout the whole ten-mile course. I was enjoying running through the city slowly and soggily. Two or three kilometers before the finish, two young men approached me from behind. One said, "Sri Chinmoy is a great spiritual master." He had read the aphorism on my T-shirt:

> The determination
> In your heroic effort
> Will permeate
> Your mind and heart
> Even after
> Your success or failure
> Is long forgotten.
> —SRI CHINMOY

These young men stayed with me until the finish. It was fun to find some English-speaking runners. These men had participated in the International Peace Marathon in June and had met other Americans then. One of the two, Yevgeniy, was especially interested in meditation. He knew of our meditation teacher, Sri Chinmoy, as a spiritual poet. Sudakkha and I met with him many times after this and got to be quite close. Although he was a Hare Krishna devotee, he was very inspired by Sri Chinmoy's spiritual philosophy on running as a way to combine the inner life of meditation with outer activities. He explained to us that Russians put a great emphasis on group sports and developing athletic capacity toward the glory of the larger team. The idea of making inner progress by competing with oneself rather than with others was a new approach for him.

It was very rare to see a lone runner in Moscow. Runners restrict their routes to the parks and tracks, and usually are part of a team that meets in the early morning or evening to train. Sudakkha and I ran fifteen kilometers with Yevgeniy's Peace Club team one Friday evening. First there was a short meeting with announcements of future events, and then the group of thirty runners assembled outside their clubhouse in Gorky Park. The group stayed together as a single unit for the first few miles. Then runners split into smaller groups according to speed. We ran with the head of the team, David, and told him about our running in America. He is an ultramarathoner in his fifties, and dreams of running in the New York City Marathon. We ran up into the Lenin Hills, and the lights of the city stretched out in the distance below. By nine-thirty we were back at the clubhouse, happy and exhilarated from the night air and our marathon conversation. David gave us some medals and flags of the Peace Club as mementoes. We walked back to the metro with a young woman who had recently joined the club through a friend at work. She had never run any distance before, and running with the club was giving her new confidence in herself.

As we crossed the finish line of the Moscow Day race, we were handed certificates by some former champions who were draped with medals. I was approached by a reporter who wanted details about me as a foreign runner. All of a sudden we were surrounded by a swarm of runners who all wanted their certificates autographed by me! This was a surprise, and also a lot of fun. The race staff people were serving very sweet hot tea in flimsy brown paper cups. Leona and Doveen had come for the finish, and we were all hungry, so we got in line for some small eclairs. The next day I read about myself on the front page of *Soviet Sport*—the largest circulation sports newspaper in the world, we were told. Under the banner headline, GREEN LIGHT ON THE GARDEN CIRCLE, it read:

> Among the many tourists from around the world, we found an American woman, Suprabha Schecter from Washington of the club, "Marathon Team" [sic]. Suprabha, a delicate, miniature woman, it turns out, is able to run 111 miles in 24

hours. She was in delight after the "Garden." "The run helped me to better understand and feel Moscow," she said, smiling.

I wanted to change my soaking T-shirt before heading for the subway, so we stopped in a building that was part of the Olympic Stadium complex. The ladies in the hall smiled when they saw my soaked running clothes and told us that runners were entitled to a special swim in the Olympic pool. I think all of our eyes must have lit up, because we had been searching for a pool to swim in for several weeks.

In fact, Sudakkha, Doveen, Barney, and I had undergone seven laboratory tests each—from multiple blood samples to foot examinations and chest X rays—in order to be deemed healthy enough to enter a swimming pool. Our final reward after all these tests was to receive the coveted swimming *spravka*, or permission slip. Once these prized papers were in our hands we discovered that there were no pools (among those considered hygienically safe by our friends) in which we could swim. Barney was the most persistent because his back required the stretching exercise provided by swimming. He had been going to an open-air public pool that required no *spravka* until we heard that there had been cases of meningitis there. The Russian Orthodox believers said this pool was cursed because it was built on the site of the Cathedral of Christ the Saviour, which had been destroyed during Stalin's time.

At the Olympic Stadium, a lady in the pool building was very hospitable and proudly gave us a tour of the pools where the Olympic competitions had been held. The pools were crystal clear, absolutely beautiful, and there did not seem to be an excess of swimmers. We asked our guide whether we might be able to use the pool, and she wrote down a list of phone numbers of various pool officials. She thought at least one of them would be helpful. We made the calls, and after extended negotiations got passes to use the pool for one hour a week. It was less than we had hoped, but at least we got to make use of our hard-earned *spravkas*.

MY GROCERY EXPEDITION

Leona is now an expert at clandestine gourmet hot plate cooking. The family members all became accustomed to the tasty three-course meals that were ingeniously produced in the Berlin Hotel sitting room, but our guests were always incredulous. Usually we would shop at the foreigners' Beriozka supermarket, where on a good day you could buy fresh produce, canned foods, various juices and jams, Russian chocolates, and even bread. Once we found Swiss muesli cereal there. Generally in Moscow you do not make up a shopping list. It is much more productive to go to the market with an open mind.

Once Leona planned to make caviar mousse to take to Yuri's birthday party. She had already located the gelatin (Yuri actually contributed this), but she still needed mayonnaise and sour cream. I volunteered to pick these things up at the gastronom across Prospekt Mira.

My mantra for this excursion was *smetana*—Russian for sour cream. (The word for mayonnaise is virtually the same.) The first store I went into was very busy, and I discovered they were out of both mayonnaise and sour cream there. I walked a few blocks in one direction, but it became clear that this was not grocery territory. Back the other way, I recognized a street that was part of our morning running route. I found a store with dairy products and huge lines. A careful scrutiny of the items in the cheese case revealed *smetana*. I caught the eye of a lady in line and, pointing to a round plastic container, asked, "Mayonnaise?" The response was affirmative.

I went to the cashier's line and paid forty-three kopecks (68 cents) for the sour cream and twenty-six (42 cents) for the mayonnaise. I joined the line for picking up the items, which by this time wound halfway around the store. Then I began to wonder if one little mayo and *smetana* would be enough for Leona's mousse. I made a sign to the sympathetic-looking lady in the beige coat behind me and returned to the cashier for another round of mayonnaise and *smetana*.

The large woman behind the pick-up counter had some kind of system for allowing soldiers and a few senior citizens to stand at the head of the line and be served intermittently with the long-term line people like me. After a twenty-five-minute wait in an atmosphere that was starting to feel like a sauna, the big moment arrived. I took a deep breath and asked for *dva smetana* and *dva mayonnaise*. The lady behind the counter did not seem to find anything foreign about my request. She handed me the items—and four kopecks change — because the regular sour cream was out and she had given me low-fat. I left the shop feeling triumphant, and had an ice cream on the way home to celebrate.

Life Without Lenin

Maxim, Gosha, Pavel, Natasha, and Lyena are a cast of characters in a story with a recurring theme: trying to find a way to get by in a society in which they could not fully believe. As Lyena and I walked arm in arm together; Maxim and I drank vodka together; and Gosha and Pavel and I laughed together; I was able to catch a glimpse of their lives through small windows into that spirit that kept them hopeful and full of life through many cold winters. They live with the constant fear of reprisals, of being caught in the acts of creation or simply in socializing with foreigners. They are trying as young people to find their identities in a world that allows them no personal freedom.

Each in his or her own experience is trying to find the scam that will get them through. How to deal with the KGB, how to find money, how to find privacy, how to be an artist, how to find work and privilege without becoming a party member. How to keep your head up high, your naïveté intact, and your integrity in a world that makes all the rules for you.

The Hermitage Group exhibitions were highlights of my stay in Moscow. The group, led by Lyonya Bazhanov, was an offspring of an earlier group of artists that had come together to negotiate with the new powers under *glasnost*. They succeeded in finding a gallery space to show paintings that had been gathering dust, some hidden for years in artists' studios waiting for a time when there would be permission to hang them. We saw several exhibits while we were there, a retrospective and a show of more current work, including paintings by artists who had emigrated. Most of the artists were there, and it was a chance to match the names I had only heard about with the people and their work.

As we all spilled out of the Berlin and into the metro, passing five-kopeck pieces to each other through the crowd, we headed to the red-line and rode it to the outskirts of the city. I came to love this ride for the time it gave us to talk to each other and catch up on the day's events. At the end of the line the walls of the station were flanked by two enormous ironwork lions, as if heralding the entrance to some great ancient city. The irony of the Moscow metro is that the palatial wonderland underground is not like real life above ground. The contrast was stark as we came out of the station at Belyayevo. As far as the eye could see were shabby blocks of fifteen- and twenty-story apartment buildings set between muddy fields on both sides of a wide boulevard. Outside the metro stop was a small outdoor market where Barney and I found fresh honey, greasy *pirozhki*, old ladies selling flowers picked from their private gardens, and one of our favorite items, watermelon, which we liked for their name in Russian, *arbuzy*, a nickname Kate has called both of us for years.

The exhibit was housed in the ground floor of one of the apartment buildings. As we walked through the mud, I felt as if we had come back to our old neighborhood. The balconies were filled with small gardens, clotheslines, baby carriages, and people who waved down to us, curious to see the visitors to the exhibit.

The opening was filled with artists, journalists, and cultural attachés from the embassies. It was a huge social gathering filled with an air of excitement and collective catharsis, a sigh of relief that this open display of forbidden art was actually happening. I met new friends who were connected to each other, all part of a network. By the end of the evening Steve had befriended Boris and Tanya, a young couple in their twenties who invited us and a bunch of their Russian friends back to their apartment to see Boris's movies. We started for the metro with a large group that slowly dwindled as people got off at stops along the red-line back into the center of Moscow.

Their apartment was cluttered, cozy, and warm, with low ceilings. The walls were covered with artwork by their friends, including several I had met. There was also a framed photograph of the poet Josef Brodsky as a young man. The films were unedited and at least three hours long, so Boris showed us only highlights on a borrowed VCR, forwarding to the parts he wanted Steve to see. A very sad girl, who had latched on to me at the exhibit, helped to translate the film for me.

The most striking scene in the film was one that began to make sense to me as we spent more time in Moscow. It opened with a young woman in a snowy, windswept, urban field, leaning over her child, squatting on the ground and breast-feeding her baby. She and a man, presumably the father, walk farther in the field until they come upon a man they recognize. He is lying on the snow-dusted ground under pieces of garbage and scrap metal, almost buried, his face wrapped in rags. He stirs and begins to rise. They help him to free himself and find a seat on some rubble. He takes a few swigs of vodka from a flask inside his breast pocket, barely able to hold it with his frozen fingers, and begins to tell the story of the men in his family. His grandfather was killed when his fighter plane burst into flames over Spain during the civil war in 1937. During the years of Stalin's rule his father was sent to Siberia, for reasons unknown. We are informed that he was an intellectual, an academic. There, in the harshest winter of all, the strongest men sneaked out of the camp at night to hunt for wolf meat. (They probably hunted deer, or other animals, but the elusive wolf became a symbol, part of the mythology, of men whose spirit could not be captured or broken.) One night his father and some others planned to escape; the others were caught, but his father managed to run away. A family took him in, he hid his identity and eventually made it back to Moscow, where now, years later, he is a professor at Moscow University. His father refuses to talk about the past; he only knows these stories from his mother.

The man who emerged from the snow explains that the legacy with which he was born, the history of the men in his family, was to die first before you could live. He wonders how he can die and be born again to find meaning in his life. He, like many others, is torn between a sense of responsibility for the past and a desire to escape the treadmills on which his parents have been trapped. He needs to atone for his father's and grandfather's suffering, but at the same time he wants to reject the past. What is his identity in a time when every aspect of his society is changing? Sometimes his world changes overnight and sometimes slowly and imperceptibly.

He says good-bye to his friends and lies down again in the cavity he has created in the ground. He begins to pull the pieces of scrap metal over his chest and legs. The woman leans over him, pulls open her clothing, and gives him milk from her breast.

I was immediately attracted to Maxim. We met at the Hermitage exhibit. I knew instantly that he was the brother of Oleg, the architect to whom Steve had introduced me. When our eyes met I saw pain and passion hiding behind an ironic smirk. Behind his sad but clear blue eyes was insight into the farce, the waltz of the viewers at an exhibition that could disappear as fast as it had been put together. There was something a little creepy about the way he and his friend Andrei descended on Barney. I thought they must be KGB or black-marketeers, something under-the-table about both of them. They explained that they were unemployed. I slapped them both on the chest and joked that they must be blackmarketeers. Barney was shocked, Andrei was insulted, and Maxim was amused. Andrei said hardly anything, and I didn't trust him. He seemed like a foreigner posing as a Russian. He was dressed like an American grad student going out for a beer; he smiled a lot and his accent was not particularly Russian. The tension I felt when Maxim looked at me was unmistakably mutual. We exchanged numbers; I played it cool while Barney wrote theirs down. I was intrigued. I wanted to find out what it would have been like if I had grown up in Moscow, to see the world through their eyes. I walked off to look at the art. I was glad I'd worn a miniskirt even though I'd been stared at on the metro. I turned my head to catch a glimpse of him across the room, and he was watching me. We both smiled. I had no doubt we would see each other again.

Maxim is at least six foot three with an intense face and haunted blue eyes, as if he had just gotten out of a concentration camp. His hands are long and bony. His voice is low and rumbling and he loves Tom Waits. Tom Waits sings on worn-out tapes in Moscow when Maxim feels the blues. There is much about him I don't know, so many stories he started and never finished, and he didn't always feel like talking. Sometimes he grew reticent and pensive. I didn't know if he was just tired of the effort of speaking in a foreign language, or if the disparity of our lives, the future and its unknowns, or the briefness of our encounter, was overwhelming him. By the middle of our next meeting, a week after we met, it was established that my boyfriend was soon to arrive from Paris and that Maxim wanted to marry a foreigner, preferably an American, so that he could go to New York. I explained that I was not the candidate, but perhaps I could help him find someone. This firmly established the limits of our friendship, but the attraction never went away. His restraint is his strength, his means of survival as an emotional exile in his own land.

Maxim's story is that he wants to leave. He is analytical and bright and realistic. He has studied French all his life and speaks both Italian and English. His father is a diplomat and this is his ticket to travel. He goes often to Geneva, and has been to the United States once. Maxim described the times his father returned from Geneva and his sons asked what he thought. "It was nice and interesting, but nothing to get too excited about," his father replied, as if to say, Don't worry, you're not missing that much. But when he came from New York, he just put his head in his hands and was unable to describe that world.

Six months before Maxim had gone to the American Embassy to see some films with friends. Later he was approached by the KGB and asked to come to their headquarters for a talk. They were very polite when he declined to meet them at Lubyanka. Instead, he agreed to meet them at the National Hotel for a breakfast meeting. At first they grilled him, politely, about whom he knew. When they realized that he was just an opportunistic young *fartsovshchik* (a Soviet youth who hounds foreigners to buy anything Western in exchange for rubles or Russian souvenirs) they asked him if he wanted to work for them by making friends with some young American men. He would go out partying with them so that the KGB agents could take pictures in a situation useful for blackmail. He said no, politely, but the agent did not want to accept no for an answer. Maxim finally said he didn't want to work for an agency of that type, Soviet or any other. It was simply not his line of work.

For the next six months he hadn't gotten any work. He repairs foreign computers on a free-lance basis. He told me that many people do not want to learn how to use the complicated software, partly out of laziness and partly because they know that no matter how skilled they become their wages will not get any higher. Recently, however, he had called his usual customers and they told him that the woman in charge of assigning him work had been out sick, but they expected her back soon. He took that as a very positive sign. In the meantime he was doing some translations from English for videocassettes.

Maxim was feeling lost. He was searching for a belief system, something with which to anchor himself inside a system in which he couldn't possibly believe. He was asking himself, should I stay or should I go? How can a man live in Russia and have American songs going through his head without feeling as if he may be going a little crazy? During a walk through Izmailova Park he asked me whether or not I would want to live in the Soviet Union. Without much hesitation I said no, and then regretted I'd said it. I felt that in a strange sense I had betrayed him and his friends. I had pointed a finger at them and accused them of putting up with it all.

One cloudy afternoon, after we had given up on the idea of waiting at the Pushkin Museum to see Chagall, he took me on a long walking tour. As he led the way with his long legs, I dodged puddles, pedestrians, and scaffolding to match his gait. Concentrating on his slow, deliberate speech, I hardly had time to take in my surroundings. We were halfway across the Moscow River, on the pedestrian side of a steel bridge, talking about what Russian students are taught about life in America. He paused on the bridge. "They tell us," he said, "about all the homeless people in America, but what strikes me is their anonymity. I've often wondered what it would be like to have no one watching me, no one watching every move."

"It's the opposite for young people in New York," I said. "Everyone's jumping up and down trying to get noticed."

"From the day we are born, someone is keeping track of us," he explained. "Are you a good Pioneer, are you a good Komsomol, would you make a good party member? I wish there was no one to care so much," he said, laughing.

I also met Gosha at the Hermitage exhibit. He must be the reincarnation of an avante-garde artist of the 1920s. With his dark Georgian eyes, black hair slicked back into a rubber band behind his head, and old suits from the 1940s that he picks up in the flea markets, he plays the part well. Like his heroes of the 1920s, he lives his life with a zeal and fervor for what he calls his "new revolutionary art." He is by far the most prolific artist I have ever met. At age twenty he has amassed an enormous number of paintings, collages, and printed textiles, which are stacked to the ceiling in every corner of his apartment. The night we met at the exhibit he told me his mother died when he was thirteen and he lives in her old apartment, to which he moved from a monastery. His father, he explained, left when he was three and lives in Paris, "as a rich and famous jeweler." He told me his story with such theatrical flair, I wasn't sure how much of it was true. "I make revolutionary art," he explained enthusiastically, "but it is not anti-Soviet!" I told him that in New York he would be called a performance artist, and he liked that. I took pictures of him posing in his hand-appliquéd vest with silhouettes of revolutionaries, workers, hammers, and sickles. The vest was wonderful, and I wanted to see more of his "revolutionary" work.

Gosha invited me to see his work, but I hesitated calling him. Then I met Pavel at the apartment of other Hermitage artists. Pavel is a photographer from Perm in the Urals. I immediately felt comfortable with him because he was so comfortable with himself. He smiled with an ease and self-assurance that was unexpected for someone with as tenuous a position as his. He came to live in Moscow without a *propiska*, and he continues to live that way, unofficially. He can't be in any public shows, because someone might ask for his papers and he could be arrested. As we talked about the difficulties of being a photographer in Moscow, he marveled at my Kodak 35-mm automatic camera. He invited me to visit his studio and his apartment, where he lives with his roommate, Gosha. I was happy for the coincidence that they were roommates, for Gosha's face had appeared in photographs on the walls of two apartments I had seen since I met him. It was unclear where Pavel was staying for the night, and then I realized that he didn't really have a place. He was living with Gosha, but more as a guest than a permanent roommate. He did not always have a bed to go home to. He is one of the many people I met in Moscow who manage to live without money. As our first meeting proved, Pavel was to be my most reliable and generous friend. He listened to my Russian with an unending patience and keen intelligence, always taking the time to repeat back to me what I had said to clarify my own thoughts in whole sentences.

I waited until Gosha returned from a jaunt to visit some underground artists in Leningrad. When he finally returned after hitchhiking with Georgian brandy as barter, I agreed to be their guest for the afternoon. From the minute Pavel met me at the Belorusskaya Station we were engrossed in conversation, so much so that the second time, when I had to get to their apartment on my own, I realized I hadn't been paying attention. We talked of architecture and photography, and what were our favorite buildings in the city. He loved Moscow, never ceasing to be excited and grateful that he was there. When I arrived at their apartment I was ushered into the kitchen, where Russians always bring their guests. They lightheartedly interrogated me: What do you do? What do you eat? How do you live here? And often they came back to, How do you live in America? They were bewildered by all the different jobs I have held because they counted each job as a different profession. They were having trouble placing me in their catalog of American ways. Gosha commanded me to beat the egg whites as he tyrannically and theatrically conducted the concoction of an apple cake. It was like the

Moscow circus act of seventeen Sumatran tigers, exhausting and suspenseful. The oven door was held shut by a broom wedged under the handle, and the faucet was opened and shut from underneath the cabinet. I explained that they reminded me of "The Odd Couple," a show on American TV about two bachelors living together, and they asked me if they were gay. I explained that they weren't, and they explained that they too were not gay; in fact, they were very heterosexual—or *normalno*, as they put it. Then they told me all the ways to say homosexual in Russian. While the cake was in the oven Gosha disappeared out the front door and Pavel showed me some of his photographs that he had taken in collaboration with Gosha.

Gosha arrived back with a tall blond woman, a very austere German TV producer who spoke not a word of Russian, but luckily some English. We drank tea in the "parlor" as they ceremoniously served the apple cake. We were surrounded by Gosha's mother's nineteenth-century furniture, her piano, and Gosha's paintings and collages on the walls and in piles in the corners of the cluttered room. The producer asked me questions in English and I was forced to translate. She was planning to make a documentary film about young Russian artists and she wanted to find out more about Gosha's hopes, dreams, heroes, and influences. Gosha was impatient with my translating abilities and I had to remind him that he should be grateful that I was doing his public relations. With Pavel's help he caught on and calmed down. He respected Pavel, who at twenty-eight was eight years his senior. They had a difficult but strong friendship. It was clear that it was Gosha's place; Pavel slept in the kitchen. They both contributed the food, never counting, they explained. Whoever could buy, did, and Gosha's uncle helped him hold on to the apartment.

Gosha spoke of his heroes of the 1920s, who included Malevich and Mayakovsky. He had tried stage design school, but had quickly gotten bored and dropped out. He was doing everything he could to stay out of trouble with the authorities, he explained, because he didn't officially have a job and he wasn't officially a student. He loved American graffiti artists Kenny Scharf and Keith Haring, whose work he had seen in books and magazines, and their influence was evident in his work. Many of his pieces had the primitive quality of the graffiti artists but were more thematic in their presentations of Communist motifs. His hand-stenciled tablecloths were reminiscent of Communist propaganda banners, but each contained a slight twist of wit and humor. Gosha put on his appliquéd vest, and had me pose with him wearing his plastic bracelets and headpieces made of found objects and Russian plastic toys. His energy and enthusiasm were unending; he was not going to waste a minute of this opportunity for showing his work. He was savvy and charming and had certainly won over the German producer by the end of the show.

A man arrived with an enticing bag of groceries and took Pavel away for a photo session of his architectural models in exchange for a sumptuous dinner. Gosha, the German producer, and I soon left to drop her off for her next appointment. He and I then went off to Prospekt Mira, to the Dom Moda, the official Soviet House of Fashion to see a show of the fashion designer Vyacheslav Zaitsev.

The contrast was hilarious. Gosha and I were thoroughly amused until he started to get bored. I managed to keep him occupied with a piece of American bubble gum. Somehow they had let us upstairs to the runway without paying; maybe we looked as if we were supposed to be there, I in my Western clothes and he wearing his flea market specials. The best part of the show was the American music. Zaitsev gave a lengthy introduction to the clothes but there was nothing original about them. They were copies of Western fashions; some looked like they were from the 1970s. The government has sanctioned Zaitsev to be its official Soviet designer, but his rise to stardom and his high prices indicated he had worked harder on his connections than on displaying original talent. His introduction to the West was supposed to bring in hard currency. Several rows of dowdy ladies fiercely applauded everything on the runway. The way they were dressed, it was evident they could not afford his clothes.

We were relieved to get out into the cool night air, and we were both starving. The problem was how to find food when there were no buffets or cafeterias open. Gosha found a pay phone and got us invited to a friend's apartment where he apparently ate often. In exchange for last-minute meals he did small errands for her and brought her pieces from the flea markets. She also enjoyed his good company. She had been a classmate of Zaitsev and was happy in her job as a designer for the state. On her balcony she kept a store of potatoes, onions, and green peppers, and she had hard dry salami made of horsemeat. We had Moscow's version of fast food while little blue parakeets flew above our heads in her tiny kitchen.

Gosha, still buzzing with energy, insisted we go visit Boris and Tanya's apartment, where I had been to see the film. Their cozy apartment was always a hub of activity. I had a chance to meet one of the actors from the film and another artist just up from Tbilisi who was collaborating with Boris on his new film. Boris excitedly showed us his models for the set designs and made us promise to keep them a secret.

With a fire in his eyes and long, curly, black hair, Boris seemed possessed with an unself-conscious excitement about all the possibilities that were opening to him. Gosha, Boris, and their friends understood that they were living an important moment in history, a rare cultural renaissance the likes of which had not occurred since before Stalin. They knew they might not have this chance again. Amid the late-night play of ideas was a realistic fear that it all might disappear as fast as it had appeared. This fear was masked by a collective wit and sarcasm that kept them from sentimentalism in this tenuous paradise.

One night, soon after my first visit to Gosha and Pavel's apartment, they invited me to join them for a party at the home of their diplomat friends. When I arrived at their apartment they were still doing the finishing touches on their hair, and Gosha was adjusting his home-made fur bow tie. Gosha and I looked like brother and sister: we had both worn black jackets and pants, black pointed shoes, and tiny pony tails. We hailed one of the many private-cars-turned-taxi and struck a deal for the outskirts of town.

The German *dacha* was a little gingerbread house in a wooded area surrounded by a tall fence with a militia post at the front gate. The little house soon became filled with cultural attachés and other diplomats from around the world. Gosha and Pavel couldn't stop drinking and eating. A four-piece Russian band was making a lame attempt at rock and roll. The hostess, in her broken Russian, begged Gosha and me to start the dancing. We obliged, laughing conspiratorially because she thought I was Russian; I didn't say too much for the rest of the evening to keep up the ruse.

Gosha flitted around the party entertaining small groups of French women. Pavel and I observed another young Russian painter surrounded by well-dressed young ladies from the diplomatic community who were asking the titles of the tiny negatives he had brought to show them. The painter's wife was eating alone in a corner, looking miserable. Lyonya Bazhanov, the organizer of the Hermitage exhibit, was getting drunk to fortify himself for the task of representing the art world to these people searching for amusement.

"How does Gosha feel about being their entertainment?" I asked Pavel.

"It's a game for him," he said. "He's using them for his own entertainment." But in the context of the party, we agreed, it all seemed a futile and demeaning act of survival. A very charming East Asian diplomat asked me where I was from and how I came to be at this party. I explained I was with my Russian artist friends. He wanted to know more about them. I explained how they live hand to mouth, yet seem to always be enjoying themselves. Later in the evening, as he was leaving, he leaned over to shake my hand, and I felt him press something into my palm. "This is for your young friends," he said, and disappeared into the night. Discreetly I looked to see twenty rubles crumpled in my hand, and whispered the good news to Pavel.

"You better keep it 'til later," he said, "in case there are people here watching. Why would he give us money when he doesn't even know us?" he asked me.

"In the Far East," I explained with a smile, "giving to the poor brings riches in the afterlife."

"In that case, I'll take it," Pavel said.

When I met Natasha for the first time in the lobby of the Berlin Hotel, she boldly came forward to greet me, slim, blond, and fashionably dressed. This meeting place was unusual in itself, and I could see she was a privileged member of society who could feel so comfortable meeting a foreigner in a hotel lobby. Unlike my other friends, she had no fear of being seen by the KGB. Her ease and confidence made me wary. We jumped on a trolley bus and rode it across town to the deserted grounds of the Olympic stadium and then to the Novo-devichiy cemetery and monastery. As we walked past the heavy brick walls and asked each other questions, her life unfolded as a series of unusual privileges and travel opportunities. She worked for *Pravda* as a foreign correspondent, and her husband worked for a branch of the Ministry of Foreign Trade that dealt with international banking. I had met my first Russian yuppie.

At twenty-nine, Natasha had been married for seven years and working at *Pravda* for six. When I asked her about people getting married so young, she explained: "It is the custom here. If I waited longer than twenty-one, people would have said there was something wrong with me." She and her husband have their own apartment. "We are lucky to have privacy; many young couples live with their parents and their marriages suffer," she said. Her mother has an apartment in the same building.

Natasha traveled to New York, Boston, and Canada in 1986, and in 1987 she visited Vienna. She covers "the lives of capitalist countries" and when I said how lucky she is to travel she replied with an ironic smile, "Of course, how can I write about them if I don't go there?" She is a five-time water-skiing champion and holds records for the Soviet Union. She explained that life in Moscow was generally pretty boring and that one had to grab hold of whatever it was that interested you. For her, sports is of great importance. She goes away on weekend trips with her horseback riding club and plays tennis with her friends.

She has been waiting for her chance to be given an overseas post. Only men have the overseas assignments, she complained. Since she is the only woman in her department in her position, there is no example to follow. If her husband gets sent to the Far East next year, she will probably go and most likely will have to give up her job, because there are no *Pravda* bureaus in the city where he would move. She said if she were given an overseas post, however, her husband would not follow her. His career is the most important. She was questioning how to find a middle ground between having a family and having a career. They don't have children yet but she has pressure from her family to have a child.

I asked Natasha if she saw her own mother as a role model for a working mother. When she was a little girl they had lived in Canada and her mother worked for the United Nations.

"There were times," she said, "when my mother made more money than my father, but they were an equal couple." She painted a picture of an ideal time when she had first learned to water-ski and her parents had been together. It wasn't until they came back to the Soviet Union and her mother was unable to find a job equal to her abilities or salary that the marriage began to fail.

As we parted on the subway platform, our toes and fingers thawing from the chilly walk, I couldn't help feeling that she was hard to read. When I thanked her for taking time out from a busy schedule, she laughed nervously and said, "Oh, don't think of it. My boss gave me permission, maybe I can write something about our talk in one of my articles about life in the West." She had absorbed all the propaganda that capitalist countries were bound for failure and that Westerners were decadent. She was playing a game with me and not letting down the mask of super Soviet reporter. We made a plan to meet the following week so that I could see her office.

On a rainy day I took the metro and then a minibus taxi from Pushkin Square, filling the tiny bus to capacity as the eleventh passenger and leaving one woman cursing on the curb. The little bus left me off on a peaceful, tree-lined side street. There were several buildings that all said *Pravda* on them, so I waited in one of them with no sign of Natasha. I ventured farther down the street and found the building with the most imposing letters on the face of it. She was waiting for me in the lobby and quickly signed me in. We paraded past the scrutiny of at least six uniformed guards. As we came off the elevator on the twelfth floor, we were bombarded by several men, all asking her questions and making demands simultaneously. She deftly appeased them with a mixture of mothering and flirtation. After a few quick, curious glances at me they disappeared. She took me down a long, eerie hallway to her office. There were at least fifteen identical black doors on either side of this long, straight, and narrow hallway. And then, as if someone were watching, although no one was in sight, she walked me all the way from one end of the hallway to the other, perfunctorily pointing to black doors and describing the people who worked behind them. Natasha's own spacious office was shared with a correspondent who was posted overseas. Amid the books on her desk was a heavily marked-up paperback copy of Adam Smith's *Paper Money*. On the wall was an anti-Reagan poster, courtesy of an East German Communist youth group.

Natasha invited me to the *Pravda* cafeteria, where we had a cup of coffee and fresh poppy seed buns. There was a meat-and-cheese counter where she could shop during her lunch hour for food to take home. The *Pravda* staff also have their own tennis courts and showers.

Two of her male colleagues, young reporters, joined us. After they finished complimenting her and flirting with her they began to question me. "How can a young girl with no experience be representing her country?" they asked me. Natasha politely told them my age, twenty-six. "Young people have many opportunities for work and travel," I explained. "What do you think about your president?" one asked. "What do you think about our country?" his friend demanded. They hammered me with questions, never waiting for my answers. They were performing for Natasha. When they finally left us there was little time left to talk before Natasha had to return to work.

Natasha told me she works a twelve-hour shift. "With such long hours and little time to shop, your husband must help at home," I said.

"No, I take care of the apartment," she explained.

"What does your husband eat when you come home at midnight?"

428

"Nothing," she said, laughing. "I cook when I get home in time for dinner. When I come home late he fixes himself tea and cookies and waits for me. He never cooks."

I didn't get to spend much time with Lyena before she became too afraid to meet me. On our first meeting, my first with a Russian away from the family entourage, we planned to meet in front of the Pushkin Museum. I had been given her name by a friend in New York. All I knew about her was that she was a student, short and blond, and had sounded a little hesitant when she spoke to me in English on the telephone.

We instantly recognized each other, and perhaps out of relief and an obvious mutual curiosity, we were instantly friends. We spent the next four hours talking ceaselessly as we wandered through the museum and the streets, warmed by the afternoon sun. Our intention had been to see the Chagall exhibit, but the line would have taken several hours of waiting, so we opted for a few minutes of seventeenth-century painters and then devoured the impressionists—Gauguin, Picasso, Bonnard, Rousseau, Matisse—they were all there, paintings I had only seen in off-color reproductions and huge Bonnards I didn't know existed.

On our way downstairs, among the plaster copies of Roman horses and Michelangelo's *David*, she told me that she was a postgraduate student in Middle English. She also speaks German and Italian. She is writing her dissertation on the origins of pagan symbols in Chaucer. She loves her studies, she explained, but it was not her calling to stay in academics, to do research, or to teach. She wanted to see the world and communicate with people. She often repeated the word *communicate* in a quiet and almost desperate tone. I could see that her free spirit was trapped by the obscurity of her subject; she wanted to live more in the present, she explained. She admitted she didn't exactly know how to find a way. "Perhaps," she said, "I could be an interpreter." Her stylishly faded denim jacket complemented her large, light blue eyes. As the sun flashed off the pools of water left from the morning showers, the sidewalks and benches shone with the brilliance of the early September afternoon. We strolled the Arbat, arm in arm. In her soft-spoken and quiet way she was bright, sensitive, and strong-willed, but I could feel her suffering underneath her pride and determination.

At twenty-four she was already doing her doctoral work, living at home with her mother and stepfather. She said her young mother, only forty-three, was like a best friend, and her stepfather was brilliant. He held a high position at the university, but, she explained, this did not allow him much privilege. Not compared to her friend Sasha, whose father was an influential figure in law and had helped the young married couple get their own apartment and him a high-paying job. She spoke highly of her stepfather, calling him generous. She was grateful to him for providing her with an intellectually stimulating atmosphere, an "open home" where students and professors from the university came for lively conversations.

She was on the rocks with her temperamental Georgian boyfriend, she explained, because he wanted to get married and she just wasn't ready. She told me that all her friends married at about twenty-one and that at twenty-four she was considered an old maid. We watched the portrait artists making their quick sketches along the pedestrian walkway. She was trying to explain the meaning of *kitsch*, but I saved her the trouble by explaining that we use the same word. Without stalls, an informal marketplace of amateur crafts and paintings had sprung up. Artists sat on tiny stools with their paintings leaning against their knees. We stopped to talk to several people she knew who were older, in their thirties, and who greeted her warmly.

We found her friend Victor furiously smoking a cigarette in front of one of the old pastel-colored, four-story buildings, which apparently held the offices of the current India Festival. Its facade was decorated with a delicate garland of plaster icing. She explained that he was an Italian specialist who spoke the language fluently but had never been to Italy. They babbled in Russian for a moment and then kindly turned to me and spoke in English. As he sucked the life out of his cigarette and eyeballed me from head to toe, I could feel anger and impatience escaping like smoke from under his clothes. I innocently asked what it was he did. He didn't catch my question, so I added in clarification, "As a profession?"

"Ah, my profession!" he spit out at me. "You want to know what is my profession?" And then, taking a melodramatic sigh, he more quietly said, "I have had so many."

He told me that what a person "does" for money in Russia has little to do with what he or she feels passionate about. He was clearly not pleased with his role as coordinator of the India Festival, and as we walked on she explained that you can study a language all your life and never go to that country. She told me that his not-so-secret desire was to marry an Italian woman so that he could live in Italy.

That was certainly the first time in my life I'd let anyone down for being the wrong nationality.

As we retraced our steps back along the Arbat, talking about love and courage and the differences and similarities of our lives, we discovered that we both kept journals and wrote some poetry. I was later to find out from an acquaintance of hers that she in fact is an extremely talented poet who rarely and discreetly gives readings of her poetry and has been compared to Mandelstam.

A Russian teenager ran up to us, imploring, "Do you speak English?" I realized we had been speaking loud enough for him to hear, and because of our jeans and sneakers he had decided to ask for something. He said to me, "My name is Kolya," and I politely replied, "My name is Doveen." Then he turned to Lyena, and she said in accented English, "My name is Lyena." He must have turned five colors of purple before he ran off down the Arbat into the crowd. She was amused, but it also seemed to make her a little uneasy. I tried to keep my voice down so that we would be less conspicuous.

On our second meeting Lyena came to the hotel for an early dinner. She was nervous about entering the hotel, yet insisted on coming. She asked me to meet her in the center of the metro platform at exactly five o'clock and escort her past the hotel doorman. As we sat around the table in our suite, members of the family returned from their wanderings and joined us. I introduced them. Lyena seemed uneasy, choosing her words carefully. She joked that the KGB had a perfect view from the building across the street and sat with her back to the window.

She spoke about her generation in a low voice, almost a whisper. "There are no incentives for the young," she explained. "Young people don't want to work hard, yet they want privilege and material goods. They don't want the same treadmill that the system offered to their parents."

Lyena told us how one weekend a month there is a mandatory field trip for students and professors. They ride the bus together to a produce distribution center in the countryside. Their duties include picking, packing, and unloading vegetables. "Aside from the huge rats in the bins," she said with a smile, "the permanent workers there are much richer than they should be from their salaries." She implied that they sold the freshest vegetables at a premium and pocketed the money.

It wasn't until Lyena and I left the hotel for a walk that she relaxed.

Her voice changed from an indoor—"the walls are listening"—third person, in which she talked about "young people" and "students," to the first person, and she began to talk about herself. The streets were quiet as we walked arm in arm. We could see our breath in the chilly night air. "How do you deal with your fear on a constant basis?" I asked. "You've really changed since we left the hotel room. I wonder how much has changed here and how much they really listen."

"I'm sure that they are watching your family," she said. "I am ashamed of my fear. When I was younger I didn't care. I said anything I wanted and I did anything I wanted, but now I am afraid and hold myself back. I have had a bad experience."

The walls of the Kremlin loomed in front of us as we headed into Red Square; but as we approached, walking over the cobblestones, we saw that it was roped off and guarded by soldiers. Bleachers had been put up and loudspeakers blared marching music over the empty square. No one was there rehearsing for the forthcoming Moscow Anniversary Day celebration. I wanted Lyena to tell me about her bad experience, but the marching music was oppressive and over-powered our conversation. So we left Red Square and set off for Gorky Street.

We walked through the underground walkway under Marksa Pros-pekt, keeping our voices down so that the young men we passed wouldn't know we were speaking English. They seemed to have a nose for foreigners and tried to trade rubles for dollars or practice their English, walking or running alongside of us. Finally, on Gorky Street we were alone.

Lyena explained that she had been an interpreter at the Friendship Games in 1986 and had had a run-in with the KGB. The Russian students at the games had been mingling with the foreign visitors, attending ceremonies and parties together at one of Moscow's largest hotels. A West German journalist had asked Lyena innocuous ques-tions about herself and her friends. Soon afterward several KGB agents asked her to come to their room for questioning. They kept her there for several hours until they were convinced that she had not said anything harmful. "You see," she said, "after this experience I am not as free. I have more to lose now because I am older and I have spent time building my career. They could ruin things for me at the university."

We walked in silence. We were far from the hotel, so we decided to part in the metro and take trains in opposite directions. It was not only the KGB we had to watch for. As we descended into the metro, a group of teenagers tried to block our way, speaking in a slang I couldn't understand. "Come on," Lyena said, grabbing my arm and pulling me through the crowd. "They won't hurt us, but let's not take any chances."

Mortified, I realized I had left the Berlin Hotel without my metro pass, and I had to borrow five kopecks from Lyena. We made our way down the escalator, where guards protected the caverns of the metro station, and found an anonymous bench below a huge arch. We leaned against the cool marble and talked as the trains pulled in and out of the station. "All I want," she said, "is to live without fear and to be able to see the world. I want to travel and decide for myself that this is where I want to live. I love my country and I think I want to live here. There is so much that is changing and growing, and I want to be a part of that. But it must be my choice that I want to come back and live here after my travels."

"You should write it down and send it to Gorbachev," I joked, and we both laughed.

"No," she said. "I am too afraid. A part of me is swallowed in that fear and I am struggling to get it back."

At least five trains came and went before we reluctantly parted. I never got a chance to pay Lyena back the five kopecks.

The hardest part of revisiting Moscow was to say good-bye. I hated the cameras by the end, resenting them not so much for myself but for the privacy they stole from my friends. I realized that the cameras had two sides: They could bring to the West the truth about our friends' lives and show the world that they were not warmongers. But on the dark side the cameras represented fear, because the film could be used against our friends by the KGB. What would happen after we left? What problems would they have from participating in a foreign film? Were we inflicting the discomfort of constantly wondering whether their fear was paranoid or real? I know my friends were constantly asking themselves, "Does the KGB really concern itself with what I'm doing? Will they find a way to punish me because I know foreigners?"

For me, Maxim was the hardest to leave behind because our friendship had grown strong and because of his analytical, discontented mind. He had been exposed to foreigners, their magazines and newspapers, and had an idea of what the other world could offer. I wanted him and Lyena and the others to have opportunities to travel, as I have had.

For my friend Katya, exposure in the West might work to her advantage, and since our departure that has turned out to be true. Katya is a young fashion designer who until recently has only shown her underground creations to her friends. Her outfits are pieced together from old army uniforms, lace petticoats, and old furs from the flea market. Her outfits are original and elegant, with details of lace and fur evoking a prerevolutionary Russian romanticism. She started out in architecture school, where she met her husband, and married at age nineteen. Now, three years later, she has a two-year-old daughter and goes to architecture classes at night. Foreign press and television have shown so much interest in her work that the Soviets finally started taking credit for her talent. She was included in a film about the Soviet avant-garde and she will be included in a forthcoming book on Soviet designers and artists.

As I watched my friends in action, creative and productive—Katya preparing a fashion show, Gosha stenciling a tablecloth, Pavel taking pictures—I tried to express to Maxim my feelings about leaving. "On one level I feel inspired, driven further to take advantage of my own freedom; on the other hand I have a sense of failure for leaving without being able to take you all with me and show you a bit of my world."

"Things will change," Maxim said. "Perhaps we'll meet again in Paris. Besides, don't worry. Katya just received a pair of shoes as a gift from a foreign woman. They didn't fit, so she sold them for two hundred rubles ($320), and she and her husband are going south for a week. Let's hope some things never change."

Return to Special
School 47

KATE

Going back to school was one of the eeriest moments of our trip to Moscow. When I walked in I felt that strange, almost dreamlike sensation one feels when seeing a place from so many years earlier that is unchanged. Everyone still hangs their coats on little hooks arranged by class and leaves their boots in rows. The gym, where Doveen and I were terrified of the vaulting horse that seemed impossible to ever jump over and the huge rope we were supposed to shinny up to the ceiling on, still sat there as if we had had gym class yesterday. Girls still wear black bloomers in gym, and all the kids have to march around in this getup while a teacher barks out military commands. The bathrooms still have no doors on the stalls, no toilet seats, and no toilet paper. Perhaps these are trifles, but it was haunting to see them unchanged after seventeen years.

Of course, much has changed since we went to Special School 47. That became apparent from our first visit to arrange the filming. Steve, Sherry, Ari, and I met with the principal and a group of twenty seniors and juniors to discuss our plans. Some of the students had traveled abroad, and two girls had lived in America. Although they had gone to the Soviet embassy school, they spoke English well and had punk haircuts. The boys knew a few European rock groups. In general, the kids seemed far more informed about the Western world than anyone had been when we were students in Moscow. They were surprised to know that we had gone to school there, but I could tell that to the students we looked like old fogies, back on a nostalgia trip. One of the older teachers, who had taught Steve, kept reiterating that Steve had been a perfect student in Russian language, brimming with pride every time Steve spoke in his flawless Russian accent. This did not go over well with the older kids, who initially tried to act jaded and uninterested. Talk of the film woke them up. They wanted to know when we would be back to shoot and became enthusiastic about participating in the film.

After the students went back to their classes, the principal confided some of the tough problems with which she had to contend. "Our biggest problem is apathy. We cannot seem to motivate our students. They have been taught for so many years how to conform to the group that now we find a lack of individuality and creativity. I am hoping that the new reforms in education will help change this problem." She spoke about plans to move out of the old school and build a new, modern facility. We said we were glad, for our sake, the old one was still there. She was hesitant about letting us film in the building because it, like everything else, was under *remont*. We reassured her we would only film where they allowed us.

DOVEEN

As the tall front doors of the school slammed behind me, I entered a familiar world. A portrait of Lenin loomed before me to greet me back. These halls had at one time been both frighteningly cold and warm with kindness. In dreams and memories I had relived these hallways, as if I had never left them behind. The building is old but carefully patched and replaced as if it too needed nurturing like the new little first-graders arriving for their first day. The smells flooded me with a rush of memories. The sweet smells of freshly baked buns and fruity compote came from the buffet. The slight smell of paint and freshly mopped floors transported me to those times I had cried endlessly in first grade, begging to see my older brother and sisters. They had been stern with me, but always kind.

I had come back to Special School 47 with Nancy on a preproduction visit to set up the shoot. I was under strict orders from Sherry not to meet with my first-grade teacher until they could capture the reunion on camera. As we sat in the headmistress's office she assured us that Lyubov Matveyevna was not in that day, so we wouldn't be running into her in the halls. We set out on a short tour of the school

436

to check the lighting, to see where the ideal spots to shoot would be when we all came back with the crew.

As we climbed the worn stone steps, the directress gave me a mock scolding. "Come now, Doveen, please don't linger," with her slightly British and Russian accent. I couldn't help but become transfixed by every room, remembering a face or an event. The gymnasium really held me, and Nancy had to tear me away. This room had been for me an echoing cavern of horrors: climbing walls and ropes, marching with wooden guns, gymnastics, and other impossible feats for a sickly child. The children looked so happy as their teacher lined them up for a game of ball. Nancy and the directress hurried me on as I took a few fleeting glances at the classrooms before we left.

EVELIND

It was seven-thirty Monday morning as we stepped out of the hotel into the raw October drizzle. Doveen, Barney, and I headed out to the corner to find a taxi to take us to school for my first visit back and to do the filming. In the warmth of the cab I felt almost the same mixed confusion and excitement of seventeen years ago, during our days in Moscow. It had been the same bone-chilling misty cold weather, and we had spent two months being driven to school from our downtown hotel until the apartment was ready.

Doveen gave the driver instructions to the school, and we soon turned off Leninski Prospekt, down a muddy side street that the driver first mistook for a construction site. Once past the road repair equipment, we could see the school, its gates almost hidden by high bushes. Inside the gates, however, it was just as we remembered it: the looming five-story brick building, the narrow front courtyard, the flight of steps up to the outer door, and the plaque announcing SPECIAL SCHOOL NO 47.

I climbed the stairs, reluctant to open the outer door. I was not sure which memories would come rushing back: the awkwardness of the early days or the familiarity of the later ones. We passed mothers and grandmothers pulling off the boots of young children in the large entryway. Two students on hallway duty opened the inner door for us. Inside was another world, safe from the chill outside. A blast of hot air warmed us immediately and pushed back the cold. For a moment I felt as if I were there for a day of school, ready to shed my coat and head up the stairs to class. Nothing had changed enough to make me feel that the place or the schoolchildren were different. I had expected to be a bit disappointed with the school; I might find it dingier than my memories. But the front hall was brightly lit, and the warm salmon-colored walls complemented the huge red flags flanking the oversized portrait of Lenin over the doorway. There was the same chatter of the younger children taking off their warm outer layers and hanging them on rows of racks set up against the windows. The same gangly teenagers conferring with their buddies as they hurried to class. Only the older students' uniforms had changed. The ninth-graders and tenth-graders could wear blue skirts and jackets with a white blouse instead of the brown wool uniforms I had worn. The recent repairs had freshened the look of the school, allowing my memories to be preserved in the new, brighter colors.

We saw Kate and Ari down the hallway in the principal's office and wound our way through the stream of students who watched us with curiosity. There was no question, in their eyes we were adults, not the schoolchildren of seventeen years ago. We were greeted by the new school principal, a pretty blond woman in her mid-forties, who I did not remember, but who said she remembered Steve. She smiled with a bemused look, mirroring my sense of displacement, seeing the five of us standing together, all very tall and not recognizable as the Schecter schoolchildren. Finally, Svetlana Semyonovna, the head of the English Department, arrived, and her familiar face and British English put me on firmer ground. She gave us all hugs and ushered us off to see the school.

We spent the morning sitting in on English classes and exploring old landmarks. I insisted on going up to the biology lab on the fourth floor, hoping that my feisty, henna-haired teacher would be there, still trying to get the students to remember their anatomy with oversized plastic organs and real skeletons. I was disappointed. The room was much smaller than I remembered, and a young male teacher was standing up front, lecturing the students.

I sat down next to one of the students to try to figure out what was going on. I noticed that the textbook had been published in 1986, confirming what we had heard about the rewriting of textbooks. (The principal told me that she expected the process of updating the textbooks to be completed within the next three years.)

This teacher may have been just as good as mine, but he did not have the same passionate delivery, and I soon slipped out of the room.

BARNEY

We found my first-grade classroom, and when we peeked in the teacher invited Doveen and me to stay. I stood at the back of the room watching the lesson in a state of contained excitement that verged on mild shock. My senses tingled as I drank in this strange privilege of seeing into my past. This room, perhaps more than any other in Moscow, could connect me with the person I had been seventeen years ago. It was here that I was most alone psychologically during those two years in Moscow. It was here that as a six-year-old I built a fortress inside and reasoned with myself whenever difficulties arose: "It's only for another year." This attitude was the source of my troubles as well as my solution to them. Had I felt it was a worthwhile investment, I might have done a little schoolwork. Instead, feeling humiliated by my substandard penmanship (the standard was very high; Evelind admitted to me that she had had to improve her handwriting so that the Russian teachers could read it) and the fact that I was left-handed, I resolved to make a fresh start in America. There, I was sure, the other children would not have the unfair advantage of perfect penmanship in wet fountain pen ink drilled into them at home by their *babushkas*. My laziness certainly did not inspire sympathy from my teacher.

Now I watched the first-graders, divided into two teams, solving math problems at the chalkboard. Each team was designated by a doll held by the team leader at the front of the room. The whole process seemed homier than I remembered. The teacher was older, softer, and gentler than the tough young one whose ire I had ignited so often. Next was a free-for-all where the teacher put a problem on the board and the children each inserted their answer, a number printed on a punch-out card, into a cardboard holder and eagerly held it aloft for her approval. The robust little children in their uniforms looked like delegates at a convention waving their endorsements from the crowded floor. They were adorable. Especially the ones who, despite the visibility of the correct answer on all the cards, got it wrong. Even they seemed to get through without undue humiliation.

During the recess, a handful of first-grade boys gathered around me in the hallway. One of them began with "What is your name?" in Russian. I had to squat down on one knee to talk to him at eye level. We introduced ourselves, and I explained that I had been in the first grade here, many years ago. They were amazed. The conversation was simple; we were looking at each other in friendly wonder. Later, when school was over, the littlest of them ran down the hall and grabbed me by the hand so we could walk down the stairs together.

KATE

One of the most interesting conversations we had that day was with a group of elderly teachers. We asked them about *glasnost* and if it was difficult to teach history now. One particularly old, wry history teacher replied, "I have always taught the truth. Even when the history books did not tell it, I knew what happened because I lived through it, and I have taught my children the truth all these years." The other teachers in the group nodded silently, but no one else contributed an opinion on the touchy subject. At one point, the same outspoken teacher started to criticize the United States, asking me why we always wanted war. I told her we did not want war and that she had been misinformed about what Americans wanted. I also said I thought that conversations where Americans and Soviets challenged each other and asked each other why the other side was so aggressive were useless. At first she eyed me coldly, realizing that I had criticized her, but the other teachers were uncomfortable with her aggression and leaped to my defense. We all smiled and moved on to more constructive conversation. By the end of the meeting we were all shaking hands, and the history teacher was hugging me.

We ate lunch in the cafeteria that day. The tastes, smells, noises, and chaos of the lunchroom brought back the most vivid sense of traveling through time. How many breakfasts had we suffered through? The wet plates of cream of wheat with a raw egg in the middle and the sweet brown fruit compote that we had stared at and left untouched. The poppy seed buns and almond cookies we had scrambled for all came tumbling back into my memory. It was hard to leave the school that day. Who knows how much longer they will let it stand, how many more chances I'll have to go back and see a piece of my childhood preserved in such strange little details?

EVELIND

The cafeteria had been emptied of the younger students after mid-morning break, and a class of seniors was filing in to talk to us. We split into groups, hoping to get an informal discussion going. Barney and I ended up with four boys, sitting around a table in a corner. Since Barney's Russian was limited and I had found that the students spoke much better English than when we had been at school there, I started in English. "Well, is there anything you would like to know about America?"

For the tenth time that day they asked about our favorite rock stars and wanted to know if we had heard of a Soviet musician who was on tour in the United States. Barney had to answer this one. One of the few problems I had from being overseas for my early teens was that I only knew the major rock groups and had never developed any devotion to particular groups or musicians. These days I am interested in a broad range of music and still can't keep up with many of the current rock groups.

Rock stars out of the way, I asked them what they wanted to do when they graduated. They all assumed they would go to a university, and skirted the issue of alternate plans if they failed to pass the extensive entrance exams.

"We're studying this spring and we'll take them this summer. We should do okay since we'll be fresh out of school. It's much harder to pass the exams after you've served the mandatory two years in the army. I'll probably start university and then go into the army after my first year," explained one of the boys.

I explained that I work in a camera factory, glossing over my actual function in finance, since there was no easy equivalent to the treasury function when one's planning and financing came from the state. I asked, "What profession will you study for?" There was a historian, an economist, an aviation engineer, and a mathematician. "What about working in a factory?" They shrugged their shoulders.

"What about *glasnost* and *perestroika*? How have they affected you?"

"Mostly we see changes in the press, there is so much being written and so many ideas being discussed," said one.

"They're rewriting the textbooks," said another.

"Yes, they are teaching us about the Stalin period in school."

"This country stopped its economic development in the 1950s and we have to do something about it."

BARNEY

I found that I was talking to the class secretary of the Komsomol, the party youth organization. He and two others were telling me how the new political atmosphere is entering the schools; how the Komsomol and the school are working together, holding meetings at which the mistakes of the past, of the Stalin years, are being discussed.

They told me that the book *Children of the Arbat* is one of the big best-sellers in the Soviet Union. The book recounts how the Leningrad party secretary, Kirov, was assassinated on Stalin's orders and how the purges of the 1930s began. "How do you know about this period?" I asked.

"Mostly our parents and grandparents told us about these things, but now these Komsomol meetings and books and the newspapers are our source," replied one of the boys. "We did not read the newspapers before. It was mostly slogans. Now I read the newspaper as if it were my favorite book," he continued eagerly, and his friends nodded their agreement.

"So there is great openness between the government and the people now," I summarized.

"Well, it is incorrect to make this separation," one boy said sharply. "The government expresses the will of the people, so they are one and the same." I suppressed a retort.

The Komsomol secretary, like the rest of our group, hoped to go to a university when he graduated. His field was history. World War II and Nazi Germany were his special interests. I could not think of a politically more correct subject. World War II had not faded from the memories of the generation of Soviets who had lived through its horrors and devastation, and they made sure the new generations would know about it. The memories of the Great Patriotic War are used to instill patriotism and as a ready excuse for national short-comings. The school had become even more sophisticated in teaching this subject than when I was there. The open recess area on the third floor was now a "museum"; it had a wall exhibit detailing the Soviet army's advance on Berlin, with maps and large red arrows pointing to major battles. A glass case displayed letters written by soldiers during the war.

I wanted to see if the students were anxious about the future, or whether the path seemed well worn ahead of them. "In America people your age are very concerned about how they are going to support themselves. The future is uncertain for them, they focus on their own problems. Your concerns must be different. Do you worry about joining the party?"

"Well, only the very best get to join the party, they are very few.

But one must not worry about getting in or not, the important thing is to participate actively in the social life, to do one's best," one of the boys answered.

"What does that mean, 'participate actively in the social life'?" If I was going to flatter them and tell them how self-centered American young people were and they were going to come back with a bunch of slogans instead of telling me what they were worried about, at least I was going to make them work.

"Your questions are very simple, but the answers are very complex," the sixteen-year-old answered sententiously. I did not mind being called simple if I was making him dig for an answer. "It can mean working hard at one's job, making oneself useful to other people." Beyond this he seemed a bit at a loss.

By the end of the discussion we warmed to each other. They said they appreciated my self-critical approach. They had met other Americans who lectured them about the virtues of America, and they were amazed that I did not. They seemed genuinely interested in my sculpting and that lightened the mood. I came up with a general statement about my work: I called it a synthesis of modern forms with traditional materials and study of the figure; that pleased them.

DOVEEN

When I entered the classroom of "2nd Klass B" my heart skipped a beat at the sight of the adorable and curious faces of the second-graders who all stood up to greet me, just as I had once done when an adult entered the room. As they stood in their uniforms and aprons, the girls with ribbons in their hair, I greeted them and asked them to please sit down. I knew Foster was somewhere close with the camera. Then I turned to see Lyubov Matveyevna. When I saw her I quickly forgot about the camera. After seventeen years she had not changed at all. Her matronly figure and soft brown hair and red cheeks were the same as I remembered them. She greeted me with a huge hug and a big wet kiss. She had been my protector and had communicated with me in hand signals before I had learned her strange and difficult language. I choked up when she hugged me again, teary eyed, and my eyes filled with tears remembering her kindness to me. She explained to the class that I had been one of her students. I told them how happy I was to see them and to be able to thank my teacher for all her kindness to me and for teaching me to read and write Russian.

443

She remembered how I had cried because I didn't understand Russian and had been frightened without my brothers and sisters nearby. Then she recalled with whom I had been friends after I had gained some courage. She proudly recounted the achievements of other classmates, now mostly diplomats, who have kept in touch with her through the years.

Swept up in the emotion of the moment, I had forgotten about the camera, but it had been there all along to capture the scene. Sherry and Foster got the warm touch they wanted and I was taken back into the warm embrace of seventeen years past.

Making a Movie (Continued)

In Leningrad Sherry witnessed a scene that left an indelible impression. She was waiting to be seated in the hard-currency hotel restaurant and overheard a party of foreigners in front of her discussing that one of them was a Soviet citizen. The others in the group said they were paying in dollars so he should not be concerned. However, when they were seated, still within view and earshot of Sherry, the waiter asked the Soviet man to leave. The man refused to get up, and his friends objected heatedly to the waiter's rudeness. The waiter explained that this restaurant, which served cuisine not to be found in any restaurant open to Soviet citizens, was only for foreign guests. The group held fast, and the waiter left in frustration. In a few minutes a man in a dark suit came to the table and told the Soviet guest that he had to leave. Still the man objected. The bouncer then informed the Soviet guest that he was from the KGB and that the guest had better get out if he knew what was good for him. The hapless citizen knew that he shouldn't push any further; he stood up and left, and his friends followed him out the door.

Sherry had permission to shoot on the afternoon train back to Moscow. Evelind and Kate were exhausted from their morning session at the oilcloth and artificial leather factory, but the opportunity to film conversations with Soviets on the moving train was too good to pass up. "It was really difficult starting conversations cold," Evelind said. "The older ladies wanted to tell us how good everything is in the Soviet Union and to say how much they want peace with the United States. A few people made it clear they didn't want to be in the film."

During the final week of shooting Sherry wanted family conversations in which we discussed our feelings and impressions of the trip. She liked best when we argued with each other about Soviet intentions; she carefully kept her own views to herself, and only smiled wryly when I took a "hard" position critical of the Soviet system.

She also needed the obligatory connecting scenes that showed how we cooked on one burner set on the floor near the window to let the odors escape, or washed dishes in the bathroom sink with a drainboard over the bathtub. She wanted a typical morning in which Jerry and I worked in the hotel suite, preparing for interviews with Soviet publishers or journalists.

One morning we began a realistic conversation in which we discussed who we would see that day. Suddenly Sherry interrupted with a question from where she sat, off camera at Foster's elbow.

"Some people criticize American reporters for coming to the Soviet Union with preconceived notions. What do you think of that? Do you think you came here with a particular mind-set?" she asked, looking at me.

She had succeeded in raising my ire by asking a provocative question on camera without telling me ahead of time. Jerry was so startled he asked her to repeat the question. It was the first time she had done that; up to that moment she had passed scribbled questions to us that we could ask or ignore. We usually managed to ask her suggested questions in the interviews.

"Yes," I began, speaking slowly to hold on to my cool. "You're right. I did come here with preconceived ideas about freedom, about rule by law, about the right of the individual to develop without repression, even about the value of free enterprise. A few days ago you saw a Soviet citizen thrown out of a restaurant, in his own country, that was reserved for foreigners. That was a government action, by an employee of the KGB. If something like that happened to me at home in the United States I would be on the phone that same night with a lawyer, probably a pro bono civil rights lawyer, and by morning we would file a suit against the government. I want to keep that option. I want to hold on to that preconceived notion."

Sherry had planned to save her most "dangerous" questions, the subjects to which she knew the Soviets would be most sensitive, for

446

the end of the shooting. Now it seemed she was turning them on us instead of the Russians, because she followed my testy answer with another question that got Jerry even madder than me.

"Tell me," she said, "where did you first meet your old friends?"

Jerry had complained earlier when Dima asked the same question. Jerry did not want to say on camera that he had made many lasting friendships outside the courthouse where Pavel Litvinov and Larisa Daniel were on trial in the autumn of 1968 for openly protesting the invasion of Czechoslovakia. I began to answer Sherry, and Jerry frantically scowled at me to stop.

"Just the other night we drank a toast together to old times. They were young then, and our children were small. It was so romantic to think back all those years, so wonderful to be together again," I said with a starry-eyed smile. Jerry relaxed.

I picked up the phone to check on the metro stop for the publisher I was going to see, a touch of realism for the camera, and left for my appointment, still seething.

Later the same day Sherry went to the apartment on Oktyábr'skaya Ploschad for a shooting session. She told the children, "You know, I think your mother is softening."

I laughed wryly, and then my anger toward Sherry melted away. I realized that her questions, at which I had taken offense, were standard journalistic fare, but in Moscow they had aroused in me a particular sensitivity. She had been trying to wrap up the shooting, including the usual questions in case she needed them later. I took a deep breath and then let it out slowly, and by that time I had softened, just as Sherry said. The combination of Moscow caution, learned twenty years before, and the pressures of being on camera had excited unnecessary passion and it was time to cool off.

The last weekend in Moscow approached, and Jerry and I began to think about giving a party at the apartment on Sunday night to which we would invite friends we had seen too briefly. "I wanted to have my friends," Steve said assertively, and Doveen echoed him, meaning to add her group. We knew, from when we lived in Moscow in the 1960s, that we should not mix friends. We knew we should not introduce Russians to each other. You couldn't just tell people to drop in; they would want to know who else would be there. The pervasive fear of being reported as socializing with a foreign journalist colored our relationships. We knew all that, but we got our signals crossed.

On Friday night, Dmitri picked me up for a dinner party at their apartment. On the way I asked him and Elena to the party on Sunday; he was surprised Jerry hadn't mentioned it to him. At the end of the evening we had an embarrassing scene in which Jerry didn't know I had invited him. Later Jerry phoned him to explain that our plans had not yet been set when we saw them, but would they please come on Sunday. Dmitri suspected that he had been left out of our plans to start with and had been invited as an afterthought. "We're going to the country. We'll see if we can get back in time," he answered, a slight hurt in his voice.

It turned out that everyone in the family had invited whomever they wanted. What should we do? "We'll invite different groups for different hours and hope they don't overlap," I said, refusing to be concerned. Parents' friends at five o'clock and the younger set at seven. The next problem was to limit the time that Foster would film during the party. How would we keep from filming the guests who didn't want to be on camera? Sherry agreed to shoot for an hour when friends were arriving and a shorter time later when they were leaving. She wanted some emotional farewells.

DOVEEN

By the night of our farewell party I had hardly slept for the previous five days. There had been much debate about whether Sherry would film the party or not. The farewell party was a chance to invite our friends for food and drink without capturing them on camera. They wouldn't have to be worried about KGB reprisals or feel self-conscious while trying to relax and have a good time. It was our chance to repay them with a small gesture of our gratitude for their time and patience in the past three weeks of filming. Sherry wanted to get shots of the party. She wanted to capture the farewells to get a feeling of continuity for the film, so that friends could be recognized as characters through the film, to give a good wrap-up. I could understand her point. So, in one of the few meetings for which we were able to pin her down, we sat around the table in the Berlin suite and compromised on what time the cameras would be rolling and what time they would go off.

I was excited about the party, and nervous. We were about to break the most important rule we had been told to follow while we were in Moscow. We were going to introduce Russians to Russians. Every time we had to introduce one Russian friend to another, we would ask at dinner and a debate would ensue as to whether that person had anything to lose or would be placed in any danger by meeting the other. Would they be uncomfortable? Would they feel threatened? It was usually not a good idea, my mother said, and there had been a few times when Steve had already invited friends for dinner, so I couldn't bring mine because they might not mix. This time we decided to test the new rules of *glasnost*. The plan was that Mom and Dad's friends would start coming around five in the afternoon and would leave by the time the younger crowd was coming around seven.

After a crazy day of running around the city, I hurriedly went back to the hotel to change, then to the apartment at Oktyabr'skaya Ploschad (October Square) to help with the party. When I arrived the cameras were already rolling and a few guests who had arrived just before me were taking off their coats. I hugged a gray-haired man, thinking he was someone else. His face lit up as he told his wife, "She remembers me!" I realized he was not who I thought he was, but I certainly was not going to disappoint him now. The rest of the party was chaos, but fun. The "adults" were enjoying themselves so much they forgot to leave. They seemed intrigued by the artistic younger crowd that started to appear. Soon both generations were consuming vast amounts of vodka and Georgian brandy and the apartment was crowded with everyone's friends, the new ones and the old ones. Amid the singing, Polaroids, gossip, and hugging, I soon forgot about Sherry and the camera, and so did the others.

LEONA

By this time we had thrown our past caution to the winds. We invited everyone we could reach by phone, and only a few Americans failed to show up. Every Soviet we asked would not have missed it, knowing full well that they would be seen by their countrymen. The party was the best proof that *glasnost* lives.

Our Russian tutor and her husband came. Dmitri and Irina arrived, he still in the relaxed clothes he had worn at their *dacha*, she in a low-cut cocktail dress. She looked glorious in a golden print to match her hair. He might have been miffed by our clumsy invitation, but Irina obviously wanted to come to the party. Dmitri's eyes lit up when he spied a political officer from the American Embassy. The two spent the next hour in a huddle, reaching each other in a way they could never do from their offices. Anatoli Pristavkin came alone because Marina was still in the hospital after giving birth to their daughter. He charmed everyone around him with his stories and even made the refuseniks smile. Andrei and Zoya Voznesensky came. In the bedroom Didier, Doveen's friend from Paris, had his camera set up and took everyone's portrait, singly and in couples.

Jerry's and my friends were still there when the parade of young artists arrived. Their colorful dress and makeup, miniskirts and artistic swagger were a show. "They're all beautiful," Yadviga Charny said. The two age groups soon got over the shock of seeing each other and settled into their own corners to eat and drink. Looking in, you couldn't tell whether it was New York or Moscow.

The guests were still leaving past midnight. We hugged and kissed them unashamedly on camera. However, the most emotional scene was not recorded: Sherry, in tears, saying good-bye to all the friends she had made in Moscow. Nobody, Soviet or American, had come through those memorable ten weeks untouched.

EPILOGUE

Jerry and Leona

In June of 1988, following the Moscow summit between General Secretary Gorbachev and President Reagan, Doveen and Barney returned to Moscow for ten days. They carried with them invitations for our friends Lyokha and Yuri to visit America. They also brought an invitation from the Washington Project for the Arts for the painter Ivan Chuikov to spend a month visiting artists in the nation's capital. They found Moscow in an uproar.

"We wish you were all here," Dmitri told Doveen and Barney over dinner at his apartment. "What is happening now is historic. The decisions that are made or postponed will affect Gorbachev's programs, his political future, and our lives." Dmitri was referring to the Communist Party Conference held from June 28 to July 3. It was the first time in forty-seven years that Communist party members gathered to debate changes in the political structure. The reformers aimed at strengthening Gorbachev's power, weakening the power of the Communist party, and enhancing the role of local governments, or soviets.

The 4,991 delegates to the conference took part in a political extravaganza, orchestrated and conducted by Gorbachev, that combined elements of an American national political convention and a group therapy session. Long-buried issues and emotions boiled over into sweeping denunciations and demands. The debate was passionate, angry, and pointed. In a bizarre, emotional moment, *Ogonyok* editor Vitaly Korotich charged that four of the delegates to the conference, seated in the auditorium, were guilty of criminal bribery, and he turned over the evidence to Gorbachev while the nation watched

451

on television. There was an astonishing call for the resignation of old Stalinist Andrei Gromyko, the ceremonial President of the Soviet Union, and a public attack on three other senior party members, demanding their dismissal. Vladimir I. Melnikov, a party official from the Ural Mountains region, said, "Those who were active in the past pursuing the policy of stagnation cannot remain and work in the central party and government organs." (Stagnation is the code word for the Brezhnev era.) Normally in the Soviet Union such an attack would mean that those criticized are about to be relieved of their duties, at the very least.

Gorbachev, sitting behind the speaker; interrupted and asked: "Maybe you have some concrete proposals? We sit here and do not know, do you mean me or him?"

Without hesitation, Melnikov answered: "I would refer to comrade Solomentsev, to Comrades Gromyko, Afanasyev, Arbatov, and others." Mikhail A. Solomentsev is a Politburo member and head of the Party Control Committee, responsible for party discipline. Viktor G. Afanasyev is the chief editor of *Pravda,* and Georgi Arbatov is the head of the Institute for the U.S.A. and Canada. Whether the call for their dismissal was prearranged is unknown, but there is no doubt it undercut Gromyko, setting him up to resign and make way for Gorbachev to step into a newly created position of President of the Soviet Union with broad executive powers.

The conference delegates approved Gorbachev's program to create major changes in the Soviet political system, but voting was divided. There was none of the surface unanimity that has been the trademark of party congresses and conferences since the early days of the Soviet state. While Gorbachev stressed political reform, the delegates hammered home the grim realities of the failing economy and the dull meanness of everyday life with lines and shortages. If the conference is any measure, he must move quickly to improve the food situation and the economy, crippled by subsidized prices, outdated technology, and an unmotivated work force. However, removing price supports and raising prices for such basic commodities as milk, meat, and bread has been postponed until 1990.

In the Soviet Union there are two competing lines of authority: an elected government, approved by the Communist party, and the Communist party, which has the final word in all matters. The government has been a rubber stamp for the party, which kept one man in power until he died or was ousted by the Politburo, the inner ruling elite of the party.

The Party Conference approved plans for a political restructuring that would curb Communist party power and move toward a parliamentary system with a president. Significantly, the conference approved a rule that would limit Gorbachev and party officials to two consecutive five-year terms of office, a total of ten years. This is a major reform aimed at preventing a repetition of the Brezhnev "stagnation" period, in which aging party officials clung to their jobs until they died. Under the proposed plan a new parliamentary body will be created by direct elections in 1989. The new position of president, to be elected by the parliament, would have enhanced power and would place Gorbachev in the formal role of head of state as well as head of the Communist party. This would free Gorbachev from restraints imposed by the party leadership and bureaucracy and consolidate his power through open public participation in the political process.

Gorbachev is trying to have the best of both worlds, continued Communist party rule and a parliamentary system. When the party bureaucracy opposes change in the economy, he can go directly to the people through the parliament to win support for his reforms. If things get out of hand, the party will still be in place, supported by the KGB and the army. At the Party Conference he allayed the worst fears of the conservatives that the party will lose its controlling hand, but he also was forced to make concessions. As part of a compromise it was agreed that even though there will be direct elections for local soviets or government administrative bodies, the Communist party first secretary will serve as chairman of the local soviets. It is an example of Gorbachev's skill in manipulating the system. Even if he must satisfy conservative demands, the reality of the changes means greater responsiveness to elected leaders and more direct democratic participation.

In a post-Gorbachev era, unless there is real popular participation in the political process and a curb on Communist party power, the new enhanced post of president could mean a return to one-man rule without the restraints of collective leadership. If Gorbachev is trying to take the best from the American and British systems with his new scheme, it will need time to take root. He could move the Soviet Union toward a multiparty system, but if he fails, the outlook is for disorder and conditions leading to police and army rule. Tampering with the power of the Communist party is the most dangerous step a Soviet leader can take. There is no precedent for success, only Nikita Khrushchev's dismissal with disgrace. Gorbachev is still struggling to put through his program, relying heavily on the Moscow intellectuals, still trying to convince the workers and party faithful that his new ideas will bring meat to the kitchen table and an end to sugar rationing.

Once Gorbachev has his modified presidential system in place, he could conceivably move to a popularly elected president and a multiparty system for the Supreme Soviet, a real national legislature. However, without the checks and balances of an American constitutional system or the guarantees of rule of law of a parliamentary system, the Communist party remains the supreme power. The party has always been coopted and controlled by a strong leader. At the Party Conference Gorbachev showed his authority and political skill, emerging for all to see him as the just but strict father, a role Russians expect their leaders to play. In his closing remarks Gorbachev said, "*Glasnost* was one of the heroines of the conference. I think I shall not sin against the truth if I say that we have not seen anything like that for almost six decades."

Boris Yeltsin addressed the Communist Party Conference and told the delegates that rehabilitation after fifty years has now become habitual, but he wanted his political rehabilitation to come "while I am alive." However, Yeltsin did not repent. "I believe my only error was to speak up at the wrong time," Yeltsin said. Then he criticized the preparation for the conference and the selection of delegates. His most damaging criticism, to Gorbachev and himself, was the charge that *perestroika* had not been properly thought through. That charge was rejected by both Gorbachev and Yegor Ligachev, who spoke of Yeltsin with scorn, yet more in sorrow than in anger. Yeltsin, he said, "has chosen the wrong path. It turns out this person's force is not constructive but destructive. . . ." He criticized Yeltsin's rambunctious qualities and lack of discipline. "Policy making is not as easy as slurping down cabbage soup," said Ligachev. "Caution should be combined with decisiveness. As the saying goes, before going into a room make sure you can get out."

Their debate went far toward defining the new political culture that Gorbachev is creating. Ligachev and Gorbachev stressed the importance of party discipline and the bounds of conduct that are considered appropriate. Ideas are fine but it is discipline and execution that count. Everyone's ideas should be listened to, but if you cannot win a consensus for your ideas, then you are not politically viable. The conference rejected Yeltsin's plea for rehabilitation.

Ligachev emerged as the spokesman for the party faithful, the man who wants to work through the party, not around it. Ligachev still has a power base to which Gorbachev must accommodate himself at the same time as he seeks to weaken it.

Ben and Yadviga Charny were given permission to leave the Soviet Union in July 1988 and were reunited with their family. They are now living in Brookline, Massachusetts.

The Krishnaites were registered as a legal religion in June 1988, as part of Gorbachev's policy to tolerate religious beliefs. He hopes to gain support from the church for his revitalization of the country.

In Moscow on July 7, 1988, Sotheby's held the first international art auction in Soviet history. Included were paintings by many contemporary artists who were unable to show their work in Moscow as recently as three or four years ago. Grisaj Brushkin's painting, "Fundamental Lexicon," which we saw at the second Hermitage Group "Retrospective," sold for the staggering price of $416,000. The painting satirizes monumental Soviet sculpture. The line is now blurred between official and unofficial art.

Democratization in the Soviet Union is a dawning concept. Our friends often spoke of the need for developing a new political culture, a long-term process; that is what Gorbachev has embarked upon. Gorbachev's efforts to change the political structure at the 19th Party Conference was a giant step forward. However, when it comes time for picking candidates for election they still have to be approved by "them," the party officials. The contradictions between democratic liberalization and one-party rule push and pull. There is movement but no resolution.

All around us Moscow intellectuals were thrilled with *glasnost*. They called it "our last hope." Living with its limitations we wondered whether *glasnost* was nothing more than a little fresh air injected to save the one-party system from its internal dry rot. The KGB and its internal police powers are still in place. Despite a resolution calling for an end to the abuse of police powers, there will be no change in laws affecting the KGB until 1991.

The core issue, profit making, is still anathema to most Soviet citizens, who have been taught that profit is a form of speculation and criminal activity. They are not considering a true market-driven economy in which people can work where they please, or start a business without the sanction of the state.

Yet even without individual enterprise, greed and privilege exist in other forms. Party members receive potatoes when they are not available for the populace. They still have special stores and hospitals. In a country where sheepskin coats are a luxury there are wives of party functionaries who wear coats made from pelts of unborn lambs.

The intensity of the debate and the criticism of Gorbachev's programs indicate that his reforms still face strong obstruction from the bureaucracy. He acknowledged as much when he told the delegates: "Spokesmen for practically all delegations said that bureaucratism still shows its teeth, so to speak, resists, and puts spokes in the wheels. As a result the reform is skidding in many directions." Gorbachev had to make compromises to win approval for his program. He has the intellectuals behind him, but the broad masses remain skeptical of his ability to improve the economy without hurting them. We heard the echo of Dmitri's prediction to Doveen and Barney that the historic decisions made at the Party Conference will affect the lives of Soviet citizens for years to come. The enormity and complexity of the political changes ahead mean that economic improvement remains a future promise.

When we left Moscow twenty years ago, we left the living past. Saying good-bye again, we pondered whether that description was still accurate. We walked the same streets, enjoyed the same warm friendships. But there was a big difference, the freedom to talk and dig below the surface and follow ideas to their conclusion. To talk of a multiparty system in the Soviet Union and a realistic approach to profit making would have been shocking twenty years ago. What we saw today was a society that had always been sophisticated and multifaceted, but had hidden its gem light under a layer of dullness not to draw attention from repressive authorities.

Now ideas and feelings are out in the open from one extreme to another. The anti-Semitic *Pamyat* organization demanded the same rights as the reformers. In the bright light of day we were able to see how alike Russians and Americans are emotionally, how many problems we share in common, especially the need for improved education. But we were also able to see with undeniable clarity that we are also very different from each other. They are still an old-world society with authoritarian traditions and psychological restraints. Change is very slow, and Soviet society must overcome its fear of change before it can move closer to the hopes of the twenty-first century. We are and will continue to be a new world, a frontier society that continually discovers and creates faster than it can absorb its innovations. We continue to be on the cutting edge of technological and social change. We have the worst as well as the best side effects of social experimentation. The sheer force of variety and freedom brings with it the slag of experiments that fail.

The Russians look at us and point smugly at our rundown inner cities and homelessness. Twenty years ago their answer to our criticism of Soviet shortcomings was, "What about your Negro problem?" This time we didn't hear that question. The cry of twenty years ago, "What about Vietnam?," was well behind us. When we asked about Afghanistan, we were greeted with a shrug because Soviet citizens heard very little about their country's nine-year-old quagmire on the southern border. Only when Gorbachev began to remove Soviet troops in May 1988 did the subject become more acceptable for discussion.

We are still very different from each other in that news, information, and travel outside the Soviet Union remain strictly controlled by a one-party system. The Soviet Union is still a country without free access to copying machines and word processors, only a country starting to contemplate life in an information revolution.

Soviet society has built-in disincentives to working hard on the job; the state is the only employer. This results in a work force that does not define itself by its gainful occupations. Rather, its emotional, intellectual, and spiritual energy is expended in long hours of discussion, drinking, and friendship. Participating in this life-style is an attractive interlude for go-getter Americans. Back in the United States, we think often about how to transplant those pleasures to our pressured lives here. It seems impossible. The two appear to be contradictory. In America our heads swirl with new ideas and unlimited opportunity; whatever money we make is never enough for the goods and services we might buy if we had a higher income. That momentum fuels our economy and leaves us exhausted at the end of the day, just the time Russians are gathering for an evening of good talk. If *perestroika* succeeds, the Russians will be as tired as we are at the end of a day's work. Their living past will then catch up with the future, but something precious, those wasteful hours of unhurried friendship, will be lost.

INDEX

459

465

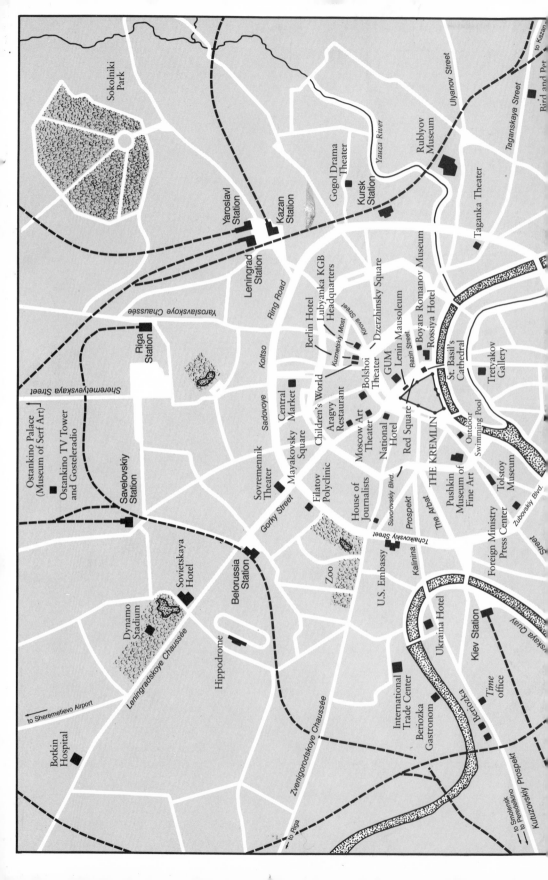